Descendants of Wounded Knee

Descendants of Wounded Knee

The Ultimate Sacrifice on the Pine Ridge Reservation

Alan Hafer
with Sandy Sauser

JOHNSON BOOKS

AN IMPRINT OF BOWER HOUSE

DENVER

Cover and text design by D.K. Luraas
Cover photos courtesy iStock

Library of Congress Control Number: 2015939489
ISBN: 978-1-55566-461-9

Printed in the U.S.A.

9 8 7 6 5 4 3

Contents

Preface

I grew up in the wheat country of western Nebraska, between the South and North Platte Rivers, the part of the United States that James Michener wrote so eloquently about in his book, *Centennial*. Listening to the farmers of my youth, I thought it to be the country of "too damn." Too damn hot! Too damn cold! Too damn wet! Too damn dry! And none of those conditions were ideal for raising the golden grain upon which our livelihood depended.

When it does rain, drops are hurled with such force to flatten golden stalks and turn freshly cultivated rows of earth into a bleached ground more representative of the Great Salt Desert than agricultural country. When the sun comes out, it won't rain again for so long that the earth cracks, wheat wilts, and dust coats the inside of houses, cars, and inhabitants' orifices. Wind is the constant. It blows from any direction, and often with enough strength to once again bend growing stalks of wheat before its wrath, making the grain nearly impossible to harvest.

For me it was, and is, a most wonderful place, for it was the home of the Plains Indians. On our farm, we had forty acres of unbroken prairie. With the few cows my father owned, it remained primeval, as it had been in the days that tribes crossed it hunting great herds of bison. In that pasture there was a buffalo wallow—a large, circular indention cut into the prairie by thousands of shaggy beasts rolling in water and cooling mud. The wallow still held water in those days, and I would lie beside it, imagining whooping warriors bearing down on the bison with bows and lances. In my mind's eye, I could see the entire village appear over the ridge and start butchering and skinning.

I grew up right in the middle of where the recorded history of the plains tribes took place. Julesburg, attacked by the Lakota in reprisal for Chivington's raid on Black Kettle's camp, was less than twenty miles to the east. Ash Hollow and Windless Hill, famous as Oregon Trail landmarks, were the same distance north. Blue Creek, where Harney's troops attacked the Brule and killed so many innocents, was only about twenty-five miles in the same direction. For me, these thrilling events had not happened that long ago. The Lakota had killed Custer only sixty-seven years before my birth, less than the life-span of many people. As a youth, I knew men and women who could remember when it happened.

I attended high school in the town of Lodgepole, Nebraska, named after the lodgepole pines harvested by plains tribes as support beams for their tipis in the Snowy Range of Wyoming, where the creek originated. There had even been a pony express station along the creek just south of Lodgepole. My friends and I spent many days, before we turned twelve or thirteen and our time was consumed by driving tractors, looking for the gold buried there by the about-to-be-killed station attendants during a furious Lakota attack.

The Black Hills were less than two hundred and fifty miles away, and the famous Sidney to Deadwood Stage Line started less than twenty miles west of Lodgepole. Fort Laramie sat one hundred or so miles west along the North Platte; Oglala with its famous boot hill, cattle drives, and Front Street was only forty miles to the east.

I grew up with a romanticized vision of the Old West, especially of the fierce warriors who had hunted buffalo on our farm less than one hundred and fifty years before. But even as I attended college and studied history, the thrill I received reading about Plains Indians cultures never faded. They were, I think, some of the freest people to have ever lived. The country was their supermarket while dogs, horses, and even their own sturdy legs provided them with the ability to go wherever they wanted—whenever they chose.

Plains Indians invented the American version of the camper. While men gathered horses and prepared weapons, women could have their houses down and packed with entire villages traveling before the sun was barely above the horizon. At night, the village was reassembled, suppers cooked, and travelers tucked into warm robes with as little fanfare as found in most RV campgrounds.

When I attended college in Chadron, Nebraska, before we were twenty-one, my friends and I would travel to Oelrichs, South Dakota, where it was legal to drink beer at eighteen. The tiny town had two bars. The establishment on the north side of the street refused to serve Indians, while the seedier place on the south side did. We soon started frequenting the south side more often because the only other people in there, Oglala from the Pine Ridge, were welcoming, friendly, funny (often in their stupor), and largely non-belligerent. But while I retained my love of Plains Indians history and cultures, I knew very little about those that were my contemporaries. Even as an adult, my contact with them was limited to books about the past.

In 2005, after a career as a school superintendent while trying to recast myself as a writer, I heard about the 1999 unsolved murders of two men on the Pine Ridge. There it is, I thought, my chance to write about the Lakota I had read so much about, and just maybe, do something meaningful. It might be my chance to make a difference.

I called a man from my hometown of Lodgepole who raised cattle on the rez, and he set me up with Sandy Sauser as a writing partner. We set out to write a true crime book, analyzing evidence from the murders and, perhaps, seeing if the investigation pointed at anyone in particular. We had no idea the Federal Bureau of Investigation had erected a barrier of secrecy (as they do in all cases), or that the families of the victims knew as little as we did. We did find the rez rife with rumors about the killings, fed by the silence of the supposedly greatest crime fighting organization in the world.

But, by then, it was too late to quit. The work had taken on a life of its own, powered by the gregarious people I came to know and to love on the Pine Ridge. Instead of true crime, the manuscript became true life—what had happened to the warriors of the plains, the freest people in the world, through almost one hundred and fifty years of colonization and forced acculturation.

We still tried to find the killers and followed the rumors together until Sandy passed away—when she died her impetuous smile kept me going. We visited homes, met people, ate and drank with the Oglala, and lived among them. Each day, our work grew further away from a true crime description of the murders and closer to finding the meaning of the inscription carved on the marker erected where the two men died: The Ultimate Sacrifice.

We had to tell the world what had happened here. How the United States had purposely sought the cultural destruction of a people and a way of life that had existed for thousands of years. The devastation of the Lakota had taken place under the guises of Capitalism, Christianity, Democracy, Imperialism, and Americanism: And it had been wrong, wrong, wrong.

The "kill the Indian and save the man" crowd did neither. The Oglala did not die, nor did they thrive. Assimilationists, missionaries, and colonists went among the people, clawed through their protective cultural shell and started tearing away societal foundations. Out went the governance of chiefs; spiritualism, norms, societal rules, and punishments were torn away as were traditional rites and ceremonies, replaced with those prominent in the Judeo-Christian tradition. White men killed the Lakota's economy for bones and hides, drove the nomadic warriors onto reservations, and sent their children miles away to learn European trades and crafts.

The Lakota culture did not die—it permutated. Unfortunately, what the Oglala acquired from the colonists was mostly bad: alcoholism, disease, and destruction of the extended family and tribalism. Personal ownership of land and private wealth replaced a societal economy based on concern for the whole. The people were forced to begin electing representatives by ballot instead of selecting leaders through traditions thousands of years old.

Replacing sacred and venerated values with American traditions exacerbated the Oglala's cultural, physical, and moral decline.

Today, the Oglala are neither what they were nor are they residents of main street America. A trip to the rez is akin to traveling to another country. What looks like home is not. In fact, the rez is an amalgamation of most of the things wrong with America.

Spend time there and you find a wonderful, warm, and brave people struggling to be Lakota while deluged by powers still trying to kill that which makes them Indian. We hope this book portrays what has gone wrong, that it illuminates the devastating effects of a one-size-fits-all approach to Americanism.

Alex White Plume, an Oglala leader profiled in chapter twenty, believes his people must return to the old values of leadership, tribe, family, humility, and spirituality to secure a better future. We agree. Certainly, there must be a better way than what has been.

Closing reservations and forcing Native Americans, at least for the Oglala on Pine Ridge, would simply be pounding the last nail into the cultural coffin of a magnificent people. What should happen is the opposite: celebrate the rez as a repository of a culture from which we can all learn. Remove all vestiges of colonialism and acculturation. Lift from the people the yoke of the Federal Bureau of Investigation and the enforcement of laws and punishments promulgated in Washington D.C.

Allow the Oglala the right of legal self-governance commensurate with their culture, history, and beliefs. Denying self-policing on the Pine Ridge ensures the continuance of violence and criminality. The policy of colonialism based on the belief that Native Americans are an inferior people incapable of self-rule must end. My friends on the rez wish to live in a better place, and it is time they are granted the opportunity to do so.

***

I, alone, am responsible for any mistakes in this work—caused because I could not or did not listen, read enough or dig far enough. However, this book is the result of the collective wisdom and efforts of many people. None of this would have been possible without Sandy Sauser and guidance from her mother, Alma, and her sister, Laurie. The same is true of Una Horn Cloud, Sandy's best friend, whose dignity and generosity helped so much, as did Mike O'Bryan and his penchant for libation after a hard day's work. I owe a special thanks to Tom Poor Bear, a tireless advocate for the Oglala, and the other members of Wally Black Elk's family including Iva Lynn Roy; Ben, Marla, and Baby Iva; Loren (always to be remembered as a real friend); and Owen. Thanks also to Rueben and Connie Quinn.

Ronnie Hard Heart's sisters Rose, Sharlene, and Sharon contributed to my understanding of those dark days of 1999. Special thanks also to Arlette Loud Hawk who plays such a prominent role in this work and has taught me so much about the Lakota culture. I cannot thank Pte San Win enough for her help with editing, photography, and guidance. She is a teacher on the rez and she taught me as well.

Walter Red Cloud contributed as did Jolene Black Elk, Bud Merrill, Jennifer Crazy Bear, Laura Red Cloud, Lupe Esparza, Doug Bissonette, Rueben and Connie Quinn, Stanley Good Voice Elk, who still owes me a hand-made Oglala bow, and all the other residents of Pine Ridge mentioned and quoted in these pages. I am proud the Oglala accepted and worked with me.

I finally met the children of the people who hunted the buffalo in that old wallow on our farm, and I found them to be my friends.

SEEKING
INFORMATION

Murder Victim

WILSON EDISON BLACK ELK, JR.

Wilson Edison Black Elk, Jr.   Ronald Owen Hard Heart

DETAILS

On Tuesday, June 8, 1999, the bodies of Wilson Edison Black Elk, Jr. and Ronald Owen Hard Heart were found on the Pine Ridge Indian Reservation(PRIR) in South Dakota, several hundred yards north of the Nebraska-South Dakota border near White Clay, Nebraska. The two victims, both residents of PRIR, were last seen on the main road to Pine Ridge, South Dakota from White Clay, Nebraska on Sunday, June 6, 1999. Authorities have determined that both victims were murdered.

REWARD

The FBI is offering a reward of up to $50,000 for information leading to the arrest and conviction of the person or persons responsible for the murders of Wilson Edison Black Elk, Jr. and Ronald Owen Hard Heart.

If you have any information concerning this person, please contact your local FBI office or the nearest American Embassy or Consulate.

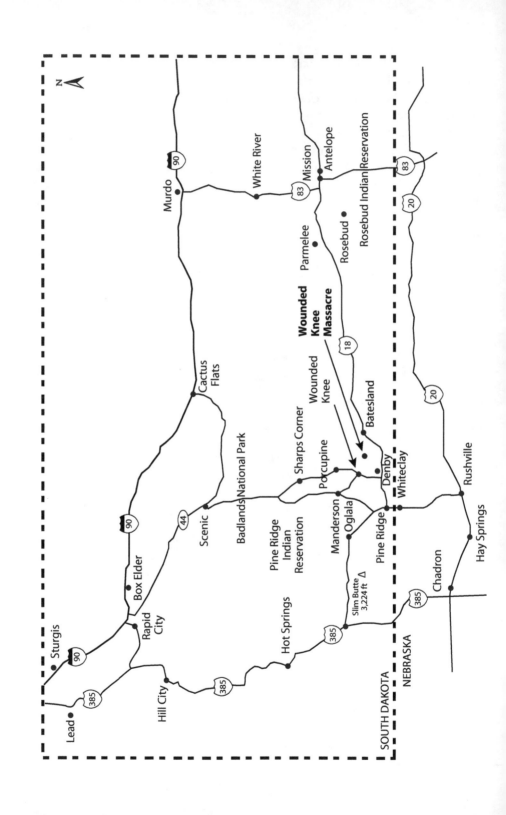

Prologue

"The Great Spirit raised both the white man and the Indian. I think he raised the Indian first. He raised me in this land; it belongs to me. The white man was raised over the great waters, and his land is over there. Since they crossed the sea, I have given them room. There are now white people all about me."

—*Mahpiya Luta (Red Cloud)*, Oglala Chief
Una Horn Cloud's seven-times-great-grandfather

The faces of American Presidents gouged into Paha Sapa—the sacred Black Hills, the womb from which the Lakota emerged through a cleft in the rocks—stare down at the countryside before them. If the men carved into stone could see, they would marvel at the view. Sprawling over plains and tree-covered white clay buttes between the Bad Lands and the Nebraska Sand Hills, the Pine Ridge Reservation—home to the Oglala Lakota, the fierce warriors who annihilated George Armstrong Custer's forces at the Battle of the Little Big Horn—is beautiful.

Spectacularly green in the spring, gold in late summer, and blanketed by snow during the winter, Pine Ridge prairies, crossed by rivers and towered over by the forested slopes of clay buttes, host large herds of cattle and buffalo. Deer, antelope, wild turkeys, and an occasional elk can be seen lazing in endless pastures. Bands of horses descended from those the Lakota warriors rode to conquer the plains race across miles of rolling hills.

It is a timeless land. Ancients walked here; the Oglala say they still do. Those who have gone before often come back to visit the living, completing the circle of life and death. The Oglala know of life on the plains before the invasion of blue-coated soldiers because their ancestors never left them. They view history not as something that happened long ago to people they never knew, but as a continuum.

Sandy Sauser hears the old ones as she sits alone among the trees she cultivates around her home, sixteen miles from the nearest town and far enough from other houses to prevent neighbors from stopping over. Except for the South Dakota public broadcasts she plays over a small radio that has never been turned off, Sandy lives in quietness. Only the sounds of an infrequent pickup on Slim Buttes Road, the lowing of cattle on the land she has leased to a rancher, or the howl of coyotes mar the silence. If those who lived before do not speak to her at home, she hikes to eroded clay buttes several miles away where ghosts gather and listens to them speak to each other.

Sandy is Oglala royalty, progeny of one of the band's most famous chiefs as well as a descendant of some of the frontier's most famous explorers and traders. She is one-eighth Lakota. Although she was raised in border towns around the reservation, life took her far from the Pine Ridge. Work and the call of adventure steered her to Denver, Portland, and Alaska, but like most Oglala who left the Pine Ridge, something—maybe the old ones—called her back.

With mixed-blood parents, hair dark enough to pass for Lakota and skin as light as her German father's, she is at home in both cultures. With a mischievous grin always lighting her face, she insists on living alone on the wind-swept prairie—her independence inherited from generations of fearless predecessors.

Sandy lives in the shadow of Slim Buttes, an Oglala landmark on land her father farmed when he wasn't working the bar he owned in nearby Chadron, Nebraska. An outdoorswoman tattooed by the scars from broken bones, she has worked enough with livestock and machinery to justify her claim as a top hand.

Since her father's passing and the leasing of her land to a rancher, she sits for hours in her smoke-clouded kitchen beading intricate designs. Through the window, she has seen eagles soaring in a cobalt sky, coyotes chasing prairie dogs across pastures the small rodents have denuded of grass, and herds of ponies racing with the wind. Occasionally a fence-jumping horse or cow, even an especially courageous antelope, stares back at her. She

Sandy Sauser, direct descendent of Chief Bull Bear, Bear Robe, Henri Chatillon, Emilie and Ben Lessert, and Wounded Knee interpreter, Philip Wells. Through her veins ran the blood of the great men and women of the American West.

doesn't watch television, seldom reads a newspaper, and except for visits to relatives in Chadron, her world stops at the boundaries of the rez.

Sandy labors to become Oglala. Educated in towns off the reservation, she grew up more Nebraskan than Lakota. Choosing life among the Indians meant becoming part of a culture she did not know because Pine Ridge is a foreign country.

Una Horn Cloud, Sandy's best friend, lives several miles down the road. A beautiful woman with classic Oglala features, she lives with Mike O'Bryan, a self-proclaimed reservation Irishman as acquainted with whiskey as he is with ranching. Their house lies near the White River in a tree-surrounded meadow where Una's garden hearkens back to early reservation days when her people had to plant to survive.

Una, if the Oglala believed in royalty, would rank higher than Sandy. She is the seventh-generation granddaughter of the tribe's most famous chief, Red Cloud. The genetic bearer of a proud people's history, her family tree includes warriors who fought Custer and women and children who died in the snow at the hands of American soldiers during the Wounded Knee Massacre.

Also an inhabitant of both worlds, Una struggles with the outside culture as Sandy does Oglala. College educated and a nurse, Una speaks Lakota fluently, can butcher animals, tan hides, and collect sinew to make sewing cord and bow strings as her ancestors did. She often speaks of cultural differences between the Lakota and the residents of border towns surrounding the reservation.

Mahpiya Luta. Chief Red Cloud, one of the most famous characters of the Old West, successfully waged war against the American army and then attempted to lead his people to peace. Under his leadership the Oglala moved onto the Pine Ridge Reservation in 1878. Una and other descendants refer to him as "the old man." (Denver Public Library, Western History Collection, B-351)

Her people belong to a society ancient long before the Christian's Christ died in far off lands. The Oglala have walked these lands for thousands of years; they believe they will still be here for thousands more—longer, most believe, than the invaders trying to change them. Mike O'Bryan, unlike Sandy or Una, does not try to walk in two societies. He raises cattle in three states but lives on the reservation because that is where he

Mike O'Bryan and Una Horn Cloud in the living room of their modern home along the White River on the reservation.

grew up, attending Indian schools, and he says, fighting his way home because he was a white kid. He says he couldn't live anywhere else. While he has many friends among the Lakota, he does not emulate them; he is content to remain different.

When Una, Sandy, and Mike drive thirty miles to a restaurant in Oelrichs, South Dakota, they usually meet with non-Indian ranchers from off the reservation. Invariably, the conversation turns to the plight of the Indians. Most, with some knowledge of the local economy, blame the reservation system for the poverty of the Oglala. They say living on government land, supported by a dole with free commodities and health care has reduced Indians to their caricature. The Oglala have, the believers say, become (maybe always were) lazy, slothful beggars, who do not work, have no desire to work, and demand that the government shoulder their support.

Mike wants to agree with them, but Sandy and Una don't give him a chance. They say this premise leaves out history. One hundred and fifty years ago, the Oglala were an ancient people living as their ancestors had for thousands of years. They had no knowledge of Aristotle, Socrates, Locke, Hobbes, modern medicine, European science, or nineteenth-century technology. The Lakota knew and believed what people who were not from the so-called great civilizations of the world knew and believed.

The Lakota were forced onto reservations in 1876, only one hundred and twenty-four years before the turn of the twenty-first century. Incorporating all the beliefs and knowledge of western civilization in that short time into a stone-age people would be difficult, if not impossible.

Sandy argues that closing the reservations, most recently attempted with only a few tribes in a policy known as "Termination" after the Second World War, would have amounted to throwing the Oglala to the wolves: bringing an end to a magnificent culture and destroying an entire people. The few who survived off the reservation would have become invisible, she says, just another demographic of the urban poor.

Long ago, Sandy tells the non-Indians, the Supreme Court found Indians to be members of dependent nations and were guaranteed lands and sovereignty by treaties. She argues that people may not like reservations, and they may covet Indian land, but they may not abrogate established law. The Lakota, she says, secured their lands and rights in battles against the American Army. While they argue for continuance of the reservation system, Sandy and Una do not look upon their land with rose-colored glasses. They see the reservation as it is. They know the Oglala are poor, eking out an existence in a beautiful place without the amenities accepted as standard in other parts of America.

"Perhaps," Sandy says, "it is the beauty of the place that makes the poverty seem so much worse."

1
Death Walk

Maybe it's Crying Woman, she thought. Most everybody who stays here [Whiteclay] sees her, wrapped in a shawl, walking Nebraska 87 through town. Maybe it's one of the Old Ones. Maybe it's someone who died in a wreck or a drunken fight—Indians die all the time in this town where they sell malt liquor.
—Patchie Black Elk, Wally Black Elk's Sister-in-Law

The sun rose over the horizon on June 5, 1999, burning brightly in the east with not a cloud in sight to cast a shadow on a beautiful spring day. Walter Red Cloud and Wilson Edison "Wally" Black Elk met at Big Bat's, the gas station, convenience store, and restaurant that is the most popular gathering spot on the Pine Ridge, for coffee and a smoke. After another of South Dakota's long and brutal winters followed by a tornado that tore through the rez a week earlier, they decided to cross the border into Nebraska and drink in Whiteclay.

Pine Ridge is one of the few remaining alcohol-free Indian reservations in the country and the reason for the existence of Whiteclay, a short two-mile walk down highway 87. The tiny community is one of the last of the Wild West's infamous whiskey ranches, where unscrupulous traders set up shop around reservations to sell alcohol to the Indians who were forbidden by federal statute from consuming it. Consisting of fewer than twenty citizens, two grocery stores, post office, café, and five liquor stores, Whiteclay sells over four million cans of beer and malt liquor each year, most of it to the residents of the Pine Ridge.

Walter, a direct descendant of the famous Chief Red Cloud, and Wally, whose renowned ancestor Black Elk is revered as the Holy Man of the Oglala, had made the trip before. They had no reason to think this time would be any different.

The two men spoke of days gone by, pretty women, the tornado, and catching catfish in the reservoir. "Catch 'em and fry 'em up," Walter said. "That's the way I do it."

Wally spoke of his involvement in the Christian religion and how it blended with the teachings of traditional Oglala spirituality. Each believes in the same God, he told Walter, "The wasicu call him Jehovah, we call him Wakan Tanka."[1]

That morning their walk took a little longer than most Americans would consider for a trip to the liquor store, but they enjoyed the day, anticipating the beverages they would soon consume. Just as they were about to cross the border, however, Tribal Police Officer Norman Brown Eyes pulled up next to them. Walter knew he was in trouble and considered dodging into the trees lining the road. Using the natural cover to hide his movement he could escape into Nebraska, but that would just postpone the inevitable.

He'd already run from the officer a couple of days earlier when Norman caught him drinking malt liquor in the small town of Pine Ridge, the largest town on the reservation with the same name. Doing his duty on the dry reservation, Norman confiscated the alcohol and put the men Walter had been drinking with in jail for the allotted eight-hour drying out period. Walter should have also gone, but he'd escaped into a vacant house as the tribal officer wrestled with another man.

Walter had figured that Norman would find and incarcerate him eventually, but going to jail had never seemed like a good idea to him. He didn't want to spoil his walk and sit in the tribal jail on that nice spring day either, but he didn't have a choice. Reluctantly, he said good-bye to Wally and climbed into the back of the squad car.

Wally walked on alone, crossed the border, and met Ronnie Hard Heart, the son of an Oglala Medicine Man. Unlike Wally, who seldom ventured across the state line to the small town, Ron was a fixture in Whiteclay, living in abandoned houses and taking any odd jobs he could get to buy booze. He got along well with the store owners, helping them out with stocking and cleaning, and playing catch with their kids.[2]

According to Lupe Esparza, a Mexican national who has lived on the rez for more than forty years, Ron was a good friend and always ready for work when he wasn't drinking.

Wally Black Elk in his uniform as an American soldier. Wally had become a Christian and was very seldom seen in Whiteclay. (Jolene Black Elk claims to have found this photo in the garbage.)

"He worked on farms, put up fences, whatever he did, he worked really hard," Lupe recalled. "Ron quit drinking several years ago, quit to pray in the old ways and straighten his life out, but then his mother died so he went back to the booze. Whiteclay became his life. He was too deep into alcohol and drugs."[3]

The same day Wally was on his way to Whiteclay, Ron borrowed five bucks from Lupe so he could buy more malt liquor.

Several days later, June 8, 1999, Darlene Red Star set off on her morning traipse, as the early hours are her favorite time. She walked in the cool air, taking food to members of her tiospaye, her extended family. She remembers it as a beautiful morning—a cool breeze battling the warming rays of the sun. Trees sported a full complement of leaves, and the soft coos of mourning doves filled the air.

As she had before on her route, she noticed coyotes, wild dogs, and turkey buzzards fighting over something on a grass-covered slope a couple of hundred yards from the Nebraska border. Her curiosity got the better of her. Holding her nose against the stench, she left the pavement, climbed over a barbed wire fence, and made her way to the side of the ravine where the animals congregated. Not watching where she stepped, she slipped in the mud left by the spring storms and fell. When she looked up, she saw that she was lying by two human bodies.

She did not recognize either man because of the damage caused by scavengers and the mutilation the victims suffered at the hands of the killers. When she noticed their chests moving up and down, she wondered how they could possibly still be alive. Just in case they were, she told them they'd better get into some shade; it was going to get hot real soon.

Only later did she realize an invasion of maggots caused the movement in their torsos. By then she'd found Wally's wallet, its contents strewed on the ground. She realized the men had been murdered and thought whoever killed them didn't do it where she found them because there was no blood anywhere around the bodies. By the time she'd flagged down a passing motorist from Florida who went to notify the tribal police, Darlene had become overwhelmed by the stench and the images burned into her brain. She would never be the same again.[4]

Officer Norman Brown Eyes was the first cop to arrive. His job was to preserve the scene, keep on-lookers away, and call in investigators from the Bureau of Indian Affairs and the Federal Bureau of Investigation. When the feds moved in, Norman's shift ended, and he went home. Later, Wally's brothers said Norman had tried to do his job, but by the time he left, half of Pine Ridge had come to see the bodies and trampled over the area.

According to Tom Poor Bear, Wally's half-brother and Ron's cousin, the killers savagely brutalized the men. Wally's face lay open—a gash ran from the corner of his mouth to his right ear with the skin peeled back. An eighteen-inch incision extended from his forehead down the back of his skull, and he had thirty-two stab wounds in the right side of his chest. The killer or killers had used a pick or a sharpened bar to punch a large hole into the middle of his lower back.[5]

Tears come to Walter Red Cloud's eyes when he remembers the murders of his friends and considers how close he came to death. Not only was he lucky Norman Brown Eyes had arrested him, he was especially fortunate that the officer forgot about him. Norman had intended to keep Walter in jail for the standard eight hours, but his stay behind bars lasted for fifteen.

"That's what saved me," he says. "If I had gotten out in eight, I probably would have gone to Whiteclay and looked up Wally."[6]

The day the bodies were found, Owen Black Elk, Wally's youngest brother, had been fishing at Whiteclay Reservoir. Not catching anything and thinking it just wasn't his day, he had headed back to Pine Ridge along Highway 87. As he drove past the ambulances and police cars while the bodies still lay where Darlene found them, an officer motioned for him to keep moving, but something compelled him to stop.

Seeing two Oglala emergency medical technicians he knew, a man and a woman, Owen ran to them and asked what had happened. His buddy told him not to go down there. "You don't want to see it," he said.

The woman threw her arms around him and said, "I have to tell you. It's Wally. He's dead."

The son of a medicine man, Ronnie Hard Heart had earned a reputation as a hard worker who would do anything for anybody. Ronnie had become a fixture in Whiteclay.

***

In most places, the almost two decades old unsolved slayings of two men might constitute just another cold case, a mystery sitting in a cardboard box on steel shelves in a police storeroom, but on the Pine Ridge the deaths persist as stark symbols of a clash between cultures. Once the proudest warriors of the plains, the Oglala have become America's forgotten people. To them, the murders of Ronnie Hard Heart and Wally Black Elk symbolize white America's treatment of their people.

The two-mile trip along Highway 87 to Whiteclay is the new Trail of Tears. Like the original, the forced removal of tribes from their eastern homelands to Oklahoma, wooden crosses and Indian symbols dedicated to those who died along the way mark this trail. Going to Whiteclay is an escape from the poverty and despair of the place the government designated as the last stop of the Oglala.

Although the Oglala have lived under a program of forced assimilation for over one hundred years, they have neither benefited from nor enjoyed their association with the dominant culture. They view themselves as a sovereign nation, winning their independence in battles against the United States Army. In truth, their lifestyle resembles that of a repressed minority in a Third World country.

Walter tries to envision what life was like for his people before the army herded them onto the reservation. He often looks across the Pine Ridge landscape imagining Oglala warriors mounted on spotted ponies racing through the tall grass. He visualizes the entire band with horse-drawn travois (horse-pulled carriers) heaped with meat and hides returning to their village after a successful hunt.

If he had lived during the time of his heralded ancestor, the wasicu (white men) would have feared him. Dressed in elk skins as soft as butter and the color of bone, draped with furs and feathers, he would have roamed a country larger than most European nations. His land would have stretched from the Canadian border to the Platte River and from Minnesota to the high peaks of the Rockies. With millions of buffalo, herds so large they ran past Lakota camps for days at a time, and plains teeming with elk, antelope, and deer, the Oglala had a well-stocked larder.

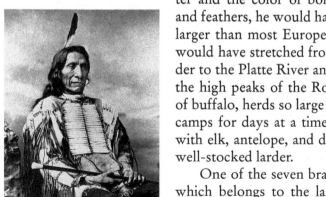

Chief Red Cloud.

One of the seven branches of the Lakota, which belongs to the larger group of Oceti Sakowin or Seven Council Fires, the Oglala were members of the wealthiest and mightiest tribe in all America. They ruled the prairies, never tasting the bitterness of military defeat. Chief Red Cloud, Walter's famous ancestor, was the only Indian leader, perhaps the only military leader, to win a major war against the United States.

Walter knows that little is left of the old days but dreams. Instead of warriors on painted ponies, he sees plastic bags scoured from the dump by howling winds clinging to barbed wire fences. Disposable diapers, fast-food wrappers, styrofoam cups, and beer bottles tossed from the windows of the battered cars that traverse the roads line the trails he walks.

Like many other Oglala, Walter has lived off the reservation; he has seen life in other parts of America and realizes how poor his people are. He knows that in 1989, the Census Bureau found the residents of Shannon County, South Dakota, wholly within the rez, to be the poorest in the nation with a per capita income of $3,714.00. And he knows their lives have not gotten any better.[7]

Most Oglala, including Walter, have neither jobs nor a car to get to work if they did; they walk everywhere they go. "Most of the cars parked around people's houses," he explains, "they are rez cars, used for two things. Either they are stripped and used for parts to keep another car running, or they're bedrooms. People, sometimes families, sleep in them. And the houses," he points to trailers and small wooden houses scattered over the prairie, "usually only one person in each place has a job. That's what you do. Live with someone who has a job. The oldest woman in the house, the grandmother, is the boss. Her daughters live with her and their families occupy one of the bedrooms, no matter how many people there are. People sleep in the living room, the hallway, and the junked cars. Many of these houses have twenty or thirty people living in them."[8]

Many Oglala live in trailer houses scattered across the reservation. They are usually surrounded by cars cannibalized for parts to keep one running and often used as bedrooms.

The need for the Oglala to live in overcrowded houses, using abandoned cars as extra bedrooms, has adversely impacted reservation economics. Since the federal government dispenses funds to the tribe by population, it is necessary for the count to be accurate. But census numbers for Pine Ridge have been inaccurate for years. Using new methods of counting in 2005, the Census Bureau accepted Pine Ridge as the home of twenty-eight thousand people instead of the fifteen thousand counted. Insiders doubt the new figures, putting the total much closer to forty thousand.[9]

The cause of poverty on the Pine Ridge is simple to understand. In Big Bat's an older couple, with not a tooth between them and tearing small pieces from chicken wings, told Walter what he already knew when he asked how it was going. "There are no jobs. Nobody can work. Nobody knows what to do," the elderly man said. His wife, probably not even five feet tall, smiling the whole time, and speaking broken English added, "It's bad. It's hard."[10]

There are no jobs, no industries, no factories, and few businesses. According to Robert Ecoffey, former superintendent of the Pine Ridge Bureau of Indian Affairs, his wife found it extremely difficult to secure a loan to buy a new sandwich franchise in the small town of Pine Ridge.[11] While it was difficult for them to borrow the funds, it would be impossible for anyone else who did not have his income and connections to the outside world.

Walter, like 90 percent of reservation residents, depends on the state and federal government for his support. As an over thirty-five, non-married, non-head of the household, he receives $83 general assistance every two weeks, energy assistance to keep from running out of heating fuel in the winter, and is eligible to visit the commodity warehouse once a month to pick up a supply of groceries. If he had his own home, he could collect $393 each month, and if he had a wife and children, his allotment would depend on the number of kids.[12]

Tribal President John Yellow Bird Steele painted a grim picture of life on the rez in 2007. He told the Senate Committee on Indian Affairs that the Oglala had an 80 percent unemployment rate and some of the highest rates of alcoholism, heart disease, and cancer in the United States. Almost half of the population over forty had diabetes. The life expectancy for men was forty-eight years, for women it was fifty-two, and the Oglala had the highest infant mortality rate in the country.[13]

Yellow Bird Steele told the committee that most of the overcrowded trailer houses, boiling in the summer and freezing in the winter, were not fit for habitation. Many lacked indoor toilets, working furnaces, windows, and leak-proof roofs. But the senators didn't need to listen to his presentation; they could have driven down any road on the reservation to see what

Yellow Bird Steele spoke of, including residents sleeping in vans and abandoned cars. On the reservation, you do what it takes to get by.

Unfortunately, the troubled economic times following Yellow Bird Steele's meeting with the Senate only served to decrease funding and help to the Oglala. It seems that when ordinary Americans must tighten their belts a few notches, the residents of Pine Ridge starve.

The residents of Pine Ridge have known only poverty for as long as anyone can remember. Leo Vocu, a tribal leader, told the *New York Times* that the Oglala constituted, "a fifth-going-on-sixth-generation welfare state."[14]

The Reverend Joseph Daniel Sheehan, a Jesuit priest whose church once overlooked the Wounded Knee Massacre site where the 7th Cavalry killed nearly three hundred Lakota in 1890, compared life on the Pine Ridge with living in India. He said Oglala poverty is a more bitter type than that found in India, where the attitude is that everybody is in it together. "Here [Pine Ridge] they feel that anything that comes to them is what's left over. They get angry at one another. It's a kind of poverty that destroys the family."[15]

Words cannot adequately describe the condition of the Oglala. They cannot convey the worry of the young mother, still resembling the wisp of a girl she had once been, as she panhandles to buy food for her babies. Teeth edged with black rot, she will soon be reduced to gumming her own meals. On the rez, few escape the ravages of tooth disease, including Tom Poor Bear, Wally's older half-brother and tribal vice president. He opens his mouth and points to one tooth in the middle of his lower jaw. "The last one," he says, proud to have it.[16]

The Pine Ridge is a beautiful place, the western scenery often only broken by herds of horses and cattle, and trailers surrounded by cars.

2

The Ultimate Sacrifice

*When it comes time to die, be not like those whose hearts are filled
with the fear of death, so when their time comes they weep and pray
for a little more time to live their lives over again in a different way.
Sing your death song, and die like a hero going home.*
— *Wasicu Tasunke (American Horse),* Oglala Chief

L oren Black Elk had started walking the streets of Pine Ridge and Whiteclay searching for his older brother, Wally, a day before the bodies were
found. Shorter than many Oglala, about five feet nine, Loren had worn his
usual jean jacket and tee shirt. His faded jeans reached the soles of his hiking boots. With his trademark red bandana headband clamped over his hair,
the man with a gentle soul looked like a town tough.

He had spoken to people on the streets, poked through the broken-down
buildings and abandoned cars where Wally and Ron might have holed-up.
Must have been one hell of a drunk, he thought. Unable to figure out why
no one knew where they were, Loren had been walking past Billy Mills Hall,
a gymnasium and auditorium in Pine Ridge named after the famous Lakota
runner, when his brother, Wayne, told him Wally was dead.

After identifying the body at the hospital, Loren said he got mad and
wanted to hurt somebody. Then he fell to his knees and cried, not only for
Wally and Ron, but for all his people who had succumbed to violence. He
swore the Oglala would never forget.[1]

Tom Poor Bear, Wally's half-brother, was the family member most
prepared to act on Loren's promise. He had joined the American Indian
Movement (AIM) in 1972 at the age of sixteen. AIM is a quasi-militant organization founded in Minnesota in 1968 to provide support and leadership
to Native Americans. He helped dig bunkers and ferried in supplies during
the 1973 Wounded Knee siege a year later.

His athletic build, conditioned by years as an AIM bodyguard and
driver, deferring to the laws of gravity with his stomach slipping toward
his belt line, hair worn in a long ponytail and sporting a heavy mustache,
Tom had become a local politician, serving as sergeant at arms for the tribal
government. He had been loading donations for victims of the spring tor-

Loren Black Elk, holding the can, with Steve Little Sky and an unidentified man. Little Sky and his brother, Beau, had been involved in the takeover of Wounded Knee. Their father, Eddie Little Sky, was a regular in Hollywood movies. He had major roles in A Man Called Horse *and* Paint Your Wagon, *among others. He also played the role of a Pacific islander in several* Gilligan's Island *episodes. Steve died of diabetes and other health problems in 2014.*

A photo of Loren Black Elk that was used at his wake.

nado when he heard about the police investigation along the state line. He jumped into his car and drove to the scene, unaware the two bodies baking under a blue tarp were those of his half-brother and cousin.

Tom waited for two weeks to learn about the investigation while questions kept swirling around in his mind. He wanted to know about possible suspects and the evidence collected. He wanted to read the autopsies and learn how his relatives had died. Had they suffered? Did the authorities suspect a hate crime? Had they questioned anybody? Who? But the Federal Bureau of Investigation, the lead law enforcement agency on the reservation, had built a wall of silence around the case.

He believed alcohol had killed Wally and Ron. Someone else had deployed the killing instruments, but they had died because of booze. And he, like many Oglala, had always believed Whiteclay existed for the sole purpose of destroying his people through alcohol. In Wally's memory, he pledged to close the alcohol outlets in the border town.

Tom phoned AIM and asked the leaders to join him on a protest march from Pine Ridge to Whiteclay, calling attention to the killings. Maybe they could convince Nebraska to close the beer stores.[2]

On June 26, eighteen days after the bodies were found, the Oglala met in Billy Mills Hall as they do every year on that day to celebrate Custer's defeat at the Little Big Horn.[3] This time they also met to discuss Tom's strategy to defeat Whiteclay's purveyors of death. Besides Poor Bear, speakers included AIM leaders Clyde Bellecourt, Dennis Banks, and Russell Means.

These three men had been active on the reservation before, and their presence placed state and federal officials on edge. There was reason to suspect that the visitors might hold a match to a powder keg as they had in 1973, when AIM and Oglala tribal members fought the American government and the FBI to a standoff on the site of the Wounded Knee Massacre. Violence had flared again on the same day as they met, June 26, in 1975 when two FBI agents and an AIM member died of gunshot wounds in a battle between the two groups.

Dennis Banks, one of the primary founders of AIM, told the crowd what they all believed. "We're up against people who think it's okay to kill Indian people. They think it's okay because they'll get away with it."[4]

Russell Means spoke next. An Oglala and a leader of AIM during the Wounded Knee takeover, Means had been jailed many times for advocating Indian rights. In the past decade, he had become an actor, playing Chingachgook in *Last of the Mohicans*. A local celebrity, he further stirred up the Oglala, "We'll go after these people who killed these people. And when we find them, we're going to get justice. … I believe we're looking at some hate crimes, and I think the members of the Klan are involved. AIM is going to start something."[5]

Tom Poor Bear used his time at the microphone to draw attention to his half-brother's death, but his words were no less a call to action. "The Great Spirit didn't call for him, somebody sent him. Wally had too many things to do here on Mother Earth."[6]

Almost two thousand Oglala left the hall heading toward Whiteclay. It was time to close the last of the whiskey ranches and free the people from the scourge of the wicked water. It was also the time to right another injustice, one that had been a thorn in their collective side for more than one hundred years—the Whiteclay whiskey traders operate on land that the Oglala believe legally belongs to the tribe.

After the Lakota victory at the Greasy Grass, known to most Americans as the Little Big Horn, the federal government reduced the amount of land given to the Lakota for reservations as punishment for killing Custer. Then in 1882, hoping to protect the Oglala from whiskey traders operating along their southern border, President Chester A. Arthur returned to them a strip of land in Nebraska five miles wide and ten miles long. Congress acted and ceded this strip of land, known as the Whiteclay Extension, to the tribe for as long as it "may be needed for the use and protection of the Indians."[7]

However, in 1904 after a visit by Nebraska Congressman Moses Kinkaid and continual hammering by irate citizens of Nebraska who demanded the land be returned, President Theodore Roosevelt issued an executive order giving the land back to the state. He acted with neither congressional approval nor Oglala consent.

The Oglala consider the land illegally occupied by Nebraska. They marched not only to shut down Whiteclay's alcohol sales, but to have the Whiteclay Extension returned to the tribe. The marchers stopped where Darlene found the bodies, offered tobacco in the Lakota way, prayed, and then surged on to reclaim their land.

Tom Poor Bear, Wally's half-brother and the Oglala tribal vice president, his sister Iva Lynn Roy, and their niece Baby Iva, Ben Black Elk's daughter.

Wally's brothers had planned the walk to Whiteclay as a peaceful, non-violent protest, but the authorities had been correct to fear an outbreak of violence. For the Oglala, there had been too many deaths, too many years of injustice and poverty, too many families destroyed by the white man's wicked water, and too many violent confrontations with the American government in the past.

When they reached Whiteclay, Russell Means yelled they were there "to tell Nebraska, all the way to the governor, that this is our land …"[8] Men pulled a sign out of the ground that proclaimed, "Welcome to Nebraska, the Home of Arbor Day," and carried it down the street. Somebody broke down the doors of VJ's Market, a grocery store that did not sell alcohol. Looters carried off cigarettes, cases of soda, and watermelons. Soon smoke wafted through holes where the doors had been.

Tempers flared on both sides. Sheriff's deputies and highway patrol officers moved in; protesters and law enforcement personnel lined up face to face and shouted at each other. Nobody moved away until Chief Oliver Red Cloud, a direct descendent of the great chief and Walter's grandfather, appeared and ordered the protesters to move back.

There were no arrests. The marchers said that people already in Whiteclay, angered by the owner's treatment of them, had broken into the store and started the fire. According to the owner, the people hurt by the action were his customers—100 percent Native American.[9] Still, the liquor stores opened for business with a brisk trade the next day.

Determined to end alcohol sales and get their land back, angry Oglala continued their protest marches. They demanded to speak with Nebraska Governor Johanns, but were met with rebuke by a member of his staff who said it was ridiculous to expect the governor to meet with anybody on such short notice, especially since he kept office hours.[10]

During the last week of June, Governor Johanns announced that he had initiated a conversation with Harold Salway, Oglala tribal president. On July 3, Tom Poor Bear led the people on another march on Whiteclay. This time they were met with a solid wall of patrol officers and sheriff's deputies standing shoulder to shoulder behind yellow tape stretched across the road.

The marchers would not be allowed to enter Nebraska; those who tried would be arrested. When nine, including Tom Poor Bear, Ben Black Elk, John Yellow Bird Steele (future tribal president), Frank LaMere (a member of the Winnebago tribe and citizen of Nebraska), and Russell Means, crossed the state line anyhow, officers charged them with failing to comply with a lawful order.[11]

To the Oglala, the actions of the Nebraskan police spoke louder than the governor's words. The state that permitted a whiskey town to operate two miles from the border had just established a new level of hypocrisy. It was legal to enter Nebraska to buy booze, get drunk on the street, and pass out on the sidewalk. Spending grocery and heating money on cheap malt liquor was legal, but entering the state to protest the sale, trying to prevent someone from becoming an alcoholic, was not.

The next day, Wally's brothers erected Camp Justice, a mixture of tipis and rude structures about one hundred yards toward Whiteclay from where Darlene Red Star found the bodies. They announced that the camp would remain until they got justice.

Tom Poor Bear and his supporters stayed busy. In July, they met with Governor Johanns, who had walked into the camp from Nebraska. His visit led to an August meeting between the Oglala and a task force appointed by Johanns. When the leaders of Camp Justice asked for a return of the Whiteclay Extension, the response from the

Ben Black Elk, one of Wally's younger brothers, pointing out the location of Camp Justice in the trees between Pine Ridge and Whiteclay.

task force gave Wally's brothers their only victory in their struggle to close the liquor outlets. The task force acknowledged that the 1904 executive order was illegal without an act of Congress. However, they also claimed it was a federal issue, and they could do nothing about it.[12]

The Oglala continued to protest. Even President Clinton knew of Camp Justice, the murders, and Whiteclay. He visited the reservation that summer, marking the first Presidential visit to a reservation in fifty-five years.[13]

In October, Attorney General Janet Reno met with Tribal President Harold Salway. While editors of the Camp Justice Update, a website published by the American Indian Cultural Support organization, reported that although Reno seemed more concerned about the Waco and Clinton scandals than the unsolved murders, she did take note.[14] During a meeting in February, the FBI told the families that Reno wanted the case solved and ordered the agency to do anything to get it done.[15]

Yet, those who committed the murders were still not identified and the effort to shut down the whiskey trade was to no avail. In January 2000, the Nebraska Liquor Commission issued new licenses to all the outlets in

Whiteclay. All through the cold winter months, Wally's and Ron's friends and relatives occupied their camp and watched cars and foot traffic heading from Pine Ridge to Whiteclay. They saw deadly traffic accidents and more people fall victim to the white man's wicked water, including Ben Black Elk's wife, Pachi, who abandoned her husband and children and lived on the streets of Whiteclay.[16]

***

Nine years later, in the boiling heat of a late July afternoon in 2008, Loren Black Elk, Walter Red Cloud, a young woman named Mary, and a couple of other friends sat around the remains of Camp Justice. They pulled chairs from under trees and untangled others caught in new-growth bushes. Intent on celebrating her birthday, Mary wanted to get the party started, but the men were focused on discussing the deaths of Wally and Ron.

Loren walked silently over to a white-enameled coffeepot hanging from braided rawhide twisting gently in the breeze. The pot had been there as long as the camp—it was a symbol of the attempt to find justice and close Whiteclay.

Mary, movements hampered by her too-tight jeans and winter coat, so drunk she could barely walk, complained about not having any fun and staggered off in the direction of Whiteclay. Loren navigated through brush and shrubs to view a clearing on the facing bank of a small ravine. The area where he stood hosts a thick forest, as does the bottom of the ravine. The south-facing slope on the opposite side of the ravine is free of heavy vegetation; a small wood-fenced enclosure stands on the grasses covering the soil. In its center sits a red stone in the shape of a grave marker. This is where Darlene Red Star found the bodies.

Ribbon in colors meaningful to the Lakota festoon each side of the enclosure. Black marks west, where the thunder beings live to send rain. Red on the east represents the home of light. The cleansing wind from the north bears a white ribbon. The yellow on the south points to where summer comes from, bringing the power to grow.[17]

Solemnly, with the deliberate and studied actions of a priest celebrating mass, Loren broke open several Marlboro cigarettes, rolled tobacco shards between his palms, and scattered them around the sacred space. Entering the enclosure, he dropped to his knees, tracing his hands along white mortar where the stone, bought with funds raised by Camp Justice, had been repaired. Several years before, residents of the camp found it broken one morning. Some believed the killers pushed it over. Loren thought lightning struck it, a sign from the Great Spirit.

The words inscribed on the memorial carry pleas from a brutally conquered people whose ancestors won all the battles but lost the war. They express the bitter frustration of men who are unable to stand against forced acculturation, turning them into caricatures of their conquerors. Powerless to strike out, they must resort to nonviolence, something that does not fit so well with their warrior heritage.

JUNE 8, 1999
IN MEMORY OF
WILSON "WALLY"
BLACK ELK JR.
AND
RON HARD HEART
TWO LAKOTA BROTHERS
WHO GAVE THE ULTIMATE SACRIFICE
FOR THEIR PEOPLE
SO THE PEOPLE WILL
ALWAYS SEEK JUSTICE FOR
THE FUTURE GENERATIONS.
CAMP JUSTICE.

The stone erected by Wally Black Elk's brothers commemorating the ultimate sacrifice made by the two murdered men.

Since the Lakota's gallant victories over the American army, the U.S. government has continually ripped away that which made them Lakota. Even the warriors' children, the grandfathers and grandmothers of today's tribe members, were sent away to schools that would not allow them to speak their native tongue.

Wally Black Elk and Ron Hard Heart are not the only Oglala to have perished mysteriously in the small town of Whiteclay, on the reservation, or in other border towns. It is impossible to understand what has happened to the Oglala without knowing their history, without walking their trails.

Understanding the history of their struggle is key to making sense of Oglala actions after the murders and, perhaps, even to bringing the killers to justice. Loren Black Elk epitomizes that history and struggle; he lives it every day, a warrior in the fight against the white intruders.

Homeless, Loren spends most of his time at his brother Ben's house. He is also a victim of Whiteclay. He has difficulty remembering the day before he turned sixteen when his father told him to drive the family pickup into town. Just as he was pulling onto the main highway, less than a mile from Pine Ridge, the inebriated driver of an approaching car must have thought Loren encroached upon his right of way. He slammed to a stop, jumped out of his vehicle and struck Loren repeatedly on the head with the barrel of a pistol. Loren awoke in the hospital. Several years later he nearly died when another man hit him over the head with a shovel.

Loren is eligible for monthly general assistance funds and also qualifies for Social Security payments for his brain-injury disability. He refuses to collect either. When told that Robert Ecoffey, BIA superintendent, would personally help him secure both categories of funds, Loren refused his help. "That's the government," he says, "we've been fighting against the government for over one hundred years. I can't start working with the government now."

Maybe the brain injury prevented Loren from realizing the economic benefit to himself and his family by taking the money. Perhaps, however, it was the heritage of the Oglala infused into his genes that prevented him from working with the people who pushed his tribe off their lands and onto the reservation. (Sadly, Loren passed away after this was written.)

3
Skid Row of the Plains

In the course of our travels, we have so often met upstanding citizens who told us, comfortably sitting by their fireside of an evening: "Every day the numbers of Indians decrease. It is not, however, that we very often wage war against them, but the brandy that we sell them every year carries off more than our arms could kill. This world here belongs to us."

—*Alexis De Tocqueville,* Democracy in America and Two Essays on America (1835)

If no drunks staggered the streets of Whiteclay or slept on the sidewalk, the hamlet would still be a dump. Squalid, whitewash-fading, paint-needing, plaster-peeling walls; weed overgrown vacant lots; abandoned houses and stores in varied states of collapse—civic pride left long ago. A Ministry Center, two grocery stores, and a cafe struggle for respectability, but with staggering drunks on the street, and liquor store owners behind metal cages and bars, it becomes what it is: skid row of the plains. Alcoholism affects eight out of ten families on the Pine Ridge; the death rate from alcohol-related incidents is 300 percent higher than the national average.

A typical business day in the small Nebraska hamlet of Whiteclay. Inhabited by less than twenty people, the town's stores sell over four million cans of beer a year, mostly to residents of the Pine Ridge.

The Oglala, like other indigenous Americans, did not come by their use of alcohol accidentally. Booze has always been a weapon in the crucible of indigenous genocide. European colonists landed on American shores with a gun in one hand and a jug in the other; they used both to destroy the land's original inhabitants. Muzzle-loading muskets killed faster, but alcohol, called sacred water by the Lakota and thought to have spiritual powers by many Indians, has killed more.

Emigrants left a world awash in alcohol and brought it to people that had never known its mind-bending powers, turning it into a profitable business.[1] The world wanted furs so American Indians, unable to handle alcohol but quickly developing a need for the pernicious liquid, struck a deal. They supplied fashionistas with pelts, and the world paid them with booze.

Colonists did not bring alcohol just for the Indian trade or see the exchange as a particularly heinous business. Spirituous liquids were an important part of their life. According to one estimate, the average colonist drank three pints of distilled beverages every week, or roughly seven shots a day.[2] Americans learned early on the problems associated with supplying liquor to the Indians. Numerous stories of drunken Indians running riot created a stereotype that all Indians drank and turned into murderous monsters under the influence. A report by Benjamin Franklin doubtlessly caused many frontier families to lay awake in bed at night fearing an attack by inebriated natives. After withholding alcohol from a group of over one hundred men, women, and children as an inducement to sign a treaty, Franklin's party finally rewarded the Indians with rum. According to the publisher of *Poor Richard's Almanac*:

> We found they had made a great bonfire in the middle of the square; they were all drunk men and women, quarreling and fighting. Their dark-coloured bodies, half naked, seen only through the gloomy light of the bonfire, running after and beating one another with firebrands, accompanied by their horrid yellings, formed a scene the most resembling our ideas of hell that could well be imagined ..."[3]

Early in the seventeenth century, Plymouth Colony passed laws criminalizing the sale of alcohol to Indians because they drank too much, "and in their drunkenness commit much horred wickedness, as murthering theire nearest relations ..."[4]

Other colonies followed suit. In 1648, Warwick, Rhode Island, passed a law that no men in the town could sell alcohol to the Indians. But the sale of booze was just too profitable to stamp out. The town fathers finally recognized the impossibility of halting the trade, allowing it as long as the Indians drank at least one mile from town.[5]

An Oglala man spending time on the streets of Whiteclay.

America's booze peddling prevailed, even though—and contrary to the stereotypical notion that Indians were drunkards who couldn't stop drinking—tribes did try to end the trade. The Shawnee in Pennsylvania threatened to destroy the liquor that came to their homes. Iroquois and Delaware Indians also tried to stop the sale.[6] One of the first Americans to establish fur trading with the Lakota in the Old Northwest noted in 1767 that the Lakota had little experience with liquor and did not take to it readily.[7]

Except there was no stopping the use of alcohol. Frontiersmen going west into Indian country brought booze along. Lewis and Clark took enough to fulfill their men's daily liquor allotment and "to create good relations with the Indians."[8] On August 19, 1804, they gave a "dram" of whiskey to a group of Otoes, a people who "… begged much for whiskey."[9]

A month later near the present site of Pierre, South Dakota, they invited a group of Lakota chiefs aboard their riverboat and "gave each of them a quarter of a glass of whiskey which they appeared to be very fond of, sucked the bottle after it was out and soon began to be troublesome."[10]

Throughout the exploration and settlement of the West, alcohol continued as a mainstay of the Indian trade, and Americans did their best to show the natives what drunkenness looked like. In fact, soldiers stationed around the West to protect settlers and immigrants from Indian depredations may have been too drunk to attend to duty. A report from Fort Larned, Kansas, showed that 34 percent of the six officers and 110 enlisted men were alcoholics and that this disease increased every year after the army began compiling medical statistics at the fort in 1868.[11]

At least the army drank real booze. Supplying western Indians with enough alcohol for commerce called for traders with creativity and a complete disregard for the health of their clients. Far from stills and necessary ingredients to make whiskey, transporting the finished product to the Great Plains and the Rocky Mountains was too expensive. It was cheaper to pack in alcohol and serve tribes a disgusting and lethal brew.

> You take one barrel of Missouri River water and two gallons of alcohol. Then you add two ounces of strychnine to make them crazy because strychnine is the greatest stimulant in the world—and three plugs of tobacco to make them sick—because an Indian wouldn't figure it was whiskey unless it made him sick—and five bars of soap to give it a bead, and half a pound of red pepper, and then you put it in some sagebrush and boil it until it's brown. Strain this into a barrel and you've got your Indian whiskey, that one bottle calls for one buffalo robe, and when the Indian got drunk it was two robes. And that's how some of the traders made their fortune.[12]

After their settlement on reservations, tribes found themselves surrounded by whiskey traders working out of ranches and towns. The federal government had banned the sale and consumption of alcohol by Indians, but merchants flocked to the borders to set up shop. On the Pine Ridge where the tribe has continued prohibition, whiskey traders still wait at the border.

Whiteclay is a twenty-first century representation of frontier whiskey ranches. Unlike the federal government that formally banned the sale of alcohol to Indians in 1834 and kept the prohibition until 1954, Nebraskans have always found the sale of booze to the Oglala too profitable to pass up. "They're going to go ahead and drink it, so we just might as well get the money," sums up the state's policy.[13]

By some estimates the Whiteclay outlets sell almost 14,000 cans of beer a day—almost all to the citizens of the Pine Ridge. This is big money for Nebraska, and in 2010, Whiteclay paid almost $500,000 in federal and state excise taxes. The whiskey traders had over $3.5 million in sales that year alone.[14]

While Whiteclay's merchants do not lace their products with strychnine, what they sell is not the garden-variety beer sold at ballparks. The Oglala call Black Ice, twenty-four ounces of 10.5 percent alcohol malt liquor, whiskey in a can. If they can't get that, they drink 6 percent alcohol-laden Hurricanes. The Budweiser website describes the brew as a full-bodied and robust malt liquor that offers a smooth, slightly fruity and slightly sweet taste.[15] If that isn't enough of a kick, the Oglala can also buy Hurricane High Gravity with an alcohol level of 8.1 percent.

Ron Hard Heart and Wally Black Elk made the walk to Whiteclay following the whiskey trade—two more Indians to die while on a trip to purchase that which white Americans have found most profitable to sell them. The traders at Whiteclay fulfill the long-standing and seemingly revered American tradition of selling firewater to the natives. The whiskey trade is still killing the Oglala, still destroying their families, and still ravaging a proud people.

A Whiteclay street scene.

4
State of Pupilage

Because of the local ill feeling, the people of the states where they are found are often their deadliest enemies. … The power of the general government over these remnants of a race once powerful, now weak and diminished in numbers, is necessary to their protection, as well as to the safety of those among whom they dwell.
— *United States v. Kagama, 1886*

Norman Brown Eyes patrolled the reservation for more than ten years as a police officer with the Oglala Sioux Tribe Department of Public Safety; he now works security for Indian Health Services. At six-feet-four-inches tall and two hundred and fifty pounds, the American cavalry would have despaired at confronting him, and so do modern criminals. A former marine, he learned his trade guarding nukes on aircraft carriers.

Norman does not have stories to tell of his warrior ancestors, except that one may have traveled with Buffalo Bill Cody's Wild West Show. He spent most of his childhood cut off from Lakota culture, attending elementary school in Nebraska before enrolling in the boarding school on the reservation. He equates that school with the movie, *Lord of the Flies*.

All Norman ever wanted to be was a cop, a result of watching his favorite television program, *Adam 12*. He had worked fatal traffic accidents, but never imagined anything like the horrific sight that confronted him when he arrived at the double homicide along the highway to Whiteclay. Ten years later he cannot forget the smell or mutilation of the bodies. The murder weapon had to be something large and heavy, he says. Echoing Darlene Red Star, Norman thinks the lack of blood at the scene suggests that the murders occurred elsewhere.[1]

If he had heard more tales of the old days while growing up, he might have thought about a killing one hundred and eighteen years earlier. Crow Dog's shot that killed Spotted Tail on the Rosebud Reservation in 1881 helped fashion a law enforcement system that still disenfranchises Indians.

***

Post-revolutionary leaders of Georgia believed that land ownership in America flowed from England to them, and Indians occupying the ground

Una Horn Cloud's grandfather, Oliver Red Cloud, the last of the traditional Red Cloud Chiefs on the Pine Ridge. (Photo by Laura Red Cloud)

had no claim to it. Heightened by the discovery of gold on Cherokee land, the state became a battleground over the rights of indigenous residents. Because the Cherokee emulated Euro-Americans, hosting a written language and constitution by 1827, the fight was waged in courtrooms instead of on the battlefield.

In 1830, a Cherokee named Corn Tassel, also known as George Tassel, killed Sanders Talking Rockford, another member of the tribe. Georgia immediately tried Tassel and sentenced him to death. Tassel's attorney based an appeal to the Supreme Court on the Cherokee's belief that the state did not have authority to try Indians, alleging treaties between the tribe and the federal government took precedent.[2] The court ordered the state to appear in January "to show cause if any there be why judgment rendered against the said George as in the said writ of error mentioned should not be corrected."[3] In December, Georgia made the case moot by hanging Corn Tassel.

Tassel lost, but two other cases filed for the Cherokee during the following years set the boundaries of tribal, state, and federal intercourse. In *Cherokee Nation* v. *Georgia,* the United States Supreme Court led by Chief

Justice John Marshall designated tribes as "domestic dependent nations ... in the state of pupilage; their relation to the United States resembles that of a ward to his guardian ... being completely under the sovereignty and dominion of the United States."[4]

While the ruling disappointed the Cherokee because the court found that they did not have the sovereignty of a foreign nation, justices did find them to be different from just another group of citizens living in the state of Georgia. A year later in *Worcester* v. *Georgia,* after the state again attempted to force its will on the tribe by jailing missionaries living on tribal lands, the Supreme Court held:

> The Cherokee Nation, then, is a distinct community, occupying its own territory, with boundaries accurately described, in which the laws of Georgia can have no force, which the citizens of Georgia have no right to enter. ... The Acts of Georgia are repugnant to the Constitution, laws, and treaties of the United States.[5]

Realizing this ruling could prevent the removal of the Cherokee to the West, President Andrew Jackson remarked, "Chief Justice John Marshall has made his decision, now let him enforce it."[6] A Supreme Court justice has no enforcement powers, and Presidential politics trumped the court. In 1838, the tribe began the infamous Trail of Tears during which more than four thousand Cherokee died.

Another murder on the Cherokee reservation, this time on the new western lands, established who is and who is not an Indian. In 1848, William Rogers, a white man married to a Cherokee woman, killed another white man. He claimed immunity from Georgia law as a member of the tribe. The Supreme Court led by Chief Justice Roger Taney held that membership in the tribe was not a political award of the tribe, but rather a matter of racial status—a decision that still defines "Indian-ness" today.

> Yet he is not an Indian: and the exception is confined to those who by the usages and customs of the Indian are regarded as belonging to their race. It does not speak of members of a tribe, but of the race generally— of the family of Indians: and it intended to leave them both, as regarded their own tribe, and other tribes also to be governed by Indian usages and customs. And it would perhaps he [sic] found difficult to preserve peace among them, if white men of every description might at pleasure settle among them, and, by procuring and adoption by one of the tribes, throw off all responsibility to the laws of the United States, and claim to be treated by the government and its officers as if they were Indian born. *It can hardly be supposed that Congress intended to grant such exemptions, especially to men of that class who are most likely to become Indians*

by adoption, and who will generally be found the most mischievous and dangerous inhabitants of the Indian country [emphasis added].[7]

***

During the latter half of the nineteenth century, Spotted Tail had been a renowned warrior and chief of the Brule Lakota. In 1854, he took part in repelling an unwarranted army attack on his tribe near Fort Laramie. Known as either the Grattan Massacre or the Mormon Cow Incident (a Minniconjou Lakota butchered an old, sick cow owned by a Mormon traveling the Oregon Trail), the short battle began the final wars between the United States and the Lakota.[8]

One year later, General William S. Harney commanding six hundred army dragoons attacked a peaceful Brule village camped on Blue Water Creek in western Nebraska.[9] Harney met with Brule chiefs as his column surrounded the village, demanding the surrender of Indians who had attacked a mail wagon and killed three men following the Grattan incident. When they did not appear, his forces opened fire on a camp filled with women and children. Spotted Tail fought heroically before suffering two near-fatal bullet wounds.[10]

Not satisfied with slaughtering eighty-six Lakota and capturing over seventy women and children, Harney again called for the surrender of the Indians who attacked the mail wagon. Spotted Tail and three other men turned themselves in, shielding their people from further assault.

Leaving behind a young wife and several children, Spotted Tail spent a little over a year in prison at Fort Leavenworth, Kansas. Imprisonment converted the warrior to statesman. Realizing that there were too many Americans, he recognized the futility of fighting. For the rest of his life, except for an 1864 raid on Julesburg,

Spotted Tail in 1870.

Colorado, in revenge for the massacre of Black Kettle's Cheyenne at Sand Creek, he remained at peace with the white invaders.[11]

Because of Spotted Tail's conciliatory practices, General George Crook appointed him Chief of the Red Cloud and Spotted Tail Agencies, when no Lakota had ever before been the leader of the combined tribes. Other Brule saw Spotted Tail as a sell-out—and a generously rewarded one.[12] As the anointed leader of the tribes, Washington politicians wined, dined, and fêted him. The government even built him a $4,000 three-story house on the reservation.[13]

His nemesis, Crow Dog, had also been a famous Brule warrior and was even more grievously wounded in battle. He received his name when he led a band north of Brule land on a spiritual quest. While he prayed a coyote howled four times, warning him that Crow Indians, traditional enemies of the Lakota, were near. Crow Dog received such terrible wounds in the ensuing battle that both sides left him for dead.

The story is that coyotes nursed the wounded warrior back to health, bringing him medicine and curling around him for warmth. On the fourth day, as a crow flew overhead cawing out warnings of danger, the animals led Crow Dog back to his people. On returning to his village, he changed his name to Crow Coyote. We know him as Crow Dog because an interpreter misstated his name to census takers.[14]

While Spotted Tail stayed on the reservation during the fight against Custer, Crow Dog took part and fought bravely. A few days after the battle, in a minor skirmish, soldiers shot him twice. Gravely injured, he returned to the reservation where he came to believe Spotted Tail worked more for the whites than the Indians. He had become "too soft on the wasicus, [and] too ready to give in."[15]

Perhaps trying to win over his rival, Spotted Tail appointed Crow Dog chief of the Akicita (tribal police), but the opposite happened.[16] Crow Dog discovered white ranchers from Nebraska grazing cattle on the reservation and demanded remuneration to the tribe. The cowboys said they had already paid Spotted Tail. When Crow Dog publicly accused the chief of taking the money and keeping it for his own purposes, Spotted Tail took away his position with the police.[17]

Politics was not the only reason for Crow Dog's enmity. Besides seeing him as a sell-out, he disliked Spotted Tail because of the chief's affinity toward other men's wives. Spotted Tail had earned the nickname "speaking with women," which meant "making love to women because of his amorous conquests."[18] Years earlier he had encouraged the young wife of one of Crow Dog's relatives to leave her husband and become one of his wives. Shortly after firing Crow Dog, Spotted Tail raided another man's tipi and took the man's wife as his own.

As proud warriors and skilled fighters, the two refused to step lightly around each other. One time they met while each carried a gun and dared the other to shoot. They had the sense to walk away that day, but the next time they did not. They met for the last time on August 5, 1881, when Spotted Tail came upon Crow Dog hauling wood in a wagon.

Depending on whose account is believed, Crow Dog was either guilty of murder or acted in self-defense. Friends of Spotted Tail said Crow Dog had seen the chief coming, got off his wagon, bent over in the road to conceal his rifle, and shot from ambush. Crow Dog said he was innocently tying his moccasins when his wife saw Spotted Tail riding toward them and threw him his rifle and he fired to defend himself.

One of Crow Dog's descendants said Spotted Tail saw Crow Dog and announced to his companions, "This is the day when Crow Dog and I will meet as men," and went for his pistol. Crow Dog was faster.[19]

Crow Dog's friends and the tribal council met with Spotted Tail's family to adjudicate the killing as tradition demanded. Both sides considered the matter resolved with the payment of six hundred dollars and a number of horses and blankets to Spotted Tail's family.

However, John Cook, the Rosebud agent, had Crow Dog arrested, taken to Deadwood and tried in the territorial court for murder. The judge in the booming mining camp sentenced the old warrior to hang. Amazingly, he granted the Brule permission to return to the Rosebud and get his affairs in order on the promise that he return for his execution. Crow Dog arrived home to find his wife making him a new set of beaded buckskins for the afterlife.[20]

Crow Dog kept his promise and walked down the rudely cut board sidewalk to the Deadwood Sheriff's Office for his execution, only to be sent back home. He was a free man. His attorney, A. J. Plowman, had appealed the case to the United States Supreme Court on the basis that South Dakota had no jurisdiction over Indians on the reservation and that the Lakota, following traditional remedies, had already settled the matter. The Supreme Court in *Ex parte Crow Dog* agreed.[21]

Crow Dog's personal court victory proved a defeat for Indian sovereignty. Writing about the savage nature of Indians and the futility of measuring a red man's revenge by the maxims of white morality in their decision, justices labeled reservations lawless lands where Indians murdered with impunity. The citizens of America reacted to Crow Dog's lack of punishment with anger.

Using the public mood as justification, Congress passed the Major Crimes Act of 1885, extending federal jurisdiction on reservations to the seven felony charges of murder, manslaughter, rape, arson, assault with intent to kill, burglary, and larceny. Federal authorities now had a duty to apprehend Indians accused of committing crimes against other Indians on tribal land. Once arrested, Indians stood trial in federal court.

A year later, the Supreme Court upheld the constitutionality of the Major Crimes Act in *United States* v. *Kagama*, and decided that Congress had complete (plenary) power over all matters on Indian reservations. The court set the stage for more than a century of forced assimilation by denying Indian sovereignty, which is still in force today.[22]

Dominated by colonial rule, America's earliest inhabitants became subject to a complex and confusing system of law enforcement over which they have no control.[23] Except for misdemeanors, Indians may not police themselves. If accused of felonies, they are neither allowed a trial in front of peers nor will they be tried in a court located on their land. Instead, as in the case of the Oglala, they will face a largely white jury in Rapid City.

If a non-Indian murders or harms an Indian on the reservation, the residents of the reservation may not investigate the crime, bring charges, or oversee the trial of the accused.[24] A federal court off the reservation with a largely non-Indian jury will hear the case. However, if a non-Indian commits the same crime on Indian land and there is a non-Indian victim, a state court will try the case.[25]

The complexity of law enforcement on reservations even confuses federal prosecutors. In 2004, Arlo Looking Cloud, an Oglala, was tried for the murder of Anna Mae Aquash, an Indian from Canada, on the Pine Ridge and sentenced to life in prison. In January 2009, John Boy Patton (Graham), an Indian from Canada, went on trial in Rapid City in federal court for his part in the same crime. The court found that the Major Crimes Act gave the federal government authority only over Indians who are citizens of the United States. Since Aquash and Patton were both Canadian citizens, the federal government had no ability to try Patton for murder.

***

Dedicated men and women like Norman Brown Eyes work without real authority locked in a charade of self-governance. As an officer in the tribal police, the first to arrive at the scene of the Hard Heart/Black Elk murders, his role was never more than to keep curious Oglala away from the scene.

Darlene Red Star discovered the mutilated bodies of Hard Heart and Black Elk while carrying food to members of her extended family.

The FBI has never questioned Norman about what he saw that day. No one has asked him to talk to anyone or learn what he can from the Oglala. He has never met with the FBI; they have never told him about their investigation.

Acting under the rights granted by the 1885 Major Crimes Act, the Federal Bureau of Investigation assumed control of the investigation and placed a lock on information about the murders. When questioned, agents invariably answer, "We cannot comment on a still-open case." They claim they might unintentionally make public a piece of evidence that only they and the killers know, making it impossible to use that evidence to gain a conviction.[26]

5

Wasicu Justice

The white man says there is freedom and justice for all. We have had
"freedom and justice," and that is why we have been almost extermi-
nated. We shall not forget this.
        —1927 Grand Council of American Indians

Six months after Ron and Wally died, the South Dakota Advisory Committee to the U.S. Commission on Civil Rights held a forum in Rapid
City entitled "Native Americans and the Administration of Justice in South
Dakota." Tom Poor Bear, Wally's half-brother, told panel members, "I
personally hold that county [Sheridan County, Nebraska] responsible for
these deaths, as many of our Lakota people do. ... Every time they say our
people die of natural causes, when they are identified by family members
they are beaten."[1]

Poor Bear also gave a poor evaluation of the Federal Bureau of Investigation, alleging that agents failed to look into the crime until the announcement of the civil rights meeting. He told the commission, "If those were
two white people that were found, the FBI would have been there in full
force the day they found my little brother and Ron ... last week the FBI did
come to Camp Justice and did a sweep and they brought a dog—six months
later."[2]

Robert Ecoffey, Pine Ridge Bureau of Indian Affairs Superintendent,
gave credence to Poor Bear's claims. A former tribal police officer, he testified, "There is a total lack of communication and timeliness of response
when it comes to either the victim or the victim's family."[3]

James Burrus, Jr., Assistant Special Agent in charge of the Federal Bureau of Investigation, Minneapolis Division, disputed Poor Bear's statement. He told the commissioners that two of their most experienced agents
were on the scene the day of the murders. According to the special agent,
they interviewed more than three hundred people, deployed search dogs
and evidence response teams, conducted aerial surveys, expedited forensic
testing, and offered a $20,000 reward for information.

The special agent left the Lakota scratching their heads by adding that
discrimination in the justice system would, "undermine the trust placed in
us by the residents. ... I believe reservation residents want the FBI to be

involved in Indian Country law enforcement, but we must continue to earn their trust by working every day for justice."[4]

The comment prompted the chairperson to express concern that the agent's testimony "lacked recognition of the long-standing mistrust and lack of confidence Native Americans hold for federal law enforcement agencies."[5]

Border Town Justice: South Dakota

The state of South Dakota fared no better at the hearing than Sheridan County or the FBI. Faith Taken Alive described the ignominious death of Robert Many Horses in Mobridge earlier that year. Twenty-two years old and afflicted with fetal alcohol syndrome, Many Horses joined four white teenagers in a night of drinking. The next morning the police chief found his body upside down in a garbage can. Taken Alive alleged, "Native American people knew from day one that Many Horses was killed and then stuffed into the trash can—that he did not merely die from alcohol poisoning …"[6]

In response, Daniel Todd, state's attorney, told the commissioners that the court dismissed the charges he had filed against the teens, which included manslaughter and aggravated assault. His only recourse would have been to charge them with underage intoxication, and he thought that would have been insulting to Robert's family.

The facts of the case are fairly clear. Less than five feet tall and underweight, Robert often bought alcohol for kids too young to buy their own.[7] He met four white teens at a convenience store early in the morning of June 30, 1999. The five young people drove several miles out of town to drink, and on the way eighteen-year-old Layne Gisi and Robert each drank a pint of Yukon Jack. Both young men became drunk, sick, and vomited. Soon Robert became incoherent and then unconscious and non-responsive.

The teenagers drove him back to town later that evening after either throwing him into a ditch or dropping him into one, a contentious point between attorneys and the prosecutor. Close to Robert's home, they shoved him head first in a garbage can. Gisi's attorney alleged that Robert fell out onto the street when they opened the car door. Thinking it would be a great joke on his drunken friend, Gisi put him in the garbage can. The attorney said maybe it was a tasteless joke, but that is what it was, a joke.

State Attorney Todd believed the position in the can contributed to the death and charged Gisi with second-degree murder; the other three teens were charged with aiding and abetting manslaughter in the first degree. None of the charges stuck. Judge Portra, whose own father was an enrolled member of the tribe, ruled the cause of death to be alcohol poisoning because Robert had a blood ethanol level of .446 percent. Robert was drunk before they picked him up—according to Gisi's attorney the frail Many Horses had consumed at least a forty-ounce bottle of Old English Malt Liquor and a beer earlier that morning.

Todd claimed the white teenagers acted with indifference to the medical condition of Robert. "Civil law imposes upon individuals an obligation to act honestly and morally toward others."

The defendants' attorney argued that Todd's statement flew in the face of his own witness, a medical doctor who said a non-medically trained person would be unable to tell the difference between someone in a comatose state and a passed-out drunk. And nobody is taken to the hospital for merely passing out.[8]

Still the Lakota's outcry continued. The ABC program *20/20* responded in September of 2000 with a program hosted by Barbara Walters. They took evidence from the case to six forensic experts around the country. At least two of them, the former deputy medical examiner from Chicago, Dr. Robert Kirschner, who had an international reputation and had been a forensic consultant to the United Nations International Criminal Tribunals for Yugoslavia and Rwanda, and former medical examiner from New York City, Dr. Michael Baden, a noted author and pathologist who had investigated the remains of Czar Nicholas of Russia and his family, called it murder. They concluded that Robert died of positional asphyxiation, a homicide in either city. Baden said that if Robert was alive when he went into the can, "positional asphyxiation was the cause. Flat-out was the cause."[9]

When the FBI launched a probe into Robert's death, the local AIM office issued a statement of support. "The unbelievable has happened. The FBI kept their word."[10] However, the investigation ended without charges. Even though State's Attorney Todd said he would look into the work of the ABC program, he later called expert shopping unethical. No further charges were filed.

In 2003, Robert's foster mother, Lila Martel, accepted a settlement in a civil case a month before the trial. While all parties agreed to keep the settlement confidential, her attorney had earlier announced that the family planned to ask for one million dollars. "Sometimes I miss that kid so bad, it's unreal," Martel said in a 2000 interview. "It hurts."

Peggy Redday told the Civil Rights Commission the story of her son, Justin, who was killed on his way home from a party in Roberts County on the Lake Traverse Reservation in the northeastern corner of South Dakota. Justin, who had been drinking, was hit while walking on the road by a pickup driven by inebriated seventeen-year-old Mark Appel.

She testified that Appel told the police Justin was passed out and lying in his lane. When asked why he hit him, Appel said because it was illegal to swerve or to cross a white or solid yellow line, and he did not want to get in trouble for swerving.[11] He drove straight ahead and ran over Justin. Unsure of what he hit, Appel backed up and ran over Justin again.[12]

A grand jury indicted Appel on charges of vehicular homicide, driving under the influence, probation violation, and underage consumption. However, Kerry Cameron, state's attorney for Robert County, dismissed the grand jury's charges and allowed Appel to plead guilty to driving while under the influence.[13]

According to Cameron, Justin was lying near the center of the road when struck by the pickup, therefore alcohol was responsible for Justin's death. The plea bargain dismissing the manslaughter charge sentenced Appel to the Department of Corrections until he turned twenty-one for violating probation by drinking alcohol. He would have received the same sentence if convicted of manslaughter.[14]

Thirteen years later, Justin's mother still disputed Cameron's testimony about Appel's sentence—and the state attorney's commitment to justice. Mark Appel never spent one night in jail for Justin's death, she said. He did, however, spend two nights in the slam for a later incident in another town, placed in jail for his own protection from angry citizens.[15]

More criticism of Attorney Cameron's racial unfairness followed when David Seaboy of Sisseton related his daughter's story. Melanie, an eighteen year old that Cameron prosecuted a year earlier, had crashed into another car while driving drunk, killing a non-Indian motorist. The court sentenced her to fourteen years in prison.

During his presentation, Seaboy listed the sentences for ten similar cases in the Fifth Judicial Circuit serving a population of over eighty thousand citizens and covering more than eleven thousand square miles. Melanie's sentence was nearly three times more severe than any other sentence for a comparable offense. The next harshest sentence for vehicular manslaughter or homicide was five years; some defendants served no time at all. Another female defendant also pled guilty to vehicular homicide but received only a five-year suspended sentence.[16]

State's Attorney Cameron, a Republican, lost his job to Democrat Kay Nikolas after the Civil Rights Commission met. According to Alva Quinn, head of the tribal realty agency, Indians were responsible for Cameron's 2010 re-election and planned to keep him in office. His assistant, not Cameron, had been responsible for the Melanie Seaboy sentence.[17]

In 2002, the newly elected Nikolas prosecuted another Indian girl, a case that graphically highlights the injustices that Indians face in wasicu courts and probably was responsible for Cameron's return to office. Adelia

Godfrey's experiences "may be the most egregious example of the legal system that preys on tribal members, especially youth."[18]

Adelia's troubles began as a fifteen-year-old in 1999. Her mother, Shirley Duggan, called the authorities for help one night when she could not find her. Adelia finally came home, but the family failed to notify the police. The following night as she walked to a movie the police picked her up as a runaway. She argued. A police officer slammed her up against a wall and charged her with resisting arrest.

Even though it was Adelia's first appearance in court, Nikolas tried to move the case to adult court, alleging Adelia had scratched an officer during the arrest. If convicted, she would have received a six-year sentence. The judge denied the prosecution's motion and sentenced the juvenile to a youth facility in Plankinton, South Dakota.[19]

Adelia and other girls in the center were four-pointed, an uncommon practice where they were chained to a concrete slab and had their clothing cut off their bodies. Allowed to wear only a paper gown, she spent her first two weeks in solitary confinement sleeping on concrete without a blanket or pillow.[20] Adelia was one of several girls who tried to kill herself in Plankinton. The facility closed after another girl's successful attempt.

When vandals broke several windows out of her home in 2000, Adelia's mom thought her daughter might have done it and called the police. Although another girl confessed to the destruction, Adelia "went ape during the booking" and ran into another room where she jumped onto a desk and sprayed an officer trying to subdue her with a fire extinguisher. Adelia then tried to bite and scratch the deputy. He went to the hospital with a rash, and the ninety-eight pound girl went to the dungeon, the sheriff's name for the basement cell where they put her.[21]

Illuminated by two ever-shining light bulbs, closed-circuit cameras followed the seventeen-year-old girl's every movement. She crouched behind a waist high concrete wall while showering, trying to shield her body from display on television in the dispatcher's office.

"At night, I get panic attacks and I worry I'll stop breathing … I get real scared and depressed," she testified about her experiences in the dungeon. As it turns out, she had good reason to be afraid. The county attorney again applied to try her as an adult on two counts of aggravated assault, charges that could have netted the youngster thirty years in the penitentiary.[22]

The judge denied the request and sent Adelia to the Heartland Behavioral Center in Nevada, Missouri, where she was placed on 300mg of Thorazine without parental consent or notification.[23] After the filing of a police report alleging molestation by a Heartland staff member, she was transferred back to South Dakota and released.[24]

Could the story get any worse? Edward Godfrey, Adelia's father, a retired substance abuse counselor, said the officer that his hundred-pound daughter was accused of assaulting stood six-feet-eight-inches tall and weighed over 280 pounds. He also said the incident with the fire extinguisher only occurred as she tried to protect her younger sister from police brutality. She was never offered any rehabilitation or treatment for alcohol addiction—and when Adelia returned from Missouri she "was a complete zombie." It took her several months to return to normal.[25] In 2012, now a wife and mother, Adelia was back in jail serving out the remainder of her ten year sentence for violating parole with alcohol-related incidents. Her husband and child travel to the prison to see her regularly.[26]

***

Jesse Taken Alive summed up the dangers facing Indians entering the judicial system for panel members. "American Indian people sit in front of juries of all non-Indian people when we are supposedly economically disadvantaged and yet they are sitting in judgment with all the stereotypical messages that they have received throughout the years."[27]

The 1999-2000 commission, led by Mary Francis Berry armed with both a Ph.D. and a law degree, and holding a lengthy career in academia and the field of civil rights, labeled race relations in South Dakota a crisis. Commission members called for Attorney General Janet Reno to form a task force and appoint a full-time mediator to deal with the situation.

However, then governor of South Dakota William Janklow, known to many as Wild Bill, called the report garbage and announced, "Mrs. Berry has seen fit to come out here and beat up on people in South Dakota with her mouth. She's seen fit to call this state names or allude to names about individuals that live in this state."[28]

The beautiful white clay buttes and forested slopes of the Pine Ridge begin in northern Nebraska and extend to the South Dakota Bad Lands.

***

Border Town Justice: Nebraska

For thousands of years the Mnitanka Mnilusa (Rapid Large Water), now called the Niobrara River, coursing through the northern edge of the Nebraska Sandhills, watered the vast buffalo herds hunted by the Lakota. The river now serves cattle ranches and provides irrigation for crops planted by descendants of late–nineteenth century European immigrants. The towns of Rushville, Gordon, Hay Springs, and Whiteclay rose among the tipi rings and fire circles left by the Indians confined to the reservation across the state line.

Sheridan County grew into a prosperous agricultural center where God-fearing, gun-toting farmers and ranchers, hunters and football fans extol the virtues of hard work. Pride in lives and livelihood etched across suntanned faces is hardened into calluses on their hands.

Christian churches stand on almost every street corner, and even in the rolling hills of the countryside steeples soar high above the pines. Peeling bells call the faithful to services every Sunday. Christian fellowship makes Sheridan County a great place to live.

Except for Indians. Since their arrival, the Oglala have regarded the newcomers as a people bent on destroying their way of life—they say it is cultural genocide. Sheridan County greets them, they say, with the scourge of racial discrimination frequently delivered with violence—both on a personal and institutional level.

Older Lakota remember signs on businesses proclaiming "NO INDIANS ALLOWED." The white population's feelings have not changed, the Oglala say, they are just a little less obvious. Ben Black Elk says the same attitude exists in nearby Chadron. While shopping in a large, chain retail store, every time he or his wife, Marla, look around they see a store employee, usually a large man, watching them. "He just stares, waiting for us to steal something. It always happens," Ben said. "We don't say anything because it would just cause more trouble."[29]

Just before the turn of the twenty-first century, discrimination existed in a formalized context in Sheridan County. In 1995, the Department of Justice charged the First National Bank of Gordon with charging higher interest rates for consumer loans to Indians than whites, a violation of the Equal Credit Opportunity Act and the Fair Housing Act. An assistant attorney general announced that the differences in rates "could not have occurred by chance and cannot be explained by factors unrelated to race or national origin."[30]

But neither store harassment nor financial exploitation is what the

Oglala fear the most—they are afraid of what they cannot see, what the wasicu, they say, keep secret.

With a whisper, afraid that loud voices could call down harm upon them, they speak of Ku Klux Klan gatherings illuminated by bonfires and burning crosses. They refer to Whiteclay as WhiteKKKlay.

"My auntie saw them on a hill behind that little church by the highway," a middle-aged woman said. "They wore white robes and carried torches. She was really afraid."

"Lights are on all night long in that church basement in Rushville," said another. "That's where the Klan headquarters is."

A younger woman, fashionably dressed and well spoken, the daughter of a Lakota mother and a wasicu father who spent years off the rez, says she is cautious traveling across the border into Nebraska. "I can take you to those places where the Klan meets, where the cops take Indians to beat them, but you have to be careful being seen with me. People will watch you if you're with an Indian woman."[31]

Other than Oglala statements, there is little to support the contention that Sheridan County is home to an active Klan Klavern. The Southern Poverty Law Center, which keeps track of hate groups, is unaware of Klan activity there.[32]

No one has marched or paraded in white sheets down the streets of Sheridan County towns since the years after World War I when membership in the Klan spread across the plains. But that does not mean prejudice does not exist. The small town of Gordon was once home to a leader of the Church of the Creator, which teaches that races other than Caucasian are mud people.[33] The church, now part of the Creativity Movement, has been called one of the most violent white hate groups in the United States.[34]

Any discussion the Oglala have about white power begins with the 1972 murder of Raymond Yellow Thunder, when four men from Gordon who had spent a winter's day coyote hunting decided to return to town and bust an Indian.[35] As outrageous as Indian busting sounds, brothers Melvin and Lester Hare, with Bernard Ludder and Robert Bayless, were not the only people to indulge in that pastime on the windswept plains and pine-covered buttes of northwestern Nebraska.

Less than a decade earlier, a few students from Chadron State College twenty miles to the west openly bragged about their favorite Indian busting method. They would drive one of the sturdy cars from the 1950s over lonely highways and dirt roads until they spied an Indian walking on the roadside. Approaching from the rear, they pulled over as if offering a ride. When the Indian, man or woman, turned toward the car, the driver stomped on the accelerator while his partner shoved open the heavy door, viciously knocking their prey into the ditch. Bragging rights were granted for how far the Indians flew; propelling one into an electric fence or a telephone pole earned extra points.[36]

The Gordon Indian busters used a more hands-on method. They took turns beating fifty-one-year-old ranch hand Raymond Yellow Thunder and then stripped him from the waist down and threw him into a packed dance at the American Legion Hall. Bloody and humiliated, he staggered back into the street where his assailants shoved him into the trunk of their car and drove around the rough streets of Gordon. With their blood lust finally satisfied, they released him from the trunk and gave him back his trousers.

Yellow Thunder struggled to the city jail, something he had done before after a night of drinking, and passed the winter night in an unused cell. He left the next morning and found his way to an unlocked pickup on a used auto lot. When his friend George Ghost Dog passed by and asked if he would be okay, he replied that he would.[37]

Unfortunately, he would not be. Raymond Yellow Thunder died; his frozen body had lain in the truck for a week before he was found. According to the autopsy, bleeding into the lining of the brain due to the beating at the hands of the Indian busters caused his death.[38]

Supposedly acting out of compassion, county authorities did not allow Yellow Thunder's relatives to view the body in its frozen state, a decision leading to a trove of speculation. Rumors swept the reservation that he had suffered cigarette burns and castration. The torture and mutilation, Indians said, was kept quiet to protect the town's reputation.

Yellow Thunder's grieving relatives turned to the newly formed American Indian Movement meeting across the state in Omaha for help. Soon, led by Russell Means and Dennis Banks, close to fourteen hundred justice-seeking Indians occupied the town of less than one thousand residents.

AIM leaders declared victory when town fathers agreed to set up a human rights commission after Indians held a mock grand jury and heard accusations of official hostility and aggression, including cops raping Indian girls. The American Indian Movement also succeeded in gaining a second autopsy, one that put to rest rumors of Yellow Thunder's castration and cigarette burns—there were no signs of either. His killers received prison sentences ranging from two to six years.

The Oglala have also never forgotten the story of John Yellow Bird, a Vietnam veteran and AIM activist whose wife Joann swallowed strychnine, committing suicide in 1980. She was buried near the Wounded Knee Cemetery next to Zintkalazi, their stillborn daughter from 1976. Seven months pregnant, Joann had been kicked in the stomach by a police officer who was arresting her husband. She said she felt the baby kick hard as a result, and then never felt it move again.

According to her account she was also arrested, and the deputy transporting her to the Sheridan County jail began swerving over the road. He said he was trying to decide whether to take her to jail or out in the country and shoot her. She replied, "Why don't you go ahead?"

"I would, but I don't want to waste any good bullets," the officer supposedly retorted.

Joann had writhed in pain for several hours in jail before she was taken to the hospital in Gordon, where doctors were unable to detect a fetal heartbeat. Three years later a non-Indian jury in federal court in North Platte, Nebraska, awarded her $300,000 in a civil suit she had brought against the town of Gordon and the police officer who had threatened to shoot her.[39]

***

Understandable for a people who still talk of battles between their ancestors and the uniformed men of an invading nation, people whose collective memory include the horrors of the Wounded Knee Massacre and victims such as Joann Yellow Bird, the Oglala fear border town cops and law enforcement agencies. Apparently, their fears are justified.

Incarceration in Sheridan County can be dangerous for Lakota prisoners. Twelve inmates, all but one of them Indian, attempted suicide between 1998 and 2005. Four of them were successful. The last to die behind bars, twenty-year-old Leno "Jay" Spotted Elk, a Sicangu (Brule) Lakota from the Rosebud Reservation, died suspiciously, causing some Oglala to believe he may not have taken his own life.

On July 11, 2005, after downing one beer at home, Jay went to hang out with friends. He told them about the family's move back to the Rosebud the next day and some of the things he planned to do there. He appeared in good spirits, happy to get back to the rez; they said none of them were drinking that night and neither was Jay.

He left them for a short walk to his girlfriend's house. On the way, a deputy sheriff picked him up on an old speeding warrant. As jailers hauled him to the cell usually reserved for those who are creating major disturbances, Jay still was feeling good, greeting one man he knew cheerfully.

Less than an hour later he was dead. His friends called it murder. They questioned why he still had his belt after jailers had removed his earrings, bandana, and shoes, and wondered if the jail staff intended to hang him with it. Noting Jay's body, arms, and hands were scratched and bruised, it was suggested that he received the injuries fighting for his life as jailers held him down and suffocated him.[40]

Arlyn Eastman, Jay's mother, filed suit but not for death at the hands of law enforcement personnel. She accused the arresting deputy of failing to report to the jailers that her son "exhibited objective signs of clinically diagnosable and treatable mental illness and suicidality."[41]

Eastman's lawyer announced at a press conference that Jay had made suicidal statements to the deputy and injured himself in the patrol car by slamming his head against the doorframe, causing an open head wound.[42]

Once in jail, Eastman contended that jailers failed to care for her son in accordance with county policies. Jay was so impaired, she claimed, that a trained jailer would have known to provide care. She also charged that her son had a constitutional right to be free from punishment and indifference.

Accusing the county of a history of tolerating misconduct, Eastman asserted that Jay received disparate treatment due to law enforcement decisions based on racial animus.[43] Four days before trial, Sheridan County settled, paying Jay's estate $100,000 and agreeing to implement suicide prevention measures specifically regarding American Indians.[44]

Does Sheridan County deserve any credit after Jay's death by trying to do the right thing, or did civic leaders attempt to sweep it under the rug? The county convened a grand jury to look into Jay's death, however, no criminal charges were ever filed. Since grand jury proceedings are sealed, no one will ever know what was discussed, but it has been reported that the jury consisted of a doctor, a jailer, and ten other members of law enforcement.[45]

***

Two weeks after Ron and Wally's deaths in 1999, Nebraska cops cordoned off the highway to Whiteclay and arrested protest marchers; the Oglala saw racial discrimination as official Sheridan County law enforcement policy.

In June of 2012, a band of women and children marching peacefully on the small beer town calling for the end of alcohol sales met armed and resolute cops as they crossed the state line. At least one ten-year-old child was sprayed in the face with mace while adult protestors were thrown into a feces-splattered horse trailer and hauled away.[46]

Protestors say the violence was planned. Autumn Two Bulls, marcher and mother of the maced boy, claims that liquor store owners hired thugs to drive them away. Deborah White Plume said the men were "trained martial arts fighters. They were screaming 'Get your fucking jungle bunny ass back where you came from.'"[47]

***

Every day on the streets of Whiteclay, Sheridan County's cash cow, drunks slumber on sidewalks, women service men for booze, and groups of drunks line the street to drink. Nowhere else in Nebraska would such a spectacle be allowed. The small town is such a hellish sight it took only one visit in 2012 for Nicholas Kristof of the *New York Times* to write, "After seeing

Anheuser-Busch's devastating exploitation of American Indians, I'm done with beer." Comparing the effect on the Lakota the same as if Mexico legalized selling crack cocaine in Tijuana, he called for a boycott. "That's why I'll pass on a Bud, and I hope you join me."[48]

Loren Black Elk often speaks of John Means, Willard Bores A Hole, and Mike Waters, friends found dead among the liquor stores and abandoned houses. Suspicious deaths, Loren always said, especially of Mike Waters, "We're supposed to believe he fell off a six-inch stump, hit his head and died?" he asked incredulously.

Even Sandy Sauser discovered death among the hamlet's ruins. Walking through the town's deserted, weed-strewn lots and dilapidated houses snapping pictures, she came across the body of Wilmer Ten Fingers. She watched as Nebraskan authorities retrieved the body lying across a refuse heap in the basement of a ruined, two-walled house.

"He supposedly stopped there to urinate over the foundation, had a seizure, and died," she said. "Pretty good trick to fall up the hill and kill yourself on a pile of garbage. He could just as likely have been killed and thrown onto the dump. How is anybody going to know how he hit his head? There was no investigation, no crime scene tape, and no questions. They just brought in the meat wagon and hauled him away."[49]

A carload of Oglala arrive in Whiteclay. (The author had to pay $5 for this photo, probably so they could buy more beer.)

6

Dead in the Water

*Whose voice was first sounded on this land? The voice of the red
people who had but bows and arrows. ... What has been done in my
country I did not want, did not ask for it; white people going through
my country. ... When the white man comes in my country he leaves a
trail of blood behind him.*

—*Mahpiya Luta (Red Cloud)*, Oglala Chief

Beginning deep in the sacred Black Hills (Paha Sapa), Rapid Creek flows
eighty-six miles before joining the Cheyenne River churning across
eastern South Dakota. Known as big water in the Black Hills, it is one of the
few streams wide and deep enough for anglers to need hip boots.

In the hills above Rapid City, impoundments impede the stream's progress. Pactola Reservoir offers acres of fly-fishing and trophy-size trout, as
does Canyon Lake found just above the city limits. In the heart of the city,
Rapid Creek is a pretty little stream enjoyed by anglers, picnickers, walkers, hikers, and photographers.

Looks are often deceiving. As if the tranquil water resents its reputation as a tamed recreational area, Rapid Creek sometimes rises and swats
humans aside. Four people died when Rapid Creek flooded in 1907 and
eight more lost their lives in 1920. In 1952 severe property damage occurred
along its banks; ten years later severe flooding destroyed 120 mobile homes
and forced 1,500 people to evacuate to higher ground. In June of 1972, the
little stream quit fooling around. After ten to fifteen inches of rain had
fallen over a sixty square mile area west of town, Canyon Lake dam gave
way, sending a wall of water roaring downstream. More than 250 people
died with over 2,500 homes damaged or destroyed.

The town's founders should have spoken with the Lakota about living
near Rapid Creek. Indians never camped along its banks because of "Too
many floods! Too many bears."[1] Of course, if they had any intention of
listening to Indians they wouldn't have been anywhere near the Black Hills.

The 1868 Treaty of Fort Laramie bearing Red Cloud's mark, ratified by
Congress, and signed into law by President Andrew Johnson, included the
hills as part of the Great Sioux Indian Reservation. The land was secured

for Indian-only use by a clause stating that no persons (other than Lakota), except governmental agents and military personnel "… shall ever be permitted to pass over, settle upon, or reside in the territory described in this article …"[2]

The Indian-only policy expired when an exploration and mapping expedition led by General George Armstrong Custer found traces of gold along French Creek in the Black Hills. For miners such as John R. Brennan and Samuel Scott, founders of Rapid City, it became Katie-bar-the-door. Neither the threat of hostile Indians nor the army charged with preventing miners from trespassing on Lakota ground could keep them from the riches.

The party left Fort Laramie in 1874, as cavalry patrols sought to arrest non-Indians sneaking into the Black Hills. Led by noted scout California Joe, who steered them away from the troopers, they made it to the present site of Rapid City. Joe knew the way. He'd scouted for Custer and guided the Jenny geological expedition only a month before.[3]

Brennan and Scott's group were nearly the last to travel clandestinely. By the time they reached the hills, the army had quit arresting trespassers. General George Crook, Commander of the Department of the Platte, decided that allowing Americans in was a better idea than keeping them out.

Gripped by recession, the United States needed the mineral wealth just

Rapid City at the turn of the twentieth century. Copyright © photo librarian at flicker.com

as Georgia did the gold-bearing lands of the Cherokee forty years earlier. Crook, unmoved by arguments of sacred ground, figured a large civilian presence would pressure the Lakota to negotiate a sale.[4] The general did not act alone. The decision to break the terms of the treaty went all the way to President Grant, who backed Crook and ordered no further resistance to miners entering the hills.[5]

Brennan and Scott's party did not find gold. Instead they laid out the town of Rapid City, named after the beautiful little stream running through the valley—the one that knowledgeable Lakota would not camp near. They built cabins and stores and became merchants. They called their new town the gateway to the Black Hills.[6]

***

The pretty little stream still takes human life. An average of one or two people die every year in Rapid Creek, victims of accidental drowning, heart attack, and exposure.[7] That is what makes the fifteen months from May 1998 to July 1999 so difficult to understand. The death toll jumped by nearly 1,000 percent when eight men drowned in the water, and three other bodies were found nearby—all but two of them Indians.

Such an increase seems unexplainable by chance, as Elaine Holy Eagle told the Civil Rights Commission. "I can't understand," she said, "how eight men drowned in Rapid Creek, and in December 1998, four men drowned in four days."[8] She may have misconstrued some of the dates, only two men died in the creek during the last month of 1998, but her disbelief characterized the feelings of the Lakota and some Rapid City cops. According to the Lakota, the men were murdered in the city they call Skinhead Central, USA.[9]

Dead in the water were: Ben Long Wolf, thirty-six, found under the Sixth Street Bridge, May 21, 1998. The coroner listed his death as accidental. George Hatton, fifty-six, found at the West Boulevard and I-90 bridge, May 31, 1998. A transient with marks around his neck, his death was also called accidental. Allen Hough, forty-two, a white male whose body was recovered at South Valley Drive, July 4, 1998. The police found no evidence of foul play in Hough's death and listed the cause as drowning. Royce Yellow Hawk, twenty-six, died from four gunshot wounds, November 12, 1998. Randall Two Crow, forty-eight, found near the East Boulevard Bridge in a pool of water close to downtown Rapid City, December 8, 1998. With a blood alcohol level of .515, authorities believe he died while sleeping under the bridge. Apparently he either rolled into the creek or rains upstream raised the water level enough to sweep over him. Lauren Two Bulls, thirty-three, found downstream of the East Boulevard bridge on December 9, 1998. An Oglala and a well-known artist, the coroner credited Two Bulls' death to severe alcohol toxicity. He had a blood-alcohol level of .531 when he died. Dirk Bartling, forty-four, a white male found in Rapid Creek, May 27, 1999. Cause of death was drowning while drunk. His blood-alcohol level stood at .288 percent. Arthur Chamberlain, forty-five, found in Rapid Creek, June 7, 1999, death from drowning, according to the coroner; blood-alcohol level of .26 percent. Timothy Bull Bear, Sr., forty-seven, found in the creek near Orchard Lane, July 6, 1999. Lonnie Isham, forty-three, his badly decayed body was found behind a store, November 2, 1999. Wilbur G. Johnson, forty-one, bludgeoned to death in an alley, December 22, 2000.[10]

Craig Tieszen, police chief from 2002 until he retired five years later to become a state senator, helped investigate the deaths. He believed the men died, except those noted, of accidental drowning. "I still believe that the evidence and the lack of evidence suggest it was a strange coincidence, but just a coincidence."[11]

Pennington County Sheriff Don Holloway told reporters ten years after the deaths in 2009 that officers had examined every lead and found nothing, but he still hoped to catch some killers. "I'm sure there's somebody out there responsible for at least some of them," he said. "We always hate to have something like this hanging out there."[12]

DeWayne Glassgow served as the deputy chief investigator and Pennington County deputy chief coroner during the investigation.[13] He also thinks some of the men were murdered and says cops did everything possible to find the killer(s). They worked with the FBI on computer models, searched everywhere along the creek, and talked to countless people. However, nothing turned up that pointed to murder.

According to Glassgow, the pretty little stream served as an active participant in the drownings and/or murders. During the fifteen months of the deaths, Rapid Creek ran unusually high. In the deeper channel, bodies floated farther in the current and investigators were never able to pinpoint the scene of the murders. They could not identify the locations where the bodies entered the water.

A lack of witnesses also hampered the investigation. Nobody knew, saw, or heard anything. More accurately, according to Glassgow, nobody remembered anything due to the alcoholic blackouts that afflicted most of the people who stayed along the banks of the creek.

The death of Timothy Bull Bear stands out in Glassgow's memory. The afternoon before his death, Bull Bear partied with a group of men along the banks. Two cops stopped to talk and played a game of catch with the men using a baseball they found in the grass. One of the officers fell into the creek trying to fish out the ball. Bull Bear and his friends pulled him out.

After Bull Bear's body was found, none of the men remembered much about the game or when the victim disappeared. Glassgow figures Bull Bear had a heart attack, fell into the water and floated nearly half a mile downstream. But no one remembered, and he has no proof.

Even though he died at the age of thirty-three, Lauren Two Bulls was another of the victims that Glassgow says probably died of medical causes. He attended the autopsy and describes the dead man's liver as bright yellow and hard as a tabletop. Lauren most likely sat down, fell over into the river, and drowned, Glassgow explains.

Two deaths that bother Glassgow most were those of Arthur Chamberlain and Dirk Bartling. Their bodies were discovered less than two weeks apart near downtown Rapid City; their blood-alcohol level lower than the other victims. The way they found Chamberlain raised Glassgow's suspicions. Chamberlain had always worn a cowboy hat with a flashy band. When they found him, the hat was gone, and the band was tightly wrapped around his throat.[14]

While the former deputy thinks Timothy Bull Bear died of a heart attack and found no evidence of foul play, the family fervently disagreed with those findings, citing claims reminiscent of the death of Raymond Yellow Thunder almost twenty years earlier. They claimed he was naked, had rope burns around his neck, and cigarette burns all over his body. They also disputed the findings of intoxication. "Everybody knew he wasn't a drinker. He was a singer at sun dances. He had just come from a sun dance when they found him dead."[15]

If there is no other evidence of murder, the timing of the deaths is, at least, suspicious. The first three died respectively on May 21, May 31, and little over one month later on July 4, 1998. The following three occurred on November 12, December 8, and December 9, of the same year.

Dick Bartling's body floated in the water on May 27, 1999, almost exactly one year after the first two. The next two on July 6 and 7 were close to the time of the deaths one year earlier. Perhaps spring brings heavy rains and the creek is the most dangerous. But that does not explain why Lonnie Isham, in keeping with the cycle of three, died July 11 on a hill above the creek.

Except for Isham who died behind a store and Yellow Hawk and Johnson, both obviously murdered, how did the men die? In the water and, as Glassgow says, that is the problem. Ben Long Wolf's demise either shows how easy it is for drunks to drown in the creek or how simple it is to kill them. Officially, he slept through his own drowning. Sitting beneath the bridge and leaning back against something, Long Wolf went to sleep, never aware of the rising water from the rains upstream. "When they found him, he was sitting half upright. It looked like Ben Long Wolf was napping, only he was underwater."[16]

How do you know if a drunk fell into the water, slept through rising waters, and died accidentally, or after passing out someone threw him into the water? What's the difference between holding a man's head underwater until he drowns and an unconscious man floating onto a rock or bridge piling and being pinned under the surface by the current?

The 1990 death of Lakota Irving Audiss Jr., still unresolved with a reward of $10,000, is one of the most perplexing of the Rapid Creek mysteries, and the best example of the difficulty in investigating the deaths. Drag marks led directly to where his body was discovered in the water. His relatives said that cops suspected foul play, but with inconclusive autopsy results they never launched a formal investigation. Apparently the coroner's inability to tell whether death by drowning was accidental or murder negated the evidence indicating the victim had been dragged into the creek.[17]

***

For the Lakota, the fifteen months of suspicious deaths along Rapid Creek, while horrifying, were not a surprise. Frank Killsright noted in 2000 that he knew of sixteen Indians who had died along Rapid Creek in the sixteen years since 1984, including his brother Timothy Red Wolf. Killsright believes that skinheads were responsible for the murders, with his theory based on personal knowledge. In 1999, six skinheads confronted him and two friends on a bridge. One of his friends was thrown off the bridge and suffered a broken arm. Killsright came away with broken glasses and a fat lip.[18]

Howard Pretends Eagle also thinks racism was behind the deaths. He reported to the police during the time of the murders that teenaged white males tried to chase him down with their car. Instead of going after the teenagers, he said, "They [the police] tried to arrest me. It doesn't do any good to report crime against the homeless."[19]

Don Holloway, sheriff of Pennington County, told the 2000 Civil Rights Commission that such prejudice did exist in Rapid City. "You've heard here today," he said, "… about prejudice and thex perception of prejudice in our community, and I think those are true or accurate descriptions."[20]

Thomas Hennies, then Rapid City chief of police, went one step further. "I personally know that there is racism and there is discrimination and there are prejudices among all people and that they're apparent in law enforcement." Then he made a courageous statement:

> When I first became a policeman here, if you found a drunk Indian downtown, you put him in a garbage can. And when he got out, he was

sober enough to leave, and that's just the way things were. ... I can tell you if these things do occur [today], and I am not so naïve as to say never, but if they do occur, they will be dealt with because we're trying to make a difference.[21]

Royce Yellow Hawk and Wilbur Johnson, a member of the Yankton tribe, were murdered. Their killers had nothing to do with patrols of skinheads or gangs on a mission to harm Indians. Yellow Hawk died following an altercation, probably a fistfight, at a party. Ralph Larvie pleaded guilty to being an accessory and received a sentence of five years, while seventeen-year-old Dustin Seegrist got fifteen years and paid $3,000 in compensation.[22]

Wilbur Johnson died of a beating with a heavy blunt object after leaving a bar with two men and then trying to run away from them. James Ray Howard of Rapid City and Adrian Gilbert Black Bear were arrested and charged with murder. According to the police, the murder was either robbery or a disagreement turned fatal.[23]

Former deputy Glasgow searched for a connection between the deaths of Wally Black Elk and Ronnie Hard Heart and those in Rapid City. Working with the FBI, he concluded that the differences in the condition of the bodies, except for Yellow Hawk and Johnson, mitigated chances the same killers were working both sides of the reservation. Hard Heart and Black Elk, he explained, had been violently, brutally murdered, while those found in Rapid Creek bore little or no marks of trauma.[24]

The deaths on opposite sides of the reservation do have similarities. They all constitute a mystery with little explanation of motive and no resolution. All but two were young to middle-aged Indian males and alcohol was a factor in each.

Were the deaths some bizarre initiation, perverted thrill, or violent prejudice? Did the deaths end around the Pine Ridge because the killers moved away or died? To the Indians, the demise of so many constitutes more evidence that they live surrounded by hostiles.

7

The Carpenter Guy

People be warned, for you can be sure of this: No immoral, impure, or greedy person—such a person is an idolater—has any inheritance in the Kingdom of Christ and of God. Let no one deceive you with empty words, for because of such things GOD's wrath comes on those who are disobedient.

—The Carpenter Guy

"It was that carpenter guy," the Oglala woman says, breath escaping in nervous gasps. She keeps glancing over her shoulder to make sure no one is listening. "He's the killer. We knew it as soon as he put everything from his house and shop on the curb and started giving it away. He told us he did it."

"It was their spirits," her friend explains, "Ron's and Wally's ghosts. They got to him every night, all the time. Wally and Ron would look in his windows, move things around inside the house. He went crazy, couldn't take it no more because of what he done."

"He confessed to the murders," the other said. "He was really in bad shape."[1]

The two women sway in the blast furnace hot wind blowing dust and trash around Highway 87, Whiteclay's main street, as they remember the day the carpenter guy confessed. They had been drinking in Whiteclay when he gave his stuff away. Like everyone else who had been in town that day, they are convinced of his guilt.

What else could explain such bizarre behavior? Giveaways commemorating life's celebratory moments such as birth, marriage, or loss of a loved one are a cherished facet of Lakota culture. But a wasicu? The guy who built small cabins and picnic tables out of logs and preached Christianity to the Indians? No way! He went crazy. Ron's and Wally's ghosts drove him insane.

He lined the street with his possessions and allegedly confessed to the Indians on April 4, 2006. The problem is that no one in authority was there when he admitted his guilt. Homer Robbins, Sheridan County sheriff, said there was no confession, at least not one that he heard. "No," he claimed,

White clay buttes dominate the landscape of Pine Ridge and northern Nebraska.

"not to me. None of my officers heard him confess."[2] However, a day later he told a reporter asking about the alleged confession, "We did take an individual into emergency protective custody. He has been taken to a hospital for medical evaluation in Scottsbluff."[3]

***

Belying its reputation as flat farmland, grass-covered, thinly populated hills of shifting sand make up more than one-fourth of Nebraska. A trip north of the Platte River is traveling back into the Old West. The Sand Hills are miles of unfenced pastures, cattle, horses, isolated ranches, haystacks, deer and antelope, and strings of lakes shimmering in green valleys as far as the eye can see. Cowboys fixing fences, riding horses and herding cattle appear as if they just climbed out of the pages of an 1880s dime Western.

In Arthur, Nebraska, cars often have to stop for deer crossing the highway in the middle of town. In 2010, the village of 145 people and 62 households served as the seat of Arthur County, which held only 444 inhabitants in an area of 718 square miles. McPherson County to the east of Arthur, listed 533 people and 859 square miles of ranchland, while Grant County to the north of Arthur had 747 people living on 776 square miles. Hooker County, directly to the east of Grant hosted 783 people on 722 square miles. The most populous in the area, Sheridan County, north of Grant, contained a population of 6,198 on 2,470 square miles, but most of those lived in Gordon and Rushville or smaller hamlets such as Whiteclay, Lakeside, and Bingham.

Being only a fraction of the Sand Hills, these counties consisted of 4,768 square miles inhabited at a rate of 1.66 people per square mile and most of the people lived in small towns. Where better for a confessed murderer driven to a mental institution by ghosts to hide? Maybe even spirits cannot find their way through such wide open, trackless territory.

Fifty years old in 2010, the carpenter guy lives in a small frame house next to his parent's home, forty or fifty miles from the closest town. Roads into their little valley require a muscled-up four-wheel drive vehicle to traverse in foul weather. His house sits next to corrals and his work yard. Two tiny cabins ready for sale stand next to the road.

He answers the door with a smile, apologizing for just coming in from working with stock, acting as if someone asking him if he is a killer is an everyday occurrence. He invites his guests into his living room, retires to a well-worn easy chair, his slim, work-hardened body garbed in a striped western shirt with blue jeans tucked into knee-high cowboy boots.

Before speaking, he takes his large, well-read *Bible* from the table. Throughout the conversation, he accentuates his words with holy text. No! He is not a murderer, he says. Taking a life is a sin; his life is about Christ and the good book, not sin, and living without sin took him to Whiteclay in the first place. He opens the *Bible* and reads the commandment, "Thou Shall Not Kill," and sighs, spirituality weighing heavily on his shoulders. No, he repeated, he did not kill Ron and Wally, but he knows who did. And then he says, "They died because of me."[4]

He tells a story of drugs, fundamentalist religion, hired killers, and crooked cops on the dusty streets of Whiteclay. It began when his wife divorced him. Traumatic for most, divorce hit him exceptionally hard. His religion, which seemed to be made up of the Church of Himself, will not permit him to remarry. He interprets the word of God to mean that marriage binds a man and woman together for eternity. For him remarrying or lying with another woman would be a sin.

Destined to live alone, he moved to Whiteclay to be near a man that he believed led a perfect life; a man who gave him land in the small town and ministered to him in his time of need. Unfortunately, the saintly man died in the same year he moved to Whiteclay.[5]

Soldiering on, trying to live as his benefactor did, he moved into a house and shop on a large corner lot and fenced his property with split logs. He befriended one of the liquor store owners and agreed to pour a concrete pad for him. He grew accustomed to his new friend showing up at the construction site, complaining about slow business and the lack of profit in the whiskey trade.

Since no one in Whiteclay is well off, he thought little about his friend's fiscal grousing—until he noticed clandestine activity that had nothing to do with the liquor business. Shipments began arriving at all hours of the day at the post office. Instead of waiting for them to be picked up, the postal clerk, who was in on the deal, delivered the packages to the liquor store at odd hours of the day. Suddenly, his friend bought a new house, and a new car, and started throwing bucks around.

With the Lord's help, the carpenter guy saw his erstwhile friend as he truly was, when toughs and intimidators began hanging around the liquor store. He was like them, the carpenter guy realized, and he carried a gun. After the fire in VJ's Market broke out during the march to Whiteclay led by Wally Black Elk's brothers, the liquor store owner had sat up on the roof of his business intending to shoot Indians breaking into his store. He expected to get hit next, telling Whiteclay wasicu that he had done more to the Indians than Vic (owner of VJ's Market) ever did.

The carpenter guy believes the statement to have been a confession. He began putting things together shortly after the march when the man he thought to have been his friend walked down the streets of Whiteclay shooting at bottles and cans with a pistol, endangering everyone on the street. In a confrontation on the sidewalk, his onetime friend aimed the gun at him. He would have been lying dead in the street if a car had not driven slowly past them.

The store owner intended to kill him because he knew too much. The carpenter guy had figured out that drug shipments were coming in through the post office, and the liquor store had become a drug trafficking center.

After the murders, God opened his eyes, and the truth came to him. Maybe Ron Hard Heart owed a large liquor bill, or maybe he took the job for money, but for whatever reason, the liquor store owner hired Ron Hard Heart to kill him.

Looking back on those days, he has identified the exact moment his death was supposed to have occurred. Several days before the Black Elk/Hard Heart murders, Hard Heart had showed up at his gate, probably carrying a pistol, and called for him. When the carpenter guy hailed him in a friendly manner, Hard Heart ran. That was the day and time he had been scheduled to die. When the amiable drunk ran instead, the store owner either killed the two Oglala himself or hired some local boys to do it. Ronnie Hard Heart was the target for failing to carry through on the contract. Wally Black Elk was just in the wrong place at the wrong time.

The carpenter guy could no longer live safely in Whiteclay. It had become the center for the sale of drugs on the reservation. The drug kingpin had already tried to kill him. He could not go to the authorities because he believed the Sheridan County sheriff to be a corrupt man who had covered up murders before. In fact, he thinks the sheriff partnered in the illegal business.

As if it backs up his claim of the lawman's guilt, the carpenter guy says life has not been easy for the sheriff as a result of his criminal behavior. Judged in heaven early, the sheriff had already paid a high price for his sins. His son died in a car wreck later that same summer.

So the carpenter guy pulled up stakes and left Whiteclay for his own safety six years after giving everything away and after the sheriff took him into protective custody and sent him away for medical evaluation. He offers no explanation for his survival during those years, and did not say why his former friend, the liquor store owner turned drug dealer who had tried to kill him once, decided to leave him alone. He also will not acknowledge the day Robbins and his deputies took him into protective custody and transported him to the hospital.

The carpenter guy has never told his story to law enforcement. When they came to talk to him about the murders, the Lord had not yet guided him to the answers. But it would not have made a difference because he refuses to testify in court. The *Bible*, he says, forbids Christians from swearing, and court proceedings require people to swear to tell the truth. Since he cannot swear, he cannot testify, even if that means sitting in jail as a martyr to his beliefs.

He stays close to his place in the valley, building cabins, tending livestock, and reading the *Bible*. He maintains a page on Myspace and describes himself as single and "searching for serious sincere faith." His interests include, among others, "praising God at the piano, getting up early, eating lots of vegetables, feeding the cows, fix the fence, ride the horse off into the sunset, keep the tummy flat, drive the tractor, build the furniture, and build the cabin." He rests between midnight and 4:00 a.m., except in February when the snow is deep, and he loves people and things in secondhand stores.[6]

He claims to have sponsored children in Third World countries through World Vision and Save the Children. He is quick to show their pictures and pray for their safety.[7]

8

The Killing Begins: Wasicu Wars

*This war did not spring up on our land, this war was brought upon us
by the children of the Great Father who came to take our land without
a price, and who, in our land, do a great many evil things. ... This
war has come from robbery—from the stealing of our land. ... It has
been our wish to live here in our country peacefully, and do such things
as may be for the welfare and good of our people, but the Great Father
has filled it with soldiers who think only of our death.*
—Sinte Galeska (Spotted Tail), Chief of the Brule Lakota

Sandy Sauser pours Una Horn Cloud coffee in her sunlit kitchen. Outside, a dazzling snowscape sparkles under a brilliant December sun.
Freezing temperatures and heavy snow had swept across the reservation
the night before; the same weather that blew across Pine Ridge December
29, 1890, when nature tried to cleanse the blood from the ground that still
flows through their veins, and snow-covered America's shame. That day
marked the last time their ancestors fought each other; the day a ruthless
government killed Una's family.

During the years the Lakota battled the wasicu invasion, Sandy Sauser's
and Una Horn Cloud's predecessors were giants of the American West.
Not just legends to Sandy and Una, these were real people who fought
and suffered for their families, often fertilizing the prairies with blood and
bones. The two women look at pictures of their forefathers and see the suffering of a warrior culture sentenced to a place where they were no longer
free etched into their faces.

Sandy and Una are Maske—more than sisters, unrelated, but with
one soul. They found each other when Sandy moved back to the rez from
Alaska. Their bond restores a piece of the Lakota Sacred Hoop symbolizing
life in balance that was destroyed nearly two centuries earlier by a killing
in their families.[1]

***

Sometime around 1830, Chief Bull Bear listened to traders along the Shell
River, the southern border of the Oglala hunting grounds, and knew they
spoke the truth. If the people left the Paha Sapa and moved closer to the

Una Horn Cloud, seventh-generation granddaughter of Chief Red Cloud. She lost many from her father's side of the family at the Wounded Knee Massacre.

Holy Road along the river that the whites called the Platte, they could trade for cooking pots, metal for arrowheads, and maybe even guns and powder—along with all the things women needed.

Bull Bear led the Oglala south. Warriors rode in the vanguard watching for Crow, Ute, or Shoshone enemies while women hauled tipis and the accoutrements of life to the buttes, canyons, and prairies along the Platte. The trading post known as Fort John, later taken over by the army and named Fort Laramie, became their center of trade with the wasicu.

Henri Chatillon, a frontiersman who later gained fame by guiding historian Francis Parkman as he chronicled his journey across the American West, took Bull Bear's daughter, She Who Wears a Bear Robe, as his wife. Though Bear Robe died young, she had given birth to a daughter named Emilie. Sandy Sauser is Emilie's great-great-great-great-granddaughter, and a direct descendant of Chief Bull Bear.

The Oglala prospered, growing in numbers and wealth until they became the greatest of all the Plains Indians. Buffalo, elk, and deer were plentiful; traders paid well for hides and furs. However, like every other society held together by personal and political relationships, schisms emerged in the tribe and conflict began pulling the Hoop apart.

Many of the young men wanted to drive the whites out of their country instead of trading with them. They saw Bull Bear, a member of the Koya Band, one of the subdivisions of the tribe, as too friendly to the whites while being tyrannical, even brutal, to his own people.[2] Parkman noted Bull Bear's take-no-prisoners style of leadership, "In his way he [Bull Bear] was a hero ... [but] it fared hard with those who incurred his displeasure. He would strike or stab them on the spot ..."[3]

One man who incurred Bull Bear's wrath was Old Smoke, leader of the Bad Face Band and uncle of Una Horn Cloud's great-great-great-great-great-great-great-grandfather, Red Cloud, destined to become a famous Oglala chief. History has recorded the cause of the hostility in two ways, probably both correct. According to Parkman, Bull Bear became angry because whites preferred to trade with the congenial Bad Face leader and called him out of his lodge to fight. Old Smoke did not appear, so the enraged chief stabbed and killed the other man's favorite horse. Members of the Bad Faces saw this as an insult and swore revenge.[4]

As an old man, Chief Red Cloud recalled that the trouble began when a young Bad Face warrior kidnapped a woman of the Koya Band and took her as his wife, an acceptable form of marriage among the Lakota. However, Bull Bear and the other Koya warriors did not like the new groom. Under the influence of whiskey, they decided to take her back.

Parkman wrote that Bull Bear and some of his warriors dropped in on Old Smoke's camp for a visit. A fight broke out after the young men of both bands started drinking, and Bull Bear rushed out to put an end to the ruckus. Red Cloud said the chief's men came to the camp looking for the Koya woman, spied the father of the man that kidnapped the woman and killed him, bringing the Bad Face warriors rushing out of their lodges.

Parkman and Red Cloud agree on what happened next. Shots rang out and Bull Bear went down, hit in the leg. Red Cloud, renowned for his courage, ran straight at the fallen chief yelling, "You are the cause of this," and shot him in the head.[5]

Twenty years later, Chief Red Cloud waged a successful war against the American military, forcing the closure of two army posts along the Bozeman Road running through the Lakota's hunting grounds in eastern Wyoming to the Montana gold camps. After securing the Treaty of 1868, granting the Lakota a part of North Dakota and most of South Dakota as the Great Sioux Reservation while allowing them to hunt east of the Big Horn Mountains in Wyoming and Montana, Red Cloud led his people to the agency in 1872.[6]

Red Cloud—Una's family calls him "the old man"—never again went to war against the United States. He believed he could best protect his peo-

The interior of Chief Red Cloud's house on the Pine Ridge. Note the star quilt: the construction of these beautiful quilts is still a trademark craft of industrious Oglala women. (Denver Public Library, Western History Collection, X-31434)

ple by settling on the land set aside for them. At least they would be free from the American cavalry's surprise attacks on Lakota bands that did not go to the reservation—raids that killed women and children and forced survivors into starvation and destitution.

***

The world of the Lakota turned upside down when Lieutenant Colonel George Armstrong Custer discovered gold in the Black Hills.[7] At first, the United States tried to enforce the treaty that Red Cloud's warriors had won. Cavalry patrolled the area, chasing aspiring miners off the land reserved for the Lakota.

President Grant held out for less than a year before caving into pressure from a recession-pressured public, deciding the United States, caught in the Long Depression, needed gold more than the Indians needed a spiritual center. After the Lakota had spurned his offer to buy the hills for $6 million or lease them for $400,000 per year, he called off the army, and soldiers no longer tried to keep gold-crazed miners from entering the hills.[8]

In December 1875, the government commanded the Lakota to move to the agencies (reservations) in two months or be rounded up by the military and forced onto the area set aside for them. The order was the opening salvo in a plan to force a war with the Indians, subdue them, and open access to the rich ore deposits and thousands of acres of farmland.

Una's great-uncle on her father's side, Beard, was fourteen and hunting in the Powder River country of northeastern Wyoming when the Lakota were ordered into the agency.[9] His family joined the bands led by Sitting Bull, Gall, and Crazy Horse, who refused to end their free lifestyle. America quickly labeled them hostile and sent the army into the field.

Academy-trained generals with Civil War experience planned a three-pronged attack to catch the Indians in a pincer movement. General George Crook left Fort Fetterman in Wyoming to hit the tribes from the south.[10] General Terry's forces, including Custer and the 7th Cavalry, moved west from Fort Abraham Lincoln in North Dakota, while Colonel Gibbon marched south from Fort Ellis in Montana.

The descendants of a warrior culture thousands of years old had their own ideas about getting caught by an invading army. Spies, scouts, and families pouring into the camp from the agencies told them that soldiers were coming. And if that were not enough, Wakan Tanka, the Great Mystery, showed what would happen to the soldiers. Sitting Bull, both a medicine man and tribal leader, held a Sun Dance in April or May, much earlier than usual. After slicing fifty notches of flesh from each arm, he fell into a trance. On awakening, he described soldiers and horses, all with their ears cut off, falling from the sky and landing among the tipis. He said the people would soon have a great victory.

Beard was left behind on June 17, 1876, when Crazy Horse led nearly one thousand men on a fifty-mile night ride to attack Crook's force of thirteen hundred men, which included more than two-hundred and fifty hated Crow warriors. In a pitched battle, something new in the annals of Plains Indian warfare, the Lakota fought Crook's forces to a standstill, eventually forcing him to fall back to the south.

A week later the combined tribes numbered close to ten thousand, one-third of them warriors. Beard had never seen so many people gathered in one place: six camp circles stretched for miles along the Greasy Grass, the river the wasicu called the Little Big Horn. June 25 was already hot early in the morning. Beard and his friends headed for a bend in the stream to swim where the water was more than five feet deep, close to where older men tried their angling skills.[11] Beard and the other boys, including Wally Black Elk's ancestor Black Elk, had to be careful not to scare the fish or else earn the wrath of their elders.[12]

The boys splashed, pushed, dunked, and swam. Sprawled on the grassy banks warming in the sun, they spoke of the time when they would be warriors. Suddenly, people hurried past them shouting, "The chargers are coming! They are charging! The chargers are coming!"[13]

Beard had figured something would happen, as his uncle had warned him at breakfast, "When you finish eating go help your brother watch the horses. Something might happen today. I feel it in the air."[14]

DEWEY BEARD, WIFE AND DAUGHTER.
Cole Photo Co
12113-12Q

Una's famous great-great-uncle, Iron Hail or Beard, fought against Custer as a teenager and heroically defended his people in the ravine during the Wounded Knee Massacre, in which several family members, including his wife, were killed. He is pictured with his second wife, Alice Lone Bear, and their granddaughter, Marie Not Help Him. (Denver Public Library, Western History Collection, X-31958)

The swimmers ran back to their lodges, sporadic gunfire in the distance quickening their steps. Horn Cloud, Beard's father, met him in front of the tipi. "Soldiers are attacking us," he said. "This day you become a man."

Horn Cloud held the reins of his favorite war horse, a big, black stallion outfitted with a mouth bridle.[15] He helped his son onto the horse, handed him the bridle rope and a war club with a stone head, turned the animal toward the fighting, and slapped it on the rump. Eager to join the fray, the black ran toward the sounds of fighting with little heed to the anxious youngster on its back.

Beard gained heart from the words of Sitting Bull, who seemed to be everywhere, seeing to the camp's defense. "Brave up!" the chief shouted. "We have everything to fight for. If we're defeated, we'll have nothing to live for. It'll be a hard time, but fight like brave men! Brave up![16]

The Lakota were, and still are, exceptional equestrians and Beard was no different, except the black stallion had only one goal, to get to the fight as fast as possible. As he raced back to the river, Beard saw an old woman kneeling in prayer, holding a staff toward the heavens. "Look out grandmother," he yelled. "I cannot stop this horse." Moments later the horse sideswiped the woman, knocking her into deep water.[17]

Beard never found out what happened to her, and he did not know the soldiers were led by George Custer. He had never heard of him before and could not have known Custer had divided his forces into three branches, sending 175 men with Major Reno to storm the camp from the south to panic the Indians and drive them north where he would attack after swinging around to the east. The plan was simple and had worked in Kansas where his troops had decimated a Cheyenne village along the Washita River eight years earlier. Perhaps, it had once been an effective strategy, but like Beard, Custer had never seen so many Indians in one place before.

The black's wild charge carried Beard onto a killing ground strewn with bodies where the angry warriors, led by Gall whose two wives and child died in the original charge, had met Reno's men in the open. As he rode through the carnage, a wounded soldier struggled to sit up and point his revolver at him. Armed with only the war club, Beard leaped off the black stallion and killed the American with a blow to the head.

By the time Beard remounted, Custer and his troops had ridden down Medicine Tail Cooley into the river across from the middle of the village. There a small group of Cheyenne warriors and older Lakota men and boys held their fire until the soldiers were in the water and then emptied several saddles. The soldiers rode their stumbling, tired mounts back up the hill as hundreds of Lakota fired at them from all sides.

Beard arrived at Custer's Last Stand in a blizzard of bullets and arrows. He searched through the smoke and dust, looking to use his club again. He heard a man named Spotted Rabbit calling for warriors to help capture the leader of the bluecoats, a tall white man wearing buckskins and shouting orders. As they galloped toward the white man, Spotted Rabbit's horse went down, forcing the black to swerve to the side. Beard had missed his chance and watched another brave ride in and kill the buckskin-clad soldier.

Beard found the man in buckskins where he had died, his horse's bridle still tied to his wrist. Another Lakota took the horse, telling Beard the dead

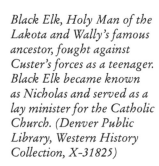

Black Elk, Holy Man of the Lakota and Wally's famous ancestor, fought against Custer's forces as a teenager. Black Elk became known as Nicholas and served as a lay minister for the Catholic Church. (Denver Public Library, Western History Collection, X-31825)

man was Long Hair. He thought it a strange name for a soldier chief with short hair.[18]

Wally Black Elk's famous predecessor, Black Elk, was only thirteen that day, but his experiences were similar to Beard's. When the shooting started, his older brother rushed off to join the battle, neglecting to take his gun. Black Elk rode after him with two pistols, one his own, the other for his brother. He had been told by his father, and again by his brother as he gave him the revolver, to return to the village. Instead, he joined the fighting and shot a wounded soldier in the forehead. He scalped the bluecoat and then rode back to the west side of the river where the women were singing a high tremolo to cheer on the warriors.[19]

***

While Una's relatives battled for their lives along the Greasy Grass, Sandy's paternal great-grandfather, Phillip Wells, was in the Black Hills, signed up to fight the Lakota. Through him, Sandy can trace her lineage all the way back to Chief Powhatan and Pocahontas. Wells grew up near the Lakota's relatives, the Dakota, in Minnesota,[20] and was the grandson of Brown Eyes and the first child born of a Santee woman and a wasicu. His father was killed during the uprising near Spirit Lake, Iowa, in 1862 while traveling with Phillip and two other sons to establish a trading post in the Black Hills.

Wells had been appointed civilian interpreter to accompany the 7th Cavalry when it took the field. Just before Custer left for his meeting with Sitting Bull, Wells and four other men were ordered to carry a dispatch to a small cavalry force near Bear Butte east of the Black Hills. On the way back to Fort Lincoln, they narrowly escaped an ambush, losing their pack and saddle horses. The five frontiersmen snuck away, avoiding pursuing warriors by traveling during the night and hiding by day. Starving, they stumbled into the fort too late to make the trip to the Little Big Horn.[21]

Philip Wells pictured with Buffalo Bill. Wells, Sandy Sauser's paternal great-grandfather, served as an interpreter for the army at Wounded Knee. (Denver Public Library, Western History Collection, Z-14173)

***

Within two years of the victory over Custer, continuously being pressured by the army and with the enormous buffalo herds nearly exterminated for their hides, except for Sitting Bull's Hunkpapa who held out in Canada until 1881, the Lakota moved onto the reservation.[22] With the surrender of the plains tribes, the tiger in Washington showed its true stripes. No longer did the United States treat tribes as dependent nations—they were now looked upon as a defeated and subjected people.

Congress took the Black Hills from the Lakota, ignoring the clause in the Treaty of 1868 that called for a three-fourths vote of all tribal males to cede any land. Officials of the commission to get it done put it simply: Deed over the Black Hills and hunting areas off the reservation or starve. Rations would be withheld until they agreed.

Now that they were wards of the state, the destiny of the Lakota would be planned by the people that defeated them. Benevolent easterners urged compassionate treatment, but they were wolves in sheep's clothing, wanting the plains warriors to become just like everybody else, surviving by losing that which made them Indians.[23] Assimilate, Acculturate and Anglicize: Own land, speak English, educate children in government schools, give up ancient religious beliefs and cherish Christianity.

The Lakota were forbidden from holding the sacred Sun Dance and even the more social Rabbit and Owl Dances in which men and women danced together. Since education was seen as the quickest route to making good Americans, rations were withheld if parents refused to send their children to out-of-state schools, which forced them to cut their long locks, speak only English, and practice military drills.

Limited to the reservation, the former nomads needed a permit from the agent to leave its boundaries. Previously the owners of vast pony herds, they were required to obtain permission to sell a horse or mule. Polygamy was forbidden, as was riding down and shooting cattle like they were buffalo. Such practices were considered savage—anathema to a God-fearing nation.

More than anything else, reformers and government officials agreed that tribalism was what most separated Indians from civilized society. Communal ownership of land and allocation of authority to chiefs prevented tribal members from reaping the rewards of capitalism and democracy. Red Cloud, Sitting Bull, and Spotted Tail were out of the past, anachronisms in a democratic society, ignoring the fact that the band leaders relied on consensus, and could easily be replaced by disgruntled followers.

In 1883, Sitting Bull told the Dawes Commission, which was instituted to convince the Indians of the advantages of individual ownership of land, that he was a chief by the will of the Great Spirit. While it probably didn't help that he admonished the commissioners that they conducted themselves like men drinking whiskey, Illinois Senator John Logan's reaction represented the low opinion Congress held of the Lakota. "You are not a great chief," he said, "you have no right to any control ... and if it were not for the government you would be freezing and starving."[24]

9

Killing: From War to Massacre

*I did not know then how much was ended. When I look back now
from this high hill of my old age, I can still see the butchered women
and children lying heapen and scattered all along the crooked gulch
as plain as when I saw them with eyes still young. And I can see that
something else died there in the bloody mud, and was buried in the
blizzard. A people's dream died there. It was a beautiful dream ... the
nation's hoop is broken and scattered. There is no center any longer,
and the sacred tree is dead.*

—*Heȟáka Sápa (Black Elk)*, Holy Man of the Lakota

L ife had changed forever. The people starved—promises of prosperity on the reservation a cruel joke. The Lakota lived in a depth of poverty they had never known before. Tipis, if they did not live in rude huts, were now made of thin government-issue canvas that the wind blew through instead of buffalo hide, which had provided shelter for thousands of years. Instead of soft, creamy buckskin they wore white man's clothing often made from the same material as their lodges. There were no wars to prove manhood, no hunts to feed the people, no journeys from hunting ground to hunting ground. The people were going the way of the buffalo. Waken Tanka had forgotten them.

It must have seemed miraculous when word flew across the plains that the Great Being had not abandoned them. He had sent the Messiah, the Christ of the Christians, back to the earth as an Indian promising His people prosperity in a heavenly paradise.

Winds of hope carried the doctrine of the Messiah, an infusion of Christianity and traditional native religion, across the tribes of the West. The Oglala sent emissaries to discover the truth of such glorious news. On their return, now zealous believers, the travelers became missionaries and spread the gospel. His name was Wovoka, a member of the Paiute tribe, and He had sat at the hand of God on the day the sun died—the solar eclipse on January 1, 1888. He had come to punish the wasicu, resurrect the dead, and restore the supremacy of the Indians.[1]

A Pine Ridge Agency scene, 1890. (Denver Public Library, Western History Collection, X-31301)

Hearing that the Lakota might adopt a belief other than that which the government prescribed, colonial rulers reacted quickly to keep the Indians in their place. When the Oglala began meeting to discuss the glorious news, Indian Agent A. J. Gallagher arrested the men who had gone to see Wovoka, holding them in jail until they promised an end to the gatherings.

Like Christians facing Roman lions, the new believers could not be intimidated. When the Messiah sent an epistle summoning them again, eleven Lakota returned to sit in His presence.[2] When they returned home, none doubted: He was the son of God, killed by the whites, and He bore the marks of crucifixion. Consistent with his first visit to earth, He brought a message of peace. According to Short Bull, a Brule Medicine Man, the Messiah told them:

> I have sent for you to tell you certain things that you must do. There are two chiefs at your agencies and I want you to help them all you can. Have your people work the ground so they do not get idle, help your agents, and get farms to live on.
>
> This is one chief.
>
> The other chief is the church. I want you to help Him for He tells you of Me.
>
> When you get back, go to church. All of these churches are mine. If you go to church when you get back, others will do the same. I have raised two bodies of men on this earth and have dropped one of them. That is the army.
>
> I want no more fighting. Take pity on one another, and whenever

you do anything that is bad something will happen to you. I mean fights between Indian and whites. All over the world one should be like the other and no distinction made. Always sing and pray about Me, for it is right.

Two days from now all nations will talk one tongue. ... Then the sign talk will be no more. Educate your children, send them to schools. You must not fight. Do no harm to anyone. Do right always. ...

Whiskey is bad. Who drinks, they cause murders and suicides. Across the ocean is a great church where He came from. That church belongs to Me. You may go as you please. But the church is one belief, one faith. ...

The whole earth is now filthy and stenches. These murders and suicides are that which now stink. You say, 'Father! Oh Father! Is that you? All that [you] will say, say thus [and] the father God will look at you. Those that have done wrong, He will shake the earth. This part of the earth will get it.[3]

Good Thunder, also a Brule and one of the original emissaries, visited the Messiah a second time and relayed His message graphically—especially the part about the shaking of the earth:

I want to tell you when you get home your people will follow My examples. Any Indian who does not obey Me and tries to be on white's side will be covered over by a new land that is to come over this old one. You will, all the people, use the paints and grass I give you. In the spring when the green grass comes, your people who have gone before you will come back, and you shall see your friends then, for you have come to My call.[4]

Wovoka taught them a dance in which the participants shuffled crab-like to the left. Only if they danced would His prophecies come to pass. They danced on four or five successive nights. Dancers often fell into trances and when awakening claimed to have met long dead relatives, prosperous and happy in the spirit world. The Lakota sang as they danced, beginning their religious observance with a promise of joyful reunions:

The father says so—E'yayo!
The father says so—E'yayo!
The father says so,
The father says so,
You shall see your grandfather—E'yayo!
You shall see your grandfather—E'yayo!
The father says so,
The father says so,
You shall see your kindred—E'yayo!
You shall see your kindred—E'yayo!

The father says so,
The father says so.[5]

Somehow, the Messiah's message changed, not just with the Lakota, but with most of the plains tribes. Either Wovoka added to his prophecies, perhaps through new revelations foretelling of the white race's destruction, or tribal delegates from all the western tribes misinterpreted the message. The Ghost Dance, originally named because it supposedly led to a happy reunion with all Indians that ever lived, now hastened the earth's regeneration and the wasicu's destruction by the hand of God.

The Lord would have vengeance. On the promised day, an avalanche would cover the ground with a deep layer of new soil while an accompanying flood poured into the mouths of whites and choked them with mud. Indians would fly to the top of the new earth and discover prairies green with grass and speckled with herds of game. They had only to dance, gather at a designated place at the time of the event, remove all of their clothes, and the new world would appear.

Although the Lakota believed the new religion would result in the destruction of the whites, the Messianic religion was no more violent than one which teaches that all believers ascend to heaven on an appointed day, the rest to spend their lives in torment, and much less violent than an inquisition that promoted torture and death by fire.

Dancing may have been the road to eternal salvation, but the federal government was determined to block the Indians access while maintaining their earthly misery. At the same time that agents did everything possible to stop the dancing, Congress decided the Indians were eating too well at the public trough when they should be producing their own food. After imposing individual land ownership of small plots in 1887 and dividing the Great Sioux Reservation into five small agencies in 1889 as a way of divesting them of one half of their lands, Congress added injury to insult by cutting beef rations.

Eastern friends and congressmen alike figured that a newly discovered farming instinct, sure to come with land ownership, would provide a surplus of crops. They must have been thinking about some other land than the freezing in the winter and bone dry, heat-stricken prairies of the Dakotas in the summer. Elaine Goodale Eastman, married to Dr. Charles Eastman, a noted Lakota physician, wrote of their plight in the summer of 1890:

> A veritable "Dust Bowl" extended from the Missouri River almost to the
> Black Hills. In the persistent hot winds the pitiful little gardens of the
> Indians curled up and died. Even the native hay crop was a failure. I had

never before seen such sickness. The appearance of the people shocked me. Lean and wiry in health, with glowing skins and a look of mettle, many now displayed gaunt forms, lackluster faces, and sad, deep-sunken eyes.[6]

Yet, the Lakota had hope and rather than planning war, they turned their eyes toward heaven, unaware their dancing sent the Americans living near them into a panic. In the minds of Americans living near the reservations, they were still crazed savages armed to the teeth. Settlers believed the apocalypse was surely coming, not at the hand of God as the Messiah promised, but spread across the land by hideously painted savages pouring from the reservations like the hordes of Genghis Khan, their rapacious thirst satiated only by the blood of innocents.

The first to sound the alarm was Charles Hyde, a citizen of Pierre, South Dakota, whose May 29, 1890, letter to the Secretary of the Interior warned of an outbreak, his information supposedly coming from a young Lakota acquaintance. Even though Indians tried to assure Washington and the public that no uprisings were imminent, fear grew throughout the summer. After all, these were the warriors who had wiped out Custer, the battle-hardened men who had ruled the plains.

By the middle of November, the stew simmering over America's xenophobic fire came to a boil. No actions or words of the Lakota turned up the heat—the melding of political ingredients in Washington provided the necessary energy. Only a month earlier, Daniel F. Royer, physician, druggist, newspaperman, and banker who had served in the Dakota Territorial Legislature, a loyal Republican who had no experience with Indians, became the Pine Ridge agent. Shortly after his arrival in October, he requested the Indian commissioner to send a police force for his protection. The Lakota soon dubbed him Young-Man-Afraid-of-Indians.[7] Believing he had narrowly escaped death when a man named Charging Thunder, whom Royer had ordered arrested, drew a knife and a standoff between traditionalists and the Indian police ensued, Royer could stand it no longer. Afraid the wasicu on the reservation were to be slaughtered at any minute, he took his family to Rushville and telegraphed Washington, "We need protection, and we need it now."[8]

An old Indian fighter with political aspirations could not have been expected to turn down the heat. General Nelson Miles had become Commander of the Department of Missouri in 1890. A self-taught soldier who read military strategy when not working as a clerk in a pottery store near Boston before the Civil War, Miles saw himself playing a role on a much larger stage. His name had been circulated as a candidate for the Presidency in the previous election.

Miles sent the army into action the same day, supported by his commanders who saw a good uprising as a means to badger Congress for more support. Troops established posts and fortifications on the reservations, soon amounting to the largest concentration of the military since the Civil War. And they needed every man—Miles estimated the fighting Indian strength at six thousand warriors and growing. Many Lakota, especially the Rosebud Brule, believing they were about to be attacked, moved to a natural fortification in the Bad Lands.

Reporters and the army convinced the country that an uprising by the united Lakota tribes was only days away. In 1890 America, threats of Indian uprisings sold newspapers, and flagrant yellow journalism upped the sales even more.

The press served the madly boiling Lakota stew across the country and politics kept the dish hot. Daily stories of Indian perfidy raised the fear level among settlers near the reservations ever higher while building a national call for military intervention. The more afraid people became of the Indians, the more they beseeched the military for help. The need to protect the frontier enabled the army to call for greater defense spending. Congress bowed to public pressure and met military demands.

On November 15, the *New York Times* quoted Miles saying that settlers were afraid, the Oglala were of the character to indicate an imminent outbreak, and he was not predisposed to wait for trouble. The *Salt Lake Tribune* reported three days later that fifteen thousand braves could become involved in the uprising.[9] The *St. Paul Daily Globe's* lead story contained the headline, "Citizens of Mandan [North Dakota] Anticipate an Attack by Frenzied Sioux Braves," and quoted Miles that the situation was extremely grave with reason to expect trouble from the Missouri to the Rockies.[10]

On November 20, the *Times* heightened the fear even though the predicted attack on Mandan did not occur. "The expected massacre of the people of that place by a band of Indians armed to the teeth and bent on exterminating every white man in the vicinity did not take place."[11]

An *Omaha Daily Bee* article on November 20 reported that chiefs Red Cloud and Little Wound had declared they would lead their warriors against the troops in battle the next day. According to the reporter, the Messiah would appear in front of the assembled warriors in the form of a buffalo and give a signal to start the conflict to annihilate the white race. The paper did not wait for an actual fight before reporting one. The article announcing the fight began with the publication of a just-received telegram reporting that troops had already met the Lakota between Rushville and Pine Ridge. The paper reported sixty soldiers and braves died. Of course, the battle was merely a figment of someone's over-active imagination—there had been no confrontation.[12]

In late November, the *Times* announced that every officer stationed on the Pine Ridge saw the situation as critical. "They know that 6,000 to 8,000 Indians are liable to swoop down on them at any moment. 'If that happens,' one officer said, 'nothing but a miracle could save us from Custer's fate.'"[13]

The most inflammatory article, published on November 27 and reprinted in virtually every newspaper in the country, came from General Miles' office. A South Dakota rancher named Scotty Phillips, an Indian scout when Custer took the field for the last time, said he had never been afraid of Indians before, but he was then. He had met a group of Lakota, who told him there would soon be an uprising. "One said he had seen the time when he used to beat out the brains of children and drink women's blood and that the time was coming soon when they would do it again."[14]

Una's ancestor, Red Cloud, tried to turn the fire down by telling Americans not to worry. On November 19, in a letter published in the Chadron paper he announced, "I have been friend to the whites that live near the reserve, and I want to have peace all around."[15] A statement of his published in the *New York World* on November 22 reported, "I don't want to fight and I don't want my people to fight. We have lots of old women and lots of old men. We've got no guns and we can't fight, for we have nothing to eat and are too poor to do anything."[16]

Using the white man's newspapers did not work for the great chief—reporters still linked him to the trouble. The *Salt Lake Herald* noted that he and Sitting Bull had been attempting to regain control of the reservations ever since they were deposed the year before for opposing the land sale. The article called them personally responsible for the agitation.[17]

On November 25, 1890, the citizens of Chadron sent a resolution to the Secretary of War proposing that leaders and instigators of criminality in savages should be punished the same as the law provides for traitors, anarchists, and assassins. They also suggested that the shortest route to the satisfactory settlement of the troubles would be to deprive the savages of their horses and give them oxen trained to the plow.[18]

Agent Royer's panic brought the army to the reservations, but the actions of Standing Rock Agent McLaughlin sent the soldiers into action. McLaughlin controlled Standing Rock with an iron fist, or he would have if Sitting Bull had not had the loyalty of the people. The finagling agent saw the Ghost Dances as a way to neutralize his adversary. He blamed the Messiah craze on the old man, calling the chief, in an interview printed on October 28, "… the leading apostle of this latest Indian absurdity."[19]

McLaughlin, with the press cheerleading, finally convinced Miles that the crafty old savage, for the sake of peace, had to be arrested and imprisoned. He sent his Indian scouts backed by the army to make the arrest.

When a scuffle broke out, Sitting Bull and two of his sons, one only twelve and hiding in a corner of his father's cabin, were killed. The chief's enraged followers attacked the police, who barricaded themselves in the cabin until the army came to their rescue.

The chief's favorite white horse, a gift from Buffalo Bill and trained to dance when fireworks sounded during the Wild West Show, lent a sadly macabre air to the murder. As Sitting Bull and his sons died under a flurry of gunshots, the horse danced in front of their cabin.

General Colby, Commander of the Nebraska National Guard and stationed with his troops just across the border from Pine Ridge,

General Colby of the Nebraska National Guard holding Lost Bird, the baby found alive in the snow after the Wounded Knee Massacre. She was adopted by the general and his wife. (Denver Public Library, Western History Collection, X-31472)

later wrote that officials had decided it would be easier to kill the old man than take him prisoner. The scouts had been ordered to kill him.[20]

America's press gloated over Sitting Bull's death. The *St. Louis Republic* announced in an extremely egregious piece that his death removed "one of the obstacles to civilization. He was a greasy savage, who rarely bathed and was liable at any time to become infected with vermin. ... He will now make excellent manure for the crops, which will grow over him when his reservation is civilized."[21]

***

On the Cheyenne River Reservation, home to Una Horn Cloud's great-great-grandfather's family, including Beard and her great-grandfather Joseph, the dry heat of the summer carried into the fall. Gardens, essential to health by adding fresh greens and vegetables to the stale and tasteless rations dispensed by the wasicu, curled into the dust of the prairies. Rib-showing livestock wandered listlessly, cracked hooves stirring clouds of dust.

Members of Chief Big Foot's band of Minniconjou returned to the old ways for sustenance. The Horn Clouds and two other families secured a pass from the agent, took three wagons, and traveled to Dog Teeth Butte near the Missouri River to hunt antelope.

Una's great-grandfather Joseph, nineteen years old and with three and a half years of white man's schooling under his belt, enjoyed the hunting and camping on the prairie. Before the trip he had heard of the Messiah, but had never seen a Ghost Dance. When his family returned home, wagons laden with meat, Joseph learned that the Minniconjou were holding a dance that day. He and Beard, his older brother who had fought against Custer, dashed off to see the spectacle.

Three men from the Pine Ridge were at the dance carrying a letter signed by Red Cloud and several Oglala chiefs. Worried about the explosive situation on the Pine Ridge with the arrival of blue-clad combat troops, they asked Big Foot to bring his people to their reservation and help make peace, promising one hundred horses if he did.[22]

Mindful of the empty bellies in his band of three hundred souls, Big Foot said his people first needed to travel to the agency for annuities. After

Every year, the Oglala follow the flight of Big Foot's band from the Standing Rock Reservation to the Pine Ridge.

that, he added, "I will see if we can go to the Pine Ridge Agency and make peace."[23]

As the band awaited the supplies distribution date, one of Chief Sitting Bull's nephews with a bullet wound to his leg and another man, both without blankets or food, stumbled into camp. They brought the story of the death of the chief and said his followers were fleeing south to join Big Foot.

Beard and ten other men set out to find the refugees and guide them into camp, narrowly avoiding a fight with another Minniconjou band led by Hump, a famed war chief whose loyalty had shifted to the wasicu, who would not allow Sitting Bull's people to join Big Foot. In the end, few Hunkpapa made their way to Una's relatives, but the fear of two bands of starving, poorly equipped Lakota merging heightened fears of an uprising.

The *New York Times* labeled the Minniconjou hostile and warned, "Should Sitting Bull's warriors combine with Big Foot's and Low Dog's braves as they no doubt will, they will greatly outnumber the troops."[24]

Several days after Sitting Bull's nephew and the other man arrived in Big Foot's camp, Colonel Sumner of the 8th Cavalry lectured the chief about harboring the slain leader's followers. He ordered Big Foot to take his people home, neglecting to mention that telegrams had already circulated about the feasibility of arresting and sending him to Fort Meade as a prisoner.[25] Escorted by troops, Big Foot, now known to America as a ghost-dancing miscreant, peacefully did just that—even though blue-coated soldiers bullied the band's women and children.

Joseph Horn Cloud and his brother William spent December 23 cutting hay along the river and piling it on wagons as livestock feed for the winter. They watched a Minniconjou on horseback tearing across the brown and gold hills toward them. The rider yelled at them to go home, soldiers were coming to fight. They did not believe him, could not understand why there would be trouble. They continued working at the same pace, not seeing any reason to hurry until their brother Frank met them on the trail. He told them a wasicu called Red Beard was in Big Foot's camp with information about the army's plans.

After delivering the hay, Joseph, William, and their older brother, White Lance, raced over to the village of canvas shelters. Red Beard, his horse still covered with foam after running hard, told the Minniconjou that soldiers were, indeed, on the way and that they needed to flee to Pine Ridge for safety.

Big Foot refused to leave, saying the agency was his home. The white man argued that he was placing women and children in danger. Sounding anything but warlike the chief replied, "This is my home; this is my place;

if they want to kill me—if they want to do anything to me let them come and do as they please."

As Red Beard ran to his horse, his words carried a chill colder than the December wind, "I heard the officers agree together to bring a thousand soldiers from Fort Meade to take all the men and bring them to Fort Meade as prisoners."[26]

The threat tore away Big Foot's reticence. He moved the band into the hills south of the river. That night he sent Beard and another warrior to look for the soldiers. They found them stuck on the far side of the ice-jammed river, unable to cross. By the time Beard returned to the new camp, the worried band had already started south.

The Minniconjou, frightened people, poorly armed, scurrying across the prairie, hardly resembled a well-armed fighting force intent on hostilities. They fled to Pine Ridge for protection and to win a herd of horses for helping bring peace. Beard traveled in the rear and cared for the weakest and slowest while watching for pursuit.

Crossing the Bad Lands, fording the White River, and spending December nights in the open proved too much for Big Foot, no longer the fit fighting man he had been at the Little Big Horn. He succumbed to pneumonia, forcing him to travel in the back of a wagon, blood from his mouth and nose pooling on the blankets covering the harsh wooden slats.

The Minniconjou traveled slowly caring for their chief, the thought of warring on the settlers never on their minds. They did not realize that they were the subject of America's most publicized cavalry chase, so demonized by the press that scared pioneers poured into communities for protection from them. Even the army seemed afraid of them. General Miles announced that the Minniconjou were such a threat that, joined with those in the Bad Lands, "These Indians in the absence of military protection could have massacred as many settlers as the Sioux did in the Minnesota troubles of 1862.[27]

Five days after Joseph and William gathered hay along the Cheyenne River, Big Foot's band approached a force arranged against them in battle order along Porcupine Creek—two rapid-firing Hotchkiss guns presented an especially hostile welcome. They probably would not have approached the army if they had known about the telegrams Miles had sent to General Forsythe. On the 26th, he instructed, "Big Foot is cunning and his Indians are very bad." The next day he commanded, "If he fights, destroy him."[28]

Beard was not going to stand by and let the soldiers turn the guns loose on his friends and relatives. He told his wife to keep out of the line of fire, dismounted, and thrust his arm into the barrel of a Hotchkiss gun. If the bluecoats intended to fight, Beard was anxious to die in the defense of his people.[29]

Major Whiteside, commanding a detachment from Custer's old regiment, rode up and asked for Big Foot. He probably expected to see a warrior astride a pony, reins in one hand, rifle in the other, and shoulders draped with cartridge belts. Instead, he found an old man lying in a pool of blood in the bed of the wagon.

"I am sick," the chief said in a breaking voice. "My people here want peace and ..."

"I won't nor will I have any parlaying at all," Whiteside commanded, backed up by the rapid firing Hotchkiss guns. "It is either unconditional surrender or fight. What is your answer, sir?"

The old veteran of fights against the Crow, Shoshone, and bluecoats from the days when Lakota warriors saw battle as honorable—the profession of hardened and fit men—must have shrunk back into his blankets at the officer's audacity. Did he believe war bands traveled in wagons filled with families and meager possessions? Would warriors committed to protecting the defenseless place them in the front lines?

Calmly Big Foot replied, "We surrender. We would have done so before, but we couldn't find you and couldn't find any soldiers to surrender to."

"I am glad to see you are peaceable," Whiteside said, and then showed his disdain for the word of a Lakota, "Therefore, I want you to give me twenty-five guns."[30]

Big Foot, afraid that giving up their firearms would leave his people at the mercy of all enemies, persuaded the officer to allow the band to travel to the Pine Ridge Agency before turning over their weapons.

The Minniconjou believed that they were on the way to join the Oglala, but that was never the army's plan. Whiteside halted the trip to the agency on Wounded Knee Creek the next afternoon and dispatched a messenger calling for more troops to assist in disarming his captives. Whiteside, as did Sumner earlier, left out a crucial piece of information. He neglected to tell Big Foot that his entire band would be sent to prison. They were to be disarmed and then escorted to the railroad in Gordon for shipment.[31]

Una's relatives, people whose ability to read signs enabled them to survive on the prairies, knew something was not right. Restless and uneasy, Beard did not sleep that night, did not even lie down until nearly dawn. Most of the camp stayed awake. With soldiers stationed around them, a larger force pouring in, and four Hotchkiss guns aimed at their ragtag collection of tents, a cloud of fear hung over the camp. Dogs barking, children crying, men and women praying, soldiers shouting orders, the creak of leather and sounds of artillery rolling into firing positions along with cavalry taking up stations—shod hoofs colliding with frozen ground—it would be a wonder anyone slept.

While the Indians worried, the soldiers celebrated. Officers wandered from tent to tent, toasting their success with alcohol. As they drank, William Horn Cloud heard them referring to their prisoners as the Indians who had killed Custer.

Alice Ghost Horse, a girl of thirteen, understood enough of what was going on to call the soldiers drunk. Describing a fairly typical combination of testosterone and alcohol, she recalled that they said many bad things about Minniconjou women.[32]

Years later a man named Swigert confessed to feelings of guilt for delivering a load of whiskey to the army.

> It was too bad those drunken soldiers were allowed to handle a delicate condition. I know they were all drunk. I am sorry because I feel partly responsible in hauling whiskey in with the supplies. If it was not for this liquor, I do not believe this massacre of the natives by the soldiers would have occurred.[33]

Just before dawn, Horn Cloud gathered his sons around him—his words those no father would wish to utter, ringing with the honor, courage, and dignity of the Lakota:

> I will give you advice—all my sons—therefore, I have come. They say it is peace but I am sure there is going to be fighting today. I have been in war all my life, and I know when my heart is growing bitter that there is going to be a fight; so I know we are going to have a fight, and I have come to tell you—all my sons, what I want you to do. If one or two Indians go to start trouble, I don't want you to go with them; don't you join them. Besides this, if the white people start trouble first, then you can do what you want to—you can die among your own relations in defending them. All you, my dear sons, stand together and keep yourselves sober and all of you, if you die at once among your relations defending them, I will be satisfied. Try to die in front of your relations, the old folks and the little ones, and I will be satisfied if you die trying to help them. Don't get excited. When one or two under the Government laws start trouble they are arrested and taken into court and put in jail, but I don't want any of you to get into such trouble, but to stand back until all the whites assail us, and then defend our people. I have come to tell you this as advice before the trouble begins. I want you to heed my warnings.[34]

Horn Cloud then looked each of his sons in the eye, dropped his hands on each one's shoulders in turn, and left for Big Foot's tent as a caller walked among the shelters ordering the men to gather in council. Men collected in front of Big Foot's tent; Horn Cloud helped carry the invalid chief out, still wrapped in blankets, and placed him on the ground.

Joseph, White Lance, and William joined the men in the council circle. Beard remained in his tent, in a hurry to get the wagons rolling toward Pine Ridge, hoping against hope that his father's premonitions were wrong.

Joseph stood next to Captain Wallace, an officer who had been with Reno at the Little Big Horn. When Wallace asked about his family, Joseph pointed out his father sitting next to Big Foot.

The voice of Major Whiteside carried through the cold, still air just as the sun began its journey to the west. "Big Foot, I want twenty-five guns. Yesterday, everybody had a gun. I want twenty-five of them."

With blood pouring from his nose, Big Foot cooperated even though the previous day the same officer had agreed to wait until they reached the agency to take the weapons. "All right," he announced. "Bring twenty-five guns. If I was able to talk I would talk for you, but I cannot talk."

When twenty-five weapons were piled in the center of the council, Whiteside called for five more. When these were produced he said, "I want them all."

Big Foot ordered, "Bring them all, boys," to which several in the crowd replied that there were no more, the soldiers had all of them.[35]

Not satisfied and believing, as did Miles, that the Minniconjou were superbly armed, Whiteside called for a search of the camp—person by person, tent by tent, pack by pack, and wagon by wagon.

As the search began, Beard's mother rushed into his tent. "My son," she said, "some soldiers are coming and gathering all the guns and powder and axes and knives, all bows and arrows, and are coming this way."

Beard quickly scooped a small depression in the dirt, laid his carbine inside and smoothed the ground over. He buried cartridges under manure in front of his tent just as a soldier walked up and demanded he go to the council.[36]

Phillip Wells, Sandy's great-grandfather, had ridden into Wounded Knee with General Forsythe the evening before. When Forsythe took over the negotiations, Wells interpreted. The general ordered him to "Tell Big Foot he says the Indians have no arms, yesterday they were well-armed when they surrendered. He is deceiving me. Tell him he need have no fear in giving up his arms, as I wish to treat him kindly."

When Big Foot replied that the weapons were all accounted for, Wells answered as directed, "You are lying to me in return for my kindness."[37]

The men assigned to search the tents brought in a few more rifles along with anything sharp they could find and stacked it all on the previously turned in firearms. Forsythe then issued what must be close to the most bizarre and shocking order ever pronounced by an American Army officer. An interpreter, perhaps Wells, who does not mention it in his writing, announced:

> This officer asked yesterday for twenty-five guns, but you did not give them, now he will get them, he would take them himself; so you pick them himself [sic] and you had better give those you have in your blankets, and your knives and belts and it will be all right. When you give the guns and knives, you will stand in one rank right along the edge of this bank [the ravine] and some number of soldiers will stand in front of you and aim their guns at your forehead, but the guns are unloaded.

A loud murmur ran through the council, the men telling each other that they had been born to the land and should not be treated as dogs. "We are people in this world," many agreed.[38]

Joseph still stood next to Captain Wallace when the order was given. In an act of army gallantry, probably the only one of the day, Wallace told him, "Joseph, you better go over to the women and tell them to let the wagons go and saddle up their horses and be ready to skip, for there is going to be trouble, for that officer is half shot."[39]

Joseph ran to follow the captain's suggestion. When the line of guards did not let him pass, the captain interceded. Joseph raced to where women, expecting to travel to Pine Ridge, were hitching horses to wagons. He told them to get ready to leave in a hurry, caught his own horse, and tied it to a wagon. Inexplicably, probably due to his father's early morning talk, Joseph then returned to the council.

Phillip Wells stood next to Major Whiteside, watching a gaudily dressed Medicine Man from the Rosebud dancing in the council area. His face painted green and his nose yellow, the shaman suddenly stooped over, grabbed a handful of dirt, and threw it into the air. "Ha! Ha," the man shouted, "I have lived long enough." Turning to the warriors, he told them of their invincibility. "Do not fear, but let your hearts be strong. Many soldiers are about us and have many bullets, but I am assured the bullets cannot penetrate us. The prairie is large, and the bullets will fly over the prairies and will not come toward us. If they do come toward us, they will float away like dust in the air."

"That man is making mischief," Wells told Whiteside.

"Go directly to Forsythe and tell him about it," Whiteside commanded.[40]

Before Wells could carry out the order, Black Coyote, a deaf man, raised his rifle above his head saying he had paid good money for it, and the bluecoats would have to pay him if they wanted it. Three sergeants pushed through the crowd and grabbed him from behind. During the struggle, the rifle discharged.[41]

Wells had kept his eye on the Medicine Man who seemed to be drawing nearer. On his left someone yelled, "Look out! Look out!" He turned and saw five or six young warriors take rifles from under their blankets, then Black Coyote's rifle fired. The soldiers fired instantly, volleys tearing through the Minniconjou men, and Wells reached down to cock his weapon. He looked up to find the Medicine Man instead of a warrior only three or four feet away, a long, sharp cheese-knife raised above his head.

Wells tried to block the thrust with his rifle, but the Medicine Man moved faster, striking inside the interpreter's defense. The knife sliced through Well's face, almost completely severing his nose. He stepped back, nose dangling from strips of skin, raised his rifle, and killed the man. Blinded by blood and smoke, he reached up to pull the remnants of his nose off and find other targets when Lieutenant Guy Preston yelled, "My God, man! Do not do that! That can be saved!" Wells followed Preston to the medical staff.[42]

The Medicine Man, who nearly cut off Philip Wells' nose and in turn killed by Wells, lying dead on the field of the massacre. (Denver Public Library, Western History Collection, X-31423)

Joseph Horn Cloud followed his instincts to safety. He hurried into the ravine bordering the camp on the west where people were trying to find shelter and then, perhaps realizing the depression was a death trap, ran back into the fight along a road that took him north of the council ground.

Lucky to be alive, he found a mixture of cavalry mounts and Indian ponies, most of them wounded by the indiscriminate shooting that troops poured in all directions at fleeing women and children. Collecting five animals, perhaps thinking he could take them to his family, a woman's shout startled him, "Brother, come and help me."

A young mother with a baby strapped to her back stumbled toward him. Joseph brought the panicked horses around and jumped off the one he rode which was saddled—it would be easier for her to ride. The horse circled sideways in fear, eyes rolling wildly at the sounds of battle. The woman had just been able to get her foot in the stirrup when a bullet knocked her to the ground. Pulling herself back up, baby still strapped to her back, and with Joseph's help, she climbed into the saddle and rode away.

Horn Cloud, Una's great-great-grandfather, had been one of the first to die. Sitting beside Big Foot, he died in the first volley as did many of the Minniconjou men. So did many of the soldiers killed that day—shot by fellow soldiers who, if they did not hit an Indian, had a chance of hitting someone wearing blue on the other side of the circle.

Minniconjou Chief Big Foot frozen in the snow on the field of the massacre. The old man, stricken with pneumonia, had to be carried to the council meeting. (Denver Public Library, Western History Collection, X-31469)

Beard reacted as a seasoned warrior. With powder smoke hiding his movement and armed with only a knife, he rushed a trooper whose brass buttons sparkled through the smoke. The soldier fired with his rifle barrel next to Beard's ear. Momentarily deafened, the action quieted into an eerie silence as Beard grabbed the weapon and stabbed the man in the chest.

The blade did not easily pass through the winter uniform, barely penetrating the soldier who had grabbed Beard by the neck. With his adversary's arms raised, Beard struck again, stabbing him in the side. Mortally wounded, the bluecoat slipped to the ground, still struggling. Beard thrust the knife repeatedly into the man's kidneys—the soldier's screams loud enough to pull the warrior out of his deafness.

Beard ran toward the ravine carrying the soldier's rifle, with bullets sounding like swarms of angry bees. One found its mark and Beard fell, hit in the shoulder. A few yards away a soldier pointed his rifle at him continuously pulling the trigger, the hammer falling on an empty chamber.

Beard fired back at point-blank range, only to discover he had not reloaded the dead soldier's rifle. The panicked trooper, continuing to dry-fire, yelled for other soldiers to help. Beard jumped to his feet and ran into the ravine just as another bluecoat climbed over the bank. Beard killed him and leaped into the chasm as soldiers began lining the banks, firing into the bunched humanity in the bottom.

A view down the ravine where Big Foot's people ran to escape the soldier's guns.

Beard was hit again just above the knee. He sat down and began picking off bluecoats lining the bank above him. He held his ground although army fire was intense, with bullets smacking into the ground like hailstones, dust and smoke filling the air. He showed a young girl, shot through the neck with her mother sprawled dead behind her, a way out of the death trap and then ran up the ravine.

He came upon his mother bleeding heavily, moving slowly, swaying as she walked, an army revolver swinging in her grasp.

"My son, pass me by," she said. "I am going to fall down now."

Before Beard could speak, bullets thudded into her flesh, ending the life of Una's great-great-grandmother. Beard fired back in a futile attempt to protect her, exchanging weapons with a wounded warrior who carried a Winchester, the bottom of the ravine now so choked with smoke and dust the defenders were virtually blind.

Beard moved again and found two of his brothers in a pit on top of the ravine that yielded some protection from bullets whipping past them. White Lance was mortally wounded and William, only days before helping Joseph load hay, had been shot through the chest.

"Shake hands with me. I am dizzy now," William said to White Lance.

As White Lance, too shot up to be of much help, tried to get William to safety, Hotchkiss guns began firing into the ravine. Soldiers still lined the banks firing into the bottom.

Beard resolved to find his wife and child. Running and holding his right thumb in his teeth to keep his wounded arm from flopping painfully, he came to another pit, this one filled with women and infants, most of them dead. Soldiers sprawled on their stomachs surrounded the depression, firing at anything raised above the banks of the hollow.

Exhausted and hurt, his people massacred, Beard decided to die among the babies. Using the ground to steady his rifle, he began firing, hitting at least two of the enemy he now hated so badly that, "Even if he ate one of the soldiers, it would not appease his anger."

With everyone else in the depression dead, he shot an officer on horseback who was exhorting the soldiers to keep firing. Forsaking his vow to die, he moved back up the gorge, continually under fire. As the sun fell low in the west, firing reduced to isolated shots, he met Joseph and four other men on horseback heading toward the ravine.

"Where are you going?" he asked.

"All my brothers and parents are dead, and I have to go in and be killed, too, therefore I have come back," Una's great-grandfather said.[43]

Able to talk Joseph out of his suicide mission, Beard led him to the Oglala camp on White Clay Creek. They found White Lance still alive and

This photograph's label is succinct: Bird's Eye View of the Battlefield. The title, of course, should be changed to "Massacre." (Denver Public Library, Western History Collection, X-31288)

learned William had not made it. In what must have seemed a small victory for Joseph, he found the young mother and infant he had helped earlier still alive. Even though multiple bullets had passed through her clothing, none struck her or the baby.

White Lance had been the Minniconjou's deadliest warrior that day, accounting for twelve of the troopers killed or wounded. Choosing a well-protected fortification, he had been able to pick his targets across the battlefield. Forsythe probably spoke of him when he wrote about a "buck" pouring out such accurate fire that his forces made the decision to leave him alive instead of trying to dislodge them.[44]

Joseph, Beard, and White Lance lost parents, their sister Pretty Enemy, Beard's wife, and their brothers Sherman and William. Beard's twenty-five-day-old son was found alive, trying to nurse even though a bullet had torn through his mother's breasts. The infant died later that spring, never recovering from the ordeal. The family believed he died from consuming his mother's blood instead of her milk.

***

Three days later, New Year's Day, a burial party contracted out to a frontiersman by the name of Paddy Starr used more than twenty-five laborers to dig a trench on the frozen, wind-swept hill where the Hotchkiss guns had delivered their deadly fire. The bodies of the Minniconjou, many naked since soldiers, journalists, and visitors had taken anything of value including Ghost Shirts and other clothing, were stacked in the trench like cordwood. Estimates run that three hundred or more of Big Foot's followers died that day, many never recovered for proper burial or ceremony.

The American Army, in a frenzy of self-admiration for service well done, awarded twenty Medals of Honor for the Wounded Knee Massacre. For the Lakota, there are only family stories of the slaughtered and a weathered slab of concrete bordered with grave markers noting the brutality of the day.

The party of civilians gathering up the dead after the massacre. (Denver Public Library, Western History Collection, X-31464)

***

For Una's cousin, Leonard Little Finger (Beard's grandson), seventy years old and living in the small community of Oglala several miles north of Wounded Knee, the massacre became more than a horror story several years ago when he received a telephone call from a museum in Barre, Massachusetts. One of the souvenirs taken from the battlefield, ending up in a box donated to the museum, was Big Foot's hair. He was not scalped, he merely had the postmortem ignominy of losing his hair to a souvenir hunter who sold it to a private collector in the East. Leonard needed to prove his relationship in court before taking possession of his ancestor's locks.

Back on the Pine Ridge along the banks of Wounded Knee Creek, Leonard and other family members conducted the sacred Lakota rite,

Keeping of the Soul. They purified the dead chief's hair with smoke from sweet grass, wrapped it in a piece of sacred buckskin to make a Soul Bundle, and hung it in a special tipi for a year. During that time, they honored the chief's soul through the goodness of their actions. At the end of the year, they burned the hair, freeing Big Foot's soul to travel the Spirit Path and reach Maya Owichapaha, the old woman who judges, and be sent on to join Wakan Tanka.[45]

***

One of the most horrific editorials ever to appear in an American newspaper ran in the *Aberdeen Saturday Pioneer* on January 3, 1891, only two days after Una's relatives were thrown naked into the trench. The writer called for genocide, advocating the extermination of an entire people.

> The PIONEER has before declared that our only safety depends upon the total extirmination [sic] of the Indians. Having wronged them for centuries we had better, in order to protect our civilization, follow it up by one more wrong and wipe these untamed and untamable creatures from the face of the earth. In this lies safety for our settlers and the soldiers who are under incompetent commands. Otherwise, we may expect future years to be as full of trouble with the redskins as those have been in the past.[46]

Ten years later, the editorialist's novel for children was published. His protagonist exclaimed the famous words, "But I don't want to live here. I want to go to Kansas, and live with Aunt Em and Uncle Henry." Dorothy may not have been in Kansas anymore, but Frank Baum, the man who wrote *The Wizard Of Oz*, did not want the Lakota to be alive anywhere.

10

Enemies Among Us

*Their Indian wives, who are patient, kind, and true, made good homes
for them. There were not many cases of desertion among them; most
of these men, though rough in their way, were kind and loved their
children. Some of them, at great sacrifice, sent their children away
to schools to be educated. Their descendants are numerous on every
reservation.*

—*Susan Bordeaux Bettelyoun*, Oglala, relative of Sandy Sauser

Bear Robe, daughter of Oglala Chief Bull Bear, survived only long
enough to be with her husband Henri and their daughter Emilie as a
family for a brief time. Her father erected her funeral scaffold on the lonely
hills overlooking the Chugwater River. Her portrait still hangs in St. Louis,
Missouri.[1] Matthew C. Field immortalized her appearance in 1843, the
night she gave birth to Emilie, using a term since considered unbecoming
by the Lakota, "The good-looking squaw of Henri, the hunter, gave birth
last night to a little female half-breed …"[2] Five years later Henri, living
a double life as a resident of St. Louis and a mountain man, married his
wealthy first cousin and built a house in the bustling frontier town. He
returned to the West when he heard the call of the mountains, but he never
allowed his mixed-blood daughter to intrude on his American family. He
found a foster home for her with the mixed-blood family of Joseph Bissonette, a friend who traded with the Lakota.

Emilie grew up in the half-world of mixed-bloods, neither Lakota
nor white, along the Oregon Trail. Her first home was a trading post near
Ash Hollow where pioneers used a windless to lower wagons down to the
Platte. As a teenager, she worked in her foster father's trading post and toll
bridge near the present site of Glen Rock, Wyoming. While serving hungry
immigrants one evening, her eyes met those of a young mangeur de lard
(greenhorn) from Missouri. Emilie turned away in embarrassment because,
as she told her daughters later, she knew this was Ben Lessert, the young
man her father brought to be her husband.

They married in a traditional Lakota ceremony and moved to the banks
of the South Platte near the present site of Denver in 1858. Using a pan

Alma Sauser, Sandy's mother, and Ben and Emilie Lessert's great-granddaughter.

to swirl in the rich waters, Ben found five hundred dollars in gold and promptly took his bride to St. Louis where they married in a Catholic ceremony in the fall of 1859.[3]

Denver transformed into a burgeoning city as thousands of miners poured in hoping to strike it rich. Sentiment ran high against the Indians in the transplanted population, driven to a fevered pitch by the *Rocky Mountain News'* 1863 call for the extermination of all Native Americans. A year later the editors praised Chivington's massacre of a band of Cheyenne living along Sand Creek under the protection of the American flag. That was the same year Emilie gave birth to their first child.[4]

Joining other mixed-blood families to escape the vitriol, Ben and Emilie moved north to the sparsely settled valley of the Cache La Poudre River near the present city of Fort Collins. Again, their little family prospered. Ben purchased footsore, weary animals from travelers, rehabilitated them, and sold them for a profit. He also farmed and partnered in the ownership of a saloon and would have been content to live out his life in northern Colorado.

As a mixed-blood Lakota woman living among the white families, Emilie felt pressure and began to speak of returning to her people. She wished to live closer to her uncle, Little Wound, a chief of the Oglala. Even though his heart belonged to the mountains, Ben knew that many mixed-blood families were pulling up stakes and moving to the new Pine Ridge Reservation in southern South Dakota.

By 1877, Ben and Emilie could no longer ignore the pull of family or the push of a bigoted white population. When Dr. James Irwin, the Pine Ridge agent, wrote a letter requesting that Ben organize one hundred Indians and four hundred horses to pull one hundred wagons, and haul provisions for the reservation, there was no reason to stay in Colorado.[5] At a pay rate of seventy-five dollars a month, men from other mixed-blood families soon joined Ben in his labors.[6]

Ben and Emilie set up housekeeping near the present town of Whiteclay in a place set aside for mixed-blood families. Their family prospered until

Valentine McGillycuddy, a longtime foe of Red Cloud, became the new agent. One of his first tasks was dismissing from agency payrolls any man who had worked for the former superintendent.

Valentine T. McGillycuddy, Pine Ridge agent, seated with the long mustache in 1883 along with policeman Standing Soldier seated on the left, and George Sword standing in uniform. William Garnett and Young Man Afraid of His Horses are the two other men.

Ben went to work for a merchant named T. G. Gogill, who had been appointed by the Commissioner of Indian Affairs in 1881. When Agent McGillycuddy accused Ben's boss of stirring up trouble with the Indians, Gogill started collecting names on a petition to have the Pine Ridge Reservation investigated. Ben signed. Gogill lost his license and Ben lost another job.[7]

For mixed-blood families, adjustment to life as a second-class citizen under the dictates of colonial rule must have been traumatic. Some, like Ben and Emilie, gave up government rations and free land. They built a ranch in the beautiful tall grass country along the Niobrara River. Others stayed on the Pine Ridge, their offspring continuing to marry into full-blood families.

The names of all the old fur-trading families are common on the reservation. Bissonette, Shangrau, Richards, Provost, Pourier, Janis, and Ecoffey are still there. Big Bat's, a gas station and convenience store, stands as a continuing monument to Baptiste Pourier, a trader and scout for the United States Cavalry, who also hauled cottonwood logs for the first building erected in Denver.[8]

Ben was not the only member of his family to have problems with Agent McGillycuddy. The agent accused Ben's son-in-law, Edward Herridge, of consorting with horse thieves and ordered him off the reservation in 1883. He did the same to Bill McWilliams, married to another of Ben's and Emilie's daughters, for pointing a gun at a man's head. McWilliams wore coveralls and a striped cap when photographed helping dig the mass grave for the dead at Wounded Knee.[9]

Ben's and Emilie's daughter, Susan, born in September of 1861 in La Porte, Colorado, married John Green in 1883. Their son, Floyd, born in 1897, was Sandy Sauser's grandfather. Sandy's grandmother, Mercy Lamaroux, was the daughter of another mixed-blood family.

Nineteenth-century Lakota called the white men who lived among them iyeska, or interpreters; they still call mixed-bloods that today. Because

The Lakota murdered during the Wounded Knee Massacre were unceremoniously thrown into a mass grave on the very hill where the rapid firing Hotchkiss guns rained down death upon them. This is now the site of the Wounded Knee Cemetery. (Denver Public Library, Western History Collection, X-31292)

the Oglala settled near Fort Laramie along the main road to Oregon and California, they had a high intermarriage rate with Euro-Americans. Too often elements of both races looked down upon the mixed-race offspring—neither fish nor fowl, they lived with a boot in one camp and a moccasin in the other.

Even after the families of the original iyeska moved onto the Pine Ridge, white men continued coming to the reservation. Married to Lakota women, they qualified for government rations and their own piece of land in a country where available real estate was rapidly disappearing. Two years after the massacre at Wounded Knee, the ratio of full blood to mixed-blood residents of the tribe stood at more than nine to one; it fell to two to one by 1925.

Coexistence, more truce than brotherhood, prevailed during the years of forced assimilation. The iyeska, at least those more willing to accept an American lifestyle, became known as progressives. They lived in proximity to the full bloods who continued to practice the old ways, however, the two groups grew miles apart culturally.[10]

With Franklin Roosevelt's selection of an eastern social worker, John Collier, as Commissioner of the Bureau of Indian Affairs, the truce, uneasy

Large crowd of Native American Lakota Sioux and white men pose in front of the Pine Ridge Agency building, South Dakota, 1890. (Denver Public Library, Western History Collection, X-31355)

during the best of times, began to mutate into hostility. The most sympathetic wasicu ever appointed to lead the Bureau, Collier believed that Native Americans deserved a New Deal as surely as the rest of the country. He devoted his life to turning federal policy away from assimilation and individual land ownership—culturally genocidal policies that he considered the primary cause of Indian failure to thrive.[11]

In January 1934, he issued a circular asserting Indians' rights to practice their own religious traditions, and recruited Representative Edgar Howard of Nebraska and Senator Burton K. Wheeler of Montana to pass his policies through Congress. Greatly altered by an assimilationist assault during a fierce congressional struggle, the Indian Reorganization Act of 1934 brought allotment to an end, and in a radical victory for Indian rights, lessened the influence of reservation agents while granting self-government to tribes.

Collier, a man who loved all things Indian, could have never imagined that his work would turn Pine Ridge into a killing ground. The beautiful country of the Pine Ridge, the permanent home of the Oglala, was destined to become the most dangerous place in America.

Pine Ridge traditionals received the commissioner's allotment policies with the same outrage that their fathers did President Grant's order for them to move onto the reservation. For many, their plot of dirt was an embodiment of the hunting grounds traversed by their ancestors. Suspicious of the government that had broken every promise it made, they saw the new policy as just another land grab. A government of iyeskas (interpreters) controlled by the detested Bureau of Indian Affairs would take their plots, their part of the old hunting grounds.

Confiscating their land was serious enough, but the section of the law calling for majority rule thrust a bayonet through their hearts. It meant the abandonment of a centuries-old system of societal organization and governance. This new voting rule felt like previous attempts to make them into white men.

Probably the most democratic people in the world, without a word for authority in their language, the Lakota had no concept of majority rule. All decisions were consensus. Bands chose the leader, or Itancan, for qualities of wisdom, common sense, and compassion. A leader who acted otherwise often found his followers gone. The Lakota had no process guaranteeing anyone or any group with tribal leadership, no heritable royalty; the notion of powerful chiefs and omnipresent Indian princesses with scores of fanatical warriors burning and pillaging at their whim was a European concept popularized by Hollywood.[12]

John Collier considered the tribes of the Southwest the natural embodiment of what Indians should be. He refused to listen to the Lakota. He never considered their traditions, practiced longer than democracy, as a viable alternative to his law. He forced majority rule onto the Oglala, sparking distrust and internecine rivalry that broke into open warfare less than forty years later.

11
Wounded Knee II

Is it wrong for me to love my own? Is it wicked for me because my
skin is red? Because I am Sioux? Because I was born where my father
lived? Because I would die for my people and my country? God made
me an Indian.

— *Tatanka Iyotanke (Sitting Bull)*, Chief of the Hunkpapa

Indian uprisings made the newspapers in 1973, just as in 1890. On February 27, the takeover of Wounded Knee on the Pine Ridge exploded into national news when the Oglala finally renounced Collier's Indian Reorganization Act (IRA) government and occupied the tiny wasicu-owned village of Wounded Knee.

> Federal officers exchanged gunfire today with between 200 and 300
> militant Indians who seized the settlement of Wounded Knee on the
> Pine Ridge Oglala Sioux reservation, taking hostages as they did so. Ap-
> proaches to Wounded Knee were sealed off. Oglala Tribal President Dick
> Wilson said the Indians had hunting rifles and might have at least two
> machine guns. U.S. marshals ringing the town, many dressed in bright
> blue coveralls, were heavily armed. The Indians were organized by the
> American Indian Movement (AIM). They seized the Wounded Knee
> trading post Tuesday night, clearing out artifacts, guns and ammunition.
> Wilson said the post recently had received a new shipment of rifles and
> the Indians could possibly hold out "for weeks."[1]

The United States reacted as it had a century earlier—troops surrounded the Indians and started shooting. Armed feds dug bunkers, lit up the night sky with flares, rained down machine gun fire from helicopters, and scarred the earth with armored personnel carriers. The rez had turned into a war zone.

Aaron Running Hawk, a Vietnam combat soldier raised as a warrior and trained to kill by the army, returned from war-torn Southeast Asia in 1973, expecting to make a quick trip home to the Pine Ridge. Instead, the army confined him to his base. Several weeks later, the army sent Aaron and other Native American servicemen to Europe.

A bunker occupied by American Indian Movement members during the 1973 occupation of Wounded Knee. Note the upside-down American flag. This symbol can still be seen on the Pine Ridge reservation. (Denver Public Library, Western History Collection, X-31923)

The Nixon Administration thought the battle-experienced Indians would head straight for Pine Ridge and join the occupation. And they were right. "Your United States government is shit," Aaron said, drawing on a cigarette in a friend's house along the White River after engaging in a bi-weekly sweat lodge ceremony.

"I would have been there if I could have because of that damn IRA government." The 1934 system of rule forced onto his people is a constant irritant. He knows exactly why it has never worked—voting and majority rule are not the Lakota way. According to Aaron, the heart of American democracy is killing the Indian and saving the man: "The idea was so you can control, and I have to be a good Indian."[2]

Aaron lived alone in Yellow Bear Canyon, a beautiful, timbered landscape of rugged hills cut by streams with excellent hunting and fishing north and east of the town of Pine Ridge. Recently diagnosed with lung cancer, Aaron could not pursue game so readily anymore. He acknowledged that cigarettes may have caused his illness, but he thought it was more likely the repeated Agent Orange drenchings he suffered in Vietnam. Even in the dim light as he crawled from a sweat lodge into the brisk night brightly illuminated by a roaring fire, his skin reflected the pall of disease.

Aaron did not like, or trust, anything wasicu. He would not go to the Pine Ridge Health doctors. He gave control of his life to the healing powers of his ancestors' ceremonies.[3]

Aaron was an inveterate reader. He worried about the damage inflicted on the earth by global warming and about the health of the Lakota. He was convinced uranium mines around the rez were dumping polluted water into the streams and poisoning the people. However, it was when he spoke of the old ways that his voice came alive. He could have been sitting among a council of the Oglala just before the Custer fight when he said, "The pipe [central to Lakota ritual] can speak to us, and its language is Lakota."[4]

He would have joined the militants not only because of the IRA government, but simply because he is Lakota, and it would have been his chance to fight the United States. He would have shot federal marshals and FBI agents because of the broken promises, the occupation of Lakota lands, the theft of the Black Hills, the massacre at Wounded Knee, and the brutal treatment of his people by whites living around the reservation. "It has been too much," Aaron remarked quietly, "it is time to fight again.

"Crazy Horse, Red Cloud, and Sitting Bull tried to live by the pipe in the old days," Aaron narrated, breaking up his sentences with Lakota, "because the pipe leads to a trail of peace. But one day, they put the pipe away and took up the cause of war. The pipe is about life. It is about peace. That is why they had to put it away. Now it is time to put it away again. It is time for the people to stand up and put on the ways of war."[5]

Collier's IRA government lives in infamy in the minds of traditionals. Many want to return to the old way of governance, the days of tiospayes and chiefs. Arlette Loud Hawk lives with her daughter, Starlight, and their family pet, Super Dog, near the town of Oglala. Pert, thin, a short-haired Lakota due to cancer treatment, Arlette said that even if the Oglala did not hate the IRA government so much, it could never succeed. "It is no good. It does not work for the people, and it will never get any better because of the poverty. Whoever you put on the council—and they get paid—they are going to start looking out for themselves and their family instead of all of the people."

Like Aaron, Arlette did not care for the ways of the blue eyes, a term Lakota women often use for wasicu. "I am Oglala. I have my own laws and customs. If you come on my land, you had better act like an Oglala."[6]

Traditionals such as Arlette and Aaron rue the day, October 27, 1934, when Pine Ridge residents voted to establish an Indian Reorganization Act government, passing the measure by just seventy-four votes, 1,169 to 1,095 out of 4,075 eligible voters. But that count is by the white man's reckoning.

Historically, Lakota respond to proposals they do not like with their feet. A nineteenth-century band leader might find himself alone, his followers simply joining another village. Rather than object to his decisions, they left. Rather than voting against the IRA government, traditionals simply stayed home.[7]

Mixed-bloods carried the day. They adopted a constitution with a preamble written by unimaginative bureaucrats in the Office of Indian Affairs,

The 1936 Tribal Council, the first Pine Ridge Council following the passage of the Indian Recovery Act, led by Iyeska President Frank Wilson, passed a resolution demanding prohibition of pre-Inca Stone Age, or other exhibits, showing uncivilized practices of the Oglala Sioux.

"We, the Oglala Sioux Tribe of the Pine Ridge Indian Reservation, in order to establish a more perfect organization, promote the general welfare ..."[8]

The new council, led by mixed-blood President Frank Wilson, who had obtained a Pine Ridge allotment in 1906 while a citizen of Lawrence, Kansas, followed in the footsteps of earlier assimilationists and passed a resolution to "protest, object and demand prohibition of pre-Inca, stone age, or other North American uncivilized practices of Oglala Sioux now exhibited for show and amusement purposes ..."[9]

Wilson mocked traditionals as the loafers who hung around Fort Laramie a century earlier, calling them unlettered and their tiospaye groupings communistic. He went so far as to try to deny full-blood participation in governance. "We also object to ration Indians [who] take the liberty of representing non-ration, progressive, intelligent members of the Oglala Sioux tribe in matters of vital tribal importance."[10] In 1942, the council tread upon sacred ground in an act that seemed to the Oglala as if they were once again under the guns of cavalry in a pre-dawn attack: They removed all buffalo from tribal lands and turned the pastures over to cattle.

After World War II, either as a consequence of governmental policy known as "Termination," which closed some reservations and dumped their residents into mainstream society, Indian soldiers not returning home, or Indians moving to cities to find work, the demographics of Native Americans changed. According to the United States Census, by 1970 one-half of the Native American population lived in urban areas.

Urban Indians seeking out their own kind led to a new phenomenon, pan-Indianism—a political and cultural movement emphasizing the cultural ties of Native Americans. Members of differing tribes became friends; their children learned about civil rights in the same schools. They believed Indians on and off the reservation should stand up for themselves and demand treaty rights and tribal sovereignty.

It was time for a national organization of Indians, time to unify, and time to take their place at the bargaining table. Enter the American Indian Movement (AIM), started in Minneapolis in 1968 by three Chippewa as an offshoot of the Office of Economic Affairs' Anti-Poverty Program.

Known for outspoken rhetoric, AIM members showed the wasicu that they were not afraid of the police or their jails. They participated in the occupation of Alcatraz in 1969, justified by the Lakota interpretation of the Treaty of 1868 that "gave the Sioux the right to claim any federal facility or real estate for which the government had ended appropriations."[11] In 1970, members gained real notoriety by painting Plymouth Rock red and seizing the *Mayflower II.*

AIM became a fixture on the Pine Ridge in 1972 when the Great Creator looked away, and the Oglala once again betrayed their heritage. Less than forty years after Frank Wilson's election, they gave the presidential nod to Dick Wilson, a 5/16 mixed-blood, progressive plumber from the town of Pine Ridge.

Ironically, the murder of Raymond Yellow Thunder in Gordon and the traditionals' disapproval of Tribal President Gerald One Finger's handling of the incident propelled Wilson's candidacy. He campaigned on assurances to full-bloods that he supported their cause to find justice and told local AIM members he was 110 percent behind them.[12] That was the last and only time he championed Indian rights. From there on, Pine Ridge politics moved from rhetoric to violence.

Several months after Dick Wilson took office, AIM sponsored a national march on Washington called the Trail of Broken Treaties—caravans of Indians from every corner of the United States drove into the Capitol. Believing they had been lied to because they had to bivouac in rat-infected basements instead of the quarters they had been promised, AIM occupied the Bureau of Indian Affairs' building and destroyed furnishings and equipment, and confiscated thousands of documents.

Oglala President Wilson became AIM's most outspoken critic. Under his leadership, the tribal council quickly resolved that the Oglala tribe did not "condone or approve any or all actions taken by the American Indian Movement in Washington D.C."[13]

After AIM left Washington, according to then Tribal Secretary Toby Eagle Bull, Russell Means, an Oglala and AIM leader, asked to use Billy Mills Hall for a victory celebration. When Eagle Bull turned him down, Means is supposed to have replied, "Get the pigs together because we're going to take Billy Mills Hall and use it."[14]

Believing Means meant his threat, again acting quickly to ward off trouble, the council pledged full support for whatever action the president took to protect "the property, interest, and dignity of the Oglala Sioux Tribe," and denied AIM's use of any building under the jurisdiction of the council.[15] Then the combative and short-haired Wilson could not resist making it personal. He threatened to cut off Mean's hair, long and braided in the traditional style, and hung a poster on his office wall offering a $1000 reward for the activist's pickled body.[16]

Years later, with a national reputation as an activist and movie actor, Means said he never made that call to Toby Eagle Bull and AIM never planned on holding a victory dance at Billy Mills Hall. When questioned about the call and his threat to over-run the hall and reservation police, Means laughed softly and exclaimed, "Bullshit. This is the first I've ever heard of it." He added that the leadership of AIM would never have made that call anyway, they would have had a local woman do it.[17]

Supporters still view Wilson as cool under fire, a decisive man who knew what had to be done and saw that it was. However, seeing the same set of actions in a different light and accepting Mean's word that he did not make the call shows Wilson's Machiavellian nature. He used a counterfeit telephone call to pass a resolution empowering him to fight a threat that did not exist.

Traditionals say Wilson picked fights with them from the day of his election, turning council meetings into power struggles. He refused to seat Birgil Kills Straight, White Lance's grandson, claiming he lived in Rushville, Nebraska, and not on the reservation. According to Kills Straight, later the head of the Tribal Parks Department, Wilson's problem with him was entirely personal. Kills Straight, a traditional and a former adjutant professor at the University of Colorado recalled, "In those days, there was a lot of animosity toward the full-bloods, and Wilson especially felt that way when he thought someone was more capable than him. A big, husky man and a bully, he made fun of the people who practiced with the pipe, probably the most damning thing you could do to a traditional."

Taking off his hat and combing his long, grey hair with his fingers, Kills Straight showed his continuing contempt for Wilson by calling his followers the remnants of the loafers or hang-around-the-fort Indians from a century before.[18] Ellen Moves Camp said that traditionals disliked him from the start and claimed he was a one-man council and a dictator.[19]

After picking fights with the traditionals and AIM, Wilson planned ahead, taking steps to protect his regime as if he knew armed insurrection lay in the near future. On August 17, 1972, only a month after Kills Straight took his place at the table (Wilson refused to administer the oath of office to him), the council passed an ordinance severely curtailing the right of assembly on Pine Ridge. Before the year ended, under the powers granted him to protect and defend the reservation, Wilson formed a militia, misappropriating $65,000 in federal funds for weapons.[20] By making up a threat when one had not existed, the dictator now had his own standing army.

Oglala Medicine Man Petaga Yuha Mani (He Walks With Hot Coals) described living on Pine Ridge during Wilson's tenure:

> He had his so-called "GOONs" travel the highways and the districts. These GOONs are keeping tabs on the people who did not like what Dick Wilson was doing. People could not get together to communicate. We could not hold meetings. No three people could get together and talk. Even when they talked about the weather, people in groups were broken up by Dick Wilson's GOONs.[21]

The enmity between Wilson and traditionals came to a head early in 1973. Council members Hobart Keith, Birgil Kills Straight, and Richard Little attempted to impeach him on charges of corruption, embezzlement, nepotism, failure to operate without a budget, and false arrest. Wilson survived the vote when traditionals on the council followed the historic practice and walked out in protest over his handling of the proceedings. Even then, the vote came only after Wilson made everyone watch a John Birch Society film about the evils of communism presented by William and Eugene Rooks, who called AIM a communist front for world domination.[22]

According to the Rook brothers, AIM's plan was to overthrow all Indian country starting with Pine Ridge to be used as a weapons depot. The allegation was Wilson's trump card. In 1973 America, still mired in the jungles of Vietnam, charges of communism brought armed might on the run.

In the days before the impeachment hearing, U.S. paramilitary marshals armed with automatic weapons and supported by armored personnel

Tribal President Dick Wilson standing by the marker at the Wounded Knee Cemetery. (Denver Public Library, Western History Collection, X-31926)

carriers and helicopters surrounded the Bureau of Indian Affairs (BIA) building in the village of Pine Ridge. Blue uniformed troops occupied three sandbagged positions on the town's main street. Inside the building, an armed command post was equipped with grenade launchers, sniper rifles, and gas masks.[23]

After the failed proceedings, a group of full-blood women marched down the main street to a machine gun nest–studded BIA building surrounded by men with fully automatic rifles who never took wary eyes off the walkers. Ellen Moves Camp, Gladys Bissonette, Lou Bean, and Agnes Lamont had formed the Oglala Sioux Civil Rights Organization, sponsoring the procession in a last ditch effort to appeal to the federal government for help.

They were met with silence by newly appointed BIA Superintendent Stanley Lyman under the pretense that he had no ability to over-rule the council—a laughable excuse to women who knew better—provoking Gladys Bissonette to comment about the poor quality of men chosen to guide the Indians. "Some hayseed like you that don't know nothin'."[24] One of the signs the women carried announced, "Lyman, we don't want your Dick," referring to President Dick Wilson. Even the embattled superintendent saw the humor.

Repulsed at every turn, full-bloods returned to Calico Hall where they had been meeting with chiefs and traditional elders. Leon Eagle, one of Gladys Bissonette's grandsons and a member of an indigenous dance group, thought it was a powwow. His group attended hoping to perform and pick up a little cash. Instead, they spent several days listening to tales of rape, beatings, extortion, and firebombing by Wilson's GOONs, a group of the president's followers believed by the traditionals to be armed by the FBI and acting as the agency's hit squad.

Women pressurized the gathering by asking where the men were who would stand up for them. They invited the eight primary chiefs of the Oglala, who according to Means were "the real power on Pine Ridge—the supreme spiritual leaders and therefore the moral authorities ... embodied our culture and our aspiration to sovereignty."[25] After meeting with the women and American Indian Movement leaders in private, Chief Frank Fools Crow told the Oglala to go to Wounded Knee where the spirits of their ancestors would protect them.

Fools Crow represented the traditionals and full-bloods impeccably, according to Birgil Kills Straight, who had worked as the chief's assistant. He recalled how the leader frequently invited people to his house and gave away horses, cattle, guns, and household possessions, leaving he and his wife with nothing but the clothes they were wearing. When Fools Crow made the decision, Pedro Bissonette, Gladys' adopted son and natural nephew, appointed to liaison with the American Indian Movement, made the call to organization headquarters in Rapid City. That night carloads of Indians, including Leon Eagle, drove into Wounded Knee.

Consisting of about ten structures, the town of Wounded Knee straddled the highway south of the massacre site. A Catholic church stood on the rise where the soldiers fired Hotchkiss guns at Big Foot's followers. Mainstays of the town were Clive Gildersleeve, a wasicu reportedly holding racist tendencies and his wife, Agnes, a Chippewa, who had been the Pine Ridge superintendent's secretary and had taken notes when John Collier met with the Lakota in Rapid City. They operated a trading post and small Lakota museum curated by Agnes's brother. Perhaps the cost of doing business with a culture not their own, they were plagued by accusations of taking advantage of their customers while commercializing a sacred site.

After years of trading with the Oglala, the Gildersleeves venture suffered even more when they took in their daughter, Jan, and her husband, Jim Czywczynski, as partners. There had been trouble after the Gordon demonstrations earlier, over the death of Yellow Thunder, when carloads of Oglala stopped in Wounded Knee and castigated Jim for brutally shaking a fourteen-year-old Oglala boy who had mocked him. Museum artifacts turned up missing during the confusion as the assembled crowd chanted "Burn, burn, burn."[26]

However, the future, not the past, turned the Gildersleeves' neighbors and clients hostile. Clive Gildersleeve had made a deal to sell the property, securing him a place on the board, to a corporation planning to transform the massacre site into a tourist trap complete with a motel and restaurant complex. Designs called for the erection of a marble monument over the mass grave. A spectacularly macabre touch was to be a neo-classic column holding an eternal flame with a splotch of red terrazzo at the base symbolizing oozing blood. A fence of cavalry sabers was to surround a sunken crypt containing the exhumed and re-interred bones of the victims.[27]

When the caravan of angry AIM members and Oglala jumped out of cars and began shooting out streetlights, Agnes called the reservation police and reported that people were about to break into their business. Within an hour, two BIA police officers drove into the hamlet, claimed they heard shots, and cautiously backed out of town.

Before long the Gildersleeves and the other non-Lakota residents, except the Czywczynski's who were at a basketball game, were under guard while the soon-to-be occupiers scavenged the trading post for food and looted the museum. The loss of stolen artifacts amounted to $150,000, according to Jim Czywczynski. Russell Means said the Oglala put them back

A family gathers at Wounded Knee Cemetery to pray.

into the earth where they came from, "so they would deteriorate and disappear, never to be robbed again."[28]

The FBI, alerted about two hours after the caravan pulled up to the store, established roadblocks on all the roads into town. Believing the militants outnumbered and outgunned the agents, marshals, and GOONs, FBI Special Agent in Charge Joseph Trimbach requested M-16 assault rifles and armored personnel carriers. The next morning, before authorities and occupiers had spoken about negotiations and demands, two Phantom jets roared low over the village.

The Catholic church on the site of the artillery at the 1890 massacre, astride the highest point, became AIM's base of operations. The occupiers matched the federal bunkers with their own. No one could get in or out of Wounded Knee.

Estimates of more than one thousand Indians and sympathizers passed through Wounded Knee during the seventy-one days they occupied the village, including two great-grandsons of General George Armstrong Custer.[29] Occupiers braved the bitter cold of South Dakota, trudging through snow or stumbling over rock-hard chunks of frozen dirt cleared of vegetation and moisture by the relentless winds when there was no snow, and the thermometer crouched below freezing. They huddled for warmth, starved, cried, lived, died, gave birth, made love, and hunkered down as automatic rounds tore fist-size holes through reinforced walls and blew washtub-size gaps out the opposite side.

Those inside like Leon Eagle, there to support his grandmother, assumed different tasks. Some cooked, some nursed, some kept watch, some engaged in firefights. Leon worked as a courier, spending many nights ferrying in new recruits while carrying ammunition and food in heavy packs. After so many years, Leon most remembers lying in a trench watching tracers zip over his head and ricochet off propane tanks. He was afraid a tank would explode and kill everybody in a massive firebomb.

Leon also admits a little sheepishly that he was in on the raid on Gildersleeve's store and museum. His grandmother said that they were cheating

Indians so he thought the stuff was rightly theirs to take. He liberated a cache of gold and put it in his backpack. Since then he has heard discussions about what happened to the Gildersleeve's gold. Leon says it went to buy food and supplies for his grandmother that he brought in from the outside.

Richard Janis's family was split; some sided with the full-bloods while others signed up as GOONs. He did not know anything about the takeover of Wounded Knee before it happened; he and some friends just followed the procession heading that way looking for excitement. Thinking to take advantage of the chaos the first night, he filled his car with fuel and turned around to leave. He did not get off the grounds—he had filled his tank with kerosene instead of gas. He finally made it out after a month.

Richard laughs when he remembers Russell Means sending some California Indians out to get some beef, preferably a young cow. They came back with an old bull. "Man, was it tough," he says. "It was like chewing bubble gum trying to eat it, the more you chewed, the bigger the wad got in your mouth."[30]

After living off the reservation for most of her life, the remains of Zintkala Nuni, the Lost Bird of Wounded Knee, were returned to the Wounded Knee Cemetery for burial.

Birdie Mesteth had had enough of the treatment her people received on the reservation and in the border towns. She fired weapons at the FBI because they were the oppressors, "enemy soldiers."[31] Birdie came away with more than memories; she had taken in a friend's baby right before the occupation and kept him with her the entire seventy-one days. Forty years later, Ben Mesteth is still known as the Lost Bird of Wounded Knee II, named after Zintkala Nuni, an infant found clinging to her dead mother after the 1890 massacre. Zintkala Nuni (Lost Bird) was adopted by General Leonard Colby of the National Guard and raised by his wife, Clara Bewick Colby, a national leader in the struggle for women's rights.

Listening to stories of the occupation, hearing the Oglala describe automatic rounds blasting through buildings while facing the might of the strongest nation in the world for seventy-one days is nightmarish. For these are not stories told by foreign-born radicals, this was not long ago in a far off place. Wounded Knee happened in the heartland of America in 1973—the besieged were neither communists nor terrorists.

There is enough evidence to suggest that the Oglala who participated, like Aaron Running Hawk would have, were there because they'd had enough. They waged war against colonialism and foreign domination, trying to rid themselves of not only an IRA administration they viewed as hostile, but the federal government as well. For them, it was a renewal of the Indian wars against the American Army. It was their chance to fight the bluecoats.

A lonely chimney, all that remains of the village of Wounded Knee.

12

The New 7th Cavalry

The power of a thing or an act is in the understanding of its meaning.
—*Heȟáka Sápa (Black Elk)*, Holy Man of the Lakota

Blue Whirlwind Woman saw her husband, Spotted Thunder, die in the council area in front of Big Foot's tent. She grabbed her two small boys and fled into the ravine. Covered with blood, in excruciating pain, she would later discover that she had been hit fourteen times by bullets and fragments of exploding cannon shells. She lay over her sons, protecting them with her body. Finally, sensing a lull in the firing, she collected herself, held a child under each arm, and bolted out of the gulch. She ran until she collapsed in a clump of long grass, knowing her sons would die if she did not keep going.

Gathering the last of her strength, she carried her sons over the small ridge, barely able to make out a rude cabin through the blood hardening on her face. She was only dimly aware of a man pulling her inside. It was not until she started regaining her strength that she realized he was blind. Nowhere else to go, everybody in her family dead, mercilessly shot down by the soldiers, she decided to stay with this man, raise her sons, and make a new life over the little hill from Wounded Knee Creek. "And that's how my husband's family got their name," Rita Long Visitor says as she tells the story. "When the census taker came around in 1890 or 1900 and found out the man couldn't see, he recorded the family in his record book as Blindman."[1]

When the shooting stopped in 1891, the army posed for a few pictures, awarded some medals, and left. Beard, White Lance, and Joseph came out of hiding; Blue Whirlwind Woman made a life with the blind man; and Short Bull's followers returned to the Rosebud. Except for the few touring Europe with Buffalo Bill and other western shows, the Lakota slipped back into anonymity.

After quelling the takeover of Wounded Knee in 1973, also using overwhelming firepower, the FBI stayed, and according to the Oglala, carried a grudge. Antipathy, plus a continuing failure to understand the indigenous people as a cultural entity not American, makes for long odds that they will ever bring the murderers of Wally Black Elk and Ronnie Hard Heart to

Always marked with colored ribbons sacred to the Lakota, the marker of the mass grave at Wounded Knee carries the name of those who died on that terrible day.

justice. "What are two more dead Indians to the FBI?" is a commonly asked question on the rez.

The killers will escape justice not because they are master criminals outwitting modern forensic labs and determined detectives; the residents of Pine Ridge believe they continue to evade justice because nobody is looking for them. Pine Ridge and the surrounding border towns, they think, are the best places in America to get away with murder—if the victims are Indians.

The Oglala view the FBI as an oppressive rather than an investigative force. They see the preeminent law enforcement agency in America, at best, as a bust. At worst, federal agents are Custer's troops reincarnated, prepared to heed the bugle's call to attack. They came by this view of the vaunted crime fighting organization naturally—it is what the FBI announced. According to Norman Zigrossi, special FBI agent in charge, Rapid City, in 1976:

> The Indians are a conquered nation. And when you're conquered, the people you are conquered by dictate your future. This is a basic philosophy of mine. If I'm part of a conquered nation, I've got to yield to authority. ... [The FBI must function] as a colonial police force.[2]

*****

Special Agent in Charge of the Minneapolis Office of the Federal Bureau of Investigation, Joseph Trimbach, orchestrated the FBI response at Wounded Knee. In 2008, he published *American Indian Mafia: An FBI Agent's True Story about Wounded Knee, Leonard Peltier, and the American Indian Movement (AIM)*. If his writing accurately records the convictions of federal law enforcement on the Pine Ridge in 1973, little had changed since 1890. Agent Trimbach seemingly misread the events in Indian Country as surely as the army had eighty-three years earlier.

According to General Miles, the army had to capture Big Foot's band before they drenched the prairies in blood; Trimbach had to break the occupation because the "objectively treasonous" American Indian Movement planned to conquer all of Indian Country. "Job one was to topple the elected tribal leadership at Pine Ridge, Russell Mean's hometown reservation, and use it use a base of operations and a weapons depot."[3]

No matter how the Lakota tried to set the record straight before the 1890 massacre, including Red Cloud's letters to the Chadron newspaper, Americans did not believe them. The same held true in 1973. The Oglala Sioux Civil Rights Organization's invitation to AIM to help after their attempts at peacefully ousting Wilson as tribal president was never sent, according to Trimbach. "Wounded Knee happened because AIM supporters, 'frustrated by lack of response from the FBI, appealed to AIM for protection.' No proof accompanies this conclusion ..."[4]

The drive to impeach Wilson was not a grass roots Oglala action. "The new meeting place was Calico Hall. Here the AIM leaders joined with local malcontents in whipping up their followers into a lather over tribal council matters, lack of jobs, and the government's failure to honor the Treaty of 1868."[5]

For Agent Trimbach, the occupation of Wounded Knee was merely a crime. He consoled himself "with the virtual certainty that this 'bank robbery' could not last long." The victims were the residents of Wounded Knee, especially the non-Lakota Gildersleeves and their relatives who lost everything they had for no reason. "Agnes and her husband Clive had lived on the reservation for almost forty years and were well accepted on the reservation, certainly more so than the outsider [AIM leader Dennis] Banks."[6]

Of course, Trimbach also wrote that Wilson was a staunch advocate for Indians and a more ardent defender of Indian sovereignty than Russell Means.[7] He claimed residents affectionately referred to the Guardians of the Oglala Nation as GOONs[8] formed with only one purpose, "to ward off the coming assault of AIM lawbreakers."[9]

Agent Trimbach looked across the frozen landscape of Pine Ridge and saw a few local malcontents join forces with a terrorist group to take over Indian lands for communism. For whatever reason, instead of local discontent, the FBI saw a ploy by actors on the world stage to further the cause of Marxist-Leninist revolution. The FBI joined with local members of the John Birch Society such as William and Eugene Rooks, who insisted the American Indian Movement was a communist front organization.[10]

Trimbach never saw oppressed people desperately trying to hold onto their culture. He seems not to have realized that the Lakota resented Christian churches overlooking their most sacred ground, or of their revulsion to sacred antiquities in the hands of non-Lakota. He did not realize that they saw the trading post and museum as exploitation of the massacre victims.

He ridiculed their wish to reinstate the Treaty of 1868 by calling prior agreements between the United States and the Lakota "old treaties long since abandoned and rendered utterly obsolete."[11] There is not a turn of a phrase on the reservation more guaranteed to invoke hostility than to mock the treaty Red Cloud's warriors won when they prevailed against the American army.

Trimbach highlighted his lack of cultural knowledge with the phrase "just a few yards away from the souvenirs, many brave warriors had died defending an ideal the village center tried to present."[12] And what could that ideal possibly have been: a government their children despised, exploitation of their culture and death by white capitalists, plans to bury them in a place surrounded by cavalry sabers, or Christian churches towering over the field where they died?

The thesis that Wounded Knee was an invasion by militant, out-of-state, and urban Indians bent on some purpose other than supporting Wilson's Oglala opponents does bear some weight at first glance. Russell Means was the only local leader in the AIM leadership, and he grew up in California.

There are traditionals, as Trimbach noted, who did not and still do not approve of AIM. Rita Long Visitor has no use for the organization and the way they came on to the reservation with guns "trying to tear everything up. If they had come in with good will trying to help everybody it might have helped, but not the way they did it."[13]

Her son, Nathan Blindman, a direct descendant of Blue Whirlwind Woman, college graduate and accomplished artist, does not agree with her. He wished he could have joined the occupation.

"Yeah, and gotten a thrashing," Rita says smiling, leaving no doubt that is exactly what would have happened to him.

Nathan is a member of the Wounded Knee Survivors Association. His passion in the defense of his people and the Treaty of 1868, and the goals of the Oglala Sioux Civil Rights Organization, erupted in a letter published in the *Rapid City Journal* in 2002:

> I am a second-descendent survivor of the Wounded Knee Massacre of 1890. My paternal grandfather, Hopa Hoksila, his mother, and little brother, Taopi Cikala, miraculously survived that massacre. As they escaped the carnage, they left their dad, Spotted Thunder, an older brother, an uncle and other relatives and friends, all killed or being killed. My grandfather, Hopa Hoksila, died in 1963. The WKSA did submit claims to the U.S. government for compensation for families and relatives killed at Wounded Knee. They were never compensated. The victims of the Wounded Knee Massacre were/are covered under the Treaty of 1868, Article I. Today, as I write this letter, the people I am descended from lie in a mass grave overlooking Wounded Knee Creek, forgotten, yet exploited to no end.[14]

Nathan supports pan-Indianism, an idea brought by AIM. Nathan says it works today, binding nations together to meet and help each other, no matter what tribe. It does not bother him that many occupiers were not local, some not even Native American. They came to help the Oglala.

Rita wasn't on the reservation in 1973, as she had already taken her two boys and moved to California for a job so she could give them a better life. However, like most traditionals on the Pine Ridge, she may not approve of AIM, but that does not mean she agrees with the Federal Bureau of Investigation, United States policy, or assimilation.

Rita, a member of The International Council of Thirteen Indigenous Grandmothers, nurtures children around the world. While she may have disagreed with AIM's tactics, she is a traditional aligned with the Oglala Sioux Civil Rights Organization. She does not like the Tribal Council of the IRA; she would prefer the traditional Lakota governance of chiefs. "These were very wise men who knew the history; they did the most they could for the people. They were strong in mind. They knew everything and the people let them decide."[15] Almost the same words Gladys Bissonette used during the occupation when she said, "We want an independent sovereign Oglala Sioux Nation. We don't want no part of that government, Tribal or BIA. We have had enough of that. They don't allow us our rights. We want our old 1868 treaty back."[16]

Rita is also a devotee of Oglala spirituality and sees Christian churches on the reservation as symbols of the oppression, of the aggressor. The same thoughts Grace Black Elk expressed during the occupation.

> And then these Catholic, Episcopal and Presbyterian, they saw a good thing, to gather a lot of sheep in the name of these dead people. They put

up their church here and never thought nothing, not one bit, of those dead people up there. Them people were not baptized at all. ... Yet the church is up there and there is a cross on top of those graves.[17]

There is no better exemplar than Wounded Knee that the United States and its Indian Country law enforcement branch did not understand the Lakota. But even cultural ignorance may not be enough to explain armored personnel carriers, machine guns, and flares lighting up the night sky for three months.

By 1973, Americans had grown used to demonstrations, protests, and even riots. Large sections of cities had burned; thousands had rioted with far fewer bullets flying at them than the FBI fired at Wounded Knee. In terms of population endangered and property destroyed, the standoff on Pine Ridge was minuscule—the only people in danger were the occupiers. The question is, why Wounded Knee? The answer is precisely what Zigrossi said, that the FBI acted as a colonial police force rather than an investigative, crime solving law enforcement agency on the Pine Ridge.

The Oglala believe Pine Ridge turned into a killing ground after Wounded Knee when the FBI declared war. If the agency is successful on any reservation, which is doubtful, agents cannot work effectively on Pine Ridge. They will probably never solve the murders of Ron and Wally because the people will not work with nor respect them.

13
Killing Ground

*When I saw this I wished I had died too, but I was not sorry for
the women and children. It was better for them to be happy in the
other world, and I wanted to be there too. But before I went there I
wanted to have revenge. I thought there might be a day, and we should
have revenge.*

— *Heȟáka Sápa (Black Elk)*, Holy Man of the Lakota

S pring had finally come to the Pine Ridge in 1973. Cottonwoods shim-
mied in pale green. Small trees and bushes cloaked in the mature leaves
of a new summer blended with knee-high grass along the river. Flowers
bloomed in soft dirt near abandoned prairie dog holes, with dark mounds
marking the omnipresent rodent's new homes. Arlette Loud Hawk's pony
ran easily, chasing the spring wind, her dog loping alongside, except when
he tore off to chase long-eared jackrabbits.

As she had climbed onto her brown and white pinto, hay bale for a
footstool, her father had warned her to stay away from houses. "Out in the
prairies and hills, you'll be fine," he'd said. He'd gotten caught up in the
trouble on the reservation. Oglala President Wilson had made it clear that,
as a tribal fish and game officer, he'd be expected to join the GOONs fighting the American Indian Movement. When Arlette's dad, Russell, not only
didn't join Wilson's private army, but made it known his sympathies were
with AIM and his oldest son, Kenneth, who had taken part in Wounded
Knee, Wilson was fit to be tied.[1]

The young girl thought she was doing what her father had said, she
didn't think riding within a quarter mile of a barely gravelled road would
matter. Maybe the Lakota have a genetic predisposition alerting them to the
whine of bullets as they gallop across the prairie. Perhaps, growing up in
the silence of the sparsely populated rez had sharpened her sense of danger.
Whatever the reason, she recognized a sound she had never heard before.
The men in cowboy hats parked along the road were shooting at her.

There is no greater bond between man and animals than Lakota and
their horses and in young Arlette's case, her dog. Calling up the courage and
sense of self-sacrifice Oglala females have forged over centuries of living

The bond between the Lakota and their horses is as strong as ever. Young people are seen riding great distances across the reservation on their ponies. Horses are often called Lakota babysitters.

with danger, she knew instantly what to do. Arlette slid off her horse and slapped him on the rump, running him over the ridge as the dog followed along. Then, she stood calmly, facing the pickup load of GOONs.

She knew why the men were using her for target practice; she had lived through the war.

> *I live[d] in Oglala. When Wounded Knee 1973 was going on I was a little girl. I looked that way and the whole sky was pink* [from the flares being shot up by the government]. *To me Wounded Knee was just right over the hill there. I was like, Oh right on! Cool! Keep on doing that, man! I was really happy. Little did I know that my nation was trying to make war with one of the big power nations of the world. I was just proud of them. And ever since Wounded Knee I've always been real happy to be an Indian and I'm proud of the fact that you mess with us, we'll mess right back.* [Italics in original][2]

Arlette's penchant for the American Indian Movement and armed resistance against the United States grew out of tragedy. Her grandmother, Dora High White Man, barely survived the Wounded Knee Massacre as a child. Her cousin, Wesley Bad Heart Bull, died in Buffalo Gap, stabbed to death by a wasicu named Darld Schmitz. Sarah, her mother's sister, received a longer jail sentence for protesting the watered-down charges against the man who killed her son Wesley than the murderer did for the killing.

Another cousin, Lesley Bandley, a member of the United States military, died when a carload of "white boys just came along and ran over him and killed him."[3] Arlette does not believe her family has ever found justice. Massacre, border town cops, and GOON bullets place her solidly among the traditionals who believe reservation problems stem from United States governance enforced by the Federal Bureau of Investigation.

For seventy-one days, Arlette watched the war at Wounded Knee as AIM and feds faced off over rifles. She saw armored personnel carriers crawling across the ground, automatic weapons

Arlette Loud Hawk.

raining shell casings onto the earth from helicopters, and snipers playing cat and mouse. The firing was loud, the night sky lit by flares—to watch and listening was terrifying—but Arlette knows that for all the ammunition used, very few people died. In what should have been a deadly arena, only two AIM supporters died from gunfire during the occupation.

A machine gun round blew through the walls of the Catholic church on April 25 and struck Frank Clearwater, known to AIM as an Apache from North Carolina, and the first to die in the occupation. The bullet hit Clearwater as he slept after hiking in the night before. His was not the only injury the day after three light aircraft dropped supplies to the destitute occupiers:

> Part of Clearwater's neck was torn, but I didn't know if it went in his skull. I see the flesh is torn off, and he was bleeding profusely, and going into convulsions. Three other people were brought in. The second man they brought in, he was shot four times. … We'll need surgery to get the bullets out.[4]

Even in death, Pine Ridge remained closed to Clearwater. President Wilson refused to allow a non-Lakota's, perhaps even non-Indian, remains to rest anywhere on the reservation. His body, the FBI identified him as a white man named Frank Clear, finally found rest on Crow Dog's property on the Rosebud.[5]

There was no question of the next fatality's identity when Lawrence "Buddy" Lamont died of a sniper's bullet eight days later. His mother, Agnes, was a leader of the Oglala Sioux Civil Rights Organization (OSCRO). He was also Gladys Bissonette's nephew and Pedro's cousin. Lou Bean, also at Wounded Knee and an OSCRO leader was his sister. Darlene "Kamook" Nichols, wife of AIM leader Dennis Banks, was his niece.

Family members buried Lamont at Wounded Knee next to the mass burial site of the 1890 massacre. Later, Buddy York, an FBI sharpshooter, said he'd probably killed Lamont since he had been one of only three agents with the type of weapon and ammunition used in the shooting. "York testified his instructions were 'shoot to kill' although official government policy was still 'shoot to wound.'"[6]

In a blow to the theory that the American Indian Movement was a subversive group bent on taking all of Indian Country and setting up an arms depot on Pine Ridge, Lamont's demise ended the occupation. According to Russell Means, his shooting, "which saddened everyone, convinced Grandpa Fools Crow and the other elders there had been enough deaths."

In addition to these deaths, and a problem for those who continue to label AIM as equipped with automatic rifles, occupiers injured only one federal agent during the entire siege. U.S. Marshall Lloyd Grimm suffered a wound in the upper right chest, paralyzing him from the waist down on March 26, a month before Clearwater died.

One agent paralyzed, two AIM members dead, and several others wounded, including Wally Black Elk's older half-brother, Webster Poor Bear. The official tally after almost three months of battle is not very long for all the shots that were fired. However, there are other lists kept by survivors and supporters of the opposing sides that are longer, and if true, a lot more grisly. These are mysteries still talked about on the rez—disappearances and deaths never recorded and if investigated, never solved.

Leo Wilcox, the first to die mysteriously, was a council member and Wilson supporter. His death was officially labeled an accident, but GOON supporters refused

Webster Poor Bear, Wally's older half-brother, joined the occupation in 1973 after serving the United States in Vietnam. (Photo by Pte San Win)

to believe it. The former marine, an outspoken critic of AIM, labeled the unrest on Pine Ridge as a struggle for control. In a radio broadcast, he announced that AIM wished to take over the rez "because the Oglala Sioux name is big and strong and it will carry a lot of weight for all the publicity they seek."[7]

Wilcox, who denied that Russell Means was anything like a new Crazy Horse, calling him instead "a genuine Fidel Castro," drove home to Pine Ridge on March 25, after a bout of heavy drinking in Rapid City.[8] He never made it. Near Scenic, South Dakota, a tiny border town whose claim to fame was an animal skull-studded saloon and a scene of at least one well-publicized murder, Wilcox drove off the black top, sinking his car in heavy, stick-to-everything gumbo. After two men had pulled his car out of the mud, Wilcox drove into Scenic and bought five dollars worth of gas.

Authorities discovered his body burned beyond recognition just off the highway. South Dakota investigators, since the crash occurred off the reservation the state had jurisdiction, determined his fuel line had been caked in thick mud and broke. Gas pouring through the breach ignited, burning the car and its driver. With his hands and feet destroyed, dental records were used to identify his corpse.

Wilcox's family and friends thought AIM turned him into a fireball because of his loyalty to Wilson.[9] A reporter for the John Birch Society wrote:

> The cause of the fire is not known, but it was definitely not the result of
> an auto accident. No authority claims that it was. Leo's car had no sign
> of collision damage, and was very neatly parked on the paved shoulder of
> the road when it was found. Leo Wilcox was unconscious but alive during
> the fire; the cause of the crack in his skull is undetermined. And nobody
> has a rational explanation of how such an extremely hot fire could de-
> velop so fast by "accident."[10]

At least the Wilcox family was able to bury his remains. Perry Ray Robinson's wife and children never had that closure. No one officially knows if Robinson, a civil rights activist and follower of Martin Luther King, died on Pine Ridge, but the evidence is almost irrefutable that his life ended there. From Alabama and a veteran of the movement for equal rights, Robinson introduced himself as an ex-boxer who practiced pacifism and non-violence.

Apparently, Robinson and a black woman also from Alabama walked into Wounded Knee on April 23, 1973. While little is known about the woman except she eventually left the village, problems supposedly started for Perry Ray the moment he arrived. He had difficulty with the lack of food, constant gunfire, and AIM's chain of command. When he began criticizing the militants, referring to Native American's as "you Indians," tempers flared. "He constantly annoyed us and got on our nerves in the bunker," said Richard Two Elk, a former AIM member who took part in the siege and later corroborated with FBI Agent Joseph Trimbach.[11]

During a firefight, insisting on staying inside, Robinson is said to have become involved in an intense argument with other occupiers. AIM security appeared, and Leonard Crow Dog told Robinson to go with them. Reportedly, Robinson swore angrily, grabbed a butcher knife off a table, and confronted the men surrounding him. Someone fired a shot and Robinson fell to the floor, wounded in the leg, his eyes rolling back in his head.

Crow Dog allegedly had Robinson taken to a makeshift hospital where he supposedly died when attendants could not control the bleeding. Chris Westerman, younger brother of famed activist, singer, and actor Floyd Westerman, is said to have taken the body to a hillside and buried it.

Robinson's wife, Cheryl Buswell-Robinson, relayed a different accounting of the shooting.

> He was sitting on somebody's porch eating oatmeal. An Indian dude came up, ordered him to go see Dennis Banks. Ray said, "In a minute— I'm eating my oatmeal—I'll go when I've finished. The Indian dude got affronted by Ray's lack of civility. The Indian shot Ray dead.[12]

According to Barbara Deming, writer and political activist, in a letter to Robinson's wife, the shooting occurred "after [Robinson] being loud and trying to lead AIM members. And the Indians didn't appreciate it. And told him so. And Ray pulled a gun. …. And the Indian he'd pulled a gun on shot him in the leg. Not with intention to kill or maim … but intention simply to get the situation under control. The wound was not a bad one."[13]

Robinson's wife informed authorities that the family had no interest in charging anyone, they just wanted the remains returned to them. The editor of *News From Indian Country* wrote that such is not going to happen. He thinks authorities would find that Robinson's remains are not alone in the grave. He believes AIM thugs were responsible for more than just one murder and hidden corpse.[14]

Not everyone in the occupation knew that Robinson or his traveling companion were in Wounded Knee. Leon Eagle acts convincingly surprised when queried about the missing civil rights worker. "Black man?" he asks. "What would a black man be doing with a bunch of us rowdy Indians?"[15]

At least, people knew Wilcox's and Robinson's names. The rumored mass murder of twelve more people forms the biggest mystery of the occupation. On April 23, the same day Robinson trekked into Wounded Knee, the tribal patrol caught twelve people described as hippies heading for the tiny village. No one knows who they were, where they were from, or if they have families still waiting for them.

Radio transmissions recorded by AIM are the only evidence the twelve were on the Pine Ridge:

> Tribal Patrol to Tribal Roadblock: We need some help up here. We got twelve guys here, hippies. Some of 'em are not Indian. Can you send some help up here?
>
> Tribal Roadblock: Someone's on their way. Cut their goddamn hair for 'em. We got two vans coming—about a dozen men in 'em. [A new voice comes on speaking with authority.] You hold them sons-a-bitches and shoot 'em if they try to run. Over.
>
> Tribal Patrol: They ain't got no fight left in 'em. Fuck 'em in the face. Twelve hippies we got and they got about eight women in there and we gonna let the women go. You want we should stand by or what? … Who in the hell is Crow Dog? They said they come from Crow Dog's camp. … Corn Dog's beating his tom-tom.
>
> Roadblock: What?
>
> Patrol: Corn Dog—I mean Crow Dog is beating his tom-tom. … I heard Dennis Banks never rode a horse in his life up until the press got there. … We caught two women coming into Wounded Knee. What should we do with them?
>
> Roadblock: Cut their hair off.[16]

According to the Wounded Knee Legal Defense/Offense Committee (WKLDOC), no one ever heard what happened to the people captured that night. Rumors of undiscovered graves in the hills continue to circulate around the reservation.

The strangest accusation involved a beating in broad daylight. On Easter Sunday, April 22, 1973, the day before Perry Robinson made his way to Wounded Knee, occupiers crucified and beat a figure dressed as a marshal on a wooden cross. Marshals and FBI agents watched the brutality through field glasses. Federal authorities felt sure they saw the savaging of a human being.[17]

"Later, authorities confirmed that the figure was only a mannequin," according to Rolland Dewing, who studied thousands of FBI documents.[18] The American Indian Movement announced the same, but Richard Two Elk said the figure was a suspected FBI informant. He claims they beat him at the request of AIM security before taking him to a federal roadblock.

There is no record of his delivery to a roadblock, leading the editor of *News From Indian Country* to speculate that Mannequin Man is now the occupant of an unmarked grave.[19]

After four decades, no one has discovered a grave or a body, even though immediately after the siege ended, federal authorities combed the area. As the finger pointing continues, especially for the family of Perry Ray Robinson, there can be no closure—there are no remains to bury or to honor.

***

Arlette and other Oglala say murder season opened at the close of the occupation. Over the next three years, called the Time of Troubles, AIM supporters died at an astonishing rate. Residents claim that more than sixty people died violently during the thirty-six month period with more than three hundred physically assaulted.[20] They assign guilt to GOONs functioning as FBI death squads ordered to decimate AIM on the Pine Ridge.

Residents of the Pine Ridge speak of the time with a mixture of sadness and anger. If their numbers are correct, "Figuring only documented political deaths," Pine Ridge's murder rate between March 1, 1973, and March 1, 1976, was 170 per 100,000. Detroit, long considered the murder capital of the United States, had a rate of 20.2 per 100,000 in 1974.[21]

Those three years appear even more tragic when compared with murder rates after the turn of this century. The homicide rate in the United States for 2010 stood at 4.2 per 100,000.[22] In all of Mexico in 2011, during a drug war, the murder rate equaled 23 per 100,000.[23]

Duane Brewer, former tribal patrol officer and leader of Wilson's private army admits that residents branded the GOONs as a virulent organization but is adamant most of the shootouts were AIM instigated. As a recently returned Vietnam vet, taunted in the Seattle and Denver airports and a newly commissioned tribal police officer, he turned against the American Indian Movement because he saw so many hard-core criminals in their ranks. "Wilson did the right thing standing against them," he says. "Otherwise they would have destroyed the reservation."

He calls the GOONs regular family men protecting their homes and no match for AIM in a firefight because the militant group had so many automatic weapons. "We had only rifles and shotguns," he insists. "We would have certainly lost in a firefight with AIM because they were better armed."[24]

Ardent in his support of Wilson and the men who sided with him, Tim Giago, founder and first president of the Native American Journalist Association, also believes AIM initiated the violence. "Those so-called GOONs lived and died on the reservation they loved ... but most of all they were decent human beings given an unfair label by the MSM [mainstream media] simply because it was colorful." Of Oglala President Dick Wilson, he wrote, "I have never met a friend of his or a member of his family that did not defend him and did not continue to love him."[25]

Giago has also been a victim of AIM violence after writing articles critical of the group's tactics and leaders. "For my efforts my newspaper had its windows blasted out and an attempt was made to burn the building to the ground in 1982, and my life and that of my family was threatened."[26]

Ronald Dewing, one of the first historians to catalog the events on Pine Ridge during and after the occupation also pointed the finger of guilt at AIM. "Although Wilson's GOONs were not blameless, most impartial reservation Indians credit AIM with initiating much of the violence."[27]

Paul DeMain, editor of *News From Indian Country,* is no fan of AIM. "From a tiny element of Native America we once looked up to, the people's movement was hijacked by false warriors, murderers, and liars."[28]

The FBI must have agreed, for sure Joseph Trimbach, the former agent in charge, did.

> What followed [AIM's growth in influence] on Pine Ridge was a period
> of unparalleled violence, virtually all of it instigated by AIM leaders
> battling a tribal government some viewed as corrupt. With a guaranteed
> prescription for unrest, the leaders thus led their membership down a
> path toward hopelessness and despair.[29]

While Wilson's side claimed victimization by AIM, their list of dead pales beside that of Oglala such as Arlette Loud Hawk and Leon Eagle. Now a mother and community leader herself, Loud Hawk is not about to forget the Time of Troubles. She is compiling her own list of GOONs and their depredations. She keeps her list because the GOONs did back in the seventies and says they killed the people on it. When asked why they did, her cryptic answer sorts out the era's politics. "Because they were the over doggies and the darker you were, you were the under doggies."[30]

Cindy Hamilton, working with the Wounded Knee Legal Defense/Offense Committee, compiled the original estimation of deaths and assaults of AIM members. The most widely published list taken from her work consists of sixty-seven names, including the twelve backpacking hippies allegedly captured by the tribal police. The list, published in Ward Churchill's book *From a Native Son*, includes:[31]

4/17/73   *Frank Clearwater*—AIM member killed by heavy machine gun round at Wounded Knee. No investigation.

4/23/73   *Between eight and twelve individuals* (names unknown) packing supplies into Wounded Knee were intercepted by GOONs and vigilantes. None were ever heard from again. Former Rosebud Tribal President Robert Burnett and U.S. Justice Department Solicitor General Ken Frizzell conducted unsuccessful search for a mass grave after Wounded Knee siege. No further investigation.

4/27/73   *Buddy Lamont*—AIM member hit by M16 fire at Wounded Knee. Bled to death while pinned down by fire. No investigation.

4/14/73   *Priscilla White Plume*—AIM supporter killed at Manderson (small town on the reservation) by GOONs. No investigation.

6/19/73   Clarence Cross—AIM supporter shot to death in ambush by GOONs. Although assailants were identified by eyewitnesses, brother Vernal Cross—wounded in ambush—was briefly charged with the crime. No further investigation.

7/30/73   *Julius Bad Heart Bull*—AIM supporter killed at Oglala by "person or persons unknown." No Investigation.

9/22/73   *Melvin Spider*—AIM member killed at Porcupine, S. D. No investigation.

9/23/73   *Phillip Black Elk*—AIM supporter killed when his house exploded. No investigation.

10/5/73   *Aloysius Long Soldier*—AIM member killed at Kyle, S.D. by GOONs. No investigation.

10/10/73   *Phillip Little Crow*—AIM supporter beaten to death by GOONs at Pine Ridge. No investigation.

10/17/73   *Pedro Bissonette*—Oglala Sioux Civil Rights Organization (OSCRO) organizer and AIM supporter assassinated by BIA Police/GOONs. Body removed from Pine Ridge jurisdiction prior to autopsy by government contract coroner. No investigation.

11/20/73   *Allison Fast Horse*—AIM supporter shot to death near Pine Ridge by "unknown assailants." No investigation.

1/17/74   *Edward Means, Jr.*—AIM member found dead in Pine Ridge alley, beaten. No investigation.

2/27/74   *Edward Standing Soldier*—AIM member killed near Pine Ridge by "parties unknown." No investigation.

2/27/74   *Lorinda Red Paint*—AIM supporter killed at Oglala by "unknown assailants." No investigation.

4/19/74   *Roxeine Roark*—AIM supporter killed at Porcupine, S.D., by "unknown assailants." Investigation open, still "pending."

9/7/74   *Dennis LeCompte*—AIM member killed at Pine Ridge by GOONs. No investigation.

9/11/74   *Jackson Washington Cutt*—AIM member killed at Parmalee by "unknown individuals." Investigation still "ongoing."

9/16/74   *Robert Reddy*—AIM member killed at Kyle by gunshot. No investigation.

11/16/74   *Delphine Crow Dog*—Sister of AIM spiritual leader Leonard Crow Dog. Beaten by BIA police and left lying in a field. Died from "exposure." No investigation.

11/20/74   *Elaine Wagner*—AIM supporter killed at Pine Ridge by "person or persons unknown." No investigation.

12/25/74   *Floyd S. Binais*—Killed at Pine Ridge by GOONs. No investigation.

12/28/74   *Yvette Loraine Lone Hill*—Killed at Kyle by "unknown party or parties." No investigation.

1/5/75   *Leon L. Swift Bird*—AIM member killed at Pine Ridge by GOONs. Investigation still "ongoing."

3/1/75   *Martin Montileaux*—killed in a Scenic, S.D. bar. AIM leader Richard Marshall later framed for his murder. Russell Means also charged and acquitted.

3/20/75   *Stacy Cotter*—shot to death in an ambush at Manderson. No investigation.

3/21/75   *Edith Eagle Hawk and her two children*—AIM supporter killed in an automobile accident after being run off the road by a white vigilante, Albert Coomes. Coomes was also killed in the accident. GOON Mark Clifford identified as having also been in the Coomes car, escaped. Investigation closed without questioning Clifford.

3/27/75   *Jeanette Bissonette*—AIM supporter killed by sniper at Pine Ridge. Unsuccessful attempt to link AIM members to murder; no other investigation.

3/30/75   *Richard Eagle*—grandson of AIM supporter Gladys Bissonette killed while playing with a loaded gun kept in the house as protection from GOON attacks.

4/4/75   *Hilda R. Good Buffalo*—AIM supporter stabbed to death at Pine Ridge by GOONs. No investigation.

4/4/75   *Jancita Eagle Deer*—AIM member beaten and run over with an automobile. Last seen in the company of *provocateur* Douglass Durham. No investigation.

5/20/75   *Ben Sitting Up*—AIM member killed at Wanblee by "unknown assailants." No investigation.

6/1/75   *Kenneth Little*—AIM supporter killed at Pine Ridge by GOONs. Investigation still "pending."

6/15/75   *Leah Spotted Elk*—AIM supporter killed at Pine Ridge by GOONs. No investigation.

6/26/75   *Joseph Stuntz Killsright*—AIM member killed by FBI sniper during Oglala firefight. No investigation.

7/12/75   *James Brings Yellow*—heart attack caused by FBI air assault on his home. No investigation.

7/25/75   *Andrew Paul Stewart*—nephew of AIM spiritual leader Leonard Crow Dog killed by GOONs on Pine Ridge. No investigation.

8/25/75   *Randy Hunter*—AIM supporter killed at Kyle by "party or parties unknown." Investigation still "ongoing."

9/9/75   *Howard Blue Bird*—AIM supporter killed at Kyle by GOONs. No Investigation.

9/10/75   *Jim Little*—AIM supporter stomped to death by GOONs in Oglala. No investigation.

10/26/75   *Olivia Binais*—AIM supporter killed in Porcupine by "person or persons unknown." Investigation still "open."

10/26/75   *Janice Black Bear*—AIM supporter killed at Manderson by GOONs. No investigation.

10/27/75   *Michelle Tobacco*—Aim supporter killed at Pine Ridge by "unknown persons." Investigation still "ongoing."

12/6/75   *Carl Plenty Arrows, Sr.*—Aim supporter killed at Pine Ridge by "unknown persons." No investigation.

12/6/75   *Frank LaPointe*—Aim supporter killed at Pine Ridge by GOONs. No investigation.

1/5/76   *Lydia Cut Grass*—AIM member killed at Wounded Knee by GOONs. No investigation.

1/30/76   *Byron DeSersa*—OSCRO organizer and AIM supporter assassinated by GOONs in Wanblee. Arrests by local authorities resulted in two GOONs—Dale Janis and Charlie Winters—serving two years of five year sentences for "manslaughter." Charges dropped against two GOON leaders, Manny Wilson and Chuck Richards, on the basis of "self-defense" despite DeSersa having been unarmed when shot to death.

2/76   *Anna Mae Pictou-Aquash*—AIM organizer assassinated on Pine Ridge. FBI involved in attempt to conceal cause of death. Ongoing attempt to establish "AIM involvement" in murder. Key FBI personnel never deposed. Coroner never deposed. Actual date of death unknown.

2/6/76   *Lena R. Slow Bear*—AIM supporter killed at Oglala by GOONs. No investigation.

3/1/76   *Hobart Horse*—AIM member beaten, shot, and repeatedly run over with an automobile at Sharp's Corners. No investigation.

3/26/76   *Cleveland Reddest*—AIM member killed at Kyle by "person or persons unknown." No investigation.

4/28/76   *Betty Jo Dubray*—AIM supporter beaten to death at Martin, S.D. No investigation.

5/6/76   *Marvin Two Two*—AIM supporter shot to death at Pine Ridge. No investigation.

5/9/76   *Julia Pretty Hips*—AIM supporter killed at Pine Ridge by "unknown assailants." No investigation.

5/24/76   *Sam Afraid of Bear*—AIM supporter shot to death at Pine Ridge. Investigation "ongoing."

6/4/76   *Kevin Hill*—AIM supporter killed at Oglala by "party or parties unknown." Investigation "still open."

7/3/76   *Betty Means*—AIM member killed at Pine Ridge by GOONs. No investigation.

7/31/76   *Sandra Wounded Foot*—AIM supporter killed at Sharp's Corners by "unknown assailants." No investigation.

14
Pine Ridge Victims

"But I'm hit, daddy!" Mary Ann cried. "Daddy they got me."[1]
—Mary Ann Little Crow, nine years old,
shot in the eye in the back of her father's car

The Oglala live in a picturesque, bucolic setting in the heartland of America. Like most residents in the middle of the country, they wave, smile, and seem genuinely glad to greet visitors. They appear to live a thoroughly American life, though many have darker skin pigmentation than their neighbors in surrounding states, and a higher percentage of them live in trailers, and keep more junked cars around their houses. But look past those differences and the Pine Ridge is like any other place.

Pretty girls with bare midriffs—skin calling to boys in football jerseys and baggy pants—are just as giggly as any place else. Athletic apparel heralding the Huskers of neighboring Nebraska, the Denver Broncos, or the Oakland Raiders is omnipresent, as in other American suburbs. The logos on tee shirts, if not advertising a sports team, may be a little different from those in non-reservation areas. One popular shirt reads, "What Happens in the Tipi Stays in the Tipi," another simply announces, "Indian Power." A few slogans may be different, but the people are thoroughly American.

Flamboyant American-

Laura Red Cloud in her high school letter jacket. Laura is Una Horn Cloud's niece and an eighth generation granddaughter of the famous Chief Red Cloud. Like so many others on the Pine Ridge, Laura excelled at basketball.

ism makes it difficult to imagine what happened forty years ago. The Time of Troubles cannot be understood in the abstract, in the names of those who died. Terror is not etched into clay buttes, it does not swirl in the milky depths of the White River, and it does not mar the faces of these beautiful, friendly people. Only when eyes mist over and voices quiver in sadness does terror appear. Tears running down weathered cheeks are monuments to lives cut short, testimony to savagery.

Wounded Knee set loose the dogs of internecine warfare, but the Federal Bureau of Investigation could not see beyond their own worst fears. Battles between friends and relatives became good versus evil, us against them. Communism could not be allowed to gain a foothold in Indian Country. If the Pine Ridge fell, other reservations would topple like dominos.

Many Pine Ridge residents still believe the FBI took sides during the three years of the Time of Troubles, equipping and supplying GOON hit squads. They say the FBI allowed the slaughter, refusing to investigate the deaths or prosecute GOONs for the killings. In fact, not until a decade or more after the names of murder victims began circulating nationally did the FBI even acknowledge the Oglala stories of rampant violence.

The unrelenting work of grieving relatives following the brutal murders of Wally Black Elk and Ronnie Hard Heart forced the FBI to respond. Without Tom Poor Bear's appearance at the Civil Rights Commission Hearing in Rapid City after the murder of his brother, the FBI might have continued their silence, ignoring cries for justice from the rez.

Six months after the hearing, the bureau published, *Accounting For Native American Deaths, Pine Ridge Indian Reservation, South Dakota: Report of the Federal Bureau of Investigation, Minneapolis Division.* With a forward by Douglas J. Domin, Special Agent in Charge of the Minneapolis Division, the FBI attempted to allay fears, reduce rumors, and convince residents that agents had served them well.

Displaying either sheer ignorance or arrogance and ignoring publications circulating for years containing lists of the dead, Domin noted that only after the hearing did the most famous law enforcement agency in the world even know who supposedly had died.

> Shortly after the forum, the FBI received a list of fifty-seven names with allegations that their deaths had not been investigated. This list came from a number of media outlets and for the first time, provided the FBI with specific information to address. We reviewed our records of these deaths and found that most had been solved either through conviction or finding that the death had not been a murder according to the law. The remaining unresolved murders were known to the FBI and remain under investigation.[2]

Even if the Oglala believed the storied agency had been unable to track down lists in books, they refused to accept the report's positive spin. AIM advocates and traditionals have not been forgiving. Ward Churchill, a prolific AIM affiliated writer, stated the document "is so full of distortions, half-truths and outright falsehoods that it literally demands rebuttal."[3]

While the bureau's report is suspect, the same is true of the lists of murder victims in books and circulated widely on the Internet. Murders are included that local knowledge or research would have shown to be erroneous.

Of the fifty-nine alleged murders (not including the eight to twelve hippies allegedly picked up by the GOONs during the occupation), the FBI records twenty-seven as homicides with the perpetrators jailed in twenty-two of the cases. Of those, a jury found one not guilty and another not prosecuted due to mental impairment, for an 88 percent success rate. The victim list and allegations, again, are taken from Churchill's work published in 1996, three years before the civil rights hearings in Rapid City. The column detailing suspects and sentences is from the FBI report.

Date	Victim	Allegation	FBI
(Note: Edith Eagle Hawk is listed as one case, however, two children died with her.)			
1. 7/30/73	Julius Bad Heart Bull	Killed by GOONs. No investigation.	Killed by Bartholomew Joseph. Second degree murder. Ten year sentence.
2. 10/10/73	Phillip Little Crow	Killed by L. R. Hand.	Killed during a quarrel. Five years in prison.
3. 2/27/74	Edward Standing Soldier	Killed by parties unknown. No investigation.	Juvenile, shot by Gerald Janis during a robbery at the Janis residence.
4. 9/7/74	Dennis LeCompte	Killed by GOONs. No investigation.	LeCompte stabbed Glenn Three Stars' son in a fight at Three Stars home. Glenn shot LeCompte. Glenn indicted by Grand Jury, found not guilty of involuntary manslaughter. Released to custody of Tribal Chairman Dick Wilson.

Date	Victim	Allegation	FBI
5. 12/25/74	Floyd S. Binais	Killed by GOONs. No investigation.	Infant killed by Marion High Bull. Had been beaten.
6. 12/28/74	Yvette Loraine Lone Hill	Killed by unknown parties. No investigation.	Killed by Marion High Bull. He received a ten year sentence for killing Binais and twenty years for murdering Yvette.
7. 1/5/75	Leon L. Swift Bird	Killed by GOONs. Ongoing investigation.	Stabbed by wife, Dorothy White Bird. Three years suspended sentence/probation.
8. 3/1/75.	Martin Montileaux	AIM leader Dickie Marshall framed for murder	Marshall later confessed. Life sentence, eventually released.
9. 3/20/75	Stacy Cotter (Cortier)	Shot in ambush. No investigation.	Shot by Jerry Bear Shield after Cotter shot him in the neck. One year sentence.
10. 5/20/75	Ben Sitting Up	Killed by unknown. No investigation.	Killed by an axe. Suspect not prosecuted due to mental impairment.
11. 6/1/75	Kenneth Little	Killed by GOONs. Investigation still pending.	Killed by Antoine Blue Bird who hit him with a tire iron during a struggle. Bluebird sentenced to seven years for voluntary manslaughter.
12. 6/15/75	Leah Spotted Elk	Killed by GOONs. No investigation.	Shot while drinking by her husband Kenneth John Returns From Scout. Sentenced to two years in prison.
13. 8/25/75	Randy Hunter	Killed by party or parties unknown. Investigation ongoing.	Shot by Vern Carlin Top Bear. Charged with second degree murder, found not guilty.

Date	Victim	Allegation	FBI
14. 9/9/75	Howard Blue Bird	Killed by GOONs. No investigation.	Stabbed by Le Roy Apple during a a fight at Apple's home. Apple charged with assault with deadly weapon. Sentence: one year.
15. 9/10/75	Jim Little	Stomped to death by GOONs. No investigation.	Beaten and kicked to death by Thomas Chief Eagle, Cecil Bear Robe, Johnson Bear Robe, and Fred Marrowbone. Chief Eagle, J. Bear Robe and Marrowbone found guilty of voluntary manslaughter. Sentences ranged from four to six years.
16. 10/26/75	Olivia Binais	Killed by unknown. Investigation open.	Killed by husband, Norman. Sentenced to eight years for voluntary manslaughter.
17. 10/26/75	Janice Black Bear	Killed by GOONs. No investigation.	George Twiss admitted spending the night with her. Pled guilty to involuntary manslaughter. Three year sentence.
18. 12/6/75	Carl Plenty Arrows, Sr.	Killed by unknown. No investigation.	Carl and Frank LaPointe shot by Glen Janis. Janis found guilty of second degree murder and voluntary manslaughter. Sentenced to twenty years and ten years, concurrent sentences.

Date	Victim	Allegation	FBI
19. 12/6/75	Frank LaPointe	Killed by unknown. No investigation.	Carl and Frank LaPointe shot by Glen Janis. Janis found guilty of second degree murder and voluntary manslaughter. Sentenced to twenty years and ten years, concurrent sentences.
20. 2/76	Anna Mae Pictou-Aquash	Assassinated on Pine Ridge. FBI tried to conceal death.	Case solved after the report's publication. Arlo Looking Cloud and John Graham charged, both received life sentences.
21. 1/30/76	Byron DeSersa	Assassinated. Two GOONs, Dale Janis and Charlie Winters serving two years of five year sentences for manslaughter. Charges dropped on two GOON leaders, Manny Wilson and Chuck Richards, on basis of self-defense despite DeSersa being unarmed when shot.	Byron DeSersa was shot and killed while driving. Billie Dean Wilson and Lonnie Dean Bettelyoun were found not guilty by a jury on 3/2/77. Co-defendant Charles David Winters pleaded guilty to accessory after the fact to second degree murder and sentenced to five years in prison. Defendant Dale Francis Janis was tried on second degree murder charges and found guilty by a federal jury.
22. 3/26/76	Hobart Horse	Beaten, shot, and repeatedly run over by car. No investigation.	Roger James Cline found guilty of shooting Hobart. Sentenced to ten years for voluntary manslaughter.

Date	Victim	Allegation	FBI
23. 5/24/76	Sam Afraid of Bear	Shot at Pine Ridge. Investigation ongoing.	Rudolph Running Shield pled guilty. Luke Black Elk, Jr., found guilty. Sentenced to fifteen years for second degree murder.
24. 6/4/76	Kevin Hill	Killed by unknown. Investigation still open.	A white male killed off the rez while hitchhiking. Stabbed. Juvenile killer charged with second degree murder. Sentenced to fifteen years.
25. 7/31/76	Sandra Wounded Foot	Killed by unknown. No Investigation.	Raped and killed by Paul Duane Herman, a BIA investigator. Guilty of voluntary manslaughter, sentenced to ten years.

Four cases of homicide remain unsolved, the perpetrators never identified.

Date	Victim	Allegation	FBI
1. 11/20/73	Allison Fast Horse	Shot by unknown. No investigation.	Bullet severed aorta. Interviewed numerous people. No suspects.
2. 9/11/74	Jackson Washington Cutt	Killed by unknown. Investigation ongoing.	Eyewitness testified Rudolph Runs Above hit Cutt with an axe. Witness recanted. No further investigation.
3. 9/16/74	Robert Reddy	Killed by gunshot. No investigation.	Repeated efforts to polygraph George White Thunder, a transient, met with negative results. Case closed—to be reopened if he agrees to the polygraph.

Date	Victim	Allegation	FBI
4. 3/27/75	Jeanette Bissonette	Killed by sniper. Unsuccessful attempt to link AIM to killing.	No positive information developed. Case closed administratively.[4] No further investigation.[5]

Allison Little Spotted Horse: The slaying of Allison Little Spotted Horse, Jr. (a.k.a Allison Fast Horse and Ellison Little Spotted Horse) struck Arlette Loud Hawk hard. Killed, she says, because his hair identified him as a traditional:

> I have a friend, we were eighth graders. He had real long hair. His name was Ellison Little Spotted Horse. He was walking down the road. Somebody just shot him dead. And we were grade school children. So the GOON squads, they started killing children. I thought I was invincible, that I would live forever and for some reason, that as a child, I had all this protection in the world. And here now they're killing children. I always remember my friend because nobody remembers him. Nobody even cares to mention his name. But he's one of the children that died in those times, all because he had long hair.[6]

The FBI reports only that a .22 bullet severed his aorta and he bled to death. Exhaustive interviews failed to identify any suspects.[7] Since Allison's body was discovered early in the morning along Slim Buttes Road, a sparsely inhabited straight line of gravel, rocks, and clay without lights, and the weapon was a rifle as common as feathers on the rez, it seems almost impossible that, without a confession, the shooter will ever be found. That the boy's family supported traditional beliefs and he wore his hair long is factual, that he was targeted for such is supposition.

Jackson Washington Cutt: The murder of Jackson Washington Cutt occurred on the Rosebud Reservation in the small town of Parmalee, population 562, in 2010. His body was discovered at 9:00 in the morning. Information from suspects and witnesses indicated that he had been involved in a fight the night before. An eyewitness told the Rosebud police that Rudolph Runs Above had struck Cutt in the head with an ax. Later, the witness recanted his testimony; Rudolph was released, and the bureau closed the case.[8]

Churchill, in his rebuttal to the FBI report, wrote, "The police took information from an eyewitness identifying a known member of the GOON squad as having re-interviewed the witness and took a statement from the GOON denying culpability."[9] While the meaning is unclear, he evidently charges that one of Wilson's GOONs from the Pine Ridge successfully prevented the witness from identifying Runs Above, who must have been another GOON.

Robert Reddy: AIM and the FBI agreed only that Robert Reddy, aged forty-one, died. Witnesses said a known GOON shot him; pathologist W. O. Brown found he had been stabbed twice in the heart.

Apparently, the bureau uncovered enough evidence to cause agents to suspect transient George White Thunder. While there may have been enough for suspicion, there must have been far short of the amount necessary to press charges. The FBI attempted to polygraph White Thunder, but he kept avoiding law enforcement and refusing to take the test.

Strangely, the FBI closed the case on April 5, 1979, but noted it would be reopened if White Thunder would submit to a polygraph. Either the suspect got away with murder and agents knew it but could not prove it— or they closed the case for other reasons. AIM would say it was because he was a GOON allied with Dick Wilson.

Jeanette Bissonette: The sniper shooting of Jeanette Bissonette, sister-in-law of AIM leader, Pedro, and daughter-in-law of Gladys, seems an archetypal GOON killing. Active in AIM and related to organizational leaders, Jeanette would have seemed to be a likely target—if Wilson's forces were targeting foes and working as death squads for the FBI.[10]

In 2010, Frank Bissonette, Jeanette's son, lived on the land where his Uncle Pedro's house once stood. Old saddles hanging from a log entrance to the driveway and an old wood-burning range sitting near the front door offer mute testimony to family history. Dressed in jeans and a flannel shirt, sitting at the kitchen table with his hands wrapped around a coffee cup, Frank talks about a past he has tried to forget, but cannot.

He speaks quietly, anxiously glancing at his wife hovering over him like a mother bird to her young. Behind him, in the corner of the living room, a backlit American flag covers a wall, a shrine to a country he is proud of, but doesn't really like.

His wife, unlike many Lakota women who find something else to do when visitors arrive, stays by his side, nurturing and comforting. Frank has never gotten over the death of his mother on May 26, 1976, the GOON invasion of his childhood home, the clubbing with a rifle butt he received at their hands that left the hair on the side of his head white, or his harrowing escape from the subsequent fire-bombing of the only home he had known.

He has suffered from fear and anxiety since. "You just don't know," he says. "That's what has always scared me. If they can shoot your mother like that, just end her life so fast, they can do the same to you." His wife envelops him in her arms when his sobbing prevents him from more remembrances.

Frank has always been afraid that someone will kill him or somebody else he loves.

Jeanette was inside Wounded Knee during the occupation. Frank was ten years old at the time. He recalls being in Calico with her when the decision to go to Wounded Knee was made. But mostly he remembers hugs, kisses, and delicious apple pie. "She was a wonderful mother," he exclaims, wiping away tears.

Jeanette left home about 9:00 in the morning on the last day of her life, taking Frank's then two-year-old brother, John, to the wake held for Stacy Cortier (also spelled Cotter) another victim of Pine Ridge violence. She picked up her sister on the way; Frank's aunt returned home at 9:00 that night. His mother never did. Frank cried as he remembered how his father, awarded the Purple Heart in Korea, told him she was dead.[11]

The facts of the case seem fairly straightforward. Jeanette's car was pulled off the road at 1:00 a.m. on land owned by President Wilson's brother. John slept either on the floor or the passenger side of the front seat.

A man was there. Her car would not start. He opened the hood and tightened a battery cable. Just as he slammed the hood shut, shots rang out on the ridge behind them. He yelled for Jeanette to get behind the wheel, she was sitting in the back seat, and take off. He ran to his pickup to drive away and found that his front tire had been hit by a bullet and deflated.

He ran back to Jeanette's car, started it, and drove away. She remained in the back seat, John slept in the front. On the short drive to the village of Pine Ridge, he spoke to Jeanette but received no response. He took her directly to the hospital where she was declared dead—bullet fragments had ripped through her heart.[12]

Early the next morning, agents found two sets of tracks made by men in cowboy boots and three expended shells, two from a .22-250 caliber rifle and one from a .35 caliber, which proved to be the killing round. Three cigarette butts scattered near the tracks indicated that the killers sat on the ridge smoking and watching their prey. After firing, the shooters ran to a house, the people who lived there were gone for the night.[13]

Later that morning a severe blizzard struck the reservation. Deep snow and fierce winds blocked travel, yet the Minneapolis office of the FBI sent a memo marked urgent to the director in Washington, "Bureau is advised there appears to be a potential for increased trouble on the Pine Ridge Reservation as from the facts available at this time, it appears there may be AIM REDACTED overtones to the killing although the investigation is not complete at this time."[14]

Did they redact the word GOONs? If so, why? AIM leaders believed that agents were trying to connect the killing to them. But murder by militants wasn't the only focus of the investigation. From the start, agents smeared Jeanette with accusations of an extramarital/sexual relationship that resulted in her death.

Her panties, along with a pink tissue found snagged on a bush, were sent to the FBI's lab on the first day of the investigation with a request to check them for evidence of sexual activity. None was found, but agents would not let it drop. In a memo sent to the director on April 2, they wrote, "There is some indication that the victim may have had sex prior to death."[15]

The day after the shooting, in the middle of the blizzard, agents requested permission to polygraph the man who had been with Jeanette. During that session, he told agents he had met her there before, and that they had been parked there from around 10:30 p.m. until the shooting. He told the agents he had lied when he first spoke to them to protect Jeanette's reputation, although he never did admit to a sexual relationship.

He claimed to have been ousted from his home earlier that day because of a fight with his wife about his drinking. He said he had been at the turn-off asleep in his vehicle for four or five hours before Jeanette showed up. She sat in the backseat, he said, because her car would not start. She wanted him to get it going and drive a ways to see if it would keep running. She didn't want to be stranded in the storm with a small child.[16]

One aspect of the investigation rings especially odd, as if agents used the inquiry to identify newcomers to the reservation. In page after page of investigative papers, one of the few names not redacted is that of Anna Mae Pictou (Aquash), murdered in one of Indian Country's most infamous crimes less than a year later. Even tribal president Wilson's name, who was drinking at a café in Rushville at the time of the murder, is redacted.

Agents interviewed more than forty people and all the names were redacted except for Anna Mae's. Most said either they were not home when the shooting occurred or, because of the blizzard, they never heard a shot. One man, possibly more, but difficult to tell in the highly redacted transcript, was questioned after being overheard drunk confessing to the shooting.

When two agents died three months later in a shoot-out with AIM near Oglala, the bureau suspended the search for Jeanette's killers because live rounds fitting the rifle that killed her were found at the scene. According to a document dated January 20, 1977, a special prosecutor, even his name was redacted, ordered all investigation held in abeyance that might adversely affect the ResMurs (FBI speak for "reservation murders") trials for the shooting of the two agents.[17]

The bureau never discovered who owned the .35 caliber rifle. A note is included in the FBI files reporting that the way weapons are traded back and forth on the reservation it would be futile to attempt to trace the weapon.[18]

The case was reopened in 1981 and became active twenty-one years later when the bureau extracted DNA from the cigarette butts stored in a freezer. These were matched against blood and hair samples taken by the Oregon State police in 2002, a Styrofoam coffee cup in 2004 from Oglala, South Dakota, and a paper cup in 2009 seized by tribal detectives in the Chinook Winds Casino in Lincoln City, Oregon.[19]

Differing descriptions of the crime and possible motives and suspects continue to haunt Jeanette's relatives. A 2012 article about Paul Bissonette, Frank's older brother, told of his resolve to find closure in their mother's death. He said she died when a car pulled up behind her stalled vehicle and the occupants opened fire.[20]

Even if the writer of that article got the shooting wrong, the story identified a sliver of evidence. According to Paul, their father found a diaper with a license plate number

Funerals on the Pine Ridge reservation usually last two to three days. These beautiful ribbon shirts, a hallmark of the Lakota, were made by Pte San Win for the funeral of her Uncle Wilmer Mesteth. (Photo by Pte San Win)

written with Jeanette's lipstick in the glove compartment. The family believed it to be the number of the shooters' car and turned it over to the FBI. According to the bureau, the writing was on a package of pampers. She had written the number 69-1934 or 65-1734, and the initials, M. W., which could stand for Morris Wounded, the man with her during the shooting.[21]

Former agent Joseph Trimbach wrote that Jeanette was a victim of AIM violence, which the propagandists do not like to talk about. According to him, the bureau believed that she was killed by a drunken AIM newcomer.[22] Adding a different twist, he tries to place the shooting one degree closer to the death of the two agents three months later, alleging the .35 caliber rifle that fired the killing shot was not seen on the rez until the arrival of Robideau, Butler, and Peltier—the three men to stand trial for the death of the agents.[23]

FBI files contain a section entitled, "Allegations Against GOONs." But the report only is about a rumor that GOONs guarding a house (Wilson's brother's home?) killed her.[24] Nowhere in the documents is an interview that Duane Brewer, leader of the GOONs, allegedly had with the producer of *The Spirit of Crazy Horse* claiming his "execution team" shot Jeanette by mistake when they meant to kill Ellen Moves Camp, who drove a similar model and color vehicle.[25]

***

For the twenty-nine cases reported as non-homicides, the FBI found a number of causes of death:

Accidental	2	Died at Wounded Knee	3
Alcohol/Exposure	5	Poisoning	3
Car Accident	7	Killed by Police	2
Heart Disease	1	Suicide	2
Home Explosion	1	Victims Unknown to FBI	2
Killed by FBI	1		

Mariah Montileaux, daughter of Iva Lynn Roy, shown as a young girl in her traditional dancing outfit, died of the scourge of suicide on the Pine Ridge before graduating from high school.

Mariah Montileaux before she took her own life.

For each of these deaths, Churchill wrote that the deceased was either an AIM member or supporter. Allegedly, each had been the victim of foul play, mostly by GOONs, but several at the hands of unknown persons. He wrote that while most of the deaths had never been investigated, the search for the killers in nine was still ongoing, and in three there had been a scurrilous effort to pin the blame on AIM. Forty years later, the truth is difficult to find. Neither side is convincing beyond a doubt. An analysis of the deaths using evidence secured from the FBI through the Freedom of Information Act, the voices of survivors, and what can be gleaned through publications posits more questions than answers.

***

The most glaring mistakes made by those who constructed and published lists of the dead concern three children reported as murdered either by GOONs or persons unknown with no investigation of their deaths. Instead, they died as a result of abuse and alcohol.

Floyd Binais and Yvette Lorraine Lone Hill: Marion High Bull, a Pine Ridge resident, killed sixteen-month-old Floyd Binais and seven-year-old Yvette Lorraine Lone Hill. He received a ten-year sentence for the involuntary manslaughter death of little Floyd, claiming he fell while carrying the infant. The discovery of Lone Hill's body, covered with scars and bruises three days after the death of the baby boy, brought High Bull another sentence of twenty years; sentences to run concurrently.[26]

Michelle Tobacco: Michelle Tobacco died, according to the FBI, when her mother fell while holding her after drinking sixteen cans of beer.[27] AIM supporters contend the mother was sober and fell when a bullet fired by a GOON smashed through a window and Michelle hit the edge of a coffee table.[28] However, a well-known Oglala matron who wished to remain anonymous, sides with the bureau. She knew Velvedine and Scoop, Michelle's mother and father, and said Velvedine frequently abused alcohol. "There was no reason for the GOONs to shoot up her house. She was a neutral person, so was Scoop."[29]

***

Ben Sitting Up: The case involving a culprit not prosecuted for reasons of mental impairment resulted from a domestic battle rather than murder. Tribal cops and ambulance drivers responding to a call at House 806, a single room white, log cabin in the small village of Wanblee on May 20, 1975, were sure they were at the scene of a brutal double homicide.

Seventy-two-year-old Ben Sitting Up, born only twelve years after the massacre at Wounded Knee, and his fifty-six-year-old wife, Isabelle, lie in pools of blood. Responders assumed so much blood—on the floor, ceiling rafters, bed, stove pipe, and other surfaces—were sure signs of murder.

As they prepared to transport the bodies to the morgue, however, both Ben and Isabelle groaned and moved. Unfortunately Ben, with head and facial lacerations and what looked to be a knife wound to the torso, never lived to see another day. Isabelle, suffering from blunt force trauma to the back of the head and wounds to her lower legs, was rushed to the hospital in Rapid City. She survived the attack but, as a result of the severe blows to the back of her head, has never remembered what happened that night.[30]

Churchill took the FBI to task for their inability to solve such a heinous crime, especially since they identified a suspect that was not prosecuted because of mental impairment. Sharpening his attack, he identified the mentally unbalanced assailant as "an especially violent member of a GOON group known as the "Manson Family."

It could have been the GOON that Churchill says Duane Brewer recalled as a freak he fired due to his intention to cut a victim in half with a crosscut saw. However, the investigation into Ben's homicide and Isabelle's assault discovered the enemy to have been themselves. And the fight that led to their injuries was not held in private, as a man said he sat on a bench and watched the entire time.

Ben and Isabelle were well liked in their community and often had visitors, except when they fought. Ben had a reputation for knocking his wife around when he was drunk and, according to neighbors, she was not a weak woman who accepted her beatings.

Apparently, they began drinking the night before and were still pulling at the bottle the next morning. Ben had set off the last bout by hoarding the last of the wine and consuming it without offering any to Isabelle. She reacted by slapping him. So drunk he had to hang on to the edge of a little table by the bed, he grabbed his cane, determined to punish her insolence. Swinging wildly, he made contact with the stove pipe four or five times, denting it, leaving paint from the cane on the metal, and knocking it to the floor before administering two crushing blows to the back of his wife's head.

Isabelle then grabbed a knife and stabbed Ben. The witness thought she missed, but medical workers in the hospital found the wound. Not about to be cut up by his wife, Ben lurched back toward the side of the bed for a small ax they kept for chopping wood into kindling. Isabelle saw Ben move and wrestled the ax away from him. Then, in what must have seemed self-defense, she chopped the blade into his head and face.

Mortally wounded, Ben grabbed the weapon and retaliated. As she tried to move away from him, he sliced her lower legs. Ben moved toward the door before falling. Isabelle lay where he had struck her.

When the ambulance personnel attempted to load Ben onto a stretcher for transportation, half his face fell loose; an eye hung out of the socket in a macabre imitation of a Halloween mask.

A search of the house found the stove pipe on the floor marked by paint from Ben's cane. Pieces of the cane lay under the bed and beneath one of two wood-burning stoves—one for heating and the other for cooking. Between the stoves lay an empty bottle of Muscatel wine and another of Gibson's Muscatel. Near the door, a box containing three twelve-ounce Schlitz beer cans also held an empty half-gallon of Muscatel.

When agents attempted to question Isabelle in the hospital, she kept asking for Ben to be present. Repeatedly told he had passed away, she seemed unable to grasp why he was not there. With a fractured skull, she had no memory of what had happened, except she knew she had been fighting, maybe with Ben. The doctors had already concluded the injuries were from mutual combat.[31] Seven months after the altercation, agents concluded that Isabelle had not committed any violation of federal law and closed the case.

Five years later, she still could not remember the details of the night she was injured and her husband killed.[32]

***

The two victims the FBI identified as accidental deaths involved the careless use of firearms.

Richard Eagle: Eleven years old, died while playing with a .22 rifle at the home of his grandmother, Gladys Bissonette.

Roxeine Roark: A teacher at the Porcupine Day School, died from a bullet in the stomach fired from a .357 magnum pistol at her residence in Porcupine, South Dakota. Paul Cedar Face and Roxeine were handling the weapon when it discharged accidentally.

***

Death from alcohol and exposure—drinking too much and succumbing to the brutal Dakota weather—does happen too frequently on the rez. The FBI reported that five of the cases AIM listed as murder victims died from the lethal combination of booze and cold.

Delphine Crow Dog: Supposedly, such was the case with Delphine Crow Dog, sister of the AIM spiritual leader. The bureau noted she suffered from acute alcoholism: just another drunk passing out in an open field and freezing. To accept that conclusion, however, is to imply that the women in Leonard Crow Dog's family purposely have woven a web of deception in denial.

Mary Crow Dog, Delphine's sister-in-law, alleged she had been "beaten to death by a BIA policeman who claimed 'drunkenness' as an excuse. Her battered corpse, her arms and legs fractured, was found in the snow, the tears frozen on her cheeks."[33]

Delphine's mother mourned her daughter as a really nice person, but with bad luck. Not only did a drunken police officer beat Delphine to death, she said, breaking her arm in the process, when "he sobered up, he asked my forgiveness."[34]

Joseph Trimbach, ex-Special Agent in Charge, doubts their story. "On the other hand, when the only sign of death is exposure to the elements after lapsing into alcohol-induced unconsciousness on the side of the road and being run over—a sad reality on Pine Ridge—there is little reason to suspect otherwise."[35]

Officially, in response to a Freedom of Information Act request, the FBI replied, "Based on the information you provided, we conducted a search of the Central Records System. We were unable to identify main file records responsive to the request."[36]

Edward Means and Lena Slow Bear: For Edward Means, found behind a mission on January 7, 1974, and Lena Slow Bear, discovered along a road on February 6, 1976, the characterization as dead from alcoholism and exposure seems reasonable. Pine Ridge is freezing in the winter and drinking oneself into a stupor is common.

The remaining two deaths placed into the category of alcohol and exposure are harder to accept.

Lydia Cut Grass: Died January 5, 1976, of over consumption of liquor and "her death was not linked to the prior beating."[37]

There is no mention in the report of who beat her, how severe her injuries were, or of her emotional state after the beating. A little more information, if the bureau knew, or cared, might have provided some answers. Since agents included nothing else, questions will always swirl around Cut Grass's death. When was she beaten? Who beat her? A GOON? How serious were her injuries? Did the beating provide any causality for her actions the night she died?

Elaine Wagner: Her death is even more mysterious. According to the bureau, she joined two carloads of people on November 30, 1974, to drink. The assumption is that she went to a Pine Ridge party. Several hours later, she walked to a nearby home, leaving the house about 10:00 that night. Her body was found the next afternoon about one hundred yards away. According to the agents, "No subject has been developed and all available investigative leads were exhausted. From all the evidence, this matter appeared to be a non-felonious death. The U.S. attorney advised that there was insufficient evidence to charge any person."[38]

There was no mention that searchers found her lying in a creekbed, nude, with thorn-type scratches from the chest down and her clothing several feet away.[39] Still, the bureau could be right, there is evidence that people in the throes of exposure and hypothermia sometimes remove their clothing, and that is what the autopsy reported.

***

Most roads on the rez are dirt, gravel, washboard, washed out, curved, rutted ribbons of high-speed death. Clouds of dust rise behind cars until even the heavens become invisible. And the Oglala walk—everywhere. Men, women, and children, alone or in a group, walk miles to town, back home again, to a neighbor's house, or anywhere else they decide.

Deaths from high-speed accidents, blown-out tires, and drunk driving are common. In the dust, curves, and steep hills, it is always possible to hit one of the many walkers, especially one staggering from ditch to ditch under the influence of Whiteclay's reason for existence. Except none of the nine deaths resulting from vehicular accidents recorded by the Federal Bureau of Investigation are that easily explained.

Edith Little Hawk, Linda Little Hawk, and Earl Janis: On March 22, 1975, Edith Little Hawk, her four-month-old daughter, Linda, and her three-year-old nephew, Earl Janis, died when a car rammed her vehicle from the rear. The collision occurred on a lonely highway near the town of Scenic, South Dakota, where three cars constitute heavy traffic. The driver of the other car, Albert Coomes, also died in the crash.

The FBI noted only that Eagle Hawk and the children died as a result of a two-car automobile accident four miles north of Scenic, South Dakota, off the reservation. The bureau attributed Edith's death to a crushed chest. "This matter was not investigated by the FBI because it occurred off the reservation, outside of federal jurisdiction."[40]

According to Churchill, the report makes no mention that Coomes, the driver of the other car, was a white vigilante known to be involved with the GOONs. There is also not a notation that Eugene Eagle Hawk, a surviving passenger in Edith's car, told officers he saw Mark Clifford, a GOON, running from the wreck.

There is also no notice that Eagle Hawk was on her way to Rapid City to testify about GOON violence on the reservation. Churchill claims she was a witness for Jerry Bear Shield, charged with the murder of GOON William Jack Steel, and that Eagle Hawk should have been under the protection of the FBI no matter where she went.[41]

"Horse shit," declares former GOON Bud Merrill. "I know for a fact that's not true. Coomes wasn't a racist, but he was a good friend of Dick Wilson, and he was married to a Lakota woman. When the accident occurred, he was on the way to Rapid City to pick Wilson up."

And how is Bud so sure? Because Coomes' car broke down in Scenic on the trip. After drinking in Bud's father's bar and adding to the load he'd already ingested, Coomes borrowed the old man's car and drove on to get Wilson. Bud's dad's car was totaled in the wreck, Coomes died in it. "That car he hit had no lights on and was parked on the road," Bud said.[42]

Priscilla White Plume: Priscilla White Plume's body was found on July 14, 1973, dead along the highway near Manderson. Churchill wrote that her death followed the same pattern as those of Edith Eagle Hawk and Melvin Spider, two road fatalities that could not have been more different.

The FBI report is concise, and confusing, "On 9/28/76, three years later, the South Dakota U.S. Attorney's Office declined prosecution in this matter because there was insufficient evidence to establish a federal crime. Further, there was inadequate information to identify a perpetrator."[43]

"That was my little sis," Alex White Plume whispers, sadness from a nearly forty-year-old death in his voice. "Yeah, we don't know what happened. She just went out riding on her horse along the road and a car hit them. Killed her and the horse. Why can't they find out who did something like that?"[44]

When queried through a Freedom of Information Act request, the FBI replied they were unable to find any file records concerning Priscilla. Yet, stuck in the middle of a request on another fatality, the bureau included one page about her. It reports that Priscilla had been fishing with friends the night before she died. The severely redacted page is too confusing to summarize.

> REDACTED, also known as REDACTED REDACTED South Dakota, advised that on the Friday night that PRISCILLA WHITE PLUME was killed, REDACTED had been fishing until about midnight. Fishing with her were REDACTED [more than an entire line]. Just after they returned from fishing she remembers that WHITE PLUME got thrown from a horse, and came to the REDACTED residence. Later WHITE PLUME left on horseback with REDACTED, a boy who stays with the REDACTED. When they left, REDACTED said they were going to her REDACTED residence.[45]

The bureau did question a woman about the use of her car that night. She replied she was in Rapid City that weekend. There is no mention in the report of a dead horse, or why agents needed to ask about a car that had supposedly killed a young girl and a horse, or what insufficient evidence to establish a federal crime means.

Melvin Spider: In 2012, Verola Spider lived near the small community of Evergreen, north of Wounded Knee. Well-traveled, Verola has taught the Lakota language in Germany. She sits in her kitchen one winter day, drinking coffee with her daughter, Angel, a graduate student in psychology at

Portland State. Even after thirty-nine years, Angel reminds her of Melvin, her brother who was killed in 1973. She still wonders why he had to die at the tender age of sixteen. She has always refused to read the FBI reports on his death because doing so would be so painful.

He had been the first in the family to graduate from high school earlier in the year he died, and that had been a time of celebration. Raised by their grandmother as devout Christians and never active in AIM, neither Verola nor Melvin drank, hung out around Whiteclay or joined other Lakota at parties.

She remembers he told his grandmother he was going out the night he died. He was with his friend, Arville Looks Twice, and while he has not been listed among the deaths, Arville never returned from that night out with Melvin. To this day, he has never shown up nor has his body been found. Verola has always thought he was also killed, and that the killer(s) used an axe. She says Melvin died of severe cerebral lacerations. They had to bury him with a toupee—he had been scalped.[46]

If Arville was with Melvin on the night of September 21, 1973, he went to the movies in Gordon, Nebraska. According to the FBI, directly contradicting Verola's statement of Melvin's abstinence, the boys drank beer and whiskey to the point of being hammered. At 12:30 a.m., they were back in Porcupine where other young men dropped Melvin off at a house and then picked him up again about forty-five minutes later.

An hour later, in a spate of bizarre behavior, Melvin and the others entered a home occupied by an older man, his daughter, and her son, Melvin's friend. According to the woman, Melvin and another boy were in the house drunk, smelling of liquor, and asking to see her son. She told them he was in bed asleep. Then the old man showed up, asking how they got into the house.

"Let's get out of here before they turn us in," the youngster with Melvin said, probably not wishing to spend time in the drunk tank. He left, but Melvin, perhaps not thinking too clearly, stayed about ten minutes before leaving. The woman went back to bed, but then Melvin's loud knocking brought her back to the door again where she found him alone. He asked for a book of matches, which she gave him, then he left again.

She was awakened later by her father, who told her a police car had turned around by their front gate. The next morning she heard that Melvin's body had been found not far away. She and her father drove to the scene.

While Melvin was in the woman's house, the young man who had left to stay out of trouble fell asleep on a haystack. He also learned of the discovery of Melvin's body the next morning and told the feds that Melvin had been carrying an unopened bottle of peppermint schnapps they were supposed to drink that day.[47]

Agents believe a car hit Melvin, resulting in the lacerations and head injuries. No one has ever proposed, as Verola suspected, that Melvin was purposefully killed with an axe. The evidence gathered by the FBI points to hit and run; several suspects were investigated, but not enough was found to sustain a trial.

A telephone tip received by BIA criminal investigators the day after Melvin died named the owner of a 1967 black Buick from Manderson as the guilty party. The caller identified the driver and five other young men in the car.[48] Since the car struck Melvin in the pre-dawn hours, it is doubtful the hit and run was seen from any distance. Agents did not arrest the driver of the Buick.

On April 4 of the following year, a Lakota who worked at a garage in Gordon, Nebraska, reported that around the day of Melvin's death a car was towed from Sharp's Corner to the garage for repair. The man said the car was a rusty-colored Chevrolet, and he had been assigned to fix the starter and generator. He saw blood splattered on the headliner upholstery on the passenger side of the car, and a long iron rod in the back seat with blood on it. He also said he did not see any dents on the vehicle that might have been caused by striking a man on the road.[49]

The veracity of the tip started to weaken when the garage's owner told agents that the man who reported the bloody passenger seat and rod was never assigned to do any repair work, had worked at the garage only for a short period of time, was not a reliable person, and only worked on the grease rack. The mechanic's story fell completely apart when the owner checked his employment records and found the man was not even employed during September of 1973.[50]

According to the owner, the only vehicle towed from Sharp's Corner at that time of the year had been a Chevrolet from Morrill, Nebraska, brought in for warranty work. The car's owner said he had been traveling through the rez when a piston went out in the engine. He'd hopped a ride into Gordon with a feed truck and turned the repairs over to the garage.[51]

On the last day of April, a resident of Porcupine reported that he had been in the Longhorn Saloon in Scenic on the night Melvin died. He returned to the bar the next night and heard a man say he thought he had hit Melvin Spider with his car. The guy wasn't sure it was Melvin, but was real sure he'd killed whoever it had been.[52]

Agents interviewed the man, by then an inmate in the Pennington County Jail in Rapid City, the following August. He said he'd stayed home on the nights of September 21 and 22 of the preceding year. He told the agents he had intended to go drinking with his friends on those nights, but they took off and left him alone. Interestingly, he said they were driving a black or dark blue Buick or Oldsmobile.

As all their leads proved futile, and with no other information, on February 18, 1975, in a memo to the Minneapolis office, Rapid City agents wrote, "It is recommended that this case be closed in view of the above and should any information be developed at a later date to identify UNSUBS, this case should be reinstituted."[53]

Cleveland Reddest: In their list, AIM alleged that Cleveland Reddest had been killed by person or persons unknown, with no investigation. The FBI reported Reddest died in a hit-and-run accident eighteen miles east of Kyle, and he had probably been prone on the road when a car struck him. Agents identified Linda and Aloysius White Crane as possible suspects. During polygraph exams, both testified that Aloysius drove the car that killed Cleveland. A federal grand jury in Sioux Falls, South Dakota, failed to bring charges, and closed the case.[54] Churchhill responded that hit-and-run hardly precludes vehicular homicide. He went on to say the autopsy revealed no alcohol or other intoxicants present in Cleveland's bloodstream, strongly suggesting he may have been beaten unconscious before the hit and run. He noted the two suspects were known GOONs, not prosecuted because the FBI abandoned its investigation before gathering enough evidence.[55]

Circumstances of the death, as found in the testimony of the White Cranes and other witnesses, deny those accusations. It seems that Cleveland, twenty-three years old, 5'8" tall, and 278 pounds, died when hit by his own 1967 blue Pontiac. His demise is the best example of what can go wrong when you get drunk, get mad at people criticizing your driving, stop the car, and get out and walk.

According to Aloysius, on March 26, 1976, his family attended a dance and, after already making one trip to Interior, South Dakota, decided at 9:00 p.m. to go back for more beer—in Cleveland's car. Besides Cleveland, Aloysius, his wife, one of the White Crane's daughters, and her younger cousin were in the car. Each of them told BIA investigators that Cleveland was drunk and driving erratically. They yelled to let Aloysius drive. Cleveland reacted angrily, stopped the car, and announced he intended to walk. The White Crane's daughter said the two younger women were the most critical of Cleveland's driving. There should have been familiarity between the family and Cleveland, as he lived with them.

With Cleveland out of the car, Aloysius, fifty years old with no driver's license, drove on to Interior and bought thirty-six beers and a pint of vodka. When they started back to the Potato Creek housing area where they lived, they looked for Cleveland.

> We thought he would be along the road someplace. I [was] traveling about 40–45 m.p.h. As we are talking and looking for Cleveland … REDACTED said, "Aloysius watch out there's a man lying on the road," she warned me a little too late, I then tried to swerve the wheel to the left but was too late. I ran into his legs, at the time I hit him, the head was towards the shoulder of the road and feet towards [the] center of the road. I stopped immediately and look back and could see the man still lying from reflections of the brake lights. I looked around and saw no other cars. I then drove on to Potato Creek to try and notify the police.[56]

Aloysius and Linda went home while their daughter took Cleveland's car to identify the victim of the accident. She arrived at the scene to see police car lights flashing near the body. She then drove back to the housing area and stopped a tribal police car. According to the cops, she was hysterical.

In the first round of interviews with the BIA, evidence from the scene had already proved that Cleveland's own car killed him. The members of the White Crane family told the police they did not know who was driving. Later during the polygraph, after a religious leader told him to tell the truth, Aloysius admitted his part in Cleveland's death.

The only mystery left is how drunk Aloysius was. During his testimony, he said he had not been drinking and remembered everything that happened. However, a record from a BIA criminal investigator noted White Crane had told him he was highly intoxicated and experiencing blackouts during the evening prior to the hit-and-run.[57]

Betty Jo Dubray: According to AIM's sources, Betty Jo Dubray had been beaten to death by GOONs in Martin, South Dakota, with no investigation of the murder. Actually, she died in a collision between a car and a truck. For her death to have been anything but a tragic mishap would have taken GOON planning beyond the bounds of conceivability.

Her killers would have had to know that she would have been drinking heavily, blood alcohol level measured at .16 percent, and traveling in a car with four other inebriated people. They would have to know the car would be driving north near Long Valley and attempt to pass a Peterbilt semi pulling a trailer. Skillfully, they would have had to cause the drunken driver of the car to sideswipe the left front fender of the truck while passing it, sending the car spinning in a complete circle on the road until it ended in a ditch. Then, with great dexterity, the GOON driving a Lil Audrey's Transportation Company Incorporated truck from Fremont, Nebraska, would have had to roll the semi over onto the car, crushing it from the top, trapping all the other passengers inside, and killing only Betty Jo Dubray. [58]

Betty Means: AIM alleged that GOONs also killed Betty Means, and the bureau failed to investigate her death. As in the case of Betty Jo Dubray, the GOONs that killed Betty Means had to have had an impeccable sense of timing and appear in a variety of guises.

The last day of Betty's life included drinking, riding in a car that became stuck in the mud east of the village of Pine Ridge, and hitchhiking—characteristics of a number of the tragic traffic deaths plaguing Pine Ridge. Betty's death, leaving the implausible GOON theory out, involved more bad luck than most people have in a lifetime.

No one really knows what led her to be alone on the highway after 3:00 in the morning. Her husband was with her that night and told authorities they had been in Pine Ridge and found a ride out of town with people he knew. He said the car slid off the road in the rain and became stuck. He passed out since they had all been drinking wine, and when he woke up the next morning, Betty was gone. He walked home and was there when the police informed him that his wife had been killed along the highway.[59]

Another man in the car with Betty did not mention anything about her husband. He said that she, himself, and another individual were in the car driven by yet another man. They turned off the highway too fast, slid into the ditch, and got stuck. He stayed in the car, the unknown man (maybe Betty's husband) walked away, and Betty left to get help. He said they both returned later.

They were all pretty high, he said. When he got into the back seat to sleep, Betty and another person were standing near the hood of the car. The other guy woke him the next morning and said he intended to walk to town for help, so he went back to sleep. Later that morning a wrecker driver told him about "some lady being found dead along the side [of] the road."[60]

Reading around the redactions, the driver of the vehicle testified that he picked up Betty and two other people in town and drove them to a residence. Apparently one of the passengers paid him four dollars for the trip. They were all drunk when his Chevrolet station wagon became stuck. He said everyone from the car then walked to a nearby house.

He recalls Betty and someone else arguing about wine. He went to sleep and didn't know Betty left the house. The next morning he walked to Pine Ridge for help and found a body in a ditch. He said it was not "readily recognizable" and thought it to be a man. He reported the body to the police as soon as possible.[61]

Was Betty killed by GOONs, targeted as she stumbled drunkenly along the highway, or was she forcibly taken from the car or the house and murdered in a staged hit and run? Probably not. In fact, two cops saw the accident happen—they just did not know it at the time. At approximately 3:20 in the morning, a sergeant in the tribal police and his partner were heading west on Highway 18. The sergeant heard his partner who was driving say, "Look at that car."

He looked up and saw a car whip off the road into the ditch, back onto the road, skid to a stop, and started sliding back to the ditch. They passed the car, turned the red lights on, and parked behind it. The car's driver told them he had a soft tire, which caused the vehicle to drive erratically.

The cops noticed two females in the front seat and a male and another female in the back. They took the driver's license number as well as his license plate number and a description of the car, a yellow 1968 Chevrolet Nova, and told him to get the tire fixed. They found no alcoholic beverages in the car, noting that the passengers were cooperative and polite.

The sergeant described the woman sitting next to the driver as an Indian in her mid-twenties with long, kinky, black hair who seemed somewhat scared. Sitting by the door was an older woman, about forty-five, also with long black hair, who told the police the car's occupants had been drinking earlier that night.[62]

The next morning, "an Indian female with maroon jeans on [inside out], yellow socks and no shoes," was found at the location where the two officers had stopped the Chevy. The autopsy showed that Betty Means had suffered compound fractures of each leg between the ankle and knee, a broken rib, broken neck, ruptured bladder, and two skull fractures. Probably blinded by the lights of the car coming toward her, she died instantly.[63]

After agents proved conclusively that the Chevy Nova killed Betty, Arlene Good Voice, the young woman with the long, kinky, black hair was arrested on charges of assault in her death and pled guilty. Arlene was placed on probation for eighteen months.[64] Her husband, John Good Voice, was charged with leaving the scene of an accident, a crime not prosecutable in federal court.[65]

Betty died because Arlene, John, and other passengers in the car were arguing about whether they should return to the Rosebud or keep on going to the town of Pine Ridge. Arlene wanted to go back home and grabbed the steering wheel three different times throwing the vehicle into the ditch. Unfortunately, the last time she hit Betty.

According to John, his wife was drunk and either jealous or mad at him for some reason. He said they were going about forty miles an hour; he saw the hitchhiker and maneuvered not to hit the person, and that was exactly when his wife grabbed the steering wheel and jerked.

***

James Brings Yellow: According to AIM, he suffered a fatal heart attack during an FBI air assault on his home. Churchill relates he had a cardiac arrest when agents kicked in his door while conducting a warrantless, no-knock search during the early stages of the ResMurs investigation. "That he died of related causes a day later in the hospital is irrelevant."

The FBI reported only that they found no file on the case.

Phillip Black Elk: His home blew apart, destroyed by a propane gas explosion. According to the FBI, a neighborhood investigation revealed problems with gas leakage over the preceding two weeks. Before he died, Black Elk said he had gone into his home and tried to light the pilot on the hot water heater when it exploded.

AIM supporters have suggested that there is a link between the explosion in Black Elk's home and the one that killed AIM leader John Trudell's entire family in 1979. "Presiding over the investigation of the Trudell family's death was local BIA police chief Benny Richards, a GOON prominent on the Pine Ridge at the time of Black Elk's death.[66]

Joseph Stuntz Killsright: Died in the volley of government firing following the murders of the two FBI agents, Ronald Williams and Jack Coler, on June 26, 1975. According to the bureau's report, "When the body of Stuntz was found, he was wearing a SWAT fatigue jacket with FBI on the back, belonging to SA Coler ... taken from the trunk of SA Coler's vehicle after SA Coler was shot."[67]

Churchill maintains that Killsright died in the same firefight as the agents, precipitating their deaths. But then he quotes two sources, journalist Kevin McKiernan and South Dakota Attorney General William Delany as saying the body had been riddled by automatic fire at close range—perhaps in retribution for the deaths of the agents.

***

The FBI found that two of the victims, Hilda Good Buffalo and Julia Pretty Hips, died of poisoning. They made a good case in suggesting Hilda's death was accidental, but Julia's is more controversial.

Hilda Good Buffalo: Arlette Loud Hawk is convinced that GOONs beat her friend Hilda Good Buffalo to death, and Churchill's rebuttal to the FBI report accepts a rumor that Douglas White and Douglas Chief killed the eighty-one-year-old woman for pay.[68] However, if Chief did it and kept the money, he has to be the least competent hit man in history.

Born only four years after Wounded Knee, Hilda lived with her fifty-seven-year-old son, Comer, in a one-room log cabin nine miles north and west of the town of Pine Ridge. On Friday, April 4, 1975, Comer picked up his paycheck from his job with the Manpower Program in Oglala. Since his mother had cashed her $90 Social Security check the day before, it must have seemed like a good day to drink.

Comer left work at 11:00 a.m. He told agents he and his mother started drinking shortly after he arrived home. Sometime that afternoon or evening, Comer's boss, forty-one-year-old Douglas Chief, showed up for a drink. Chief was a relative, Hilda and his mother were cousins, and he considered Comer a brother. According to Comer, Chief often came over and drank with Hilda.

Comer flagged down the tribal police around 3:00 a.m. Saturday morning. He told the cops the house was on fire, and his mother was dead. When they entered the smoke-filled cabin they found Hilda's lifeless body, and Douglas Chief, so drunk he defecated in his pants, holding himself up by a bedstand. The smoke came from Comer's burning mattress. After carrying Hilda and the mattress outside where the flames could be extinguished, the cops noticed a cut on Hilda's neck and assumed she had been stabbed in the throat and murdered.

Like so many other tragedies on the Pine Ridge, the truth is somewhat harder to pin down. According to pathologist W. O. Brown, the man who had the least credibility on the rez, Hilda did not die of the neck wound that extended into deeper tissues for only 1.5 cm and involved no vital structures. The elderly woman died of carbon monoxide poisoning. The extensive soiling of her hands due to carbonaceous material "indicated she probably tried putting out the fire before succumbing to the fumes."[69]

Was her death murder? She did have multiple contusions of the scalp, which appeared recent, however, there was no edema or fracture related to the wound. Unfortunately, neither Comer nor Chief could shed any light on Hilda's demise.

Comer claims to have walked to another house more than a mile away to play cards. Since he was crippled, the trip took him more than an hour. He returned a little before 3:00 a.m., found his mother dead, Chief passed out, flames leaping out of the wood stove that had the lids removed, and his mattress on fire. He rushed to get water, but since the well was three hundred yards away, he had little effect on the flames.

He also claimed that the dresser was pushed over on the floor, and a trunk was opened with the content spread around the house. Since he could not breathe in the smoke-filled dwelling, Comer awakened Chief and ran outside where he eventually flagged down the tribal police. In his official statement to the FBI, he mentioned Hilda drank quite often and quite a bit. She drank both beer and wine, he said, but he never argued with her, and certainly did not stab her.

Douglas Chief's story differs only concerning Comer's alibi. He said he drank with the mother and son until midnight when he fell asleep. He knew nothing else until Comer woke him and told him the place was on fire. He did not fight with Hilda that night and had no idea how the fire started—except that all three of them were smoking.

Further investigation found flaws in each man's statement. First, Comer's card playing alibi could not be substantiated. In fact, agents were told he had played cards the night before Hilda died. Second, Douglas Chief said he did not fight with Hilda, but the police found blood on his clothing and on one of his two pocketknives. While there was not enough blood to quantify in those pre-DNA days to prove it was or was not Hilda's, Chief could not explain the blood or whose it was. He also told interviewers he was very drunk and did not really know what he had done that night.

Comer's later testimony describing his non-verifiable card game should have given agents another reason for pause. After saying Chief was a relative who often drank with his mother, Comer told them he did not know why Chief was in the house. He suggested that since Chief arranged work for the elderly, maybe he had been in the house for that reason. Comer's testimony and failed alibi and the blood on Chief's knife and clothing certainly raised questions about Hilda's death.[70]

The case grew even more mysterious five months later when an unlisted source told agents she had secondhand information that Chief and a man named Douglas White were paid $60.00 to kill the elderly woman.[71]

Douglas Chief, supervisor of the Manpower Program on the rez, seemed a good fit for the accusation. With only a fourth-grade education, Chief had been arrested twenty-nine times between his twentieth birthday in 1944 and 1967. Most of his troubles with the law were for drunk and disorderly behavior and disturbing the peace, but he had been sentenced to one and a half years for third-degree burglary and had served four years in prison for second-degree manslaughter—a charge reduced from murder.

The case against Douglas Chief was taken to a Sioux Falls grand jury a year after Hilda's death. After consideration, jurors labeled her death non-felonious and requested no further investigation.[72] For Chief to have killed Hilda Good Buffalo for $60.00 and then stay in the house, set it on fire, pass out, and defecate in his pants seems incredulous.

The following list of symptoms appeared on Hilda Good Buffalo's autopsy. Her death serves as a reminder of the hardships of life on the Pine Ridge:

Cause of death: carbon monoxide poisoning.
Final diagnosis:
  1. Carbon monoxide poisoning
  2. Acute alcoholism

3. Cerebral contusion
4. Subarachnoid hemorrhage of the brain
5. Recent stab wound of the neck
6. Senile atrophy of the brain
7. Cardiac hypertrophy
8. Generalized arterial sclerosis
9. Arteriosclerotic aneurysm
10. Multiple contusions of scalp
11. Fibrous pleural adhesions
12. Chronic cholecystitis
13. Cholelithiasis
14. Chronic pyelonephritis
15. Old otitis media, right
16. Acute conjunctivitis, bilateral
17. Chronic thyroiditis
18. Cystocele
19. Rectocele[73]

Julia Pretty Hips: According to AIM, Julia Pretty Hips was killed by unknown assailants and her death never investigated. The FBI reported that she died of carbon tetrachloride poisoning that led to pneumonia.[74] Not satisfied with the autopsy finding, Churchill retorted, "No suggestion is offered as to why, if this were so, the body would've been found outdoors rather than home in bed."[75]

Sadly, circumstances surrounding Julia's death and her last days on earth are probably grimmer than the bureau's explanation. Her death raised more questions than it answered; murder certainly seems possible.

Sixty-four years old, five feet tall and weighing 125 pounds, Pretty Hips had a reputation as a heavy drinker. Two middle-school girls discovered her body near their school, reporting her as a passed-out drunk. She was on her back on a piece of cardboard extending from her knees to her head between two propane bottles. Agents noted that she was found in a modest fashion, dress smoothed over her knees. There were no signs of struggle where she was found and no marks signifying rape or assault on her body.

Apparently, she had hitchhiked on May 6, 1976, from Porcupine to Gordon, Nebraska, sleeping for as many as two nights in an abandoned car behind the American Legion, her usual lodging in the small town. On May 8, she sat on a bench near the Pine Ridge Post Office along with several other elderly women.

Those are the facts of her death as found in the FBI's file. However, the unanswered questions are more important.

1. Why did she die of carbon tetrachloride poisoning? The colorless, sweet-smelling liquid, also known as Halon or Freon, is used in dry cleaning and refrigeration. Earlier in the century it was used in fire extinguishers. Exposure to the chemical affects the central nervous system, damages the liver, and may result in death—as happened to Julia. There are reports, however, of people drinking carbon tetrachloride to become intoxicated even though more normal methods of overcoming the system with the dangerous chemical are by breathing the vapors or having it enter through the skin.

Where did she come into contact with carbon tetrachloride? Did she drink it to become or to stay intoxicated? Did someone give it to her in Whiteclay thinking it would be a great way to get high?

2. If she died of poisoning, lying modestly with her dress smoothed over her knees, why were her "soiled" white panties torn apart at the crotch and encircling her chest?

3. Was the sperm found in her body from rape or consensual intercourse? And was she the elderly woman, appearing intoxicated, arguing with an older man in the vicinity of the middle school on the night of May 8?

4. Was it her body a man was reported as dragging down an alley by the propane tanks that same night? Who was this man wearing cowboy boots and a cowboy hat? Was this the man agents polygraphed that was already being processed on a charge of assault with a dangerous weapon? Why did this man lie about knowing Julia, and where was he on the night she died?[76]

These questions will never be answered. On December 6, 1976, Norman Zigrossi, Assistant Special Agent in Charge, informed the Bureau of Indian affairs, "Due to the FBI laboratory finding no physical evidence on submitted materials, and the pathologist unable to contribute death beyond carbon tetrachloride for poisoning which led to pneumonia, this matter is being closed administratively."[77]

***

Clarence Cross: AIM supporters claim Clarence and Vernal Cross received wounds in a GOON ambush, and that cops initially charged Vernal with the crime but later released him. Rex Wyler, author of *Blood Of The Land* claims the brothers were "sitting in the car on the side of the road in June when hit by rifle fire, according to Vernal, who survived the shooting." Wyler goes on to say that nine-year-old Mary Ann Little Bear, riding in a car going the opposite direction received a wound to the eye. According to Wyler, GOONs Francis Randall, John Hussman, and Woody Richards did the shooting.[78]

Arlene Cross, a relative of the brothers, had charges filed against tribal officers whom she says shot and wounded the two men as they resisted arrest. Vernal was treated at the Gordon Hospital while Clarence, with wounds to the stomach and thigh, succumbed to peritonitis and generalized sepsis at Fitzsimmons Army Medical Center in Colorado. A grand jury in South Dakota refused to indict the officers involved.[79]

Pedro Bissonette: Former GOON Bud Merrill remembers Pedro Bissonette, founder of the Oglala Sioux Civil Rights Organization and an Oglala leader indicted for the Wounded Knee occupation, as his best friend. "I loved that Pedro," he said.[80]

Bud liked him as a friend and for his toughness and fighting skills. Pedro had been an amateur boxer who trained rez kids after retiring from the ring. Everybody on the reservation who knew him remembers him as the toughest man around—anywhere.

Pedro grew up to be a venerated Oglala leader even though his hobby in his younger days may have been driving around border towns and beating up white guys.[81] For his part in the Wounded Knee occupation, Pedro was arrested on May 8, 1973.

While jailed, his court-appointed attorney—there is some evidence the presiding judge refused to allow him to speak with AIM attorneys—presented him an offer from the federal government to turn state's evidence and testify against AIM. If he did, the feds would release him on parole. If he refused they said he would get ninety-nine years in prison.[82] He did not testify and was released on $25,000 bond.

In an affidavit presented to the court on June 27, 1973, in response to the government's offer, Pedro Bissonette responded:

> I will stand with my brothers and sisters. I will tell the truth about them
> and about why we went to Wounded Knee. I will fight for my people. I
> will live for them, and if it is necessary to stop the terrible things that hap-
> pen to Indians on the Pine Ridge Reservation, I am ready to die for them.
> But the judge and his lawyers must know by now I will never lie against
> my people, crawl for a better deal for myself. I stand with Russell Means,
> Gladys Bissonette, Carter Camp, Ellen Moves Camp, Clyde Bellecourt ...[83]

On September 26, the government filed assault charges against Pedro, alleging he discharged a firearm in a Whiteclay bar. GOON Charlie Winters, later found guilty of the murder of Byron De Sersa, supposedly witnessed the shot and agreed to testify. Pedro left the rez.

He was back October 17. Two cops following his car alleged he fired a rifle at them. Around 9:30 that night, he was pulled over and supposedly came out of his car with a 30.06 rifle pointed at the officers. One of them discharged his weapon, and Pedro fell dead, hit in the chest and heart by a full load of seven buckshot pellets from a twelve gauge.

But nobody on the Pine Ridge believes that. They say the supposed rifle has never been found or entered into evidence. Like Bud, most believe Pedro Bissonette, ex-boxer and all-around tough guy, would have never resorted to guns—he would have used his fists. His death was either execution by cop or the result of a frightened police officer who would have been no match for Pedro in a fight.

Like most stories on the Pine Ridge, there is more to this one. WKLDOC lawyer Mark Lane said Pedro had been shot seven times in the chest by a pistol, probably because he refused the government's offer.[84] Some Oglala offer a different, more personal, reason for the shooting. BIA police officer Joe Clifford, who gunned him down, was the brother of Pedro's common law wife. Allegedly, the ex-boxer had beaten her severely on several occasions and even sent her to the hospital once. Clifford shot him out of anger—to get even.

The American government tried to get a court order barring AIM leaders from attending Pedro's funeral. Dick Wilson refused to allow non-Oglala AIM members from entering the reservation to attend.

***

According to the FBI report, Aloysius Long Soldier and Andrew Paul Stewart committed suicide.

Aloysius Long Soldier: Long Soldier's designation as a suicide seems fairly non-controversial, but his sister still questioned his death. In a voluntary statement to the FBI, she claimed he died of a gunshot wound to the head outside Mary Ellen Bull Bear's home, killed by Mary Ellen's gun. While the sister, Germaine, questioned the finding of self-inflicted injury, she could offer no new evidence. Agents accepted the BIA's suicide theory and closed the case.[85]

Andrew Paul Stewart: The 1975 death of Andrew Paul Stewart, nephew of Leonard Crow Dog, allegedly by his own hand, is a difficult assumption to make. As reported by the bureau, the autopsy revealed the cause of death as "probably a self-inflicted gunshot wound, such as a suicidal injury."[86]

Leonard Crow Dog tells a different story, one of an alcohol-fueled wasicu terrorizing the Rosebud Reservation while protected by the FBI. Crow Dog claims a drunken Robert Beck, a white man living on the rez, invited Stewart and two women to go hunting. Before the dawn of the next day, the women with Stewart ran down from the hills screaming in terror. Responders found Stewart dead with a bullet in his forehead. Beck's rifle had fired the shot, and there was blood all over his car.

Rosebud Tribal Police told Crow Dog they had arrested Beck seven times in 1975 for acts of violence. He had broken into houses and shot at the inhabitants, including Crow Dog's sister. He had even driven past Crow Dog's place and shot at him. When arrested he had told the Indian cops, "I'm immune from arrest. You can't hold me. All I have to do is make one phone call."[87]

On the second day of September, residents claim to have observed Beck driving around the rez with FBI agents. Later that night, he and a friend, Bill McCloskey, beat up Crow Dog's sixteen-year-old nephew in Parmalee, South Dakota. With two alcohol-fueled women in tow, an hour after midnight, the pair drove through the gates of Crow Dog's property, jumped out of the car, and started beating the same boy they had accosted earlier that night. Crow Dog's security, including the boy's father, joined the fight. Beck left with a broken jaw.

Three days later, armed with automatic weapons, helicopters, and even portable boats in case anyone tried to escape across the Little White River, 185 federal agents carrying John Doe warrants roused everyone out of bed early in the morning. Crow Dog went to jail. Beck remained free, continuing his violent ways until several years later when he killed a man named No Moccasins in front of witnesses and went to jail.[88]

***

Sandra Wounded Foot: Una Horn Cloud remembers Sandra Wounded Foot, a neighbor and older girl she looked up to, as she hugged her goodbye and left the house. She told Una she had a date but could not tell her the man's name. Sandra, dressed beautifully as always, left for her date on Friday, August 13, 1976. Three days later, a Mr. Pascall, driving along a fence-line on Gooseneck Road, came upon the nude body of a female. Her garments were found in a field a half mile down the road; they had been removed and not ripped off.

The autopsy confirmed what investigators had already found; the victim had been shot twice in the head with a .357 magnum pistol. The pathologist could find no other physical trauma suffered by her, and then identified her as fifteen-year-old Sandra Ellen Wounded Foot. She had been drinking before she died; her blood alcohol measured at .14 percent.

BIA Officer White Buffalo, assigned to investigate, asked fellow BIA Investigator Paul Duane Herman to assist. Herman, respected among Pine Ridge law enforcement as a "policeman's policeman," acted jumpy from the start. When first asked to go, he told White Buffalo he had just had a steak and hoped the body wasn't ripe yet.

At the scene, he refused to look at Sandra's body or search for clues. He pressured White Buffalo to leave before the FBI got there because he needed to attend a conference. Finally, Herman explained to White Buffalo that he had been with the victim on Friday night. He said he had picked

Sandra up along the road, soaking wet, and drove her to the Evergreen Housing Complex to dry off and change. When she did, she got back in the car with him, and asked him to drive around until they found a brown and white car. They never found the car, so he took her back to Evergreen.

Probably to hide the trail of a smoking gun, Herman also told White Buffalo that Sandra had stolen his .357 pistol from under his front seat when he left the car to urinate. He had not kept his liaison with Sandra a secret from anyone. At one time that Friday when she was in his car, tribal police pulled up next to them and spoke to Herman. Ironically, in the car were two of the three cops Sandra had accused a month earlier of raping her as they arrested her for drunk and disorderly conduct. Herman had asked to handle that case, but it had been assigned to another officer who concluded the charge was without basis.

Following the exchange with his brother officers, Herman found another friend, Roger Cline, and asked him if he wanted to join the party. Cline declined, leaving Sandra Wounded Foot alone with Paul Duane Herman.

Federal agents arrested Herman on a charge of first-degree murder a little over two years later on September 24, 1978. His one-time friend, Roger Cline, serving time in a federal prison in Pennsylvania for the murder of Hobart Horse, was flown back to serve as a prosecution witness. The presiding judge dropped the charges to voluntary manslaughter. Paul Herman pled guilty and received a sentence of ten years in federal prison. In one of the court papers, the prosecutor outlined his theory of Sandra Wounded Foot's last moments alive.

> [T]hat in fact Mr. Herman was having whatever he was having with her, and that she got out of the car for some reason and at that point, from her previous behavior and activity, which would have been evident, that it's highly likely that she started screaming rape at him, or whatever, and at that point he took his service revolver and shot her.[89]

Unfortunately, a prison term did not control Herman's sexual predilections. In 1999, he received a 108-month sentence, out of a maximum of 135, on five counts of sexual contact with a minor and one count of sexual abuse.

He admitted that he used his size and strength to compel his girlfriend's thirteen-year-old daughter and her twelve-year-old sister to have sex with him. Terrified, and with good reason, the girlfriend turned him in; he had threatened to kill at least one of the girls if anybody ever told what had happened.

So, the former cop, the man who killed Sandra Wounded Foot and threatened to kill other young girls if they told anyone about his sexual assault on them, pled guilty. The prosecutor's response:

The United States will join the defendant in asking the court to find that the defendant clearly demonstrates a recognition and affirmative acceptance of personal responsibility for his criminal conduct ... and reduces the defendant's offense by two counts.[90]

If Herman's criminal behavior was not enough to damage the reputation of Indian Country cops for a long time, what has not been reported should. After his 1978 arrest on charges of first-degree murder, he was released on his own personal recognizance. Unable to find work in South Dakota, he was working as a BIA investigator on the Fort McDowell Reservation in Arizona until his date in court.

***

In a large white cowboy hat, his long black hair hanging in braids, his voice soft but firm, Vice President of the Oglala Sioux Tribe, Tom Poor Bear, stood before the U.S. attorney and pleaded, "Just one case. Can't we solve at least one case?"[91]

Due to the work of many, including Poor Bear, on August 18, 2012, National Public Radio announced:

> Today, widespread mistrust of the federal government continues, so much so that the Oglala Sioux Tribal Government recently asked U.S. Attorney Brendan Johnson to look at the forty-five deaths the tribal officials believe have not seen justice. The cases include two unsolved execution-style murders in 1998. Johnson says he agreed to re-examine all forty-five cases in question.[92]

"I hope, I pray, that a lot of people will come forward and we will achieve justice," Tom Poor Bear said at a recent Rapid City meeting with Johnson. "Every day someone calls me or stops me and says this has opened their hopes again."

Lakota hopes for the future are now in the hands of the young such as Laura Red Cloud, now a mother, pictured with her daughter.

Pte San Win's six-foot-eight-inch son, a fifteen-year-old attending a large Omaha, Nebraska, high school soars to block a shot. A high school phenom, he excels at basketball, the most popular sport on the rez.

15

ResMurs: Rule 35 and COINTELPRO,

A Ticket To Get Out Of Jail

*They made us many promises, more than I can remember, but they
never kept but one; they promised to take our land, and they did.*
—*Mahpiya Luta (Red Cloud)*, Oglala Chief,
Una Horn Cloud's seven-times-great-grandfather

Nineteen-year-old Jimmy Eagle woke up and poked through the cupboards of his grandmother's kitchen on June 26, 1975, looking for anything to fill the hole in his belly. Half-sick from all the booze the night before, Eagle ate dry cereal out of the box. He sat at the scarred kitchen table, warming in the sunlight streaming through a small window. After all the wind, rain, and whiskey, a better day had to lie ahead.

He thought back to a couple days earlier when Herman Thunder Hawk, Hobart Horse, and he had been at Teddy Pourier's house drinking with Jerry Schwarting, a white cowboy they had known most of their lives. It all happened in a blur that day when he ended up with another assault charge and his name on an FBI wanted list. Why did the feds make such a big deal out of his taking Jerry's boots? Sure, he deserved the assault charge for shooting James Catches last May; thankfully, he had not died. But cowboy boots? How did that become so serious?

Jimmy knew about crime on the rez. He knew about the killings terrorizing the rez since AIM had held out at Wounded Knee. His family and friends believed that Wilson's GOONs were committing murders while the FBI looked the other way. Some people were maybe even killed by tribal cops. And now the feds were working overtime to find him for taking a drunk's boots at a party? They had searched a house, tearing it apart looking for him, only the night before. Luckily, nobody on the Pine Ridge would tell them anything.

How about his Aunt Jeanette Bissonette? They still hadn't found out who killed her. What about his uncle Pedro? Rumor had it the cop gunned

167

him down in cold blood. Then there was his little brother Richard, killed by the gun Grandma Bissonette kept to protect the family from GOONs. Made no sense they were after him for a party and a pair of boots that didn't even fit.

Leon, his older brother by one year, had returned from New Mexico the day before, and they had sure celebrated. The brothers intended to stay at their grandmother's house all that day; Leon would make sure the feds did not find him.

Jimmy was still hiding when the moccasin telegraph brought a strange message: Two FBI agents had followed him in a red pickup in to the Jumping Bull compound, a collection of houses, cabins, and tents where some AIM guys were staying. There had been a shoot-out and Jimmy was said to be right in the middle of it—maybe even killing the agents as they begged for their lives. That was bullshit; he had not been out of the house.

Unbeknownst to their grandmother, the brothers jumped out the bedroom window, crawled into the back seat of a girlfriend's car, and drove to Wallace Little's house near the compound. Jimmy stayed there while Leon and Kenny Loud Hawk rode horses toward the compound. As the sun disappeared over the western ridge, Leon and Kenny spotted a group of Indians sneaking away and rode up to them. Knowing the country and armed with a .22 rifle and six shells for protection, they showed the escapees how to get away, avoiding the feds carrying automatic weapons combing the area. They rode their horses over the trail, covering footprints so no one could track them.[1]

***

Eight months after the death of FBI Agents Jack Coler and Ronald Williams and AIM member Joseph Stuntz in the shootout, a rancher checking fences discovered the body of an Indian woman lying at the bottom of a cliff along a highway.

Following standard procedure, the feds turned the body over to pathologist W. O. Brown of Scottsbluff, Nebraska, who performed twenty to thirty autopsies every year on the rez. Even though nurses at the hospital noticed blood on the back of her head and a smear on the table where her head had rested, Brown listed the cause of death as exposure. He concluded she had intercourse not long before her death—and then cut off her hands to be sent to Washington for fingerprinting.

Declaring the body too decomposed for embalming, the mortician sprinkled it with disinfectant and stored it in his garage—his cold storage unit—as he had done for many others over the years. While he thought there was no hurry to put her in the ground, as the body would keep as the search for her identity continued, the police chief ordered her interment.

The tribe buried the Indian woman with no identity and no hands in an anonymous grave at the Holy Rosary Cemetery with a Catholic ceremony.[2]

A few days later, fingerprint analysts identified her as Anna Mae Pictou Aquash, a Mi'kmag Indian from Canada and an active member of the American Indian Movement, who had married her boyfriend during the occupation of Wounded Knee. Eight days after her body entered the prairie soil, she was exhumed for a second autopsy at the combined requests of her family, AIM, and the FBI.

After waiting in the hospital for an FBI pathologist and being finally informed there would not be one, a physician from Minneapolis brought in by AIM as an observer used a butcher knife from a local store for the procedure. He found a bullet hole surrounded by powder burns at the base of her right ear and a lump caused by a .32 caliber bullet in her temple. He also found that Brown had reported on procedures he had not done.[3]

Friends buried Anna Mae Aquash near the grave of Joe Stuntz in a tiny cemetery just down the road from the Jumping Bull compound. The ceremony was remarkable only by the lack of attendance by any AIM leaders. In 2004, her family had her remains exhumed for a second time and reburied in Nova Scotia where she had lived as a child on the Indian Brook Reserve.[4]

***

More than forty years later, the deaths of Coler, Williams, and Aquash remain controversial. There is little agreement about what happened in the murders of the three non-Oglala (four if you count Joe Stuntz from the C'our D'Alene tribe) victims on the Pine Ridge. The violent deaths of people who did not have to die blackened the reputation of both the FBI and the American Indian Movement, leaving the Oglala trying to make sense of what happened on their reservation.

Hidden under an FBI counter-intelligence program called COINTELPRO, the truth has been all but lost. J. Edgar Hoover's followers honed the program on foreign-born communists during the Red Scare following World War I, and then they turned their bag of dirty tricks on legitimate domestic organizations during the struggle for civil rights. The list of victims contains some of the most well-known names of the late twentieth century, including Martin Luther King, Phillip Berrigan, the Black Panthers, the American Indian Movement, and probably the Democratic Party.

The definition of clandestine, COINTELPRO surfaced in 1971 when a "Citizens Committee to Investigate the FBI" confiscated files from a Pennsylvania office and handed them to the press.[5] The documents revealed a rogue agency; its purpose was "to maintain the existing social and political 'order' by 'disrupting' and 'neutralizing' groups and individuals perceived as threats."[6]

In the pursuit of this mission, agents have been accused of lying to courts, falsifying evidence, spreading rumors about individuals, violence, and anything else that could be thought of—in short, the subversion of America's citizenry. Four tactics have been identified in the bureau's bag of dirty tricks.

1. Infiltration: Agents and informers did not just spy on political groups, they worked to discredit and disrupt them. They created a sense of paranoia by smearing activists as agents, turncoats, and informers.

2. Psychological Warfare from the Outside: Agents planted false media stories, published bogus leaflets, forged correspondence, made phone calls based on fake evidence, and created pseudo groups run by government agents. They manipulated and intimidated parents, employers, landlords, school officials, and anybody else with enough influence to cause trouble for activists.

3. Harassment Through the Legal System: The FBI indicted activists on charges more serious than warranted, keeping them in court with a myriad of trials and appearances. They gave perjured testimony and fabricated evidence as a pretext to false arrests and wrongful imprisonment.

4. Extralegal Force and Violence: Agents threatened and bullied. Break-ins, vandalism, and assault were tactics used to frighten dissidents and silence their followers.[7]

Integral to the story of Pine Ridge during the Time of Troubles and GOON oppression, white hate groups across America such as the KKK, Minutemen, Nazis, and racist vigilantes functioned as an arm of the bureau against activists. These groups received funds, information, and protection, suffering only token FBI harassment as long as they directed violence against COINTELPRO targets.[8]

The 1975 Church Committee to Study Governmental Operations with Respect to Intelligence Activities, a senate committee chaired by Frank Church, concluded, "Many of the techniques used would be intolerable in a democratic society even if all the targets had been involved in violent activity, but COINTELPRO went far beyond that."[9]

On its website, the FBI states only:

All COINTELPRO operations were ended in 1971. Although limited in scope (about two-tenths of one percent of the FBI's workload over a 15-year period), COINTELPRO was later rightfully criticized by Congress and the American people for abridging First Amendment rights and for other reasons.[10]

While the relationship between the GOONs and the FBI fits securely into the agency's use of hate groups to foment violence, the clandestine web of counter-intelligence struck Pine Ridge hard in 1975, beginning with Jimmy Eagle's stolen boots. As a result of a party turned rowdy, agents wanted him for robbery, kidnapping, and assault with a deadly weapon.[11]

On June 25, FBI Agents Coler and Williams, escorted by Robert Ecoffey of the tribal police, showed up at a cabin in the Jumping Bull compound looking for Jimmy. They were told he was not there and asked to leave.

The next morning, while traveling in separate cars, Williams radioed that they had spotted a red vehicle matching the description of one Jimmy was reported to have been in and followed it on to the compound, disregarding the virtual state of war on the reservation. There are differing stories of who fired the first shot, but the two agents soon sprawled face down, dead at the back of Coler's car.

The search for Jimmy intensified. He was included in the list of suspects who might have committed the murders. Agents went to the house where the two dead agents had looked for him the day before and ransacked the place, after surrounding it with twelve police cars and fifty men equipped for war.

Circumstances surrounding Jimmy swirled into a maelstrom. Teddy Pourier, host of the cowboy boots party, had been arrested the day before the shootout. The FBI considered him so dangerous that the agent transporting him to Rapid City asked for an escort. Thunder Hawk and Hobart Horse, Eagle and Pourier's fellow partiers, were arrested several days later. For a reason never known by Jimmy's family, Thunder Hawk told authorities that Eagle had participated in the shoot-out and had been wounded.

A non-wounded Jimmy Eagle turned himself in on July 9 for sentencing on the charge of shooting James Catches; when he did, agents arrested him on the cowboy boots charge. Three weeks later, the justice department arraigned him for assaulting a federal officer and two counts of murder in the first degree—the first arrest in the death of the two agents.

The evidence against him, besides Thunder Hawk's statement, came from criminals who shared his cell, including Marion High Bull serving time for the murders of little Floyd Bianas and Yvette Lorraine Hill. High Bull said Jimmy spoke like he was at the shooting and threatened to kill yet another agent.

Gregory Dewey Clifford, a convicted rapist, said that Jimmy described how one of the agents begged for his life before he and his friends took turns shooting him with a Thompson sub-machine gun.

Yet another inmate said that Jimmy told him stealing the cowboy boots was a trick to draw the agents to the compound so they could be killed.[12]

Marvin Stoldt, a GOON and off-duty tribal cop said he spotted four men running away from the compound at eight hundred yards around 1:20 p.m. the day of the shootout. Using a scope on a rifle, he saw only a blur, but when he switched to binoculars he recognized Jimmy Eagle dressed in a black shirt and black pants as the last in the line of running men. Stoldt was not sure it was Jimmy until he had time to think about it; by the time of his interview with an agent on September 4 (almost two months later), he had convinced himself it was.[13]

Jimmy never went to trial. After AIM members Dino Butler and Bob Robideau were acquitted of killing Coler and Williams a year later in Cedar Rapids, Iowa, federal prosecutors dropped the charges against him.

The FBI fabricated the entire story according to Leon, Jimmy's older brother. He calls the report that Jimmy was seen in a car pulling into the compound the day of the murders a complete lie.

Leon has never been able to figure out why agents were looking for Jimmy at the Jumping Bull compound. His brother never ran with AIM, he did. He thinks the cowboy boots story was an excuse to drive onto the property and start shooting Indians.

He admits Jimmy turned violent when he drank and was too often in trouble. After the charges for shooting the agents were dropped, Jimmy served six years for the shooting of James Catches; he was paroled in 1977. In October of that year, he nearly killed his uncle with a gun resulting from a drunken argument over car keys.[14]

Jimmy Eagle's reported participation in the deaths of Coler and Williams has COINTELPRO fingerprints all over it. He was never in the Jumping Bull compound during the shoot-out but supposedly confessed to a notorious child murderer and convicted rapist. He was identified running away from the firefight from over eight hundred yards away, a nearly impossible sighting.

Gregory Clifford, the rapist who allegedly heard Jimmy say he shot the agents with a sub-machine gun, entered a federal witness program. Under the feds protection, he strangled his girlfriend so violently that she remained comatose in a nursing home ten years later. In 1989, Clifford was indicted for stabbing a woman eighteen times and dismembering her body; a jury convicted him of first-degree murder.[15]

As a young man, Jimmy Eagle shot at least two people, but the pursuit of charges based on dubious testimony by unsavory cellmates made his name synonymous with Indian Country murder. Jimmy died in 2006 in Casper, Wyoming.

✳✳✳

The FBI may have fabricated felony charges against Jimmy Eagle to investigate AIM activities in the Jumping Bull compound, and they may have freed a vicious killer from jail for testimony against him, but his treatment was nothing like that suffered by Myrtle LuLu Poor Bear—the poster child for COINTELPRO abuse. Myrtle, an Oglala woman with the mind of a child, fell victim to a federal agency determined to convict AIM member Leonard Peltier for killing Coler and Williams.

With Robideau and Butler freed and charges against Eagle dropped, Peltier remained the only suspect in the murders of the agents. He had fled to his native Canada seeking political asylum, hoping to spend the rest of his life there. Considering the acquittal of his friends and the near state of war on the Pine Ridge, he believed he had a chance of avoiding trial in the United States.

Then Myrtle Poor Bear entered his life. The United States filed two affidavits she had signed in the Canadian court where he fought extradition. When he first saw them, he felt, "shocked and sickened." The next day was worse when headlines in the Vancouver newspaper announced, "Peltier's Girlfriend Testifies Against Him, Claiming to be an Eyewitness."[16]

An Oglala woman he had never met signed legal documents stipulating that she was not only his girlfriend but had watched him shoot the agents, her head held by the hair so she could not look away. He had allegedly also told her what it had been like. "He said one of the agents surrendered, but he kept shooting. ... He said he lost his mind and just started shooting. He said he shot them and just kept pulling the trigger and could not stop."[17]

For a girlfriend, Myrtle was brutally honest about what her boyfriend had done. In fact, she signed three affidavits detailing his guilt.[18] The first document, dated February 19, 1976, noted she was his girlfriend and that he and other AIM members had plotted to kill BIA cops, marshals, or FBI agents when they came on the Jumping Bull compound. According to Myrtle, Peltier had a detailed plan of the proposed murders, which included an escape route.[19]

On the day of the shootout, Peltier had everybody ready because he knew the feds were going to come looking for Jimmy Eagle. To protect Myrtle, Peltier had her fill her car with gas and leave the compound. When she saw him again in August, he told her the story of how he could not stop pulling the trigger.[20]

The second affidavit, dated February 23, 1976, hosted a substantial change. Instead of leaving after filling her car with gas, Myrtle stayed and witnessed Peltier shoot the agents.[21] In only the last of the three documents she signed did someone grab her by the head and force her to watch. She also said she knew one of the men to be an agent (so their identity was no mistake to anyone), and after freeing herself from the head grip, pounded Peltier on the back as he shot one of them. He killed the other as she walked away.[22]

Myrtle Poor Bear died in 2005. Her daughter Marty, a short, middle-aged woman, lives in Allen, South Dakota. She has never heard the whole story from her mother, but what she knows is enough to sink a disreputable federal program even lower, consigning it to the hell of Hitler's Gestapo and Stalin's KGB. "They would take my mother away from us for long periods of time, and I was raised by the neighbors," she says, bitter memories etched on her face, emotion stirring her voice.

Agents knew Myrtle because she worked for the police department—they picked her for her vulnerability. As a seven-year-old, she had fallen ill with an extremely high fever. Marty's grandfather said her mother was never right again. "The FBI saw that; they exploited her, and they preyed on her from the start."

Myrtle told her daughter that when the FBI needed her, "They would pull me out of the box, and put me on show again."[23] Agents had her on public display for the first time at Dickie Marshall's murder trial for shooting Monty Montileaux in Bud Merrill's family's bar in Scenic.

The prosecution's case was riddled with holes. Nobody identified Dickie in a line up, the assailant described by witnesses didn't match Dickie physically, and they had no motive. But South Dakota's problems went away when the FBI supplied them with a witness, Dickie's former girlfriend, Myrtle Poor Bear. At the trial, Myrtle testified that Dickie told her he'd killed Montileaux and would never forget the look on the guy's face. She even provided Dickie with a motive; she said Montileaux had beaten him up in a bar in Gordon, Nebraska.

FBI records show that Myrtle was in the custody of agents Price and Wood between February 19 and 23, the dates of the first two affidavits. Price said he first met her while investigating a shooting in Allen and had put her in a motel for protection since she was feeding them so much information.[24] Her family became so desperate to find her when she was in FBI custody that they even viewed Anna Mae Aquash's body to see if it could have been her.

None of what her mother signed or said was true according to Marty. She was never Dickie Marshall's or Leonard Peltier's girlfriend and was nowhere near the Jumping Bull compound on the day of the murders. Two men she did not know, Marshall and Peltier, certainly never admitted anything to her.

Why did she sign affidavits and testify? Agents told her she would never see her daughter again, they even threatened to kill baby Marty.[25] They said she would end up like Anna Mae, dead with her hands cut off. To make it real, "They showed me certain parts of her body that were decomposed. They said that's how I was going to end up if I didn't cooperate with them. They said they would kill me and get away with it. I was very scared."[26]

Myrtle—who supposedly said that Jimmy Eagle and eight other AIM members raped her one night when her boyfriend Peltier was away, as did Dickie Marshall and numerous others—hated the FBI. Marty said hate is a strong word, but she shared her mother's sentiment.

When she finally returned home, Myrtle was a bundle of nerves, and it tore their family apart. Even though Marty was very young, she became the mother and Myrtle the daughter. "She had been victimized by every tool the FBI had to get to Marshall and Peltier," Marty says, "and she really believed they would kill me."

Before she died, Marty and her mother had built a better life, and Myrtle seemed to be getting better. "She was a wonderful person," Marty recalls about those days, quietly breaking into tears.

Marty puts all the blame for Myrtle's distress on the FBI, but she has no use for the American Indian Movement because of the way her family was treated. They were ostracized from the community, no one would talk to them, and Myrtle became a recluse, never leaving the house. Marty says AIM was nothing to her.[27]

The United States Justice Department fell into the COINTELPRO vortex with Myrtle Poor Bear's testimony. After using her affidavits to extradite Peltier, Federal Prosecutor Evan Hultman did not put her on the stand at his trial. It turned out to be a smart move. During an "offer of proof" session away from the jury—a tactic used by the defense to have her testimony heard—Myrtle recanted. She admitted to not knowing Leonard Peltier and said she had not been close to the Jumping Bull compound the day of the shooting. The presiding judge rejected the offer of proof and refused to have her heard by the jury. "The credibility of the witness for any purpose is so suspect that to permit her testimony to go to the jury would be confusing the issues …"[28]

Hultman not only refused to use her at Pelletier's trial, he told the judge at his subsequent appeal why he did not call her, "because she was so incompetent in the utter, utter, utter ultimate sense of incompetency. … There was not one scintilla that showed Myrtle Poor Bear was there, knew anything, did anything, etc. …"[29]

On the same day Hultman labeled her as incompetent, April 12, 1978, the Supreme Court of South Dakota cited Myrtle's testimony in its decision to deny Dickie Marshall's appeal of his life sentence. "The court is not satisfied nor reasonably well-satisfied that Myrtle Poor Bear's testimony at trial was false."[30]

The most incredible statement Marty makes about her mother denied the Federal Bureau of Investigation credibility and any hope of respect on the reservation. "What is so weird is that there are no FBI files on my mother now, they have been destroyed."[31]

A federal agency destroying or not maintaining records of an eyewitness to a notorious murder, a witness who heard two men confess to two different murders, and whose testimony proved responsible for another suspected killer's extradition is almost unbelievable. Yet even Peltier's attorney cannot acquire them. When he sent the bureau a Freedom of Information Request for Myrtle's files, the chief of the record keeping section replied, "We were advised the records were not in their expected location and could not be located."[32]

Twenty-five years after she signed the affidavits, Myrtle declared, "I was forced into this, and I feel very awful. I just wish that Leonard Peltier will get out of prison."[33]

In 1999, Peltier wrote, "They knowingly and with despicable cruelty manipulated and terrified a poor and helpless Indian woman into giving false testimony to convince the Canadian government to extradite me, another of their victims."[34]

Not all Canadians were impressed with the maneuvers of the United States Justice Department to get Leonard Peltier back on American soil. Warran Allmand, a longtime member of the Canadian Parliament wrote:

> By what right do law enforcement authorities take the law into their own hands by manufacturing and withholding evidence, and by conspiracy and illegality attack legitimate dissent and lawful aboriginal advocacy. ....
> We should have vigorously protested the use of a false affidavit and, at the very least, requested a new trial.[35]

***

Many Pine Ridge residents believe COINTELPRO reached ascendancy when the fatal bullet tore through Anna Mae Aquash's skull. They say she died a victim of FBI snitch-jacketing: "neutralizing a target by labeling him a 'snitch' or informant, so that he would no longer be trusted—was used in all COINTELPRO."[36]

By 1975, Anna Mae was becoming a force in the American Indian Movement, developing into a leader of the group despite its chauvinistic reputation. Involved in the struggle for Indian rights since moving to Boston from Canada, Anna Mae had helped organize the Boston Indian Council, which offered support and counseling to the city's Native population. Through the council, she took part in the 1970 demonstration at the *Mayflower II*, joining Russell Means and other members of the newly formed American Indian Movement.

Anna Mae traveled to South Dakota, staying in Wounded Knee for nearly a month during the occupation where she married Nogeeshik Aquash in a traditional Indian ceremony. She did not just stay in the kitchen or the infirmary either, Anna Mae was one of the few women to dig bunkers and take part in night patrols. She was the first to suspect that a reporter and photographer sent by a small Iowa newspaper may not have been who he claimed. She thought he was a fed and refused to work with him.

Douglass Durham, the man she suspected, supposedly part Indian, became a trusted advisor of Dennis Banks, one of the organization's founders and leaders. But Anna Mae's suspicions proved correct, as Durham was exposed as an FBI informant and provocateur two years after Wounded Knee. He admitted to spying for the feds during a joint press conference with AIM leaders. Cast out of the group, he toured for the John Birch Society speaking about the evils of the American Indian Movement.

Anna Mae's influence continued to grow in the organization. She earned a reputation as a spiritual woman through her study of traditional ceremonies. And she began a love affair with the already married Dennis Banks.

Simultaneously, Anna Mae became the subject of federal informant rumors, probably snitch-jacketed by Durham. When Theda Clark, arraigned as an accomplice in her death in 2010, publicly identified her as an informant at the 1975 AIM conference in Albuquerque, suspicion metastasized. Vernon Bellecourt ordered Leonard Peltier, Bob Robideau, and Dino Butler, all later to stand trial for the murder of agents Coler and Williams, to question her. Some believed Bellecourt had ordered her killed on the spot if they did not believe her answers. She survived, but told friends Peltier had shoved a gun barrel into her mouth during the interrogation.

AIM blamed the FBI for killing her in a COINTELPRO operation, primarily accusing David Price, an agent who allegedly told Anna Mae she would be dead in a year if she did not cooperate.[37] The FBI claimed AIM leadership ordered her death because they believed she had become an informant.

During the years of FBI and AIM finger-pointing after her death, Anna Mae was not forgotten. In 1976, Robert Ecoffey, a young Indian cop working as a jailer while studying criminal justice at the college in Chadron, Nebraska, claimed he heard the sound of a woman crying over the Pine Ridge jail's intercom. He searched the building but failed to find her. He told the story to his medicine man grandfather. After performing a Lakota ceremony, the old man had the answer. "A young woman was killed before her time, and it wasn't right. She came to you because you have a good heart. You don't understand it now, but one of these days you will be in a position to help her."[38]

Ecoffey, who had traveled to the Jumping Bull compound with Coler and Williams the day before the shoot-out, advanced rapidly through federal law enforcement ranks, becoming the first Indian marshal in the history of the service. In 2004, he was appointed Deputy Director of the Office of Law Enforcement Service for the Bureau of Indian Affairs, supervising BIA law enforcement on reservations across the country.

He was working as the administrative manager for the Pine Ridge Bureau of Indian Affairs in 1993 when Gladys Bissonette, Jimmy Eagle's grandmother, came into his office. He asked her if she knew anyone who could provide information about the murder of Anna Mae, the woman he decided had spiritually appealed to him in an empty jail.

Gladys gave him the name of a relative in Denver. From there, with the aid of Denver Detective Abe Alonzo, he followed the trail to Arlo Looking Cloud, a one-time Pine Ridge resident who had become a full-time homeless derelict in Denver.

Perhaps as a result of years of substance abuse, Looking Cloud had not concealed his involvement in Anna Mae's death. Within the Indian community, many knew of his participation; he did not pull the trigger, but he had stood on that dark, lonely cliff when she died.

During the subsequent investigation, Looking Cloud took Ecoffey and Alonzo to the place Aquash died and told them the story of her ordeal. She had been staying at an AIM safe house in Denver, he said, when a call came to take her to Rapid City. Looking Cloud, John Boy Patton, also known as John Graham, and Theda Clark, a tough Denver bar owner and member of AIM, put her in the back of Clark's red pinto station wagon, and drove to Rapid City.

Once in Rapid City, they stopped at a trailer occupied by Thelma Rios, an AIM member allegedly in on the plot to kill Anna Mae. The travelers drove on to a house on the Rosebud Reservation where Theda and John Boy went in while Looking Cloud stayed in the car with Anna Mae. Then they took her out on a deserted highway and led her to the place where John Boy shot her in the head and pushed her over the cliff. Fearing for his life, Looking Cloud took the gun from John Boy and emptied it into the ground. They buried the pistol under a bridge.[39]

For Arlo Looking Cloud, it had been such a horrifying moment that he never had anything to do with the American Indian Movement again. Maybe the memory and guilt led him to his destruction by drugs and alcohol; he never recovered from the ordeal. He had told too many people about the role he played in one of America's most famous murders to remain free.

The fourth grand jury to meet on the Aquash murder indicted Looking Cloud. In a four-day trial in February 2004, the prosecution presented twenty-three witnesses while the defense brought forth only one. The prosecution's case consisted of little evidence of the actual murder; no one testified who saw the shooting or who was there when it occurred, except Looking Cloud. Looking Cloud never took the stand, but the prosecution played his videotaped confession made on March 27, 2003. He acknowledged he was under the influence of alcohol during the taping and admitted to his role in the killing. He named John Boy Patton (Graham) as the shooter with Theda Clark and Thelma Rios as accomplices, although Rios was not at the murder scene.

He had heard that Anna Mae was an informant from Theda Clark, but maintained his innocence of the murder conspiracy. He went to the safe house where Anna Mae stayed only to look for his friend Joe Morgan. He traveled with Clark and Graham only because they asked him to ride along; he had no idea of a plot to kill anyone. The truth of Anna Mae's death hit him only when she pitched off the cliff. Strangely, he also admitted to calling Anna Mae's daughters, Denise and Debbie Pictou, and telling them the story of how she died.[40]

Then the prosecution brought out their blockbuster witness who told the court very little about the guilt of Arlo Looking Cloud, but struck at the heart of the American Indian Movement. She condemned AIM leadership for the murder in a testimony based almost solely on what she had heard other people say. While Looking Cloud's attorney continually objected on the basis of hearsay, the judge admitted her testimony on the grounds that it was for a limited purpose only, at one point explaining, "It is hearsay, at least on the basis of the record that we have at this point, and it is not received for the truth of whether or not those things were in fact said, and so it is limited."[41]

The witness was Darlene (Kamook) Nichols, Dennis Banks' wife of seventeen years, mother of four of his children, and the woman Anna Mae and Banks cheated on with their affair. Asking a Rapid City jury, as well as the press, to accept what she said without judgment of truth seems akin to unringing a bell.

According to Nichols, rumors of Anna Mae's disloyalty sped through the convention in Farmington. She said of Peltier's New Mexico interrogation, "I heard that he had taken her away from the camp in the car and had put a gun to her head and that he wanted to know if she was an informant."

She also noted that Leonard Crow Dog had kicked Anna Mae off his property because he thought she was a fed, and that she had observed Dave Hill, Leonard Peltier, and Dennis Banks forcing Anna Mae to make bombs so her fingerprints would be on them.

Her most damning testimony directed at the movement her former husband founded came as she recounted the trip she had taken with Anna Mae, Leonard, and Dennis, among others, to Washington in Marlon Brando's camper. With no bearing on Looking Cloud's guilt or innocence, the court allowed her to tell how Leonard Peltier had said he had killed the FBI agents at Jumping Bull compound. "He said that motherfucker was begging for his life, but I shot him anyway." She was convinced on that trip that Anna Mae was along so they could keep her from going to the feds, "and I knew that she was scared of Leonard and Dennis at that point."[42]

Nichols contacted the FBI after she separated from Banks in 1989 and started wearing a wire, tape recording members of AIM as they spoke to her. She began turning against AIM, she testified, on February 24, 1976, when Dennis phoned and told her they had found Anna Mae's body. She put two and two together when she learned the FBI did not identify the body until March 3, concluding AIM had something to do with the death of her husband's former lover.

While she said the phone call made her realize Banks knew what had happened, she did not hate her ex-husband and would never want to hurt him because he was the father of her children. But she admitted to wearing a wire with the FBI listening in as she spoke with him. Among the people she spoke with and tape recorded in her role as FBI informant were Arlo Looking Cloud and Troy Lynn Yellow Wood, Theda Clark's niece and Anna Mae's friend in the Denver safe house.

Under cross-examination, Nichols said she worked in Hollywood casting and had helped on the movies *Dances With Wolves* and *Last of the Mohicans.* Some years she had earned as much as $35,000, although she had made only $9,000 the year before the trial. She also admitted to receiving $42,000 from the federal government for working with the FBI.

Richard Two Elk, an Oglala living in Denver who referred to Looking Cloud as his brother because they were so close growing up on the Pine Ridge, also testified for the prosecution. Looking Cloud sought him out for help in 1994 after Ecoffey's interrogation, Two Elk said, because of his military experience, which he claimed gave him knowledge of institutional processes. Looking Cloud's former childhood friend also testified that he had helped arrange the call Looking Cloud made to the daughters of Anna Mae because he believed anyone with information about what had happened to their mother had an obligation to them.[43]

Angie Janis, formerly Angie Begay, another young woman who had befriended Anna Mae at the safe house, joined the list of witnesses. She testified that Looking Cloud saw a leader of the Denver Crusade for Justice make a hand gesture signifying they cut informer's throats and watched

Anna Mae being carried out of the house tied to a board.[44] Even though she was living with John Boy Patton at the time of the murder, she worried so much about Anna Mae's safety that she considered calling the police after the murder party drove away.

Except, Troy Lynn Yellow Wood testified that when she had tried to call the police, Angie took the phone away saying that involving the cops would just cause more problems. Throughout Janis's and Yellow Wood's testimonies, the defense made the same objection to hearsay, which constituted most of their statements. The court admitted it with the same limited-use allowance.

Looking Cloud never presented a defense, although his attorney called former FBI Agent David Price, the man with the most notorious reputation on the reservation. After explaining the job of an informant, he testified he never asked Anna Mae to be one.[45]

In an interview from the Pennington County Jail, Looking Cloud said his video confession was a set-up. "They [Ecoffey and Alonzo] were giving me drugs and alcohol. ... He [Alonzo] met me at the liquor store every day [before the arrest] and bought me the booze and gave me drugs. I was really into Chiba. You know what Chiba is? ... Heroin. I loved that stuff. He was getting it for me. All I wanted."[46]

The Pine Ridge vortex continued to spin. Darlene Nichols, Dennis Banks' wife of seventeen years, a woman who was in Wounded Knee and lost her uncle Buddy Lamont there, married Robert Ecoffey seven months after the trial. Their marriage culminated a five-year relationship, which must have started about the time she became an FBI informant.[47] Since then, Ecoffey was appointed BIA superintendent of the Pine Ridge, although he is still remembered by many residents as a GOON. He and Darlene opened a Subway Restaurant almost directly across from the BIA building.

Angie Begay, who lived with John Boy Patton when Anna Mae was taken to Rapid City, changed her last name to Janis when she married one of Ecoffey's relatives. In the always-tight job market in Pine Ridge, at the time of the trial she was employed by the Pine Ridge Bureau of Indian Affairs.[48]

***

During Arlo Looking Cloud's video confession, Ecoffey asked several times if the murder party stopped at Dickie Marshall's house on the way to the cliff where Anna Mae died. Each time Looking Cloud denied they stopped until reaching a dwelling on the Rosebud. Even when Ecoffey told him Cleo and Dickie Marshall said the killers had stopped at their house, Looking Cloud replied, "I don't remember right now, I don't remember that, I thought we just went straight to the Rosebud."[49]

Four years later during Dickie Marshall's trial, charged with supplying the weapon that killed Anna Mae and the second person to be tried in her death, Looking Cloud changed his mind. He remembered stopping at the Marshall's house and said he had been in Dickie's bedroom along with Theda and John Boy. "He [Dickie] opens a box, and there's a pistol in it."[50] Looking Cloud said Marshall gave the pistol to Theda Clark, who handed it to John Boy Patton to kill Anna Mae.

Looking Cloud also remembered more about the stop on the Rosebud where he allegedly saw the son of a prominent South Dakota senator. When asked by the prosecutor why he had not told the investigators about it earlier, he said, "I was fearful for my family as I didn't trust no one." He added that he had been threatened by both AIM and the authorities.[51]

In rebuttal, the defense's first witness, Denver Detective Alonzo, said in all of his time working on the case, Arlo Looking Cloud had never once mentioned Dickie Marshall.

Next, Looking Cloud's alleged childhood friend and confidant, Richard Two Elk, took the stand and testified that Looking Cloud owned a revolver like the one used in the shooting.[52]

Dickie did not give Theda a pistol, Dana Hanna, defense attorney, told the court. When the murder party stopped at the Marshall's house, they were looking for directions and a change of clothes for Anna Mae, not a gun. At the time they did not plan to kill her, they had expected her to stay on the run—the reason they asked Dickie and Cleo to let her stay there. He told the jury that the killing order came at the house on the Rosebud, apparently the home of Bill Means, Russell Mean's brother.[53]

In his final arguments to the jury, prosecutor Bob Mandel summarized his version of the events. Looking Cloud, John Boy Patton, and Theda Clark brought Anna Mae to Marshall's house and asked if they could leave her. "Dick says, 'No, you can't leave her here. Here's a gun. Here's the ammo.'"[54]

To show that Looking Cloud made the decision to talk by himself, without an offer of federal reward, his attorney was sworn in and he stipulated that the government had not made his client any specific promises in exchange for his testimony. However, the government had agreed to provide a statement regarding his cooperation that could be used to seek a reduction of his life sentence.[55]

The prosecution put Darlene (Nichols) Ecoffey on the stand, primarily to repeat her testimony from four years earlier about the culpability of the American Indian Movement. The blockbuster witness was to be Serle Chapman, a British writer living in Wyoming, who testified he had interviewed Dickie Marshall while researching a book. In a taped interview, Marshall told him he respected Anna Mae, had never known her, and hoped whoever killed her got what was coming to them.

In a non-taped interview, Chapman claimed to have asked Marshall about a rumor that he had supplied the gun used to kill Aquash. According to the Englishman, Marshall replied that back in the day when someone asked you to do something, you didn't ask too many questions.[56]

An all-white jury in Rapid City took less than two hours to find Dickie Marshall not guilty after he had spent two years in jail awaiting trial. The judge read the verdict and said, "Mr. Marshall, you're free to go."[57]

So was Serle Chapman, with money in his pocket. The United States paid him more than $69,000 in the failed attempt to send Dickie Marshall back to prison.[58]

✳✳✳

As Robert Ecoffey's investigation into the death of Anna Mae gained steam, Arlo Looking Cloud placed the murder weapon in John Boy Patton's hand. John Boy left Denver and the United States after the ill-fated 1973 trip to Pine Ridge, returning to the Canadian Yukon without trying to hide his trail. Along with another Pine Ridge investigator, Ecoffey interviewed him in the small city of Whitehorse in 1994.

John Boy maintained his innocence, declared his friendship for Anna Mae and expressed his sorrow at her death, yet two of his statements played to the jury in his trial sixteen years later in 2010. After hearing the case against him, Ecoffey testified at the trial that the accused had said, "Well ... looks like you guys have my future planned for me. You have your case." Later he told the investigators, "Well, I'm ready to leave the place anyway ... I will probably spend the rest of my life in jail."[59]

Investigators and prosecutors played up those statements as a subliminal confession, however, John Boy has continued to deny any part in the murder. His story has always been the same—he traveled with Anna Mae to the Pine Ridge but dropped her off at a safe house on the reservation.

Ecoffey and his partner were not the only American law enforcement officers to visit the suspect in the Yukon. FBI agents made several trips to question him while carrying offers of immunity.

> And they wanted me to name leadership that would have given the order to that effect, to kill Anna Mae. And they were trying to tell me they would put me in a witness protection program, they would change my identity, they would relocate me if I would go to testify in front of the federal grand gury in South Dakota against the AIM leadership.[60]

John Boy Patton might not have made a deal, but almost everybody else negotiated one with Robert Ecoffey, upon whose shoulders John Boy's Canadian lawyer put all of the weight of the extradition. "This whole case has been concocted by Ecoffey," he said. He told a Canadian justice she was being misled by the United States. "They have been negligent, if not deceitful."[61]

Ecoffey's concoction secured a victory in the guilty verdict against Arlo Looking Cloud, but had suffered a stinging rebuke in Dickie Marshall's acquittal, leaving Theda Clark, Thelma Rios, and John Boy Patton to add to the mix before the grand finale—the prosecution of AIM's top leaders.

Over eighty years old and battling Alzheimer's in a Nebraska nursing home, Theda Clark must not have seemed worthy of the chase; she was never charged in Anna Mae Aquash's murder. Thelma Rios was indicted on the same day as John Boy and proved to be an easy notch on Ecoffey's belt. Arraigned on one count of premeditated murder, she pled guilty to being an accessory to the murder three weeks before she was to stand trial.

Thelma received five years in prison, the maximum sentence. The court suspended all but ninety days with credit for time served and her testimony at John Boy's trial. Thelma was severely ill with lung cancer and did not attend John Boy's trial. She died in February 2011, one and a half months after John Boy's sentence.

The justice department's original plan had been to try Marshall and John Boy together in federal court. But John Boy's attorney, John Murphy, filed a motion to dismiss the charge, asserting the federal court did not have jurisdiction since neither Anna Mae nor John Boy were members of a federally recognized Indian tribe. Eventually, Murphy was proved correct; in anticipation of that judgment, the State of South Dakota indicted John Boy.

South Dakota charged him with one count of felony murder related to kidnapping, one count of rape, and one count of premeditated murder. His trial played out between November 29 and December 10, 2010. In the end, the jury found him guilty of murder in the commission of a felony and not guilty of the charge of premeditated murder. Sentenced to life in prison, he turned to Anna Mae's daughters as the judge announced the sentence and professed his innocence.[62]

Before the jury was seated, Dickie Marshall's attorney had met with the judge, prosecutor, and John Boy's attorney, arguing Ecoffey's concoction had plans to send his client back to jail. Because of Marshall's acquittal on federal charges, prosecutors gave him immunity from future state charges and compelled him to testify in John Boy's trial. Since he had previously violated the terms of his parole twice, once more and the government would send him back to prison to complete his life sentence. His attorney charged such was the state's intention.

> And my argument here is that the government seeks now, and intends now, to elicit testimony which if it conflicts with their latest version of,

quote, the truth, that Mr. Marshall is going to be punished by being sent to prison for the rest of his life through parole violation.[63]

The prosecution's case against John Boy consisted of Arlo Looking Cloud's testimony that put the murder weapon in his hands when the trigger was pulled. Attorney Murphy put investigator Ecoffey's case on trial, eliciting answers that detailed how evidence and testimony had been adapted to fit the official theories of the crime.

The prosecution's problems with changing testimony first appeared when Angie Janis, John Boy's former girlfriend and Ecoffey's relative and employee, took the stand. Since viewing the crime scene photographs, Ecoffey had contended ligature marks marred Anna Mae's wrists—an accoutrement to kidnapping. Even though neither doctor identified the marks during the autopsies, he insisted she had been bound by the wrists.

Janis testified at the two previous trials (Looking Cloud's and Marshall's) that Anna Mae had indeed been tied and said so again at John Boy's trial. In cross examination, Attorney Murphy tried to help the jury understand the inconsistencies in her memory.

She had not mentioned the fetters, Arlo Looking Cloud, or who took Anna Mae to the car during her first interview with Ecoffey. During her second session with the cop, she remembered Anna Mae's hands were tied, but did not know if they were in front or back, and that was the first time she mentioned Looking Cloud. She recalled Anna Mae's hands were tied behind her back during the third session. She had told one grand jury that Anna Mae's hands were tied but did not remember in which position; she also told the jurors she did not see who took Anna Mae to the car because she did not go outside the house.

Her lucidity had dramatically improved for Looking Cloud's trial. She recalled Anna Mae was tied to a board and carried out of the house. In fact, before John Boy's trial, her changing statements caused the now BIA Superintendent of Pine Ridge and her employer, Robert Ecoffey, to walk down the hall and ask if her story was going to stay the same or change again. She didn't seem to get the message.

Murphy questioned her about the testimony she gave to another grand jury on September 9, 2009, approximately a year earlier:

Q. And on that occasion, a couple years after the trial in Arlo Looking Cloud's case, you told the jury that Anna Mae Aquash walked out of Troy Lynn's house on her own, correct?

A. I don't recall.

Q. Okay.

Q. I will show you—I am going to show you a question asked to you.

Okay. Very good. Was she walking on her own power? Your answer,
yes. Is that what you told the grand jury at that occasion?

A. Yes.

Q. All right. And so she was no longer tied to a board and carried out,
now she's walking out voluntarily?

A. Yes.

Q. Yes?

A. Yes.

Q. All right. And in fact, you told the grand jury at that occasion
you didn't see anybody push her, shove her, or force her out of
the house?

A. Yes.

Q. And the group of people that left the house, just walked out together, is that correct?

A. I don't recall.

Q. Okay. Well, what do you recall now?

A. I know she was tied up.

Q. Okay. So now you know she was tied up. But at least back in 2009,
you said on that occasion whether she was tied up or not she walked
out of the house on her own, correct?

The stories of Anna Mae's bound hands continued to vary. Troy Lynn
Wood recalled that she was not tied, walked out of the house on her own,
and sat in the back of the small Pinto station wagon with her arms around
her knees. In an interesting aside, Troy Lynn also remarked that the victim
told her during a personal discussion she was very much in love with Dennis Banks.

George Palfrey, who also hung around the safe house, said Anna Mae's
hands were tied in front by Theda, but Anna Mae was okay with it. He testified he never saw Arlo Looking Cloud around Theda's house the day they
took Anna Mae away. The people in the car, he recalled, were Theda, John
Boy, Anna Mae, and Ida Mae, Theda's twelve-year-old daughter.

If Anna Mae had been a kidnapping victim, bound to a board or tied
up and closely guarded, the prosecution had difficulty proving it. Candy
Hamilton, AIM legal advisor, testified she saw her at the WKLDOC building in Rapid City, that she and Anna Mae drank coffee, and while she did
not believe Anna Mae thought she was free to leave, she was never guarded
or bound, and could have walked out the door at any time. Cleo Gates,
Dickie Marshall's ex-wife, agreed. She said Anna Mae could have simply
walked out the door and disappeared when Theda, John Boy, and Arlo met
in the bedroom with Dickie.

The trial moved into a more confrontational stage when Darlene Ecoffey took the stand. The prosecutor asked only five questions, directing her

to describe Leonard Peltier's confession to the murder of the FBI agents in front of Anna Mae.

John Boy's attorney was not so brief. Besides questioning her veracity, he put Federal Rule 35, the get-out-of-jail ticket, on trial. He brought out answers to show that Robert Ecoffey's concoction was put together with purchased testimony, if not from outright pay, then reimbursed in the dismissal of federal charges and reduced prison sentences.

While she insisted she was not paid for her work with the FBI but reimbursed instead, Darlene had to admit she took the cash up front. She had received one payment of $17,000 and another of $25,000 for expenses in advance of incurring the costs. As expenses, the payments were non-taxable.

The future BIA superintendent's wife had also evaded federal charges. When a car she was traveling in exploded in Kansas, authorities charged Darlene with a federal explosives violation. When the camper she rode in with Anna Mae in Oregon was stopped, she was charged again with possession of explosives—including grenades and dynamite. Darlene agreed that she had faced eighty years in federal prison. She must have been quite relieved when Oregon dropped the charges and Kansas sentenced her to three years probation after the felonies were reduced to misdemeanors—around the time she started working with the feds.[64]

The FBI did not send her out alone either. After tape recording Arlo Looking Cloud for six hours in a car, Serle Chapman of the Dickie Marshall case joined her in the vehicle. He told her he was not sure the feds heard everything that Looking Cloud had told her over the wire, and said, "You need to be very positive when you go in and say he went through it. He put himself there, said he was, you know, he, John Boy, shot her."[65]

The seventeen years between Arlo Looking Cloud's first conversation with Ecoffey and John Boy Patton's trial improved his memory—or he could have been following a well-established pattern of behavior. Previously he had been convicted forty times, twelve of those for providing false information. During John Boy's trial, Attorney Murphy found so many changes in Looking Cloud's testimony that he referred to it as the ever-changing story.

During this round of questioning Looking Cloud said he did not fire into the ground but off to the west, solving the state's problem of failing to find the slugs at the top of the cliff. He also remembered the gun was silver with red grips, when earlier he did not remember ever seeing it.

After leaving Marshall's house, the jury learned the murder party siphoned gas from Looking Cloud's grandmother's car and then rested quite a while, answering the perplexing question of what they did from the time they left Marshall's house with the gun and Anna Mae's death in the early light of dawn.

Then Rule 35 took center stage. Looking Cloud had started brokering deals in 1994. The first time saw an earlier charge of felony assault on a police officer disappear when he agreed to cooperate with Ecoffey's investigation. For agreeing to testify against Marshall and John Boy, the feds transferred him from a dangerous prison in Louisiana to county jails in South Dakota where he said he watched television all day.

Until 2008, Looking Cloud's story had been that John Boy and Anna Mae played cards or talked in a bedroom in Thelma Rios's house. He changed card playing to hearing sounds of people having sex after the authorities announced that John Boy raped the murder victim, answering yes to the question if his Rule 35 motion was dependent on what he said about John Boy.

When Defense Attorney Murphy asked, "You know my client is the only guy on trial right now for the crime, right?"

Looking Cloud answered, "Yes sir."

Then Murphy asked, "And in a way that makes him your meal ticket out of federal prison, doesn't it?"

Looking Cloud said, "Yes sir."

Arlo Looking Cloud's life sentence was reduced to just twenty years for his testimony.[66] The judge sentenced John Boy Patton to life in prison where he will remain unless he finds, if he is of the mind to do so, someone higher up in AIM to accuse of ordering Anna Mae's death.

***

In the end, it did not matter if Anna Mae Aquash had been snitch-jacketed by the FBI or if she had been an informant. The results were the same. The American Indian Movement held its unity through the Time of Troubles, the siege of Wounded Knee, and the murder of two federal agents, but collapsed following her death.

AIM leaders, previously so focused on identifying racist America, the federal government, and the FBI as the enemy, began pointing fingers at each other. No one survived unsullied.

Fueled by the murder and battles gone by, the movement split in 1993. When it did, every leader, any person who dared step onto a broader stage, was labeled informant and traitor. Behind every disagreement, behind every rock, leaders saw antagonists as puppets skillfully played by COINTELPRO.

The chasm developed around battles that Russell Means and Ward Churchill had with Vernon and Clyde Bellecourt. In 1993, Means and Churchill started an alternative faction that AIM called the International Confederation of Autonomous Chapters of the American Indian Movement centered in Colorado, where Churchill taught at the university.

During a 1999 radio interview in which Churchill and Vernon Belle-court took part, Churchill called Bellecourt a fed and the person behind Aquash's death. "The execution of Anna Mae came at the order of a federal operative. I happen to believe that federal operative is Vernon Bellecourt."

Bellecourt had already hurled a slur at Churchill in response to a question of how to end pain and suffering in Indian communities. "Well, if we get all these phony, wannabe Indians out of our community and running education programs that should be run by Indian people, I think that's the first step."[67]

The same year, five years before Arlo Looking Cloud's trial, the leaders of Autonomous AIM held a press conference on the plaza of the federal office building in Denver. They praised Detective Abe Alonzo for his work on Anna Mae's murder and identified Looking Cloud, John Boy, and Theda Clark as people with knowledge of the shooting. They announced that Vernon Bellecourt made the call to kill Anna Mae when the murder party stopped at Bill Means' house on the Rosebud.

Concluding the press conference, even though the presenters had identified Indians as the perpetrators, Ward Churchill could not resist blaming the feds. "The implication being that someone is being protected and that someone being protected was inserted by the FBI into the American Indian Movement for the purposes of creating these types of situations in order to discredit the movement ..."[68]

The leaders of Autonomous AIM backed the prosecution of Arlo Looking Cloud and John Boy, believing the orders for the hit came from Vernon Bellecourt. No one from the leadership of AIM has ever claimed responsibility for the murder.

Vernon Bellecourt and Russell Means are dead. Ward Churchill publicly lost his position with the University of Colorado on charges similar to those hurled by Bellecourt when the two shared the airwaves, "Mr. Churchill is a literary, and an academic and an Indian fraud ..."[69]

While the sides have quieted, the feud continues. Clyde Bellecourt still calls Autonomous AIM a bunch of federal operatives.[70] A woman speaking for the Leonard Peltier Offense/Defense Committee in 2012 said that they have nothing to do with the split-off group, and a person answering the phone for AIM's Interpretive Center claims to never having heard of one of Autonomous AIM's most noted leaders.

Tom Poor Bear, ever the ultimate AIM loyalist, took the acrimony to a new dimension. He believes AIM has photographic proof that Ward Churchill served as an FBI operative in full battle dress and armaments during the siege at Wounded Knee. The American Indian Movement has even posted pictures on the Internet of the unknown agent purported to be Churchill.[71]

***

FBI agents used another of COINTELPRO's dirty tricks following the killing of Coler and Williams by issuing announcements designed to inflame the public. While each man had been shot three times, the bureau reported their bodies had been riddled with bullets. Although no one has ever admitted being near the agents as they died, reporters heard they had been dragged out of their cars and executed as Williams pleaded for mercy for the sake of Coler's wife and children. The publicity following the shoot-out was so exaggerated that an investigator for the United States Civil Rights Commission accused the FBI of manipulating the media, calling many of the statements "either false, unsubstantiated, or directly misleading."[72]

The most notorious publication came during Butler's and Robideau's 1976 trial in Cedar Rapids when the bureau circulated a series of communications within the federal intelligence community. On June 21, a memo was leaked to the media announcing that two thousand Indian Dog Soldiers had been going through guerrilla warfare training and planned to begin a series of violent actions between July 1 and July 5, 1976, the dates of America's bicentennial celebrations.

Among their alleged terrorist activities, the Dog Soldiers intended to assassinate the governor of South Dakota, snipe at tourists on South Dakota highways, assault the state penitentiary, and blow up the Bureau of Indian Affairs building in Wagner, South Dakota. They would be armed with modern assault rifles, which they would get when they met at Charlie Abourezk's house in Porcupine.[73]

Called to testify at Butler and Robideau's trial, Clarence Kelly, FBI director, admitted that there was no evidence to support the Dog Soldier memo. When asked for one shred of proof that anything in the memo would occur, he replied, "I know of none. We're in the business, the profession, the occupation of preventing violence."[74]

***

WKLDOC also did not escape the death of the agents and the murder of Anna Mae with a clean reputation. Attorney Bruce Ellison, who lived with Thelma Rios at the time, has been accused of interrogating Anna Mae when the killers stopped at the WKLDOC office before driving to the rez. According to Joseph Trimbach, the former FBI Special Agent in Charge, "[FBI] ASAC Zigrossi was not alone in his suspicions that Ellison was somehow involved in the conspiracy [to kill Anna Mae]."[75]

At Arlo Looking Cloud's trial, Prosecutor Mandel said of Ellison, "[He] exercised his Fifth Amendment right. He is a co-conspirator, it is a co-conspirator's statement made in the furtherance and course of the conspiracy."[76]

How Anna Mae's wallet came into the possession of WKLDOC lawyer Ken Tilsen also casts doubt on the group of legal workers. Tilsen mailed it to her daughters in May 1976. According to Tilsen it came to him on a circuitous route, but "for the life of him," he could not remember how.[77]

16

The Beautiful Girl, the Governor, and the Psychotic

During the time he was holding me down and saying those things he unbuttoned my blouse. I was hitting him with my right hand during this time. I kept telling him that I wanted to go back into town, but he didn't pay any attention to me ... at this time he unbuckled his belt and zipped his pants open. He then pulled my skirt up and tried to pull my pants down. He finally got my pants off both legs. He then got on top of me and had intercourse with me for about ten minutes. He then got up and told me to put my pants on.

—Jancita Eagle Deer

The highway stretched for miles, climbing hills and dropping into lake-filled valleys while winding around enough curves to double the distance traveled. They had to slow down to keep from hitting deer savoring early spring, green grass on the pavement's edge, huge eyes reflecting the car lights. They hadn't seen another human since leaving Valentine, Nebraska. Even the lights of an on-coming car might have made her feel not so alone, not so scared. Slumped against the passenger door of the car driven by her onetime boyfriend, she feigned sleep. He would think she had passed out from the booze he had poured into her.

Yeah! Her boyfriend. Once she even thought he would marry her and take care of her daughter. Onetime lover! Now a violent man, he beat her, and kept her away from the people who loved her. She didn't even know who he was, only that he never had been who he said he was.

Maybe they would come up behind a slow-driving farmer in a pickup. She would jump out when he slowed down. Better to die in a ditch trying to get away than wait for what he had planned. When people told her they thought he'd killed his first wife she had felt better, knowing her suspicions weren't crazy after all. Now she couldn't stop thinking about it, and the thought terrified her.

She opened her eyes enough to see, hoping he wouldn't notice and realize that she'd faked passing out. Maybe they were near a town; he would have to slow down. She could jump out and run to a house. But there was only her fear and the dark interrupted by racing moonlight between hurrying clouds. The intermittent sweeps of light made it worse; the endless hills looked like waves on a vast and deserted ocean.

Ever since he picked her up at her brother's house with some story about her daughter's safety, acting weirder than ever, Jancita Eagle Deer couldn't get over the thought that this was it. He meant to get rid of her as he had done with his wife. He had bragged too much about how bad he'd been, trained by the government to be a killer. She knew too much—how he'd sold drugs, stole stuff, and ran prostitutes in Iowa.

People were going to pay him to go on this big tour around the whole country. John Birchers he called them. Paying him to talk about Indians, how bad they were, and how he had fooled them. They wouldn't like it if they learned their new star had made her sleep with other men, beat her, threatened her daughter, and kept her prisoner. He had told so many lies, he needed to get rid of her so he could start over on a new life.

The motor strained, topping a hill higher than the others. She glanced out the window again. Her heart jumped—lights traveled both ways on a highway in front of them. More lights twinkled against the black backdrop. Houses, farms, towns, people. Through the fleeting light, Jancita saw the outline of trees, the moon reflecting on water. She knew it was the Platte River. That meant people. A chance to get away. A place to hide.

At the first opportunity, even if he didn't stop, she was out the door. Anything would be better than staying in the car. Why hadn't he killed her back in the isolated Sand Hills, thrown her into a lake or deep blowout? She fought the terror, she had to get away.

Suddenly, the tires made a different noise. They were on a bridge. Out the side window, she saw the river flowing beneath them. If he would slow down, she could jump over the railing and into the water.

Now they were off the bridge. Jancita felt the car slowing, stopping at the intersection with the other highway. He swore as he braked. She knew if cars had not been coming from both directions he would have blown through the stop sign. He couldn't afford to have police officers stopping them. For what he had in mind, nobody could see her with him.

Slow enough. Fighting terror, fear numbing her fingers, she fumbled for the door handle. Almost frozen in panic, she hoped she could focus enough to pull the latch and fall out of the car. How much booze had he given her? When she got out to run, would she be able to control her body, make her legs work, get away?

Pushing the door open, she realized it didn't matter anymore. No more thinking, no more worrying, just run. She fell through the opening, landing on her head and shoulders, momentum from the car's movement spinning her through broken pavement and gravel down into the grass and weeds of the ditch.

Willing herself, driven by fear and the desire to live, Jancita rolled to her feet and ran sobbing onto the highway, waving at the lights coming toward her. She stumbled and swayed, alcohol coursing through her veins playing havoc with her coordination. She screamed at the top of her voice for the car to pull over, yelling there was a murderer at the stop sign.

Jancita stumbled, caught herself, and raised both hands above her head again, standing directly in the middle of the lane. They had to stop. Why didn't they stop? Disbelief fired through her consciousness. How could this be? They weren't going to stop. Slowed by booze, she threw her body toward the edge of the road, headlights now so bright, so piercing, and so close. She screamed, never feeling the car hit her, never knowing she was free as the impact threw her 145 feet. She did not see her one-time boyfriend turn his car onto the lonely highway and drive toward the lights of town.

Two teenage boys, the seventeen-year-old driver and his sixteen-year-old passenger hit Jancita without trying to stop. There were no skid marks on the highway at the scene of the crash. They drove several miles on to a house before stopping and calling the police. Her death did not even matter enough for the driver to receive a ticket.

Her former in-laws, the Sheldahls, drove from Des Moines, Iowa, to Aurora, Nebraska, to identify her body. She now lies near St. Francis, South Dakota, with a small gray headstone inscribed, "Wife—Mother, Jancita Eagle Deer Sheldahl, 1951–1975."[1]

Fifteen years later, the FBI dispensed of Jancita Eagle Deer, Delphine Crow Dog's stepdaughter, with one cryptic paragraph. "She was the victim of a car/pedestrian accident, and her death was reported as accidental." Since her death occurred off the rez in Nebraska, the agency did not investigate and reported that Jancita "was standing in a lane of traffic at night and was hit by a driver who did not see her."[2]

Jancita's story began in 1967. Fifteen years old, she attended the Rosebud Boarding School in St. Francis, South Dakota. Her folks were victims of alcohol that had claimed so many since Lewis and Clark brought it to her people, so she lived with John Arcoren and his wife twenty miles from school. The Arcorens (friends called him Johnny Cakes) were adopting the strikingly attractive teenager remembered by schoolmate Ida Marshall forty-three years later as a tall, beautiful girl with classic Lakota features.[3] A young wasicu attorney and head of the tribe's legal services program was helping them with the process. Jancita often babysat his children.

Saturday night, January 14, the attorney invited her over for a home-cooked meal with his family in Mission, a small rez town about fifteen miles away. He said he would take her into town after dinner to see if anybody was holding a dance. Bolting down her meal, anxious to get going, Jancita persuaded the attorney to leave early. They pulled up in front of the dance hall a little before eight only to find the doors locked. He asked what she would like to do. When she replied she would like to see a movie, he insisted she drink with him. When she demurred, he turned predator.

Parked on a hill miles from the nearest house, he pushed the lever and reclined her seat, telling her he had been crazy about her since first laying eyes on her. He pulled off her clothes and raped her. During the throes of lust, he asked her to go away with him. "To hell with my wife and my children, I'll divorce them," he uttered. After finishing around ten till nine, he gave her three dollars and asked her not to get him into trouble. He dropped her off in town and told her to walk back to his house later.[4]

Understandably, she never made it back that night. He found her with friends wandering the streets of the small town the next morning. As soon as he took her back to the boarding school she reported the rape, showing a discoloration of the skin on her left breast and a hickey on her neck as proof. She also said her left leg was stiff and sore and that going to the bathroom hurt.[5]

While being questioned by school authorities, warned she could get in trouble for lying, her assailant called to speak with her. When told she was distraught, he thundered into the school, found her alone in an office, and yelled loud enough for school personnel to intervene. He again instructed her not to get him into trouble and increased his payment for her silence.

Unfortunately, school authorities did not take Jancita to the rez doctor until Monday. The doctor told BIA cop Peter Pitchlynn that, "... due to the long period of time that had elapsed before the examination, there was little possibility of there being any evidence discovered."[6]

After Jancita had repeated her story to Pitchlynn, he investigated and recommended charging the attorney. Six weeks later, after taking over the investigation, Special Agent in Charge Richard Held claimed, "... insufficient evidence, allegations were unfounded; we are therefore closing our files on the matter."[7]

The young girl, brave enough to accuse a wasicu attorney of rape, quickly discovered what justice was, and still is, like in Indian Country. Her grades fell; she became despondent and developed an attitude; she didn't care anymore. She began drinking heavily and finally left the Rosebud, afraid of what else the attorney might do to her.[8]

While Jancita was away from the Rosebud, a maelstrom on Pine Ridge drew her out of obscurity and cast her into the national spotlight.

Unwittingly, she became a pawn in the war between the American Indian Movement, the man she accused of rape (then a candidate for South Dakota attorney general), and the Federal Bureau of Investigation.

By 1974, William Janklow, the alleged rapist now called "Wild Bill," had turned his back on the Lakota, riding a reputation as an Indian fighter to a political future.[9] A prosecutor in the South Dakota Attorney General's Office, Janklow had the job of trying Arlette Loud Hawk's aunt, Sarah Bad Heart Bull for rioting in Custer, South Dakota, after her son had died at the hands of Darld Schmitz.

An effective prosecutor, Janklow garnered a sentence of one to five years for Sarah, who, after being choked by a cop with a baton, seems to have been more victim than lawbreaker. One month after the trial ended, Janklow entered the race for attorney general against his boss Kermit Sande. The campaign soon turned into a mudslinging affair and brought Jancita into the fray.

Sande announced in July that he had fired Janklow for betrayal of his office and the state for political gain. Janklow said he had quit, like others from the office, because of low morale and the attorney general's ineptness. From there the war of words heightened, including a charge by Sande that a teenage Janklow had engaged in an "incident" nineteen years earlier that bore some likeness to Jancita's claims, and had earned him a criminal record. Janklow admitted something happened but denied any legal charges. Asked at a news conference if the incident involved rape, he replied, "It didn't go that far. ... It was preliminary to that type of thing."[10]

The candidate for the top legal job in South Dakota did not seem fazed by the accusation and neither did the state's constituency. Janklow remained in the race. Building on his get tough with the Indians reputation, a month before the election, Janklow reportedly said to a friend of Dennis Banks, "The way to solve the AIM problem is to shoot the AIM leaders ... put a bullet in the guy's head and he won't bother you anymore."[11]

Banks, under indictment for his role in the Custer riot, with no love lost for Janklow and fresh from the dismissal of all charges against him for Wounded Knee, decided to expose the Indian fighter. He'd heard Jancita's story several years earlier and talked the Chief Tribal Judge on the Rosebud, Mario Gonzales, into pursuing the alleged rape. Sworn in as a tribal attorney, Banks took the role of lead prosecutor in a case against Janklow.

Since the tribe could not prosecute anyone for rape, Banks wanted Janklow disbarred from the Rosebud Tribal Court. To build his case, he needed the victim's testimony, and no one knew where Jancita was.

Anna Mae Aquash finally located Jancita in Des Moines, Iowa. Banks knew just the person to send after her, keep her safe, and bring her back to the Rosebud: Douglass Durham, the organization's security director.

An ex-cop, claiming to be one-quarter Chippewa and thrown off the Des Moines police force, Durham became an AIM member shortly after visiting occupied Wounded Knee as a reporter and photographer. Discovering a predilection for AIM's work, he became vice-chair of the Des Moines chapter. He advanced quickly through the ranks until Banks appointed him director of security and his right-hand man.

Banks told Anna Mae he'd have Durham secure Jancita for the trial, but she said, "I would feel safer if I took the assignment and went down there to locate her."[12] Anna Mae had not trusted the ex-cop since she and other women saw him dying his brownish-grey hair to a blackened sheen and wearing contacts to color his eyes in Wounded Knee.

Anna Mae secured Jancita's agreement to testify, but after surreptitiously discovering Jancita's location, Durham thrust himself into the plan. When Anna Mae received a call from him telling her of his involvement, she informed Banks, "Guess what! That goddamn bastard, Doug Durham, called me. I don't want anything to do with him. I told you that."[13] She refused to fly with him to Minneapolis, leaving the young woman to fend for herself.

Since her move to Des Moines, Jancita had married a wasicu her own age named Eric Sheldahl and became the mother of a little girl, Annette. Unable to exorcise her demons, she drank heavily. The marriage broke up in 1972, but Jancita remained close to her in-laws. She sobered up and lived with them.

Director of AIM security, a pilot, and accomplished photographer, Durham seemed an impressive find to the young woman from the plains of South Dakota. She became his lover, wooed in part by pictures of her and her daughter snapped earlier when Durham had chanced upon them on the street. He said he took them only because they were such a "pretty pair."[14]

Soon they lived together. Jancita believed she was going to marry the handsome flier and help cure him of leukemia. Durham kept her hidden away while he gathered evidence for the trial. All AIM had to go on was Jancita's word, and they needed more.[15]

With the help of Paula Giese, AIM's legal advisor, Durham found Peter Pitchlynn, the original BIA investigator who agreed to testify that, in a search of Janklow's car, he had found one of Jancita's earrings and her watch with a broken band. The boarding school educators also agreed to tell their stories. To get the ball rolling, Durham arranged for a South Dakota state legislator, who owned a small newspaper in Sioux Falls, to hold a press conference just before the trial, and only eight days before the election for attorney general.

Appearing exhausted, Jancita relayed her story in a weak, frail voice. She told how she often babysat for Janklow's family, but on the night of January 14, as he took her home he drove into the country, stopped the car, tore off her clothes and raped her. "I fought and screamed but it was hopeless, we were in the middle of nowhere. ... He showed me a pistol he kept in his glove compartment and said he'd use it if he had to."[16]

Next up, Pitchlynn described his investigation and said he had believed Jancita at the time and still did. He closed by telling reporters that he had recommended that the U.S. Attorney's Office prosecute Janklow.

There are differences between what newspapers reported Jancita said that day and what she told educators and Pitchlynn seven years earlier. In 1967, she did not mention a gun, and said he was driving her to a dance, not home or back to the boarding school. When questioned why she came forward after seven years, the Lakota woman's explanation, laden with emotion and dignity, maximized her credibility. "I feel that if I can get this out of my system, maybe I can live a little better with myself." To the same question, Pitchlynn simply replied, "I've always been an advocate of law and order."[17]

Janklow immediately called Jancita's story "a complete fabrication." He told reporters, "I have turned the matter over to my attorney and the proper lawsuit will be filed and brought against those who were involved."[18] And he didn't wait to mull it over. His attorney served Barnes, Pitchlynn, and Jancita with summonses at the conference, calling their remarks, "maliciously slanderous."

There is a record that Janklow's attorney played a larger role at the AIM press conference than mentioned in stories carried by the press. Stephen Hendricks, author of *The Unquiet Grave,* had a tape of the conference and related how the lawyer took over the questioning, attacking Jancita's story and her credibility.

He began by telling her that to be raped there had to be penetration and the doctor's report said there was none. He then asked Jancita how it could have been rape. When she replied she had been raped, he again insisted there was no penetration, no marks, and nothing had happened. She said that wasn't true; he replied it was in black and white in hospital reports.

Then he must have thought he was lowering the boom. "Isn't it also true that you showed up on Bill Janklow's doorstep since he's been in Pierre? You've been to his house, you've called him on the telephone?"

Jancita tried to explain that she hadn't been to his house, but had called him. "I figured he would probably do me some good if he would just help me." Perhaps, not a strange thought for a woman whose alleged attacker had once been a legal aid lawyer, who had helped with her adoption, and whose children she babysat. Maybe, she simply supposed he might have a guilty conscious and felt he owed her. While there are several explanations for her behavior, Janklow's attorney continued trying to discredit Jancita and Pitchlynn and prove his client's innocence in front of a jury of the press.

Just before handing them the summonses, he could not hold back: "Somebody's after Bill Janklow's ass," he said. "I've never been so upset in my life, but there's a man out there with a family, with some kids that he's got to explain to in the morning things that were put on the television about him."[19]

As Jancita's story differed in some respects from what she told Pitchlynn in 1967, if reported correctly, the attorney's statements vary from medical evidence and perhaps even ethical practice. The doctor did not examine Jancita, who was fifteen and possibly sexually active, for thirty-six hours. The charge that there was no evidence of penetration was a red herring. Medical science could not prove penetration after that amount of time. And whether or not he examined the medical records is open to speculation. What is not, however, is that without a court order or Jancita's permission, he should not have.

When the trial opened on the Rosebud, even though subpoenaed, neither Janklow nor his attorneys appeared. Prosecutor Banks entered five reasons for disbarment including rape, obstruction of justice, perjury, dereliction of duty, conflict of interest, unprofessional conduct, and conduct unbecoming to an officer of the court.

Jancita agreed to a polygraph. While the examiner could not comment on her truthfulness, his opinion, like her statement at the press conference, revealed the inner demons rape could unleash. "The emotions displayed by this subject when questioned regarding the issue was such that she must be considered unstable at the time."[20]

The court also heard evidence that Janklow had ridden a motorcycle through a residential area on the rez shooting dogs and had committed to helping residents obtain credit but did not follow through.[21]

One of the most damning charges, bolstering Ida Marshall's statements that Janklow didn't like the Lakota, came from another reservation. Robert G. Philbrick tendered a notarized affidavit of an incident that occurred in February 1973 while he served as tribal chair of the Fort Thompson Indian Agency. Tribal officers had arrested Wild Bill and thrown him in the tank for driving while intoxicated—naked from the waist down. Although he did not remember where he left his clothes, Janklow did recall the law about whites in Indian country. "No son of a bitch Indian can arrest me," he said, "as no S.O.B. has jurisdiction over me."

After awaking in the tank the next morning, jailers presented Janklow with shoes, socks, underwear, and pants. Clearly, the Indians did not care to see him nude, even if he didn't mind driving around in that state.[22]

Federal support for Janklow, beginning with the FBI and the U.S. Attorney's Office in 1967, never waivered throughout his trial on the Rosebud or his public career. When presented with a subpoena by Gonzales for the original rape investigation records, the Bureau of Indian Affairs refused to release them. Judge Gonzales immediately found Norman Bear, Acting Agency Special Officer, who had the records, in contempt and jailed him. Just as quickly, U.S. Judge Andrew Bogue, the man who sentenced Sarah Bad Heart Bull, issued a writ of habeas corpus ordering Bear's release.[23]

Mario Gonzales barred the one-time legal services provider from practicing on the Rosebud on October 31, 1974. On November 5, 1974, he signed a warrant for Janklow's apprehension for: (1) assault with intent to commit rape in violation of section 46, and (2) carnal knowledge of a female under sixteen in violation of said section 45 ...[24] The same day, citizens of South Dakota elected Janklow attorney general.

No longer in the spotlight, Jancita remained with Durham. She traveled with him to Arizona for the AIM conference. When she tried to call the Sheldahls from a phone booth, he ripped the phone away and knocked her to the ground. When they arrived in Phoenix, she ran into an apartment shared by two AIM women shouting, "He's an informer! He's an informer!" Right behind her, Durham yelled that that was a serious charge to make and wrestled her outside. Later he blamed the incident on jealousy between women.

Shortly after the trip, she escaped from him and returned to stay with her in-laws, but not for long. He turned up at their door in December with the story that AIM had ordered him to marry an Indian woman before the first of the year, and Jancita was to be his new bride. She called it a phony marriage; he threatened that AIM would take her daughter Annie and raise her on the reservation.[25]

Durham took her to Gresham, Wisconsin, where the Menominee Warrior Society, with AIM's help, occupied the abandoned Alexian Brothers Novitiate. As soon as the Brothers ceded the abbey for one dollar, Dennis Banks and Vernon Bellecourt summoned him back to Des Moines. They showed him an FBI 302 form—documents that agents use to report or summarize an interview—with his signature. His face turned white as he read his name. Stammering, he admitted to spying for the agency, and asked if he was a prisoner or if he could go.

Telling Durham he could leave, Banks said, "Doug, this hurts me right here inside me. I always thought you were my friend." The spy replied,

"Well, what can I say? I work for the FBI. That's my job. That's what I get paid for."[26]

On April 4, 1975, Jancita was staying at her brother Alfred's home south of the Rosebud near Valentine, Nebraska, when a dark-haired man in a dark-colored Chevrolet picked her up and drove away. Alfred saw the man but did not get a clear look and could not identify him. Eight hours later, the coroner's physician in Aurora, Nebraska, examined her body.

Several months later, Paula Giese, AIM's legal advisor, received an anonymous phone call telling her that the license plate on the car that picked Jancita up belonged to Douglass Durham's father—the description also matched his automobile.[27] If Durham was responsible for Jancita's last ride, and there has never been another explanation, few who knew his personal history would have been surprised. The FBI should have checked their informant's credentials and background more carefully.

In 1972, acting as an undercover agent for the Des Moines Police Department investigating a series of thefts from a clothing firm, Durham sold company goods to police officers at fire sale prices. His unauthorized sales brought the force under the scrutiny of a grand jury, resulting in suspensions and censure for the top brass.

The grand jury rebuked the chief for hiring Durham in light of his earlier forced resignation from the department in 1964. At the same time, a story broke that another county had tried and found Durham guilty of larceny while he worked undercover for Des Moines. Only the Iowa Supreme Court's reversal of the conviction on a technicality saved him jail time.[28]

Paula Giese dipped further into his past, uncovering a series of allegations that, if true, makes the FBI's employment of him even more suspect. After clandestine training with the CIA, and some role in the disastrous Bay of Pigs invasion of Cuba, Durham did work as a Des Moines cop. Giese claims he immediately became involved in burglary, prostitution, and taking bribes, "for which he was investigated and reprimanded several times."

He allegedly ran hookers out of the Why Not? Grill in July 1964. After brutally beating his wife, she subsequently died and he was investigated for second-degree murder. According to Giese, a police psychiatrist pronounced him "a violent schizoid 'unfit for office involving public trust,' and recommended committal and treatment at a mental institution." While Durham never saw the inside of a ward, it probably didn't help his cause that five weeks after the death of his wife he married one of the Why Not? women.

Durham also may have been a front for the mafia, smuggling drugs and fencing stolen goods. He once bragged that he headed up the largest criminal organization in the state of Iowa.[29] Douglass Durham died in Las Vegas in 2004 at the age of sixty-six.

***

William Janklow, after one term as attorney general, served sixteen years as the governor of South Dakota, and won the 2002 election to represent the state in the United States Congress. He continually denied raping Jancita, initiating legal action against the media for repeating the allegation. In February 1983, he filed against *Newsweek* over an article entitled, "Dennis Bank's Last Stand," which centered on the rape. The article defamed him, the governor claimed, by asserting he prosecuted Banks in revenge for the Rosebud trial.

The majority of the United States Court of Appeals, Eighth Circuit Court, found against Janklow in 1986. But the judges were also critical of the magazine, stating: "We can agree the story would have been fairer to Janklow and more informative to the reader if the chronology of the rape charge against Janklow and the riot prosecution against Banks had been more fully explained."[30]

On a legal roll in 1983, the governor also filed against Viking Press and Peter Matthiessen over the book, *In the Spirit of Crazy Horse.* This time he went directly after the charges filed in Mario Gonzales' court, asserting there was no truth to any of them, including the rape, and that repetition of the accusations defamed him.

Insisting that he never shot dogs from a motorcycle, suffered an arrest for driving drunk naked from the waist down, or raped Jancita Eagle Deer, Janklow wanted his name cleared. He relied on the examining doctor's deposition to refute the charge of rape, contending that much of Matthiessen's documentation came from two convicts: Russell Means and Dennis Banks. He argued that if Matthiessen had done more research he would have discovered Janklow's innocence.

He also considered a statement that the alleged rape was "speedily smoothed over" by the FBI to be defamatory and took offense at the term "Indian Fighter," calling it a smear on his character and career. The Supreme Court of South Dakota ruled against Janklow in 1990.[31]

While successful in neither suit, passages in court findings drove to the heart of the conundrum surrounding law enforcement on the Pine Ridge. The judges found against the governor in the *Newsweek* case, but even though denying his claim of libel, they inserted a small statement in parentheses recognizing the governor's innocence of assaulting Jancita. Reacting to the charge of rape they penned, "(now acknowledged to be false) that the plaintiff had raped a teenaged Indian girl five years before."[32]

One justice, dissenting against the majority, went even further. "When *Newsweek* ran as a news item this thoroughly discredited fifteen-year-old's claim against the defendant, now governor of South Dakota," the judge argued, "it engaged in journalistic conduct more commonly associated with tabloids like the *National Enquirer* or *Globe*."[33]

The majority opinion in the case against Matthiessen and Viking Press did not deal with the charges of shooting dogs and naked drunk driving. However, a dissenting justice noted, "Derogatory comments about our former governor abound in this book in question and is then spliced with allegations of rape, drunkenness, nudity, and violence." He labeled the statements as "hostile and defamatory remarks."[34]

There are two postscripts to Jancita's story.

On August 23, 1976, Frederick W. Lambrecht sent a letter to the Wagner Public Health Service Hospital in Wagner, South Dakota. He wrote in the process of probating Jancita's estate, "In this regard, I have been furnished an executed affidavit by the decedent's former husband, Eric Scheldahl, wherein he states the decedent was raped on January 13 [sic], 1967, and that as a result, a child was born to the decedent. Mr. Sheldahl states that he does not know the name or whereabouts of the child, but was quite sure it was male."[35]

On August 16, 2003, during his first term in the House of Representatives, William "Wild Bill" Janklow blew through a stop sign and killed motorcyclist Randy Scott. The trial judge kept his driving record of twelve tickets and seven accidents from the jury. Janklow claimed a diabetic reaction had caused confusion, lethargy, and fatigue resulting in the accident. He resigned from the House of Representatives and, convicted of manslaughter, received probation. South Dakota returned his law license two years early on February 16, 2006.[36]

***

As recently as 1968, the Ninth Circuit Court of Appeals upheld a law that imposed a harsher penalty for the rape of a non-Indian woman than an Indian woman, presumably because Congress viewed Native women as immoral and, therefore, unworthy of protection.[37] The law was finally repealed by the 2013 Violence Against Women Act, signed into law by President Obama.

17
The Murder of Shelli Poor Bear

Lipstick Pro: One time we were cruising around five-people deep in a
small sports car on the rez. Shell was driving putting on make-up. I
told her to watch the road and her response was ... "This is how the
pros do it, ReAnn give me some light!" It was time for the lipstick! She
drove and had ReAnn turn the light from the passenger visor mirror
on her as she applied her lipstick ... LIKE THE PROS! She said,
"That's how it's done!" One hand on the wheel, one on the lipstick ...
one eye on the road and one on her mouth ... like the pros, I guess.
She was cool like that. I will always love you and have you in my heart.
　　　　　—*Love,* Mia, Oglala and cousin of Shelli Poor Bear,
　　　　posted on Memory-of.com (Shelli Poor Bear 1979–2005)

L ife on the Pine Ridge is a never-ending struggle for survival, a continu-
ous battle of life against death. For the Black Elk and Poor Bear families, tragedy did not begin with Wally's death, and it did not end with the
discovery of his mutilated body. Eyes tearing, Loren Black Elk described
the murder of his beloved niece, Shelli Poor Bear, her brutalized body
found on the road in an area of Pine Ridge known as Three Moccasin Park.
"She ran over her like a dog and left her to die. She went to jail for a couple
of years, but brags about how she did it and would do it again."[1]

Shelli Poor Bear died on November 3, 2005. That night as the moon
waned, the Milky Way took on more opulence, glittering brightly over
the plains and forests, heightening the dimming light. The galaxy's radi-
ance served a higher purpose than mere visual beauty; the stars brightened
the Trail of Spirits for Shelli's soul. Freed from her earthly fetters, Shelli
followed Wanughi Tachanka, the Milky Way, until she came upon Maya
Owichapaha, the old woman who judges each spirit. With the worthy,
Shelli traveled on the path to the right, reaching unity with Wakan Tanka.

Anpo Wicahpi Yuhapi Win, Woman Born Under the Morning Star,
Shelli Poor Bear died at the age of twenty-six, leaving four children to live
with their aunties. So sweet as a child they called her Sugar, Shelli's family
grieves for her every day. They miss her sense of humor, her gift of cooking,
and the love she brought into their lives.

Shelli Poor Bear (Anpo Wicahpi Yuhapi Win—Woman Born Under the Morning Star),
Annie Poor Bear (Cante Suta Win—Strong Heart Woman), and Babe Poor Bear (Pte
San Win—White Buffalo Calf Woman). One of the last times the sisters were together.
(Photo courtesy of Pte San Win)

A beautiful young woman who wanted to be a teacher, cut down for any reason is a tragedy, but Shelli's murder gives a macabre meaning to the word senseless. Her death is an ode to evil—a tribute to the brutality of existence on the Pine Ridge. Shelli's children have grown up without her, but her love for them lives on, immortalized on the Bahama blue headstone imported from India that marks her grave. It's the stone her children chose and the inscribed words were taken from a note she wrote to them before she died.

To My Children:
I love you first of all. I am glad that you were a part of my life. I will be by your sides forever. I want you to make the most of everything you ever have.

I love each of you always.
Your Mommy.[2]

Shelli's older sister, Pte San Win Poor Bear, sometimes called Babe— a Wakan (Holy Woman)—is haunted by the murder. Almost guiltily she recalls the day it happened; she should have known something bad would happen. "Being Lakota," she said, "funny things happen to us. Like right before someone dies, the family is always together."

Working as a Dean of Students in Rocky Ford, about forty miles from the town of Pine Ridge, she caught an unexpected ride back to town. On the way, she phoned Shelli and asked what was up. "Cooking dinner," Shelli replied. "Lasagna, shrimp, bread, and dessert."

"Have enough for me," Shelli's older sister said, "I'll be there." Shelli laughed and admitted she was making Hamburger Helper for her kids. After eating, the sisters, along with their children and mother, Wilma, sprawled across the bed, laughing, joking, and talking. The family was together.

Suddenly, Shelli was gone. Her older sister later discovered she went outside to call Warren Chord, a family friend who owned a television cable business in Whiteclay—people called him the "Cable Guy." Without saying goodbye, Shelli left with Warren for Rushville, Nebraska. Pte San Win never saw her again. Three months later, she posted on an Internet memorial set up for Shelli, "I am mad. I am hurt. ... How dare you go and put yourself in danger ...? Why didn't you think of your babies? Why didn't you do that?"[3]

Shelli didn't believe she was in danger. She was going out with a friend. There was no reason to be afraid. Yet, shortly after 8:00 a.m. the next morning, nineteen-year-old Sam Nelson found her body on the road as he walked to school.

On July 28, 2006, in a signed Statement of Factual Basis to the United States District Court in Rapid City, Jessica Twiss took sole responsibility for Shelli's death.

> On or about November 3, 2005, near Pine Ridge, while driving a vehicle, Jessica Lou Twiss became involved in an altercation with Shelly Poor Bear, a passenger in the vehicle. During the physical altercation between the two individuals, Twiss forcibly shoved Poor Bear from the vehicle and drove away, running over Poor Bear in the process. After striking Poor Bear with the motor vehicle, Twiss, aware that she had struck Poor Bear, left the scene of the accident without reporting the accident or obtaining necessary medical assistance for Poor Bear, which resulted in the death of Poor Bear. Twiss' actions were committed in a grossly negligent manner with actual knowledge that would reasonably enable her to foresee the peril to which her acts might subject another.[4]

The judge sentenced Jessica to thirty months in prison followed by three years in supervised release and ordered her to pay $4,000 in restitution. Released from jail on June 27, 2008, Jessica had paid most of her debt and her life began getting better. She completed Moral Recognition Therapy (designed to enhance ego, social, moral, and positive behavioral growth) and married Ed Hoof, a young man also on supervised release.

Except for a verbal reprimand for consuming alcohol and the struggle to keep a job to pay the court-ordered compensation, Jessica stayed out of trouble until 2010. Then the wheels started coming off her wagon. On January 1, while she and Ed were drunk and fighting, someone called the cops. Not arrested, but forced to go through yet another alcohol treatment program, Jessica managed to stay straight for a year.

On January 21, 2011, the wheels came completely off. She reported to the police that she had been the victim of an assault by a stranger. She lied. Ed had hurt her in another fight. Three months later she was arrested for driving under the influence. Judge Batty of the United States District Court sentenced her to eleven months beginning July 19, 2011.[5]

According to people who knew them both, Shelli and Jessica had never gotten along. The two young women, rumors attest, fueled by booze, fought over a man while sitting in Chord's truck. According to reservation police, Jessica pushed her out, drove forward, and killed her. Even though she knew Shelli could die, Jessica kept partying.

While she was out of prison, Jessica avoided the rez like the plague, with good reason. Among Shelli's friends and relatives, the rumor spread that Jessica not only admitted her guilt, but relished in it. "Yeah, I killed the bitch and I would do it again," many claim to have heard her say.

But Jessica had admitted her guilt, served her time, and even went back to prison five years later.

While anger toward the convicted murderer remained high on the rez, the case seemed closed. Pte San Win thought so, too. She had gained as much closure as she could find with a letter to the court at Jessica's 2006 sentencing—the Wakan Woman invoked Lakota spirituality to warn Jessica there was more judgment yet to come.

> As Lakota people, we have something that no one but Lakota people can understand and this is Spiritual or Universal Law. Under this law, there is no black and white document that dictates your future, unlike constitutional law when you violate another human being. Under Spiritual Law, you violated the human rights of my sister, which was to live. So, therefore, because of this you have to answer to a higher entity that is far more powerful than the outcome of you going to prison for a mere 21 to 27 months. Please understand that your fate has yet to be determined in the eyes of Universal and Spiritual Law. The most important thing that I don't want you ever to forget is that you could have saved her life. You could have called the ambulance, the police, or anyone. You chose not to. For this, I pray that one day you will be able to understand the Spiritual Law of our people.[6]

Everybody knew Jessica did it—until Shelli came back and said they had it wrong. In the first three years after her death, Shelli often came back, even appearing before her older sister's daughter as the family camped at Bear Butte. "It was a true blessing, and it also showed me that you walk with me and you are guiding me through all this pain and heartache," Pte San Win posted on the memorial site.[7]

The Wakan Woman calls the return of the soul a common belief among the Oglala:

> We really have to think about Shelli and the type of person that she was. Let's think about where she is at right now on the other side. She is happy. She loved her journey home to the other side. She said it was neat. As Lakota people we have that connection, as hard as it is to be Lakota and forgive this traumatic event, it has its perks; the ability to connect with Shelli where she is at. So this is the message that she brought to the Sun Dance last week.

Then Shelli dropped the bombshell. On a visit back to the land of her relatives, she told her older sister that Jessica had not sent her on the Trail of Spirits. She said that someday Pte San Win would speak to her accused killer and learn the truth. Texting to avoid hearing the voice of the woman she thought had killed her little sister, the Wakan Woman began communicating with Jessica.

Expecting to hear Jessica say she did it and would do it again, Pte San Win was surprised to hear the same story as Shelli told her, and she believes her. Jessica didn't kill Shelli, never threw her from a moving pickup, and never ran over her. Instead, three men beat and murdered Shelli. Jessica only took the blame because they threatened to kill her and her children if she did not. Jessica's admission of guilt was an act of self-defense and the time in prison a testimony to the love of her children.

"Three men killed Shelli. They still walk the streets of Pine Ridge. They got away with it." Pte San Win says, lamenting the inability of tribal police and the FBI to bring the culprits to account. Not only does she see them often, the ringleader always flips her the finger in a non-spoken message, "Yeah, we killed your sister, and we can kill you, too."

The Wakan Woman's story of the murder is entirely different from the case the FBI arranged against Jessica. After leaving the family gathering, she says Shelli and Warren proceeded to get drunk in Rushville. At her insistence, Warren drove to the Twiss home to pick up Shelli's longtime friend Joanie, Jessica's older sister. They wanted her to drive back to the rez with them and continue the party. Joanie wasn't home, so Jessica invited herself along.

Warren didn't make it. About eight miles south of Whiteclay, the Nebraska Highway Patrol arrested him for driving under the influence. The officer took Warren to jail, and because Shelli was obviously inebriated, the cop turned the truck over to Jessica. The two women stopped in Whiteclay, bought beer and met three men who were in a small black car. After making plans to drink together, Jessica and Shelli followed the men to Three Moccasin Park, a pretty little site of woods, a meandering stream, and grassy pasture between Whiteclay and Pine Ridge.

The police assume Shelli died around midnight at the place where Sam Nelson found her body—roughly one hundred yards off the highway. Pte San Win says they have it wrong, citing evidence that both cars drove farther into the park, over a ridge, and down along the creek. She says the Nelson family, who lives at the end of a drive branching off from the intersection where the body lay, a distance of less than seventy-five yards, was outside most of the night Shelli died. According to her, they heard nothing and never saw the drinkers parked at the intersection. Surely, she says, they would have noticed two cars with the motors running on a cold night.

A woman who lives as much as a mile from the Nelson's house along the northwest border of the park told Wilma, Shelli's mother, that on the night of the murder she heard a woman screaming, "Help, they're killing

A cross marks the place in Three Moccasin Park where Shelli Poor Bear's body was discovered. (Photo courtesy of Pte San Win)

me." She wasn't the only person to hear Shelli that night. Orville Oldson who lives next to Wilma insists that Shelli called him around 2:30 a.m. trying to score some cocaine.

A search of the area west of where the body lay, closer to where Pte San Win says they parked, turned up Shelli's charm bracelet and lip gloss. All of this, plus the visit from Shelli and what Jessica told her, causes her to believe the three males killed her sister, although she doesn't know why they killed her.

Why did Jessica go to jail and not the three men? Pte San Win says the feds blew it. "Just two drunk Indians fighting and one dying," is her depiction of the official response. The FBI never contacted any of the people who could have given evidence to the contrary; they simply wrote it up to drunken Indians and closed the case.[8]

If she had not suspected the bureau's laissez faire reaction before, the agent in charge of the investigation convinced her. Several years earlier, Pte San Win left Jason, her children's father and significant other at the time and, as happens with such matters, emotions ran raw. Now, not knowing where else to turn and needing answers about the investigation into Shelli's death, she asked her former spouse, Jason, a tribal police officer and graduate of the renowned federal school for police officers, to go with her to Rapid City to meet with the FBI.

When they entered the office, she came face to face with an agent she'd met when she and Jason had their problems. He recognized them, and asked Jason why he would be back with such a woman. Ignoring the barb, she asked about how Shelli died. She was shocked when the agent responded with anger, yelling he had worked on the rez for fifteen years and was tired of the f*cking Indians questioning his integrity.

Pte San Win resolved that he would not see her cry, a wasicu would not break her. She steeled herself and asked for written reports on the investigation. The agent threw them at her, again yelling the same vulgarity, angry with Indians accusing the bureau of prejudice. Asking for Shelli's personal effects brought even more abuse. He threw them at her, lacing the air with more profanity. Without tears, even though she hugged the articles her little sister last carried, she left the offices of the FBI knowing they would look no further into the case.

Pte San Win didn't cry, but Shelli's death and what she calls the botched investigation forever changed her life. She realized that life was no longer about her, it was about children growing up on the rez, about the Lakota culture she needed to cherish and nurture. Now she is a Sister of the Knife, a group of women who carry razor sharp knives with antler handles, pledged to prevent rape and child molestation. While they would use the knives in self-defense or to prevent an assault, the Sisters keep them as a symbol of their call for a return to the old ways. They want rapists and abusers marked with a scar beginning at the bridge of the nose, following under the eye, and curving downward along the ear. With that mark, much like wasicu sex offender lists and pictures, the people would know who among them was guilty.

Pte San Win has become an activist. She protests mining and pollution, including the Canadian pipeline once designed to cross the rez, and wasicu oppression of her people. She says the whites feared the Oglala when they rubbed out Custer and that they will learn to heed them again.

She is not the only member of her family changed by Shelli's death. "It killed my father," Pte San Win says. "He couldn't handle it, couldn't live with it." She tried to nurse him, but her ministrations were no use. Webster Poor Bear, the terror of the Viet Cong, who took scalps in the manner of his forebears, wounded in Southeast Asia and Wounded Knee, died four years after Shelli's murder of alcoholic hepatitis. "He drank to forget her death," she says.[9]

Shelli's younger sister, Annie, still rages at the injustice of her death, taking it on herself to work over all Twiss family members she comes across.

The stone chosen by her children marks the final resting place of Shelli Poor Bear. (Photo courtesy of Pte San Win)

Shelli's friend, Joanie, told Pte San Win she also grieves that she lost her best friend and didn't deserve to be beaten by Annie.

Word is out on the rez for Jessica—come back and you will never leave again. Not because of Pte San Win, who tries to spread the word that Jessica is innocent, but because the irrepressible Shelli had so many friends.

> One time I was sitting on my mom's couch and Shelli was walking by sexier than ever, wearing a pretty summer dress, hair all done up, looking beautiful as ever …. so there I was sitting there looking at her as she walked by and thinking … I was thinking damn Shelli is beautiful and pretty damn sexy. At that very moment when I was thinking she let out this HALACIOUS cough, all loud and disgusting. Her arms and one leg flew out in front of her. I even jumped in my seat. I said, "Holy shit Shelli, you were looking sexy until you coughed!" Then we both sat there and laughed. She was nuts like that … always doing something crazy … I love you & miss you forever sis … Love Babe[10]

LeShell Poor Bear, Shelli's oldest daughter, models her senior prom dress. Her mother would have been so proud.

18

The Abused Life of Jolene Black Elk

*South Dakota reported 445 forcible rapes, which doesn't include
statutory rapes, in 2009, according to FBI statistics. The state's rates
appear high compared to the 225 rapes reported in North Dakota in
2009 and the 185 in Wyoming.*

*The rates of prosecution of rapes in this country are horrendous
to begin with, and in Indian Country they're far worse.*

—*Lynn Taylor Rick*, "Rape on the Reservation: Criminal
Convictions Tough to Come By in Indian Country,"
Rapid City Journal, November 2, 2010

The Black Elk family lived in a collection of trailers haphazardly placed along the Little White River east of the town of Pine Ridge. The compound surrounded the cabin where their parents lived. The Lakota have always lived in extended family groups. During their days of plains dominance, social order required warrior ancestors to marry outside of their village due to the camps' close degrees of sanguinity.[1]

Ben Black Elk and Marla Under Baggage (named for an ancestor who hid from enemies under a travois laden with robes and family supplies as a child), occupy a trailer recently moved to the site.[2] Forced from their home when a distant relative moved into the trailer they had rented from Ben's sister, they spent the summer of 2010 finding another. Luckily, Ben's adopted brother, Randall, had an old one out on the prairie. The couple paid two hundred dollars for it. Like the others in the compound, it was of indiscriminate age and quality.

Ben, Marla, and their three-year-old daughter, Baby Iva, lived that summer in the back of Ben's old pickup. Cooking and eating with relatives during the day, they slept under the stars at night sprawled on blankets amid household goods piled into the back of the truck.

They moved the newly acquired mobile home to the site, bringing along thousands of angry yellow jackets that had made it their home. Ben installed a wood stove, their only source of heat, while Marla cooked over hot plates and electric skillets. They had no running water and, like the others, had never lived in a rez home with a working sewage system.

Just recovering from open-heart surgery when they moved, Ben could do little work. Marla cleaned and repaired the well-used trailer while holding the little girl in one arm, putting her down only to swat another wasp. Marla also brought home the bacon by working at

Marla Under Baggage holding Baby Iva and cleaning the new trailer she and Ben Black Elk moved to after living in a pickup one summer.

Sioux Nation, a grocery and general store. Sometimes Ben raised pups and sold them for pets or ceremonies.

Loren Black Elk stayed with whatever relative put him up, mostly Tom or Ben. A victim of Whiteclay, he was declining from liver failure. Clifford, Owen, and Iva also lived in the compound. Owen stayed with Iva; she worked for the tribe and lived in their parent's house.

"It's hard," Ben said, adding wood to the stove while Marla worked in the kitchen, and Baby Iva played with the newest puppy. Outside, the January (Moon of Popping Trees) wind howled through the trees. "We were lucky to get this trailer. If we didn't find it, I guess we would've stayed with family this winter, if anybody had room."

Even considering their hardships, Ben's open-heart surgery, Loren's liver failure, Owen's inability to find a job, and the host of friends and family lost to Whiteclay, they consider themselves to be the lucky ones. With homes to live in, commodities, welfare payments, and relatives with jobs, they have survived, and they have one another.

They all wish Wally's daughter, Jolene, would visit more often. Maybe she could get a job, or get married, or move in with the rest of the family. But when they spoke of her, hurt and anger colored their voices. "She's just a Whiteclay girl. Always hanging around over there," Ben said.

"Jolene's always drunk," Marla mutters as she dresses Baby Iva. "Her uncles are really mad at her. She should straighten up and come home, we could help her."

"You know," Ben lights another cigarette, careful to blow the smoke away from the little girl, "I always wonder if the family of the man Jolene killed could have murdered her dad. Maybe they killed Wally out of vengeance. It's happened around here before."[3]

Jolene isn't likely to take them up on their invitation to move home anytime soon. She is an outsider, purposely staying away. For her, it is better this way. She stays with friends, women that let her alone and protect her. That she might have been responsible for her father's death never leaves her thoughts.

Even for a land of tragedy where stories of death, disease, and even murder abound, Jolene has consistently drawn the low card. Just after her birth, her mother, Bonita, and Wally split up over Bonita's drinking. Determined not to have her raised by an alcoholic, Wally gave Jolene to his parents to raise. Jolene did not really know her father until he took her to Rapid City to live with him when she had just turned thirteen. It was there that evil first touched her.

One night while sleeping on the couch, Jolene awakened to a hand pressed over her mouth while another savagely groped between her legs and ripped off her underwear. She struggled, fought, and kicked, but it was no use. The man, maybe a boyfriend of Wally's ex-wife from Montana, was too strong. He raped her. As he finished, she pushed him onto the floor and ran into her room. Petrified he would follow but thinking clearly, she stuck butter knives into the door's hinges, locking him out. Her screams and cries brought her father rushing from his bedroom.

As Wally ran into the room, Uncle Loren came in through the front door after a night on the town. Hearing her screams, they saw immediately what had happened and chased her attacker out of the apartment. She doesn't know if they ever caught him or what they did to him. They never spoke of him again.

Jolene soon succumbed to alcohol, joining friends drinking themselves into oblivion. One night when she was sixteen and passed out on the bed along with her mother and auntie, it happened again. As a younger cousin watched, too frightened to scream or move, Jolene's boyfriend's brother and cousin crawled through the bedroom window. Jolene awakened just as they were sneaking out after they had finished. They had cut away her shorts and panties and raped her.

Jolene roused her mother and aunt. The three women rushed to the hospital. The examination proved rape, and the police were called. One of her attackers spent the night in jail, the other never saw the inside of a police station. There were no arrests, no charges. Jolene doesn't know why, except to say, "You know, sometimes evidence just disappears. Especially if it is drunk Indians raping another drunk Indian."

Life continued in a downward spiral for Jolene. At nineteen, she shared an apartment with her mother and aunt. They made it real nice for her—she had her own room, decorated as she wanted it.

One day, friends in the apartment complex threw a big party and Jolene, her mother, her aunt, and her aunt's boyfriend, a Brule from the Rosebud named Iron Shell, attended. After a couple of hours, Jolene stumbled home alone and passed out on a mattress on the living room floor. She awakened to find her aunt standing over her, shouting. Naked from the waist down, she saw Iron Shell also without any pants on cowering behind her aunt. She had been raped for a third time.

Sick from the booze and humiliated, her auntie made her feel even worse. She scolded Jolene, screaming that if she hadn't dressed so sexy, acted so wantonly, poor Iron Shell could have resisted temptation.

Angry, hurt physically and emotionally, Jolene returned to the party. Several hours later, her aunt, forgiving her for enticing Iron Shell, asked her to run back to the apartment. She had lost her key and wanted to make sure they weren't robbed. Jolene should find the key, Auntie said, lock the door, and come back to the party.

On entering the apartment, Jolene saw her rapist passed out cold on the same mattress where he had assaulted her. She had been drinking again and wasn't thinking clearly—rage and pain took control. She wanted revenge. Jolene looked around the room for anything to use as a weapon, wanting Iron Shell to feel her pain and humiliation. Her eyes landed on her diabetic aunt's insulin vials and hypodermic needle.

Jolene claims she didn't know what would happen. She figured an injection would make him sick, and she knew how to give shots from helping her aunt. She found it easy to inject the drunken, passed out Iron Shell in the buttocks—more than once. Hoping he would be sick for a long time, she returned to the party.

"My baby's dying. My baby's dying," Jolene's aunt yelled hysterically, running back into the party shortly after she had left for home. Jolene thought she meant her daughter, Jolene's cousin; Jolene couldn't imagine her auntie calling the rapist Iron Shell her baby. Wally, also at the party, raced to the apartment, saw the stricken Iron Shell and started performing CPR. His efforts futile, he told Jolene she'd better hide on the rez. That was the last time she saw her dad alive.

The feds arrested Jolene in Kyle, South Dakota, on May 2, 1997. For five months she had lived in fear, knowing the cops would come one day. She thought, and still believed, she didn't deserve to go to jail, but the Pennington County district attorney said she had acted as judge, jury, and executioner. He charged her with murder and asked for a sentence of ten to twenty-five years.

She is grateful to the judge who listened to her story of repeated assault. He told her he thought she'd been through enough and sentenced her to only three years. She went to jail pregnant. The father was a man she had met while hiding on the rez.

One of the first of her fellow prisoners she met was a woman named Iron Shell, a cousin of the man she had injected. Iron Shell was serving a life sentence for killing her baby after the father left her. She swore to kill Jolene. But male relatives of Jolene's in the men's prison saved her life when they put out the word to leave her alone. Soon, other inmates protected Jolene. The Iron Shell woman was never able to gain any converts to her cause since prisoners shun baby killers.

Jolene left prison on July 26, 1999, the same day Darlene Red Star found Jolene's father's brutalized body along the highway. She found out about his death the next day when her uncles Loren and Ben came to Rapid City to take her back to the Pine Ridge.

After the funeral, Jolene married, quit wandering, and settled down to raise a family. She still believed in romance and marriage, and she wanted more children. She had given the child she bore in prison up for adoption to a good home in North Carolina.

She fell in love with the son of the leader of the Wounded Knee occupation GOONs. They met on supervised release. With a weak smile, almost a grimace, she says she should have known better than to take up with him—he had been incarcerated for trying to scalp his previous girlfriend with a chainsaw.

She stayed with him for four years and two more children, claiming she suffered through made-for-Hollywood-TV abuse. He didn't just beat her, one time he kicked her so hard the bones in her ankle had to be pinned. Her forehead carries two parallel scars from the time he clenched down with his teeth and almost tore out a mouthful of flesh. The injury that still gives her the most pain is the broken tailbone from when he threw her down a flight of stairs.

Their marriage ended in an argument over her mother Bonita's White-clay life. They were both drunk. Jolene says her husband lost it, picked up a kitchen knife, and thrust it into her throat. She bears a large scar just to the left of the center line; fortunately the blade went straight in, barely missing her jugular and esophagus.[4]

With blood covering her throat and chest, Jolene crawled to the back porch to get away. That is the last she remembers for three days until she woke up in a Rapid City hospital. Rushed by helicopter, the surgery to save her life lasted more than twelve hours.

Her husband had saved her life by running to the neighbors, sobbing he had killed her. He went back to prison for five years. Jolene's children live with his parents, whom she respects and cares for, and says they are doing a great job of raising her children. She calls or visits them every day.

Jolene spends a lot of time in Whiteclay, just as her uncles said. An article titled, "On the Bootleggers' Trail in Indian Country," published in the fall of 2010, told of her stabbing.[5] After three assaults and a violent marriage, she didn't like men. She could not trust them.

She agrees with her Uncle Ben that it might have been the relatives of the man she killed who murdered her father, so she stays away from her family. She doesn't want the harm she caused to plague any more of her relatives.

There is another reason she doesn't live in the Black Elk compound. Her uncles were associated with the American Indian Movement. She said they had a hard time with the relationship she had with her ex-husband's parents. When her children were young and playing with cousins, she had to live with remarks such as, "Look at the little goons." Or, "A whole bunch of little goons here." Those still hurt, she says.

Jolene Black Elk is a tough woman; she has to be. She is a wanderer, just as her father was. What does the future hold? She can only say she tried the marriage and family thing, and it didn't work out so well. As for Wally, Jolene hasn't cried for him yet. Someday, she says, but not yet. Maybe it is just too difficult to cry for any man, even her father.[6]

Oglala women are still noted for their beautiful star quilts. This one hangs above the chapel where Iva Lynn Roy got married in 2014.

19
The Bones of Dan Titus

Out of the Indian approach to life there came a great freedom, an intense and absorbing respect for life, enriching faith in a Supreme Power, and principals of truth, honesty, generosity, equity, and brotherhood as a guide to mundane relations.

        —*Heȟáka Sápa (Black Elk)*, Holy Man of the Lakota

Dan Titus left behind a broken family when he went missing on February 28, 1998. His daughters, Monica and Carrie, believe that, Mary, the woman he lived with, killed him. Mary says that while she would stand toe-to-toe with him, she would never have hurt him. After moving to Nebraska to be near relatives after his disappearance, she had to read about his funeral in the *Rapid City Journal.* Nobody let her know that hunters had found his sun-bleached bones nine years later.

Cousins of the Black Elks and Poor Bears, Monica and Carrie have never stopped grieving the mysterious loss of their father. They met in Carrie's trailer in Pine Ridge, wincing as the stiff breeze rattled the walls. Sunlight peeked through the tin shack's worn, discolored paneling. The trailer rocked precipitately from side to side, joints holding the walls to the floors and ceiling long before surrendering to the harsh winds of South Dakota.

Sparsely furnished, blankets covered the open windows and plywood propped over the entrance served as a door. "I don't know what this will be like in the winter," Carrie says of her house that had no central heating. "I just moved in this summer. I guess the kids and I will cuddle under a stack of covers during the cold weather." If she could afford them, she would buy a couple of space heaters. Resigned to the harsh life on the rez, she adds, "If you have a place to live, you had better keep it."

Dan was a good and decent man, according to his daughters. A cowboy and a member of AIM, he had many friends. He was a traveling man, though, and never stayed in one place too long. They hoped for the best and feared the worst all the time they looked for him, wanting to believe he had just wandered off, hoping he would turn up again. But they also knew it wasn't like him to leave his friends or his family for that long. "Besides," Monica says, "he really loved his grandchildren."

During the winter of 1998, Dan often visited Monica while she was in a treatment center for alcoholism. Around the end of February, already concerned because she hadn't seen him for several weeks, Mary surprised her by visiting and asking if Dan had been around. When asked why, Mary told her that Dan had disappeared one night, and there had been no sign of him since. Monica began to worry—disappearing for a while on the rez is common, but Dan seemed to have been gone quite a while.

Owen Black Elk, Wally Black Elk's youngest brother, is also a cousin of Carrie and Monica Titus.

Monica and Carrie reported his disappearance to the police who, according to Monica, "didn't do one damn thing" to look for him. The cops figured he had walked out of the relationship with Mary and just hadn't told the girls. Without official help, they took it upon themselves to organize foot and horseback patrols; they had twenty-seven riders searching pastures and riverbanks near the house.

When Dan did not turn up, Monica and Carrie broadened the hunt for him. Still in treatment, Monica moved to Rapid City and organized an electronic search. She called, mailed, and messaged treatment centers, hospitals, and missions around the area. Back in Pine Ridge, Carrie passed out cards, hung posters, and tacked notices to poles and bulletin boards urging anyone with any information to come forward.

In the fall of 2009, two men on four-wheelers hunting whitetail deer along the river near the house found Dan's bleached bones covered by remnants of clothes, his wallet still in his back pocket. The mystery deepened for Monica and Carrie, however, when they considered the location of his bones. "We searched there," Carrie exclaims, "and they weren't there a couple of months after he disappeared." They insist the killer moved his body after they quit searching.

Monica and Carrie believe Mary murdered Dan. They remember her as crazy, under psychiatric care, and taking too many pills long before she ever hooked up with their father. Carrie stayed with them for a while when she had a baby and recalls Mary acting okay until she ran out of pills. "Then she went crazy. Her hair messed up and sticking out, she sat in her room for hours, rocking back and forth in a catatonic state." They never knew her to act violently, but said she often told Dan, "If you ever leave me, I will kill you." They believed that is what he tried to do, and she carried out her threat.

They also consider the possibility that Mary simply ran out of pills, lost her mind, and killed him in a fit of insanity. Whatever her motivation, they concede she must have retained some of her wits because she had to have moved his body after she hid it the first time.[1]

Dan's nephew, Don, an Oglala resident, agrees with his cousins. "I believe she was responsible for his death," he said. "She was all the time giving him pain pills, kept him real high. She carried around a big bag of them." In a strange twist on the story, he believes scavengers found Dan's bones under the floor of the house where he had lived with Mary.[2]

***

Mary can recall the number of years, months, and days since the man she loved disappeared; her story cannot be more different than the one told by Dan's daughters. She says their relationship began while they were both on supervised release from the Nebraska penitentiary. Wanting a fresh start, they moved to the Pine Ridge not far from the White River, near the small settlement of Oglala. They had a real house with stucco walls, not one of the widespread, worse-for-wear trailers dotting the plains.

She remembers the problem began on the night of February 27, 1998. An alcoholic, Dan was trying to dry himself out, "and had the D.T.'s something terrible." He didn't know who she was, where he was, or even who he was. He became belligerent and agitated, thrashed out and broke a lamp. Exhausted when she finally had him calmed, she took a sleeping pill and climbed into bed.

Mary woke up alone early the next morning; it was still dark and the house was freezing. She called for Dan to build a fire and come back to bed. When he didn't answer, she crawled out from under the warm covers and went to see what he was doing. She found she was alone; cold winter wind blowing through the open door.

"Oh shit! What has he gone and done now," she remembers as her initial reaction. But she wasn't really worried. Dan often went on drinking binges, disappearing for a day or two, usually staying with his brother. Maybe he had even gone into Pine Ridge or was hanging out in Whiteclay drinking beer. Maybe he'd stopped at one of his kid's places in town.

She shut the door, started a fire and went back to bed. After Dan had failed to appear within a couple of days, she became very concerned and drove over to his brother's house and asked if he knew where Dan was. The reply baffled her. "He's gone and doesn't want to see you." She asked again and received the same response.

Mary didn't believe Dan was hiding from her, so she went to the tribal police to report his disappearance. Her spirits lifted soon after when they called and said they had found him walking along the road out to the Lone Wolf School on his way to see his girlfriend. "The cops didn't know the difference between him at forty-eight and his son," Mary said.

Agreeing with Carrie and Monica, Mary says the cops "just pissed it off." They never did anything else, and she never heard from them again. The subject of law enforcement on Pine Ridge still rankles her. "The only thing they do is harass people."

Mary recalls vividly one day when she and Dan were in Pine Ridge doing their laundry and shopping and then drove over to Whiteclay. Dan had to pee; she calls him the "pissingist" man she ever knew, and stopped on a dirt road on the west side of Whiteclay to do his business.

While he was in the trees, Mary busied herself sweeping mud out of the floorboards of the truck. Suddenly, a Nebraska cop pulled up, asked what she was doing, and if he could search the vehicle. She told him to go ahead, he wouldn't find anything, but to be careful not to get her clean laundry dirty. He searched and messed up her freshly washed clothes. Unhappy not to find anything illegal, he gave her a ticket for littering. She took it into the Rushville sheriff's office and left it there, telling whoever was around that she would never pay it.

With no help from the cops, Mary searched for him alone. Going through the house looking for any evidence of what might have happened, she found a bottle of aftershave she had just purchased for him. "It was empty. He drank it all before he left."

Mary knew Dan had made it down their lane to the intersection with the main road; she found his soda can there. But when she pictures him swallowing aftershave, drunk, spaced-out, and stumbling down the road, she doubts her own story. Shorty, Dan's dog, went everywhere with him. Yet, the morning he disappeared Shorty was in the house, even with the front door open. She doesn't believe it possible he wouldn't have gone with Dan.

She can think of only one possible explanation. A resident of Pine Ridge, a man the FBI questioned when Ron and Wally were murdered, told her, "I put him in so deep nobody will ever find him." Perhaps someone from law enforcement spoke with him about Dan, but Mary doubts it.

Mary claims that she arranged the search parties; getting horses from a man named Waters, and does not remember Monica and Carrie as being there or having much interest. She rode on horseback with Russell and

Kenneth Loud Hawk, Arlette's brother and father. Following the Lakota tradition of hospitality, they kept telling her that if they didn't find Dan, she could always live with them.

As for her mental illness, Mary claims to suffer from anxiety and post-traumatic stress disorder caused by living with her soldier husband in Germany during the violence of the Black September Movement and the Bieder-Mienhoff Gang. She drove to her job on the base, forced to search under her car for bombs since the soldiers at the gate refused to help her. The resulting fear and worry caused her emotional issues.

Mary says she is the only Irish-Catholic democrat in the part of Nebraska where she has lived since Dan died. Latoya Marshall, Lakota and Dan's niece, lives with her and has since her mother died. And Latoya's older sister did until she married and moved to another part of the state. Mary says she will never get over Dan's loss.[3]

Monica and Carrie admit the BIA could send Dan's bones to a lab and discover the specific cause of death, but that would take several years. He was gone from them too long already, they say. Dan's family buried him in the Catholic cemetery on Pine Ridge.

"Now why did they do that?" Mary asked. She says he was an Episcopalian and wanted to be buried in their cemetery next to his brother. And why did they say in the obituary that he was sixty-one? He was forty-eight when he went missing and would have only been fifty-seven when they found the bones.

About Dan, the FBI responded succinctly to a Freedom Of Information Act Request: Based on the information you provided, we conducted a search of the Central Records System. We were unable to identify main file records responsive to the FOIA.[4]

20

Sweet White Root Medicine

*In 1868, men came out and brought papers. We could not read them
and they did not tell us truly what was in them. We thought the treaty
was to remove the forts and for us to cease from fighting. But they
wanted to send us traders on the Missouri, but we wanted traders where
we were. When I reached Washington, the Great Father explained to
me that the interpreters had deceived me. All I want is right and just.*
 —Mahpiya Luta (Red Cloud), April 1870

During the heat of battle, Oglala warriors braved arrows and bullets, galloping into enemy ranks and striking opponents with feathered, painted staves. Counting coup—touching a man trying to kill you and living to tell about it—was more prestigious than killing an enemy.

Oglala have counted coup on the wasicu since the two cultures collided. Captain Fetterman bragged that he could ride through the entire Lakota nation with eighty men. Red Cloud and American Horse showed him the error of his ways. Crazy Horse and Sitting Bull did the same for Custer. Fourteen years later, the 7th Cavalry avenged their comrades by massacring Big Foot's Band, and no other action so stains the fabric of the American Armed Forces.

In 2011, Alex White Plume was still counting coup. A former soldier who guarded Rudolph Hess at the Spandau prison in Berlin, and a member of the Crazy Horse Band, White Plume emulates his ancestors. He yearns for the Oglala's return to the old ways. On many days, he holds court in the screened outdoor kitchen and living room he built near his house, teaching Lakota spirituality and wisdom.

The second highest-ranking traditional leader of the Oglala and assistant to Una's uncle, Chief Oliver Red Cloud, Alex is his people's best hope for a cultural renaissance. He sees going back to the old ways as their only hope for progressing to a brighter future. "It is in the blood," he says, pointing at his herd of more than seventy horses climbing a pine-covered ridge. "Our blood is different, we are different. It carries our culture and traditions. We cannot live like the white men. We do not thrive."

Alex explains that individual Lakota are subordinate to the group. "The

Alex White Plume raises and races horses. The love of the Lakota and horses can be found in the bands that run wild on the Pine Ridge. This group was photographed on Una Horn Cloud's land.

tiospaye, the extended family, is supreme. We are not a tribe. That was the Germans, Irish, and French in Europe. We have rejected that word. We are clans, family groups."

The White Plume family is configured along matrilineal lines. Men in council make decisions, but women control the household as heads of the family. The arrangement, he says, had broken the cycles of alcohol and spousal abuse in their tiospaye.

Alex's voice takes an edge when speaking of Americans and capitalism. "They need to know their history because today everyone is stuck in the rut of capitalism. They don't worry about their relatives. They don't worry about themselves, they just worry about how much money they can make, and they take, take, take from the earth, and they never give anything back."[1]

As had other Lakota, he chooses poverty over materialism, living with the land instead of working at jobs and industries that despoil the earth. "The Lakota are givers; we give everything we have away every year, never take more than we need. We need to educate all of America about the horrible things they are doing to our lands, our sacred sites, our grasslands."

He believes that returning to the traditional rule of chiefs, pre-Collier's IRA government, would end the turmoil that plagues the Oglala and thinks his people should also abandon the colonist's language. "I came to the realization that we created all these problems by using the English language because that's a general rule of thumb; now we're trying to solve the problems using the same language, and it's not working."[2]

Native American struggles with European ego-centrism, Alex teaches, go back to the 1493 Papal Bull issued by Pope Alexander VI, which labeled

Indians as members of barbarous nations. The edict commanded the subjugation of indigenous peoples who should be "brought to the faith itself."[3]

Known as the Doctrine of Discovery, the Bull gave Europeans the right to claim Indian lands and dispossess the original inhabitants. According to Alex, the Pope gave Christians the moral imperative to enslave and murder more than sixty million Native Americans—the church's failure to repeal the order sticks in his throat.[4]

For Alex and other traditionals, restoring their 1851 and 1868 Treaty rights secured in war by their grandfathers had to accompany restoring the old ways. "We are still being mistreated because of what we did to Custer at the Little Big Horn. A lot of our people don't choose to be alcoholics. A lot of them are just stuck in the suppression so bad they wish for another way out. They don't want to come back to this pain, the shame of not being able to provide."[5]

A warrior-philosopher, Alex stands in the front ranks of the fight for treaty rights. Characteristic of old-time warrior chiefs, he did not seek leadership—the mantle was thrust upon his shoulders. Setting out to follow the 1868 Treaty, which encouraged the Lakota to become agriculturalists, he has become America's most embattled hemp farmer.

He fights for industrial hemp cultivation on the Pine Ridge, an initiative that many thought would lead the Oglala to economic recovery. Industrial hemp, wahupta ska pejuta, "sweet white root medicine," perhaps the most complete food source and the strongest natural fiber on earth, grows generously on the rez, needs little water and nurturing, and is kind to the earth.[6]

Joe American Horse, grandson of a famous warrior, sweat lodge leader, former tribal president, and one-time Olympics hopeful took the lead to se-

Lupe Esparza, a native of Mexico, has lived on the reservation for more than forty years. He was married to Sandy Sauser until they divorced several years before her death.

cure hemp as the Oglala's cash crop. Because of his work, the Oglala Tribal Council legalized the cultivation of *Cannabis sativa L*, hemp with a chemical make-up of less than 1 percent tetrahydrocannabinol, the psychoactive ingredient in marijuana. The tribe continues to ban cannabis with a THC concentration of more than 1 percent.[7]

Alex believes wahupta ska pejuta could feed men and animals while decreasing American dependence on foreign oil and easing the strain on world forests. Uses for the sweet, white root include food, cosmetics, paints, varnishes, clothing, canvas, and medicinal treatments for arthritis and premenstrual syndrome, as well as papermaking, plastics, and glass-reinforced auto bodies.[8] The original Levis jeans were hemp canvas; Thomas Jefferson and George Washington grew it. Ben Franklin owned a mill that made hemp paper, and our founding fathers wrote the Declaration of Independence on hemp.[9]

During World War II when the Japanese cut off exports of Manila hemp, the Department of Agriculture promoted the "Hemp for Victory" campaign, placing almost one million acres under cultivation. After researching the ubiquitous crop, everything about industrial hemp agriculture seemed right for the Lakota and America.

Alex's tiospaye planted their first crop of 68,000 plants in 2000, investing $9,000 in seeds. That same year the Slim Buttes Association (Joe Amerian Horse was a member and Sandy Sauser the secretary) put in a crop. Five months later, two weeks before harvest, Alex's family sent invitations to dignitaries in Washington D.C., Nebraska, and South Dakota to come and watch. The tiospaye had nothing to hide and an economic resurgence to celebrate.

Alex sipped coffee in his kitchen four days before the harvest, enjoying the tranquility of the forest in the predawn hours. Suddenly, the tightly wound engines of helicopters and light aircraft abraded the hills and canyons. Through the window he watched the dust cloud raised by a convoy heading toward his field. Jumping into his old pickup, he raced to his crop, sliding to a stop in four inches of powdery dirt on the road. Reminiscent of the cavalry's early morning raids on unsuspecting villages, thirty-six black-clad, heavily armed drug enforcement agents, FBI agents, and federal marshals surrounded him.

An agent ran through the swirling dust yelling, "Halt. Halt."

When Alex rolled down the window and asked, "What do you think you're doing?" the fed raised his fully automatic rifle and pointed it directly at him.

Ignoring their weapons, Alex tried to get past the agents to protect his precious plants, his evasive maneuvers causing his sister to remark, "I didn't know you could dance like that."

He was no match for so many armed men. Employing weed-whackers, they cleared his entire crop in forty-five minutes, allegedly costing American taxpayers over $200,000.[10]

Government officials—still mistreating his people because of Custer according to Alex—had not ignored the family's invitation to the harvesting ceremony; they just did not think the Oglala Tribal Council had any right to legalize hemp. They considered Alex, a school board member for thirty years, and his family to be criminals, growing and selling illegal drugs.

The feds sent in the agents to enforce the Controlled Substances Act signed into law in 1970 by President Richard Nixon, which made *Cannabis sativa L* illegal to grow. The act did not distinguish by TCH levels:

> (16) The term "marihuana"* means all parts of the plant *Cannabis sativa L.*, whether growing or not; the seeds thereof; the resin extracted from any part of such plant; and every compound, manufacture, salt, derivative, mixture, or preparation of such plant, its seeds or resin. Such term does not include the mature stalks of such plant, fiber produced from such stalks, oil or cake made from the seeds of such plant, any other compound, manufacture, salt, derivative, mixture, or preparation of such mature stalks (except the resin extracted therefrom), fiber, oil, or cake, or the sterilized seed of such plant which is incapable of germination.[11]

> * The common spelling in 1937 when Congress passed the Marihuana Tax Act. The 1970 Congress used the same spelling and definition.

Alex knew why the agents were there, he knew why they destroyed his crop. Yet, neither he nor any of his tiospaye went to jail even though growing the number of plants they did was punishable by up to ten years imprisonment. The feds simply took the crop and left. Unrepentant, and even more convinced of the plant's value, the family began planning the next year's crop.

They didn't need to replant, the weed whacking agents scattered seeds everywhere. A year later new plants sprang from the soil like a phoenix rising from the ashes. This was brother Perry's crop in the tiospaye rotation. Except, right before harvest the feds came back, this time threatening Alex and Perry with life imprisonment if they did not agree in writing to the destruction of their hemp. In an act of defiance, sisters Ramona and Alter with some of their children gathered in prayer around a ceremonial staff in the center of the field as agents confiscated about 330 bundles of twenty to thirty plants.

A year later, the family harvested their first crop. "It really felt good,"

Alex said. "Just like a sense of relief."[12] Although they gathered and sold the hemp, the White Plumes could not deliver it. The United States District Court in South Dakota had granted a declaratory judgment and a permanent injunction forbidding Alex and his relatives to be near hemp. Instead of arresting them, the feds outlawed them from growing cannabis on the reservation without a valid Drug Enforcement Agency registration. In 2004, the 8th Circuit Court of Appeals affirmed the decision.

What the United States views as controlling illegal drugs, the Oglala regard as a violation of the Fort Laramie Treaty of 1868, signed following Red Cloud and American Horse's successful war against the army. With language such as "to insure the civilization of the Indians entering into the treaty," government agents tried to steer the Lakota toward joining the pioneer farmers scurrying onto the land. Heads of families taking up the plow could select three hundred and twenty acres to farm while men with no family could place eighty into cultivation. When the novices convinced the agent they were bound to the plow, they would receive seeds and agricultural tools for three years plus instruction from government farmers. The ten Lakota, who grew the most valuable crops for the first three years, were to receive five hundred dollars in presents.

Alex believes the courts misread the treaty and the rules handed down by the Supreme Court for interpreting Indian treaties. He cautions that, as documents between sovereign nations, Indian treaties are not open to casual reading. Interpretation had to begin with setting aside personal or cultural biases and the common misperception that treaties granted rights to Indians. Treaties must be read with the knowledge that tribes ceded some of their sovereignty to the United States instead of the other way around.

Because treaty negotiation procedures often included a government-named nation-chief when none existed, outright misrepresentation, and the distribution of alcohol and gifts to gain favor, the Supreme Court developed special rules dictating treaty interpretation. Alex referred to the rules developed by the court as Canons of Construction. Without the Canons, he says, Indians would lose their sovereignty and identity:

1. Ambiguous language must be resolved in favor of the Indian parties concerned.
2. Treaties must be interpreted as the Indians themselves would have understood them.
3. Treaties must be liberally construed in favor of the Indians.[13]

The district court first ruled the Controlled Substances Act applicable to reservations and not ambiguous. "*Cannabis sativa L* plant is illegal to cultivate without a valid permit from the federal government." The White Plumes may not grow it. The court also found, "the Controlled Substances Act is a general federal criminal law intended to be applicable to all those in the United States including the Native American Tribes."[14]

The court dispensed with questions of treaty violation and abrogation cynically, seemingly with no regard to the Canons. Finding that no articles in the treaty specifically preserved the right to grow cannabis the judge wrote, "Since the treaty requires the government to provide the seeds and implements for the members to use in cultivating crops, it is unlikely that the Tribe thought they could choose which crops would be planted."[15]

What the treaty holds is entirely different. The framers specified that Indians who satisfy the agent that they are taking up the plow in good faith are "*entitled* to receive seeds and agricultural implements [emphasis added]."[16]

Apparently the judge granted the injunction chiefly on the notion that neither nineteenth-century Indians nor government farmers would have thought of raising hemp. He concluded that no one in South Dakota Indian Country would have figured out that cultivating plants springing up all over, commercially farmed in other parts of America, could make up a valuable crop.

Such reasoning mystifies the Oglala. "You must go back then," Alex says, "to the interpretation of the treaties as Red Could and the others would have understood them. Would they have realized they could only do as the government said? Would they have considered the sweet white root medicine to be a plant they could not grow and use?"

He could have added: What would give anyone reason to believe the Lakota warriors were so docile that they would have only done what they were told in the first place? Indeed, history provides a far different picture of their often intractable nature.

White Plume believes the plant, which provides food, clothing, and shelter, would have been the crop chosen to replace the vanishing buffalo. Had they desired to farm, his ancestors would have planted, consumed, and sold hemp. According to Alex's lawyer, "There's no doubt that American Horse and Red Cloud could have gone right from the treaty meeting and planted some industrial hemp."[17]

The legality of enforcing the Controlled Substances Act on the rez does not concern Alex; the Oglala wish to keep harmful drugs out of their community. He just thinks that judges should study history as well as law. With a little research, the court could have discovered hemp was a valuable crop in the eighteenth and nineteenth centuries, and the first to be subsidized in Canada.

Old Ironsides carried more than sixty tons of hemp rope and sails.[18] The United States Census of 1850 listed 8,327 hemp plantations. A lamp burning hemp oil provided light as Lincoln wrote the Emancipation Proclamation. Two years later the United States produced 12,287,999 yards of bagging from flax, hemp, and jute; 1,215,000 yards of gunny cloth, 942,864 pounds of cloth, and 767,206 pounds of yarn. Farmers realized an income of $473,260 from other products made from those crops for a total of $4,507,664 per year.[19]

Alex believes transforming "entitled" to "required" was not the court's only mistake, noting his right to grow hemp predated the Controlled Substances Act. In a 1905 case, *United States v. Winans,* the court ruled that treaty negotiations reserved rights (for tribes) not explicitly articulated.[20] In Winans, the rights were for Yakima Indians to fish unimpeded, and White Plume believes the same is true for the Oglala's right to plant.

Both South Dakota courts dealt with the argument in a circular way. They found the treaty did not provide for cultivating particular crops, and since growing marijuana without a permit was illegal, Indians may not grow it.

> The district court and the appeals court in White Plume acted not only in apparent ignorance of the doctrine of reserved treaty rights, but also declined to follow the canon requirements to interpret the Fort Laramie Treaty as the people of the tribes who entered into it would have understood at the time.[21]

The notion that Indians would think they could grow only what government farmers required is historically inaccurate, ignoring the fierce independence of the plains warriors who refused to knuckle under to BIA agents. At best, these decisions are paternalistic, culturally denigrating efforts to protect the Oglala when they do not require protection. At worst, the courts justified, as Alex believes, the actions of a colonial power that takes, takes, takes, and never gives anything back.

Alex does not strike his enemy with traditional coup sticks; he eludes their jails and continues to campaign for hemp. For many, counting coup like this might have been enough. It might, except for Alex, fostering his people's cultural and economic renaissance and the role the hardy, ubiquitous plant could play in it, has become his mission. Watching his horses descend through the pines single file, reminiscent of his warrior ancestors approaching their village, Alex shrugs and finds little wonder that his people think the government is a colonial agency with no intention of helping the Indians.

21

Ten Thousand Rumors, But Nobody Has a Clue

I went to Washington and to other large cities, and that showed me that the white people dug in the ground and built house that could not be moved. Then I knew that when they came they could not be driven away.

—Man Who Carries the Sword (George Sword),
First Oglala Chief of Police

Tom Poor Bear says there are ten thousand Pine Ridge rumors about Ron and Wally's deaths, and he knows that while reservation and border town cops may have a theory, they don't have any evidence. They may have suspects in mind, but like everybody else, they merely have opinions.

Robert Ecoffey, BIA superintendent and the former tribal cop credited with tracking down Anna Mae Aquash's killers, believes Whiteclay drinking buddies murdered the two men. Fights break out over there all the time, he says, and this one got out of hand and became a lot more violent than most.[1]

After identifying Aquash's killers through the moccasin telegraph, he thinks the Hard Heart and Black Elk murderers will be found the same way. They cannot stay silent forever. They'll talk about it, he says, get drunk again, let it slip to the wrong person, and the cops will hear about it.

In his scenario, a group of Whiteclay people including Ron and Wally drank together and decided either to walk home during the night or, tired of sleeping on the hard streets of Whiteclay, thought to camp out in the woods and sleep it off. Something happened and a fight started. Someone picked up a club or a tree branch while someone else pulled out a large knife or hatchet. Ron and Wally were on the wrong side. They died where they lay. The murderers took off back to Whiteclay or Pine Ridge.

Of course that meant Ron and Wally would have to have been walking home with violent, well-armed (especially if they used the machete the FBI said they discovered near the bodies) drinking companions. And those men would have had to have enough lucidity and coordination to carry out a

232

vicious attack and then make their way back to town without anyone noticing their blood-stained clothing. (Ecoffey seems to leave out the fact that no blood was found at the scene.)

An Oglala Tribal Police supervisor thinks a reservation gang killed them in an initiation ritual. Admittance to the ranks, he says, took a witnessed killing. He believes Ron and Wally were walking back to Pine Ridge when a car full of members pulled up alongside. Probably unsuspecting in their stupor, the two men stood mute as initiates jumped out and attacked them. Managing to break away, they ran to the side of the gully where the gangbangers finally killed them.[2]

Homer Robbins, Sheridan County sheriff, believes he was responsible for the murders. He knew Ron Hard Heart, liked him, and says he used him as a snitch, providing him with drinking money to eavesdrop on Whiteclay gang members, drug dealers, and thieves.

Ron's career as a snitch supposedly began when the sheriff busted him on a drunk charge. Indignant, Hard Heart told him he should be arresting real criminals like the guy drinking in a bar in Rushville near the courthouse. How Ronnie knew that, Robbins doesn't know, but he rushed back to Rushville and arrested a wanted man.

Robbins believes the regular criminals who habituate Whiteclay discovered Ron's part-time job or else he overheard big-time criminals setting up an operation. Either way, they killed him to keep him quiet—Wally was collateral damage.[3]

The Oglala, who suspect the Rushville deputy, think he drove them in his patrol car to the Beaver Wall, a heavily wooded area in Nebraska between Chadron and Rushville and killed them there. They also claim a hitchhiker found Hard Heart's shoes along the road near the Beaver Wall.

Ben Black Elk saw tire tracks marring the vegetation of the crime scene. He believes the deputy hauled the dead men back from the Beaver Wall in the trunk of his car and placed them on the ground.

Pine Ridge residents who believe the sons of a well-known GOON killed the two men also hold to the off-the-reservation theory of the murders. They say the brothers killed them someplace else and deposited the bodies where they were found. Tom Poor Bear gives this story some credence. A worker at a garbage dump on the outskirts of Whiteclay told him he saw the brother's clean bloody rags out of their pickup, throw away bloody clothes, and wipe blood out of the truck's bed.

Tom says the disposal worker asked them why there was so much blood. They told him they had poached a deer; the blood came from the gutted animal. He still is angry at the employee for telling him the story several years later and not reporting it to the authorities when it happened. He labels the story of the poached deer as ridiculous. "Nobody," he said, "shoots a skinny June deer just starting to put on weight after a hard winter."[4]

A logical theory, in terms of place, is the carpenter guy as the killer. Ron and Wally had to walk near his place on the way back to Pine Ridge. With the sharp, heavy tools needed for his business, he could have killed them in his shop. In the dark of night, he could have loaded them into a pickup or even physically carried them 150 yards to where Darlene found them. Unfortunately, the authorities never searched the building, and it has since burned down.

Crucial to each theory is the location where the killing took place. Darlene Red Star, Tom Poor Bear, Ben Black Elk, and the medical technicians who worked the scene believe they were not murdered at the site. Just not enough blood, they say, and no evidence of a struggle. They all say Wally would not have gone without a fight.

Most agree the men did not die where their bodies lie, insisting the murders occurred in Nebraska. They were carried back and dumped on the rez to make it FBI jurisdiction. They think the killers counted on the bureau's "what's two more dead Indians" attitude, figuring they would never be caught.

Agent attitudes aside, the location and position of the bodies, lying side by side as if sleeping in a double bed, lends credibility to the notion that the killers transported and arranged them. Tire tracks into the area are common. Passersby would have thought either drinkers or lovers occupied a car parked in the area that night. There would have been no need for haste and little worry of identification in the deserted woods.

The positioning of the bodies discredits the theory, even though espoused by the FBI, that Ron and Wally were killed where they were found. Imagine them walking home from Whiteclay along the highway. Suddenly, a carload of criminals or gang members pulls up alongside and screeches to a stop. Men armed with clubs, baseball bats, and a machete leap from the vehicle and attack.

Since no one found blood and body parts on the pavement, they were not killed where they stood. Either they surrendered without a fight, allowing their assailants to march them like sheep a hundred yards to the killing ground, a notion Wally's relatives completely disregard or, realizing they had no chance, ran for the trees. They would have had to run, drunkenly, thirty yards down a fairly steep slope to a three-strand barbed-wire fence. After scrambling over or under the fence, they would have had to flee in the dead of night through dense forest and brush.

It is inconceivable Ron and Wally would have remained shoulder to shoulder during their flight, much more plausible they would have sepa-

The Arrowhead Inn is the first Whiteclay building and business the Oglala see after crossing the border from the Pine Ridge.

rated and died some distance apart. It's even harder to imagine the killers with a car parked along the highway taking the time to drag the bodies from where they died through the small drainage and arrange them on the slope.

Why were they killed and how does the reason relate to location? Superintendent Ecoffey's belief that drinking partners killed them offers no motive other than alcohol-fueled rage. Yet, he based his theory on the notion that Whiteclay drunks could kill two men, stumble back to town with blood-soaked clothing, and keep quiet for thirteen years.

The gang initiation scenario seems equally implausible. The Wild Boyz are the largest gang in Pine Ridge. According to Alex Dillon, one of the founders and leaders, they would not have killed a couple of old AIMers even if they were winos. They respected the men who fought the government during the seventies. If the brutal murders were a rite of passage to membership, he points out, it should have happened more than once. It didn't. No one has died so brutally, in such secrecy, since Ron and Wally.[5]

The people who knew Ron deride the sheriff's theory that criminals had figured out that Ron was a snitch. No one has heard in the intervening years that he snitched on anyone, and they say nothing like that could have been kept secret.

The motives of the carpenter, the Whiteclay deputy, and even the sons of the racist are either based upon racial hatred or retribution by a beer store owner for a ninety dollar unpaid tab. Again, as with the gang initiate theory, it seems that motives such as these would not have started and ended in June of 1999. Yet there have been no others—even though the murderers got away with their deadly work.

Location and lack of motive cast doubt on any of the more widely an-nounced theories of the murders. Knowing and walking the terrain in the dead of night, observing the behavior of Whiteclay drinkers, and watching the daily march back and forth from the border town to Pine Ridge seems to illuminate only one possibility. Ron and Wally climbed into a car with people they knew—armed men who were predisposed to kill them.

Perhaps, people paid to murder them.

22
Trip to the Dark Side

Whiskey is bad. Who drinks, they cause murders and suicides.
—Tȟatȟáŋka Ptéčela (Short Bull), Oglala Chief

Bull Bear had listened to the Wicasa Inticans, the tribe's executive council, and even his wives. It was time to decide. Several weeks earlier, wasicus leading pack mules swaying with top-heavy loads came to his camp. Warriors surrounded them, bows and lances ready, expecting treachery from the bearded men while women and children sought shelter along the creek's banks.

Never before had they seen the whites so bold. Placing their rifles on a robe near their horses, leaving only a single buckskin-clad man to watch over their possessions, the strangers entered the camp unarmed. It had been strange to hear the one with the biggest beard, hair growing out of his nose and ears, speak Lakota. The familiar words coming from such strangeness created a stir among the men and sent the women and children racing back into the camp ululating with amazement.

Bull Bear had heard Indians from the tribes to the east, along the river the whites called Missouri, speak about traders. They brought knives, cooking pots, steel for arrow and lance heads, and even powder for the few with guns to barter for furs and robes. This was good. The Oglala hunts south and west of Paha Sapa, the Black Hills, had been successful. They could sell elk and buffalo hides, and if these white men wanted skin from other animals, it would be easy to find them.

As people laughed, some even groaning with excitement, the wasicu took packs off the mules, placing things never before seen by the Oglala on robes covering the ground. There had been the metal Bull Bear expected, plus bright ribbons and beads, powder, and even some whiskey.

"Great Bull Bear," the red-bearded one who spoke the language said, "bring your people south. Come down to the Holy Road on the Shell. We built a post there. You can trade for anything you want. We have Mini Wakan and guns."

Bull Bear would not hear of it. "This is my home. Here, where we can go into the Sacred Hills any time. This is the place the people were born. Wakan Tanka is here."

He hadn't expected the reaction from the members of his band as they poured over trade goods, bringing fine robes in hopes of profiting from men who had brought such wonders. Many wanted to leave at once. Men and women proclaimed there were so many buffalo and elk that surely the Great Spirit intended the Oglala to trade skins to make life better.

But Bull Bear would not make a hasty decision based on the elation of people. He would pray alone in the hills, and he would ask his advisors. The Great Creator would show the best trail for the Oglala.

Finally, he decided. He would lead the Oglala south—all the bands would go. Scouts had told him the wasicu spoke the truth. There were many buffalo, elk, deer, and antelope there. This would be the final move for his people. This was why they had left the rivers and forests of the east and moved west. The Oglala would become the richest and most feared of the tribes.

In less time than it took a warrior to don sacred paint, lodges were down and bands on the move. Women walked, leading horses bearing packs and hauling travois. Children sat on the backs of older horses, sometimes three or four per animal. Gaudily dressed warriors raced through the camp, tearing off in yet another race to see whose horse ran the fastest. The prairie seemed alive with movement.

While not choreographed, there was an order to their journey. The wise old men known as the pipe owners had designated the route, even noting the order of the various bands. Everyone obeyed, except for a family from the Bad Face band led by an old man who fancied himself the greatest of hunters. Always antagonistic, often refusing to abide by the norms of the villages, he turned the small group away from the march. Instead of moving south, they broke toward a rise guarding a lush meadow where scouts had spotted a great herd of buffalo.

The Wicasa Inticans had ordered the herd unmolested, if left alone Tatanka would stay in the valley with a stream running through it, luxuriating in thick grass. The societies would plan a hunt at the next camp. The people would rest for several days after taking many animals. There would be skins, and they would fill their larder for the next winter.

But the Bad Face group was jumping the hunt. They would spook the herd and chase them away. Such could not happen. Before the wayward group crested the rise, before the dim eyes of Tatanka saw them coming, the Akicita, the appointed policing society, drove their ponies into action. They surrounded the contrary family, whipping their backs with quirts and rawhide ropes. Those knocked off their horses threw their arms up, shielding their heads from the blows of the incensed Akicita as they raced back to their place in the march.

Warriors of the Akicita knocked the family's leader, known for jumping hunts before, to the ground. They beat him with bows, lances, and handles of war clubs. Face and chest covered with blood, lying on the grass as warriors raced back to their position on the sides of the march, he remained motionless until finally struggling to his feet and staggering after the band. Later that night he crawled into camp, only to find his lodge torn in shreds, his homeless family weeping, shunned by their fellow Oglala.

***

"It's called a tune-up," Bud Merrill, one-time GOON, says. "You gotta remember this is a lawless place; it's the Old West, the last frontier. Sometimes people just gotta be tuned-up."[1]

"Yeah," agrees former jailer Tony Hawk. "You know, an attitude adjustment. When I worked at the jail, the cops usually gave prisoners a tune-up before they got to the station. Stop somewhere and adjust them. That always caused us a lot of trouble. We'd just get the prisoners settled, everything quiet, and they bring somebody in, arms handcuffed behind his back. Make him lie on the floor and then they'd raise his hands up as high as they could. His screaming would get everything going again. Why a lot of cops had to retire someplace else. People remembered and would go after them."[2]

The dark side of the Pine Ridge, beyond the alcoholism, poverty, and disease, is a place of intimidation, beatings, and fear. The work of the warrior Akicita society is carried on today by people remembering the past, but without chiefs to order it, without the rules of the camp to follow. The Akicita no longer exists, people are not subject to rules enforced by a policing society, they are beaten by thugs paid to do the job. It is not a secret, it is not talked about, but everybody knows it happens.

Marty Red Cloud, one of the originators of the Wild Boyz, a youth gang made infamous by television and YouTube, now approaching thirty and father to his girlfriend's two young boys, has taken part. He has never thought Ron and Wally were killed by whites or border town cops. Somebody on the rez either went too far tuning them up or set out to kill them.

"Yeah, I've done it." Well over six feet tall and more than two hundred pounds of muscle, it is easy to see why he was paid to administer beatings. Marty claims tribal council members are some of the worst offenders. People who criticize them, make fun, or talk against them, often will have their attitude adjusted. "They are beaten to stay in line."

Both sides of the law participate. He was once paid by a drug dealer to watch over her house when she was away. Some guys kept hanging around her place, and Marty took care of them for her.

Hawk had it right about the cops, according to Marty. "People are afraid of them." He has been picked up, thrown into the backseat of a squad car, and pistol-whipped. He says he's also been pulled out of the backseat in cuffs and clubbed. "You put up no resistance," he says, "because the cops are brutal."

He is anxious when he goes out at night to look for his nephews or girl-friend's sons, fearing they have fallen victim to violence. Showing the scars on his torso inflicted by knives and clubs, he says he is often challenged to fight. Like Old West gunfighters, younger men think they will gain a repu-tation by beating him.

To protect his home from paid thugs or people looking for trouble, Marty keeps three pit bulls tied in front of his house. He trusts them, not law enforcement. If you want to get to him or his family, he says, you have to go through the dogs.[3]

Ben Mesteth, often called the Bluebird of Wounded Knee II because his adoptive mother, Birdie Mesteth, kept him with her as an infant during the 1973 occupation of Wounded Knee, agrees with Marty about the beatings and the killings of Ron and Wally. "Other Lakota killed them. People can say what they want, but they do it all the time, fight and die for nonsense." He believes the owner of a beer store in Whiteclay paid to have them tuned up, and it went too far. His theory jibes with the report of Renée Black Elk, who says she heard one of the owners threaten Ron Hard Heart over ninety dollars.

Calling himself one of the terrible people of Pine Ridge, Ben used to hang out in Whiteclay, something he does a lot less since injuring a knee so badly he cannot climb stairs. Huge, over six feet four inches and more than three hundred pounds, he admits to his role in the dark side. "I used to beat people up. I was paid to beat people up. And I was good at it. You know, break some arms or legs if you get paid enough, that way people remember." He says the practice is ubiquitous and agrees with Marty about the tribal council, saying members rule with an iron hand and don't let anyone get out of control.

He knows firsthand the role of Whiteclay proprietors in the beatings. He related the story of how he was paid to work over one man and drag him bleeding and broken into the beer store because of an unpaid bill. But the dark side of Whiteclay is more than just beatings for nonpayment of liquor accounts, he says. "Owners extend credit, get people in debt on pur-pose. When they are in debt, they're forced to steal or become bootleggers. They do what they are told or get beat up again."

Naming a Pine Ridge/Whiteclay regular, a Vietnam veteran, Ben says he was one of the primary thugs at the time Ron and Wally died. "That's why the FBI questioned him, because he was one of the main guys beating people up. He's crazy. Agent Orange in Vietnam made him crazy."

Prostitution also exists in Whiteclay, according to Ben and his wife, Katrina. They say the Indian men on the street aren't involved; the bar owners bring in young girls and pay them with booze. They both feel Nebraska should close the town because of prostitution, killings, beatings, and fencing stolen property. "People steal and sell anything for booze."

The real lawbreakers in Whiteclay, Ben says, are the beer store owners. "People that buy from them are poor and alcoholic, but not criminals. The bar owners are." He claims the sheriff of Sheridan County looks the other way when something happens in Whiteclay.

Ben doesn't only condemn the wasicus. "Don't expect the tribal council to close Whiteclay and make booze legal on the rez, even placing it under their control and using the profit to create treatment programs as Russell Means suggested years ago. The tribe will never go for that, because of the money. If you follow the money, you will see why the reservation will stay closed to booze. Too many people are making money off of it, taking kickbacks to prevent its legalization."[4]

***

Hidden in the dark side of the Pine Ridge, given credence by almost no one, there is a chance the murders of Black Elk and Hard Heart were expedient and self-protective, far removed from bad cops, crazed wasicu, and white supremacy. Their deaths may have been just another tragedy in a lawless society.

This premise hosts only losers—only victims. The heinous deaths of Ron and Wally may have involved no ultimate sacrifice, no struggle for sanctity or dignity. Different from conjecture, it is based on a confession by a person who says she wanted one of the men dead. It explains why the bodies suffered such savage mutilation—even though one of the men died for being in the wrong place at the wrong time.

The Oglala maintain large, even expansive, extended families. Any older woman relative, no matter how far consanguineously removed is a grandmother or an auntie. Whether the people have ever met, the relationship is real. The same is true with males. The profuse number of uncles and grandfathers claimed by tribal members can be entirely confusing to a non-Oglala. Cousins abound; children and grandchildren are commonly claimed by older relatives without the blood lineage familiar to the rest of America.

Families grow larger with the Hunka ceremony, in which two people are bound by ties of fidelity even stronger than brotherhood or family. An ancient practice, the gregarious and caring Lakota adopt each other as brothers, parents, siblings, and any other relationship. Thus, a Hunka may be of no actual relation, but still real to the people.

One of the murdered men had a Hunka daughter. Why the relationship was created is unclear, but it was important to the two. Because of this, Wally and Ron's journey toward violent death may have begun in the late 1970s, several years after the standoff at Wounded Knee and almost twenty-two years before Darlene Red Star discovered their lifeless bodies.

The Hunka daughter's mother was a Whiteclay woman. Pregnant, she drank heavily, stumbling along the streets of the border town, occasionally working her way back to Pine Ridge to dry out. Heavily into her cups at the time she gave birth, she can still be found on the streets of Whiteclay.

While she displays no physical characteristics of fetal alcohol syndrome, the Hunka daughter appears to display emotional characteristics of the condition that include problems in thinking and social skills, inability to concentrate, impulsiveness, and anxiety. Add to the possibility of suffering disability from alcohol at birth, the trauma of her adolescence, living with different people, moving from family to family, and suffering both rape and assault certainly must have affected her psychologically. Her life consisted of drinking and partying, often in Whiteclay, but it didn't matter, it was wherever she could find booze.

At least one of the men in the family claims to have observed her servicing men in the cab of a pickup on a Whiteclay street for booze. All of her Hunka relatives say she is so full of little stories that she cannot be believed, and suggest she is capable of violence.

During the hot, dry days of summer in 2011, the adopted daughter said she had not cried for her father. She knew she would in the future but had not been able to find the tears yet. By the cold winter days of January 2012, her story had changed dramatically. Instead of observers, mere recorders of events, she made the authors of this book players in a diabolical drama, pulling them into Pine Ridge's dark side.

Alan Hafer asked the Hunka daughter if she could arrange an interview with a notorious character known as Dark Mark, the former tough that Ben Mesteth had spoken of who had been questioned by the FBI about the murders. With a reputation for violence and, according to Lupe Esparza, present at a fight between Hard Heart and several young men in Whiteclay just before he and Wally disappeared, Hafer figured Mark had to know something.

Several days later the Hunka phoned Hafer and told him Dark Mark was with her and willing to talk. Hafer would need to convince him he wasn't a fed, and he would need to give him some money, the customary trade on the rez. With the agreements made, she put him on the phone. Inebriated, slurring his words and mumbling, Dark Mark told Hafer he knew everything about the murders and would tell him what happened.

The Hunka daughter suddenly came back on the line, insisting Hafer give her money since she had Mark on the phone. Hafer replied he had learned nothing yet and needed more. She gave the phone back to Dark Mark, who said he would only tell Hafer in person.

Hafer had him put the young woman back on the phone, assuming he would have to drive to the reservation to talk with Mark. She again asked for payment, assuring Hafer that Mark knew everything about the murders, even the names of the men who had killed her father. Hafer said he needed more to warrant a trip. Then, in a voice the authors had not heard before, the trembling, weak voice of a small child instead of a binge drinking Whiteclay woman, she said, "This is for my father, right? You're doing this for my dad, right? You are trying to help my dad, right?"

When Hafer replied that he was, a deep silence broken with an intake of her breath on the phone followed. In her little girl's voice, she said, "It was me. I did it."

Stunned, Hafer asked if that meant she killed her father and Ron Hard Heart. She said it did. He asked incredulously, "How could you have killed anyone?"

With a stronger voice, she said, "I paid two men to do it. I gave them five hundred dollars each." She named them and told how she had arranged it. "I did it," she said, "so he wouldn't send me away."

Still in disbelief, Hafer asked, "Where could you have found a thousand dollars?"

Her reply, instant, without time for thought, made sense. "I was dealing drugs out of a halfway house. I had sold drugs before. I had the money."

Beginning to see the possibility of her story, Hafer asked why she did it. "What was your father going to do that was so bad?"

"He was going to send me to Rivendell, a mental hospital in Kentucky. I didn't want to go there. Besides he told the police where to find me when I was arrested."[5]

Hafer told her that he would be on the rez to see her within a week if she would tell him the entire story. She said she would.

Her story gained credence when the authors discovered Rivendell is what she said, and no one else on the rez, including her family, had ever heard of the place. Hafer met her the next week at Big Bat's; she had been staying with her sister who drove her into town. She walked in and sat down, and Hafer met another person in her body. Instead of the hardened Whiteclay woman or even the little girl on the phone, he sat across the table from an anxiety-ridden, paranoid woman sobbing and shaking with fear.

"You got me in trouble," she cried. "You got me in a lot of trouble, and you have to help me out."

Hafer had no idea what she was talking about. He had not spoken with anyone about her confession except for Sauser, who had not told anyone. Not that, she said, still admitting her role in the death of her father. Her angst stemmed from a conversation the authors had with her former father-in-law weeks before.

"You got me in trouble with them," she cried again. "They say I'm getting their son in trouble. They don't want to read their names in any book."

Hafer assured her all they had done was ask if he and Sauser could speak to them about life with her. Barely able to find her voice, she said her in-laws had accused her of telling lies. And then she said, "Now you got me into a lot of trouble, and you have to help me out. You have to give me money." Implying that there had been a physical threat, she said, "I need to get away and hide."

Hafer assured her that her former father-in-law seemed to be a reasonable man. He had also told the authors not to believe all of his former daughter-in-law's little stories. They had assured him they would do their best not to display his family in a bad light based only on what the young woman had said.

Her sobs grew louder; she shook so violently she could barely light a cigarette. "You don't understand. They'll get me. You have to give me money to hide. I have to go now."[6]

She left Big Bat's with enough gas money to get to Rapid City. Stunned, Hafer sat in Big Bat's amid coffee cups and cigarette smoke. A man with no legs and artwork that showed some talent rolled over in his wheelchair and asked him to buy something. All around it was just another day on the rez, yet this was no longer a place Hafer wanted to be. There was a good chance he had just given a woman responsible for the deaths of two men enough money to run away and hide.

With Sauser ill, Hafer needed a cultural guide, someone who knew the young woman, someone who knew the dark side.

There are some people you trust from the first time you meet them, who quickly convince you of their humility, intelligence, and sensitivity. Pte San Win Poor Bear, Shelli's older sister, the Wakan Woman, and a Poor Bear/Black Elk family member had done that for Hafer. After speaking with her about Shelli and her father, the Wakan Woman had become his friend. He turned to her.

They met at her mother's home. As Hafer relayed the confession of the Hunka daughter, a person the Poor Bear sisters had grown up with, telling how she had taken credit for her father's murder, he witnessed first-hand the power of Lakota spirituality. Pte San Win seemed to age, but not as an older, wrinkled, white-haired woman; she metamorphosed into a ma-

Pte San Win often prays in the Bad Lands.

triarch, a keeper of ancient mysteries, a woman of ageless wisdom. She belonged to the past.

Her first words were, "It is true. I feel it." And then she said, swept by the power of her medicine, "I must find my center, pray, listen to the old ones."

Hafer and the Wakan Woman drove to the summit of Sheep's Mountain, a high point in the Bad Lands, accompanied by her two young daughters and her medicine bundle. On a beautiful day in May, temperatures warming into the seventies, patches of snow hanging in shaded terrain and the Black Hills rising in the distance, she scattered tobacco in the breeze so that it fell across an expanse of the eroded, gouged, and scenic land.

Her voice rose in a beautiful, captivating tone. She sang an ancient Lakota hymn, thanking the Creator for all living things. Her youngest daughter, seven years old, giggled and gathered rocks like any other American girl would, as if this were a normal moment in life. Wakan Woman centered, pronouncing herself ready. She wondered if banishment from the rez would be an appropriate punishment for the Hunka; it was the way the tribe had always treated murderers before the white men brought their laws.[7]

Hafer and Pte San Win discussed their options. The first was to give the Hunka a chance to tell her story to the authorities. Through confession, she would help her father find justice as she had said she wished, and she could also help herself.

The Hunka was homeless, drifting from place to place, shelter to abuse center, relative to friend, alley to alley, and drunk to drunk. She had no money or place to live. Neither Pte San Win nor Hafer thought, with some concurrence by an attorney, that the feds would be interested in putting her away for life or seeking her execution. Turning herself in could be the ticket to a fresh start. She could receive the treatment her father realized she needed, kick alcohol and do something productive with the rest of her life. And she could turn in the men who had brutally killed her father with a machete.

But behind the young woman's sometimes confidence, almost braggadocio, accompanying her anxiety, escapism, and hiding, there was real fear. Pte San Win knew it. Hafer had seen it in Big Bat's and would again. When he had suggested turning herself in, her first words were not of what would happen to her in custody, if she could see her children, or if the reward could be directed to them. She blanched and said, "They will get me. They're still out there. I lied to you about the men I paid to do it. They're still here."[8]

Do not try to tell a resident of the rez that the FBI will protect them. It doesn't work. When Hafer told her the feds had an obligation to help her, she just started to cry.

Pte San Win volunteered to enlist the help of the family. Several days later, Hafer received a call from Ben Black Elk, who was laughing and hollering while Marla giggled in the background. "Your book is done. It's all over," he shouted into the phone. "She did it; she killed Wally." Between fits of laughter, he said nobody would believe her; she was a pathological liar. She couldn't have paid to have them killed, he said, thinking along the same lines Hafer had originally, because she never had any money.[9]

Tom Poor Bear's call was somber, without a laughter sound track. He also said the young woman was a liar, a woman without means to have paid anyone and incapable of doing it herself. Because of her lies, he said, she was no longer welcome around any of the family. Instead of banishment for murder, the Hunka daughter became an outcast for saying she had the men killed.[10]

Quietly, the Wakan Woman said, "I knew they would act like that. They just can't see."

A month later, Hafer arranged to see the Hunka during the 2012 Veterans Pow Wow weekend. Coincidentally, it was also the anniversary of the murders. Tom Poor Bear led the Thirteenth Anniversary March from Billy Mills Hall in Pine Ridge to Whiteclay.

With about one hundred Lakota and thirty wasicu wannabes, including a woman wearing a sign that announced lawyer, another labeled press, and a young man dressed as a court jester in horizontally striped hose (a different color on each leg), voluminous many-colored shorts, a black shirt, and tinsel-draped long blue hair with a tiara to hold it down, the march blocked the highway for several hours. The group stopped four times to pray. After reaching Whiteclay, they walked back to Camp Justice where a tipi had been erected and a beef barbecued.

The young woman did not march. She had a weekend pass from an alcohol treatment facility in Gordon, Nebraska, where she had been sent by her sisters to dry out and get her life on track. She had been arrested several weeks earlier and jailed on a charge of child abuse. She had not abused anyone; she just had not been selective in her places to drink. It is against tribal law to become inebriated in a way that endangers children.

Friday night, the day before Tom's march, she had stayed with her sisters in a tent pitched near the pow wow grounds, less than a mile from Billy Mills Hall. She could have marched in honor of Wally and Ron, but chose not to be around the mourners.

The Hunka's sisters found Hafer and asked him for help. The Hunka was in the wind. Earlier, when they had driven to a house in Pine Ridge, she had jumped out of the car and raced away. Drinking was more important than either the pow wow or her treatment. Hafer and the two women returned to the housing area and drove the streets, stopping at houses of relatives and friends. They searched for over an hour, but no one knew where she was. Her sisters said there was a party going on, and people were hiding her.

After the search party had returned to the pow wow, the young woman called her sisters. She was ready to go back to the tent. With no explanation where she had been, she waved them down as they drove along the street.

Her first words to Hafer were, "You got me in trouble again. I'm in so much trouble, and it's all your fault."

Her accusations continued for the short trip to the pow wow grounds where Hafer could finally speak to her alone. On that day, wearing makeup, freshly washed hair billowing behind her in the wind, perhaps too much rouge on her cheeks, the young woman could have donned the elk dresses of her ancestors and appeared as the Oglala must have to the first wasicu visitors. Proud, haughty, and indignant, she pranced more than walked, confident and soft in each step as though she had been raised on the prairies.

Her anger was not soft. She pulled down her shirt, baring the top of a breast and displayed a bruise. "My auntie hit me for saying I had them killed. None of my family will talk to me. They don't want anything to do with me."

Suddenly she started sobbing, returning to the scared, anxious woman Hafer had spoken with in Big Bat's. "I just love my family," she said. "I love them so much and now they hate me."

When Hafer told her that if she had been responsible for her father's death she should expect the rest of her family to be angry, her tears increased. He explained her family members were still angry she had gone to Whiteclay during her father's wake instead of being there with them. By her admission, he reminded her, she purposely had been staying away from them, never making contact.

She backed up against a large cottonwood tree, hands over her face, bent over from the waist. Hafer had once again been pulled back into the dark side. Had her family done this? Would there be more violence? He only knew that he could no longer walk this trail with her, he could not stay in the dark side, so he provided her an out. He said. "Did you do it? Did you have your father killed?"

She looked up at him, anger flashing in her dark eyes. Tears rained down and black mascara streaked her vermillion cheeks.

"Did you do it?" he asked again. "If you tell me no, I will explain to the families that you just wanted money. I'll tell them you're sorry for your lies and want to be with them. I can try to make it better."

"I lied," she said, not with the same little girl's voice she'd used to confess, but sounding weary and resigned. "I didn't do it."

Why had she lied? Why endanger her relationship with her family? Did she just want money?

"No," this was the scared woman's voice. "Someone told me to lie to you. To say I did it so you would quit looking."[11]

23
Life on the Rez

A very great vision is needed and the man who has it must follow it as the eagle seeks the deepest blue of the sky.
—*Tashunkewitko (Crazy Horse)*, Oglala Lakota

The men who killed Wally Black Elk and Ron Hard Heart will probably never stand trial, but the relatives of the victims continue trying to make their deaths relevant. They seek a meaning to the carnage that will elevate their lives, and those of all the Oglala.

Led by Tom Poor Bear, elected tribal vice president in 2010, Wally's brothers have made the war against Whiteclay their personal mission. They

Bloketu Win (Summer Solstice Woman or Bella) wearing glasses and Wicahpi Yuha Mani Win (or Choppi) with paint on her face, Pte San Win's daughters, are learning the ancient skill of turning a freshly killed elk into the winter's meat supply. (Photo courtesy of Pte San Win)

have made his legacy an end to whiskey ranch predation, the first step in ending the unjust treatment of Oglala in border towns.

Soon after the murders, the brothers erected Camp Justice, beginning a tradition of demonstrations and protests, placing the blame squarely on the whiskey ranch traders: "One of these proprietors threatened one of those who died over an unpaid 'tab.' He said if it was not paid, then the 'boys' would take care of the debtor, or maybe the deputy sheriff would. A town of racists, making a living from people they hate, protected by racist law enforcement. The very breeding ground for murder."[1]

A list of demands for justice by Camp Justice included an investigation of all the civil rights violations the residents of Pine Ridge have suffered in Sheridan County. They also called for the establishment of a permanent civil rights office in the border county, closure of all Whiteclay alcohol outlets, removal of Sheriff Robbins for covering up Deputy Randy Metcalf's criminal actions, and data collection on all traffic stops in an attempt to prevent profiling.

Fourteen years later, the whiskey ranch was still in business and business was booming. Whiteclay was still a skid row populated by drunks sleeping in the streets, gathering around fires among the abandoned houses, and panhandling passing motorists for change. While the tribal police are more noticeable along the border, the tiny booze hamlet remained a lawless place.

Whiteclay still sold more than five million cans of beer a year, raking in over $12 million dollars a year at the expense of the nation's poorest people. After the murders, however, it was never really back to business as usual. The Oglala kept the pressure on Whiteclay.

In February 2012, the tribe filed a $500 million federal lawsuit against Anheuser-Busch, Molson Coors, Pabst, Miller Brewers, and retailers and distributors of booze in Whiteclay. Not a scheme for alcoholics to get rich, the money was to be used for treatment centers, helping to repair the damage to a population afloat in Nebraskan alcohol. But as usual, the Indians received no help—in October of the same year a judge ruled the federal court had no jurisdiction.

Still, the mission to close the whiskey ranch picked up steam. In 2012, protesters set up camp near Camp Justice where they could continue daily demonstrations. They created human roadblocks to prevent trucks carrying booze from reaching town.

Nebraska, Sheridan County, and Whiteclay reacted as they always have. When Tribal President Bryan Brewer joined the blockade and told Sheriff Robbins that beer trucks were not going to make it into the alcohol hamlet that day,[2] Brewer was arrested. Digging into the bag of dirty tricks border town lawmen always seem to have at their disposal, he was not arrested for blocking traffic, but for an outstanding warrant on a bad check. Charges were dropped when the check was made good—but the blockade had been handled for another day.[3]

In July of 2013, Tribal President Brewer met briefly with Nebraska Governor Dave Heineman about the whiskey ranch. The session proved to be a microcosm of the demonstrations, protests, and communication between Pine Ridge and Nebraska. Heineman informed Brewer it was not up to the state to solve alcohol problems on the Pine Ridge. Brewer heard him say, "It's not my problem, it's your problem. Solve it."[4]

President Brewer walked out of the meeting just a few minutes after it started. A spokesman for Nebraska said the Oglala president was confrontational. In turn, Brewer said the Nebraska governor had blood on his hands for failing to end the exploitation.[5]

After fourteen years of demonstrations, arrests, court proceedings, and dealing with a state government making a lot of money off the Lakota but unconcerned with the misery caused by Whiteclay's reason for being, Tom Poor Bear and the Oglala started looking inward. One plan, led by Brewer, was to construct a port of entry on the highway from Whiteclay, search all cars headed for the Pine Ridge, and confiscate all the booze they found.

Taking a more permanent solution, the tribe voted to end alcohol prohibition and sales on the rez in August 2013, now on hold due to an injunction, and to use the profits to establish treatment centers. Beer sales in Whiteclay will probably plummet, except it will be illegal to be intoxicated on the streets of the Pine Ridge, and that may be Whiteclay's primary attraction for the addicted—the ability to drink and sleep in public and panhandle passersby for beer money.

With the vote, Wally's brothers may have gained a measure of justice. Without the senseless deaths of the two men in 1999, business may have stayed the same in the whiskey ranch. It seems after fourteen years of activism, the days of Nebraskans making money from Oglala addiction are numbered.

***

There has been little economic progress on the Pine Ridge since the discovery of the bodies. Shannon County, wholly within the Pine Ridge, is no longer the poorest county in America. More than signifying an economic resurgence for the Oglala, statistics show the declining fortune of the residents of Todd County on the Rosebud Reservation, the second poorest, and the inhabitants of Ziebach County on the Cheyenne River Reservation, who are now the poorest in America.

As usual, no one really knows the per capita income of the Pine Ridge, listed in the 2010 census as $7,880, because there are no accurate counts of the population. The Census Bureau put the number at a little over eighteen thousand; the tribe says it is more than twice that number. Most residents continue to live far below federal poverty guidelines.[6]

Since the research for this book began, Loren Black Elk has succumbed to liver failure. Physically, he shrank in size; weight poured off his robust frame while fluid he could not pass distended his abdomen. His skin color changed from the sun-baked, weathered tone of a man who spent a good deal of time outside, to gray.

A warrior, Loren faced his impending demise with hope and courage. He fought until he could withstand the ravages no longer. During his battle, he lived in a small room in Ben and Marla's trailer, his papers and personal possessions kept in a small pouch.

Loren never collected the welfare money for which he was entitled, and he never was able to secure disability funds as a result of the brain injury he received as a youth. His wake and funeral were AIM-sponsored ceremonies.

Dead at the age of fifty-two, surrounded by AIM warriors, he lay in a coffin in a teepee erected in Billy Mills Hall. Loren wore his traditional AIM jacket and red headband. Both Bill Means and Clyde Bellecourt spoke; no one from Autonomous Aim attended. His son, Wendyll, who suffers from cerebral palsy, brought documents to prove that he (Wendyll) should be named the Chief of the Oglala band once led by Sandy Sauser's relative, Bull Bear.

Aaron Running Hawk, the Vietnam combat soldier who would have participated in the siege of Wounded Knee if the army had not confined him to base, died of lung cancer in 2011. Eschewing modern medicine and physicians, he placed his faith in the traditional ceremonies of his people. Perhaps a victim of Agent Orange, and certainly cigarettes, he died shortly after a Yuwipi, or healing ceremony.

Iva Black Elk's daughter, Mariah Montileaux, Ben and Loren's niece, committed suicide on November 18, 2009, at the tender age of fourteen, a victim of another rampant epidemic on the rez. The teenage rate for suicide is 150 percent higher than the rest of the United States.

Sandy Sauser, descendant of Bull Bear, Bear Robe, Emilie and Ben Lessert, great-granddaughter of Wounded Knee interpreter Philip Wells, suffered from intense back and sciatica pain for years. Stricken with vaginal cancer from which she seemed to be recovering, she always believed the pain in her back and down her legs was caused by a lifetime of hard work, most of it for her father, "that damned old German."

Preparing for Christmas with her family in 2012 on Christmas Eve,

The land that Sandy loved so much on the Pine Ridge. The house was removed after her death. The site of her marker is located next to her father in the hills back of this plot, surrounded by trees she faithfully watered.

probably sitting at her kitchen table beading, or rolling cigarettes, her dogs napping at her feet, the pain in her back became too much to bear. Flown to the Rapid City Regional Hospital by helicopter, tests showed cancerous tumors along her sciatic nerve; the diseased cells also resided in her stomach, lungs, and brain.

Joking, grinning mischievously, and refusing to give up life on her beloved rez, she made it only until February 25. In the summer of 2013, Sandy's family interred her ashes in the same little plot on the hill as her father, surrounded by trees she planted.

24

The Heart and Soul of the Oglala

Arlette Loud Hawk is a traditional. In 2013, she discovered Facebook; her posts open the heart of her people. She begins each with "Hello Relatives," *Mitakuye Oyasin*, perhaps the most commonly heard Lakota phrase, meaning all are related—everything is connected.

On Being Lakota
Hello Relatives:

Ake yapsopsose howaetanyin tke.

Pine Ridge Indian Reservation ... how is it living on the reservation? *Eya Sicawaepektesni, ikceyakes,* it is GRAND. Yes, it is beautiful, the land, the sky, the sun, moon, stars shine for me every night. I am home on the land. I love the land of Crazy Horse. As you enter our reservation a sign says, Welcome to the Land of Crazy Horse. WOW.

What makes me so strong? This comes naturally, the DNA of the Greatest Buffalo Hunters and Greatest Warriors of the Plains.

If I don't teach you who you are and where you came from, will it be a white man teaching you who you are and where you came from? It is going to be a German telling you your history, the history of the Lakota. He wouldn't know. This is your history.

Le nitawa iksuyape!

Okay. A German is going to teach us who we are—so sad.

I am a Lakota. Abide by natural law, customs and laws of the Lakota society. First I was born a Lakota so to my nation, I am loyal. I am at all times Lakota first. I identify with my own nation always. *Lakota ki he tokahe.*

Next, identity is what makes you the person you are, Lakota, with the values and belief system of the Lakota. I then will act accordingly. I have the manners of a Lakota, my behaviors and actions will be like a Lakota. *Waunsiyelakte*—you will love your fellow man. Big white man word again, but it describes the concept. Fellow man is the love of all creation, the trees, the animals, the sun, moon, stars, earth, water, wind, and fire. These are all sacred. We are all related.

So you *unsikila* [love] everything in creation as living and as your relatives. Okay, so I am a Lakota. I know who I am. My sacred role and duties to my family is as a mom. I am a teacher to my children. This is my God-given duty, to raise my children well. I never went into the employed strata of life. I stayed home with my children, did the best I could as a single parent. Next, a single grandparent.

Identity, I look like a Lakota. I have the characteristics of a Lakota. I act like a Lakota. I am quiet by nature. I am not quarrelsome, I don't gossip, talk bad about my neighbors. Identify as a Lakota, love the Lakota ways first. You will love your people first. You will marry within your nation to promote the nationhood of the Seven Council Fires.

Ma Tuwe ki slolwakiye, wanna.

On Chief Crazy Horse and the American flag

We are seven sub-bands, ours being the Oglala Lakota. Our band is the fiercest in all history books. The Battle of the Greasy Grass, when the Seventh Cavalry and their General, George A. Custer, met his defeat that day. Crazy Horse and Sitting Bull were victorious. In war, your war lance is taken if you are defeated. Custer's lance was the United States flag. The flag goes to the victorious. Crazy Horse's flag was the American flag upside down. The people of Crazy Horse have ownership to hang it upside down—telling everyone this is the Crazy Horse flag.

At the site where we are told Crazy Horse was buried, I stood, listening in awe of the land. My heart was happy to be at his favorite camping place. The creek ran by in his day; the cherry trees must have been plentiful. It was so moving, touching my heart, reaching the sky—my spirit was happy.

On Alcohol and Whiteclay

Hello Relatives:

I have been at the Whiteclay blockade for many days now. Every day, I hear insults to my warriors standing up to Whiteclay. I look at the young men in our group: I know the Creator has touched their spirit. I look at them, and I stand there and pray for them. I pray that everything goes good for them. I ask Grandfather to protect them from harm, danger, and evil.

Yes, after a day at the council meeting at the casino, I sadly go back to Oglala. I was happy to be with all the lady warriors, now we go our separate ways. I am happy my niece has taken up the shield, which is for protection, now we hold signs and protest, protecting our nation from alcohol.

WE have taken up our spears, our war lances, which are our canes, the staff of our nation. WE have our Sacred Bow and Arrows to shoot off into the sky, calling on the Grandfathers of the Universe and the White Buffalo Calf Woman for help, to stop all alcohol from coming into our reservation.

WE are the last reservation to be a dry reservation. Pray for the children, pray for the women who stand up to the council. Please pray for Me. I am the one who has a sharp tongue.

***

Wakan Woman Pte San Win Poor Bear fills her Facebook posts with Spiritualism. Religion to her, as it was to her ancestors, has never been a once a week only on Sunday activity. It is a constant part of her life.

Ina Maka na Mahpiya Oyate na tate topa [Earth Mother & Sky Nation & Four Winds] I am *lila* [really] thankful for the life that you bring to my sacred soul. This morning, in the wee hours as I sat at my house in the COUNTRY, I sat and watched as GAKA WI [Grandfather Sun] made his sacred and beautiful journey to the sky. I looked to the NORTH and I saw the sacred silhouette of our beautiful and healing BLACK HILLS. I looked to the EAST and I saw you grandfather sun blessing me like CLOCK-WORK on this sacred RED day. I looked up above me and I saw the different shades of pink and purple glistening across the sacred SKY NATION. Ahhh, it is beautiful to be connected. Ahhh, it is sacred to be LAKOTA. Today, I give thanks for all the LIFE that surrounds me and I pray with all my heart for those who forgot ...

Hecetu Ksto [That is the way it is]

Mitakuye Oyasin [We are all related]

Lililililililililililili—the Thunder Beings are here and my daughter and I are on our way to inipi [sweat lodge] and ceremony.

My love for you and your children and families is so real and so deep that it makes me want to cry. I love our elders. I love our language. I love our stories. I love our rich and vibrant history. I love all the bands of the Tetuewan. I love my great-great-great grandchildren. I love being LAKOTA!!

Mitakuyapi, may today bring you many blessings, may Creator encourage you and embrace you as you face the day as well as the week that lies ahead. *Mitakuye Oyasin.*

Wicahpi Oyate Heciya—Star Nation You Are Alive!

Thank you for the balance.

Thank you for the stories.

Thank you for the pathways.

Thank you for the doorways.

Thank you for the presence of our ancestors.

Thank you for sustaining history and future.

I know you are in the vastness of *Mahpiya Oyate*—Sky Nation watching over ALL of us. You were so beautiful in your Earth Walk. I could only seek forever to follow in your footsteps.

CREATOR has a plan for all of us and we, as human beings, are the decision-makers that were given the fit of 'choice,' it is truly up to us whether we follow the long road or the short road. Either way, we will get to the destined point that the CREATOR knew all along.

As I stand upon our Sacred Mother's flesh, I look to the north at this time, at this hour, at this moment, and I see ... I feel ... I am you *Tatanka Oyate*—Buffalo Nation, who resides in the north. You who give us courage, bravery, and strength as well as the ability to remain and sustain upon this Earth Walk through your ancient ways. ... To the north where I see you sacred Red Willow constellation ... You are distant, yet close. I love you and thank you for being our guide. My mother, grandmother, and great-grandmother's guide, for you are OUR spiritual calendar in the sky. I look to the west where brother *Wakinyan* [lightning] resides as well as *Sunka Wakan Oyate*—Horse Nation. Ahhh, I am alive!!! Thank you for the energy *Mitakuye*. Han, I see you Sacred Hoop in the sky resting in the west. Huh? Do I see you leaving? Yes, I do. I am going to miss you. Thank you for being part of this winter cycle with us as we carry on in this universe as one with everything that is alive—*Taku Skan Skan. Hecutu Ksto. Mitakuye Oyasin.*

Earlier when I went to see my sister in the tipi and camp set up for our babies at WHITECLAY BORDER it was cold and windy and snowy and the tipi was standing strong. I parked on top of the road for if I drove in I would have got stuck and got out of the car and ran down. Maybe if I were on my horse I could have ridden to the front door with no fear. As I went into the tipi I saw *Maka*—the flesh of Earth Mother—used to be alive or otherwise called DIRT. I felt her flesh beneath my feet. There was a fire going. All around the rim of the Hocoka was all their belongings, bed rolls, and such. We sat down and visited. It was so calm and peaceful, most of all COZY. Meanwhile, the world around them in a state of panic over our sacred Sky Nation relatives because of the blizzard and no electricity.

Time for us to move toward living in the dwelling of our ancestors.

Appendix

Loren Black Elk: The Search for Justice
Camp Justice was established after the bodies of our Brother Wally and Cousin Ron were found north of Whiteclay, Nebraska. They were brutally murdered. From there on, we knew it was a battle that would be tough. For it was a battle with a people who worked for the government of the USA, who think that if a Native American is found dead, it doesn't matter how the person died, for he or she is only a Native American. This has been going on since who knows when. Think back and you can realize how many of our people were found dead and the investigations, which only went as far as the blood sample, were ruled out as exposure due to alcohol. So like it has been said, our reservation is the killing field of South Dakota.

Camp Justice met with the National Council of Churches, the Justice Department, and the Civil Rights Commission. It's nice these organizations took Camp Justice into consideration, as to where they stand. I believe the Civil Rights Commission members are the only ones who got to see how this investigation is being conducted. However, it seems when the FBI

Ronnie Hard Heart's sisters, Rose, Sharlene, and Sharon, listen to a presentation about an investigation into his death. They have never stopped grieving his loss.

caught wind that the Civil Rights Commission was coming to our reservation, I guess they thought they could make themselves look good. So, the FBI came in full force, in what they thought was a thorough investigation. They even brought a dog. We didn't know what this was all about. All we asked was why six months later, what are you going to find? The FBI was walking around where the bodies were found. They even went down to where the monument was built and trampled everything around it.

All we asked them was why six months later? Don't you think this should have been done in the first few days after the discovery of the bodies? We also told the FBI that the Civil Rights Commission had already been there the day before. You should have seen the reaction!

At the big meeting in Rapid City, that's where everybody should have been. They would have seen the FBI lie about a double brutal murder investigation. However, the Civil Rights Commission made liars out of the FBI, in front of everyone, totaling close to two hundred people. It was a blessing!

For I have been here since Day One, and I have seen how they conducted their so-called investigation. Wherever they received their training, it sure wasn't for the kind of tragedy that fell upon the families in the past. So people, I ask that you pray with us that justice may be served for all these deaths, and for all the uninvestigated investigations. Or are they just a cover up?

The March for Justice was organized from Pine Ridge to Whiteclay and held every weekend for justice. Whiteclay was the protest point, because we believe that due to all the alcohol that is sold out of there, alcohol that played a role in these brutal murders. A lot of the talk points to the involvement of some of the merchants, like a threat being made by one of the merchants to one of the brutally murdered victims, and to some of the town's residents being connected to racist groups in the surrounding area.

You've probably heard of the Camp Justice Warriors. They were arrested for crossing the state line. Their court hearings have already started. It all comes down to where they violated every right we had to act on. So people, it's very interesting to be there, to see these brothers along with their attorneys, who are going to prove Nebraska wrong.

As to the jurisdiction, that also is a winner, for under the 1868 Treaty, Whiteclay sits within the reservation boundary line and was illegally established.

These brothers are doing the same thing Crazy Horse would have done. They are saying, "This is our land and we have every right to it." Come join the struggle, the struggle for Justice.

Also, people, Camp Justice supports the Oyate's issue, for we are a part of this tribe also. All that is going on for a better future for the people and future generations. All the injustices that came out of the issue so far? Well, if you can't see these, then definitely there is something wrong. The arrest of three councilmen and a director, who was trying to cover up for them, well doesn't this show how the rest of them are? Especially the treasurer. He is supposed to be watching, but actually works with these council people in betraying our Nation.

So with this I say support is needed here and at the Tribal Building. Our Nation has been hurting, hurting since 1934, since the IRA Government was formed. The council was designed to fail at the change of every administration. That is why we are stuck at this poverty level and it's why we don't have any jobs. For more information, you can call the Tribal Building and talk with someone there about what's going on and where they stand now, as of today.

So people out there pray with us for justice, maybe you are not going through what we are going through, but a prayer for justice for all wouldn't hurt. And, we here at Camp Justice are trying our hardest to have things heard about these so-called investigations that go nowhere.

How can someone be so blind as to not understand what we are here for? We are a symbol for justice, justice for the double brutal murder of our brother, Wally, and cousin, Ron. And we do speak for the other deaths that occurred in and around our reservation, which all happened within a certain time period and stopped. If no one stood up and demanded justice, nothing would be done, and the killings would still be happening.

I bet everyone thought we gave up and closed the camp down. Well, for your information, we are still here, and there is a long-range plan. As in building an office where a computer, typewriter, and such will be available for our use. So, hopefully, this can be a plan that will come true and all the injustices that fall upon our people can be heard.

So, with this, I close, however, until next time, may the Great Spirit watch over you all always.

Dok-Sha [Later]
s/ Loren Black Elk
823 Camp Justice
Pine Ridge, So. Dak. 57770

Sharon Hard Heart: Tribute to Her Brother Ronnie

One rainy day morning, I woke up and made a pot of coffee like I usually do and waited for my brother Ron to come up from downstairs or walk in the back door and say good morning to everyone. It was like this for about a week. No sign of my brother. So my boyfriend and I went looking for him but no one had seen him. We went clear to Chadron, Nebraska, but couldn't find him.

On our way back through Slim Buttes Road and into Pine Ridge, we went toward Whiteclay and I kept smelling like something dead, like a dog. The whole time it was my brother and cousin Wally in the ditch, dead. As we were passing through, this lady named Darlene Red Star was trying to stop us, but we just drove on. If we had stopped, I would have seen my brother. Nowadays I feel so bad that I didn't stop for Darlene.

I miss my brother a lot. Back in high school we both joined cross-country and he and I used to go out running together in the hills. We had our ups and downs every now and then. We had disagreements, like over drinking. I am a recovering alcoholic and its been twenty years for me since I had a drink. Today, I am alcohol and drug free and in focus on my job and grandchildren. I'm hoping to go back to school one day.

I'm a proud grandmother of eleven. I'm also a single parent raising three boys and three girls all by myself. I've been working at the Prairie Winds Casino for seven years. And there hasn't been a charge in my brother's death.

Ron, my mother, Ruth Poor Bear [Hard Heart], and I were my father's helpers when ceremonies were held at my parent's home, five miles north of Pine Ridge. My father is Edward C. Hard Heart, a veteran of the Korean War. He was a traditional dancer and bronco rider, and he used to teach Lakota classes at Pine Ridge high school. My father always went to Cheyenne Frontier Days and my mother was the head cook for the Red Cloud School for twenty years.

We are a family of nine, but we lost our oldest brother and two older sisters from drinking, and Ron was murdered. My parents died of cancer. Right now we have one brother left and three females left.

My brother used to be a Medicine Man. I still believe in his way of life. Sometimes I sit here and wonder if the criminal investigators are really looking for leads in his death. It feels like they just tell us anything to keep us quiet and not bother them. Ron wasn't the fighting type and he wasn't a troublemaker. He always told the truth and was really helpful. Hopefully, they find the people that murdered my brother and cousin. Its been sixteen years and no one has come forward, even for the $50,000 reward.

I have a bad feeling the Rushville sheriff had something to do with my brother Ron and cousin Wally's death. I pray every night for my brother to calm him down and rest for a while till they find the murderers. I know his spirit is still walking the earth with hunger and thirst and pain. But I pray Tunkasila eases my brother's pain. All I can say right now is we really miss our little brother.

Cante Suta Forever.

Hard Heart Family

Sharon, Rose, Sharlene, Carol, and Bernadette

Endnotes

Chapter One
1. Walter Red Cloud, in discussion with the author, July 2008.

2. Stew Magnuson, *Death of Raymond Yellow Thunder And Other True Stories from the Nebraska-Pine Ridge Border Towns* (Lubbock: Texas Tech University Press, 2008), p. 276.

3. Lupe Esparza (Sandy Sauser's husband) in discussion with the author, 2008.

4. Darlene Red Star in discussion with the author, July 2008.

5. Tom Poor Bear (Wally's older half-brother and Oglala Tribal Vice President) in discussion with the author, 2008.

6. Walter Red Cloud, discussion.

7. U.S. Bureau of the Census, Per capita income by County: 1959, 1969, 1979, and 1989. Housing and Household Economic Statistics Division, Bureau of the Census. Washington, DC, 2000. http://www.census.gov/hhes/www/income/histinc/county/county3.html

How poor are the Oglala? The average of the poorest counties in each state amounted to $8,152.80 or $4,735.82 per capita more than the Oglala.

The 2010 census listed the Pine Ridge as the third poorest in America, following two other South Dakota reservations. The yearly per capita income is listed as $7,880.

8. Walter Red Cloud, discussion.

9. Tom Crash, "HUD Accepts New Census Numbers: Population Soars from 15,000 to 28,000." *The Lakota Times*, July 27, 2005.

The new census numbers were developed by Dr. Kathleen Pickering of the Department of Anthropology at Colorado State University and David Bartecchi, Pine Ridge Project Director for Village Earth. http://Villageearth.org/pages/Projects/Pine Ridge/pineridgeblog/2005/07/hud-accepts-new-census-numbers.http.

10. Elderly Oglala man and woman (did not wish to be identified), in discussion with the author, July 2008.

11. Robert Ecoffey (Bureau of Indian Affairs superintendent), in discussion with the author, July 2008.

Ecoffey is credited with solving the 1975 murder of Anna Mae Aquash, a Canadian born Micmac Indian drawn to the Pine Ridge reservation in 1973 during the seventy-one day standoff between the FBI, the Oglala, and members of the American Indian Movement at Wounded Knee.

12. Patty Duchman, (Bureau of Indian Affairs Pine Ridge Social Services representative), in discussion with the author, February 2009.

B.I.A. General Assistance payments are stipulated to be at the same rate as the state the reservation is located in has set for Temporary Assistance for Needy Families payments.

13. Senate Committee on Indian Affairs. Oversight Hearing on Indian Housing. Testimony given by John Yellow Bird Steele, President of the Ogallala Sioux Tribe, March 22, 2007. http://indian.senate.gov/public/-files/Steele0322.

14. Peter T. Kilborn, "Life at the Bottom—America's Poorest County /A Special Report; Sad Distinction for the Sioux: Homeland is No.1 in Poverty," *New York Times*, September 23, 2008. http:\\www. nytimes. com\archive.

15. Kilborn, "Life at the Bottom."

16. Tom Poor Bear, discussion.

Chapter Two

1. Loren Black Elk (Descendant of the Holy Man of the Lakota and Wally's younger brother) in discussion with the author, 2008.

2. Tom Poor Bear (Oglala Tribal Council member and Wally's older half-brother) in discussion with the author, 2008.

3. On June 25, 1876, the Lakota, led by the great Oglala War Chief Crazy Horse, defeated George Armstrong Custer's 7th Cavalry at the Battle of the Little Big Horn. One day later, with the remnants of Custer's command isolated on a bluff, the victorious Indians left the field of battle.

4. Joe Duggan, "They Marched for Their Dead Brothers," *Lincoln Journal Star*, June 27, 1999. http://www.journalstar.com/articles/2007/09/24specialreports/whiteclay/p6/doc4286955a8c20a147804020. txt

5. Magnuson, *Death of Raymond Yellow Thunder*, p. 280.

6. Duggan, "Marched."

7. Steven Hendricks, "Promised Land," *Orion*, July/August 2005. http://www.stevehendricks.org/writings/promised-land.pdf.

8. Duggan, "Marched."

9. Joe Duggan, "Rally Leaders Promise to Return," *Lincoln Journal Star*, June 28, 1999. First Nations Issues of Consequence. http://www.dickshovel.com/wc3.html.

10. Duggan quoted Chris Peterson, a spokesman for Nebraska Governor Johanns, as saying, "the governor doesn't deal with demands. Making a demand that the governor traveled two miles or two hours seems foolish, considering the governor's open door policy. His home phone number is listed and he is always willing to listen and work with people." Joe Duggan, "Marched."

11. Camp Justice Home Page. http:www.aics.org/justice/camp.html.

12. Camp Justice update 9/3/1999. http://www.aics.org/justice/0903.html.

13. At least one prominent Oglala was not impressed with a visit from the President of the United States. According to Magnuson, *Death of Raymond Yellow Thunder*, Russell Means said he "didn't give a damn if the 'sleaze of all sleazes,' as he called Clinton, came to the Pine Ridge." p. 7.

14. Camp Justice update 11/4/1999. http://www.aics.org/justice/1104. html.

15. Camp Justice update 02/22/2000. http//www.aics.org/justice/0222.html.

16. Pachi Black Elk's picture and a story about her life in Whiteclay were published in a sixteen page special report, "Standing at the Crossroads." *Lincoln Journal Star*, May 15, 2005.

The paper quoted Pachi as laughing and saying she was just killing herself with alcohol. She told the author in 2006 she wouldn't talk to any more newspapers because they made her look like a drunk.

17. John G. Neihardt, *Black Elk Speaks: Being the Life Story of a Holy Man of the Oglala Sioux* (New York: Pocket Books, 1972), p. 2.

Chapter Three

1. Peter C. Mancall, *Deadly Medicine: Indians and Alcohol in Early America* (Ithaca and London, Cornell University Press 1999), p. 20.

2. Mancall, *Deadly Medicine*. 14.

3. Benjamin Franklin, *Autobiography and Other Pieces*, ed. Dennis Welland (London: Oxford University Press, 1970), p. 115.

4. Alden T. Vaughn, ed., *New England Encounters: Indians and Euroamericans. ca. 1600–1850* (Boston: Northeastern University Press, 1999), p. 65

5. Vaughn, *Encounters*, p. 92.

6. Mancall, *Deadly Medicine*, p. 114.

7. Mancall, *Deadly Medicine*, p. 111.

Jonathan Carver met the Lakota in 1767. He wrote, "Some of these chiefs could not be prevailed upon to taste any spirituous liquors on any account as they look upon it as a bad medison, ... The Naudowessee of the plains have scarcely any knowledge of spirituous liquor and are not at all inclind to it," p. 41.

Still this knowledge did not keep Carver from striving to set up a still to produce alcohol in the region. As Mancall wrote, "The significance of the plan lies in Carver's assumption that the prosperity of the fur trade was linked to the expansion of the liquor trade. In his imperial fantasy, Carver betrayed the Indians who had adopted and conferred a great honor upon him. Though he knew that alcohol disrupted their communities and brought suffering to individuals and families, he hoped to serve the king and to profit himself by bringing more liquor to them," p. 166.

8. Meriwether Lewis and William Clark, *The Journals of Lewis and Clark* Abr. ed. (Washington DC: National Geographic Adventure Classics, 2002), p. 53.

9. Lewis and Clark, *Journals*, p. 69.

10. William E. Unrau, *White Man's Wicked Water: The Alcohol Trade and Prohibition in Indian Country, 1802–1892* (Lawrence: University Press of Kansas, 1966), p. 19.

11. Unrau, *Wicked Water*, p. IX.

12. Edward Charles Abbott (Teddy Blue) and Helena Huntington Smith, *We Pointed Them North: Recollections of a Cow Puncher* (Norman: University of Oklahoma Press, 1955), p. 124.

13. A Nebraska farmer (did not wish to be identified), in discussion with the author, July 2008.

14. Frank LaMere, "Frank LaMere Speaks About Whiteclay," Common Ground Common Sense On Line Community. http://www. commongroundcommon sense.org/forums/lofiverson/index.Php/t30469. html.

15. Anheuser-Busch Companies. http//www.anheuser-busch.com/beerVerified .html#hurricaneHG

Chapter Four

1. Norman Brown Eyes, in discussion with author, August 2009.

2. Jeff Mather, "To Raise Up an Interesting Commonwealth: Jackson's Reaction to Worcester And Nullification." http://jeffmatherphotography.com/jeff/ Worcester.html.

3. Sidney L. Harring, *Crow Dog's Case: American Indian Sovereignty, Tribal Law, and United States Law in the 19th Century* (Cambridge: Cambridge University Press, 1994), p. 29.

4. *Cherokee Nation* v. *Georgia*, 30 U.S. 1 (1831). http://www.law.cornell.edu/ supct/html/historics/USSC_CR_0030_0001_ZO.html.

5. *Worcester* v. *Georgia*, 31 U.S. 515 (1832). http://scholar.google.com/scholar_ case?case=6938475705816460383&hl=en&as_sdt=2&as_vis=1&oi=scholar.

6. There is contention among historians on the accuracy of this statement. Harring, *Crow Dog's Case*, used the quote but noted the dispute. However, he wrote, "but his actions clearly indicate his intention." (25) Paul F. Boller and John H. George, *They Never Said It: A Book of Fake Quotes, Misquotes, and Misleading Attributions*, say the actual statement was written into a letter as "the decision of the Supreme Court has fell stillborn."

7. *U.S.* v. *Rogers*, 45 U.S. 567 (1846). https://bulk.resource.org/courts.gov/c/ US/45/45.US.567.html.

8. Along the Oregon Trail near Fort Laramie in eastern Wyoming, a cow belonging to a Mormon traveling on the trail wandered into the Brule camp of Chief Conquering Bear. According to the Brule, the cow was old and footsore, only skin wrapped around bones. A young man named High Forehead shot and butchered it. The traveler went to the fort and complained about the illegal killing of his cow. Lieutenant Grattan, not long out of West Point and inexperienced with plains Indians, demanded the arrest of High Forehead. When that didn't happen he took a squad and two cannons to Conquering Bear's camp. A shot was heard, a cannon fired, and Conquering Bear fell dead. The Indians took revenge by killing Grattan and all of his men.

The different names for the battle or incident are reminiscent of Tecumseh's famous quote about Indians, white men, and battles. "When a white man kills an Indian in a fair fight it is called honorable, but when an Indian kills a white man in a fair fight it is called murder. When a white army battles Indians and wins it is called a great victory, but if they lose it is called a massacre." http://www.friendsofthefrontier.org/Frontier/tecumseh.asp.

9. After the battle, Harney would be known as "Woman Killer" by the Lakota—perhaps, an unfortunate name for the highest peak in their sacred Black Hills.

10. George E. Hyde, *Spotted Tails Folk: A History of the Brule Sioux.* (Norman: University of Oklahoma Press, 1961), p. 73.

Susan Bordeaux Bettelyoun was the daughter of a French trapper and a Brule woman. She says Spotted Tail ran to fight partly undressed. He grabbed a sword from a mounted soldier, knocked him off his horse, jumped onto the animal and unhorsed thirteen other soldiers, killing some of them. Susan Bordeaux Bettelyoun and Josephine Waggoner, *With My Own Eyes: A Lakota Woman Tells Her People's History* (Lincoln: University of Nebraska Press, 1998), p. 57.

11. At Sand Creek, in eastern Colorado, Major Chivington, an ordained Methodist minister, led the Colorado First and Third Cavalry against a peaceful village of Arapahos. When asked about the children, he is reported to have responded, "Nits make lice." Striking on a November morning, Chivington's nine hundred men killed around 138 Arapaho, of which two thirds were women and children. It was reported that his men returned to Denver with women's breasts tanned into tobacco pouches and scalps taken from female genitalia. Margaret Coel, in an excellent biography of Arapaho Chief Left Hand, records Chivington said, "Men, strip for action. I don't tell you to kill all ages and sex, but look back on the plains of the Platte, where your mothers, fathers, brothers, sisters have been slain, and their blood saturating the sand of the Platte." Margaret Coel, *Chief Left Hand.* (Norman: University of Oklahoma Press, 1981), p. 276.

12. Jeffrey Ostler, *The Plains Sioux and US Colonialism from Lewis and Clark to Wounded Knee.* (Cambridge: Cambridge University Press, 2004), p. 69.

13. Harring, *Crow Dog's Case*, p. 106.

According to Hyde, the chief's family didn't really live in the house, using it only on ceremonial occasions. Hyde, *Spotted Tail's Folk*, p. 40.

14. Leonard Crow Dog and Richard Erdoes, *Crow Dog: Four Generations of Sioux Medicine Men* (New York: Harper Perennial, 1996), p. 22.

15. Crow Dog, *Crow Dog*, p. 33.

16. Eileen Luna-Firebaugh, *Tribal Policing: Asserting Sovereignty, Seeking Justice.* (Tucson: University of Arizona Press, 2007), p. 18.

That the Lakota traditionally had a legal system and it was enforced became very important in the Crow Dog murder case. Lakota enforcement societies were called Akicitas. They were appointed by the camp leader from the membership of certain societies and served terms of one year. They were empowered to regulate buffalo hunts and enforce tribal laws and customs. They served as both judge and jury.

17. Hyde claims that Crow Dog always blamed Spotted Tail for the loss of his job but that police records show Spotted Tail was visiting Pine Ridge when the dismissal occurred." Hyde, *Spotted Tails Folks*, p. 315.

18. Crow Dog, *Crow Dog*, p. 34.

19. Crow Dog, *Crow Dog*, p. 35.

20. Crow Dog, *Crow Dog*, p. 37.

21. *Ex Parte Crow Dog*, 109 U.S. 556 (1883). According to modern day Oglala, Crow Dog promised to take care of Spotted Tail's family for four generations.

22. *United States* v. *Kagama*.

23. Embry, Carlos B., *America's Concentration Camps: The Facts About Our Indian Reservations Today.* (New York: David McKay Co., Inc.), p. 38.

Religious ceremonies such as the Sundance and the Rabbit Dance were forbidden as was giving away of property (giveaways have always been a hallmark of Lakota culture). So were frequent and prolonged periods of celebration and any excessive performance that promoted superstitious cruelty, licentiousness, idleness, danger to health, and shiftlessness—with severe penalties for violation.

24. The ability of reservation residents to enforce laws over themselves as defined in the Indian Civil Rights Act of 1968 is limited to imprisonment of up to one year and a fine of $5000 or both. For everything else they are at the power of non-reservation, usually non-Indian, Americans.

The adjudication of criminal behavior on the reservation regarding law enforcement agencies and tribal status of the accused is complex. If an Indian commits a major felony against another Indian, the crime falls under the Major Crimes Act, is investigated by the FBI, and adjudicated by a federal court in a city off the reservation with the makeup of the jury composed of a cross section of that city's populace. In terms of state responsibility, with an Indian on Indian crime, the reservation, because of sovereignty, is invisible to the state. However, if a non-Indian commits a crime against a non-Indian on the reservation, the state has jurisdiction over the investigation and adjudication of the crime.

25. Making adjudication on reservations even more confusing, Public Law 280 passed in 1953 changes this system for the six states of Nebraska, Wisconsin, Alaska, California, Minnesota, and Oregon, giving the states the powers reserved to the federal government in the rest of the United States.

26. In a surprise announcement, the FBI increased the reward and offered new information about their investigation in August of 2009.

Chapter Five

1. South Dakota Advisory Committee to the United States Commission on Civil Rights. "Native Americans in South Dakota: An Erosion of Confidence in the Justice System," 2000, p. 20. http://www.usccr.gov/pubs/sac/sd0300/ch1.htm/.

2. Ibid, p. 20.

3. Ibid, p. 14.

4. Ibid, p. 5–6.

5. Ibid, p. 6.

6. Ibid, p. 15.

7. Jon Lurie, "Harvest of Death." http:www.dickshovel.com/lsa27.html.

8. Eric Davis, "Lawyers file briefs in Many Horses Case," *Native News*, September 14, 1999. http://www.mail-archive.com/nntivenews@mlists.net/msg0428.html

9. ABC Transcript: The Death of Robert Many Horses, *20/20*. http:groups.yahoo.com/group/aim/message/9347.

10. American Indian Movement; Still Strong, "Aim Reaction." http://www.mailarchive.com/native news@mlists.net/msg04577.html.

11. Appel reportedly said, "It is illegal to cross the white line, or if it is a solid yellow line, or even if it wasn't, it is illegal to swerve." Suzy Buchanan, "Malign Neglect," Intelligence Report, Southern Poverty Law Center, #24, Winter 2006.

12. Ibid.

13. Ibid, p. 21.

14. Ibid, p. 11. Cameron's statement is disputed by Redday's mother and the Southern Poverty Law Center.

15. Peggy Redday, phone interview with author, 2012.

Buchanan, "Malign Neglect," reported Appel received a sentence of thirty days in jail and a $300 dollar fine.

16. Ibid, p. 22.

17. Alva Quinn, in discussion with the author, 2012.

18. Ruth Steinberger, "Strange Case of Adelia Godfrey Supports Suspicions." *Lakota Journal*. http://www.dlncoalition.org/dlncoalition/2002septgodfrey.htm.

19. Lee Williams, "Adelia Won't Be Tried As An Adult!!!!!" *Argus Leader*, April 20, 2002.

20. Ruth Steinberger, "Juvenile Justice," *Native Times*. http://www.dlncoalition.org/dln-coalition/2002septgodfrey.htm.

21. Lee Williams, "Teen's Jailing Angers Tribe." *Argus Leader*, March 3, 2002. ttp://www.dlncoalition.org/dln_coalition/adelia_godfrey1.htm.

22. *Associated Press*, "Tribes Charge Double Standard Used." March 4, 2002.

23. Thorazine is used for the treatment of schizophrenia (severe disruptions in thought and perception). It is also prescribed for the short-term treatment of severe behavioral disorders in children, including explosive hyperactivity and combativeness; and for the hyperenergetic phase of manic-depressive illness (severely exaggerated moods). http://www.healthsquare.com/newrx/tho1441.htm.

24. Ruth Steinberger, "Juvenile Justice," *Native Times*. http://www.dlncoalition.org/dln-coalition/2002septgodfrey.htm.

25. The officer Adelia sprayed with the fire extinguisher testified, when asked by her lawyer why he grabbed her, that it was for her protection. "It's been my experience with Adelia that if I did not do something, she might trip and fall to the floor." Williams, Adelia Won't be Tried As An Adult!!!!!

26. Edward Godfrey, in discussion with the author, 2012.

27. South Dakota Advisory Committee, p. 27.

28. Denis Ross, "Janklow Seeks Meeting," *Rapid City Journal*, May 3, 2000.

29. Ben Black Elk after buying giveaway items for Loren's funeral, in discussion with author. February 2012.

30. Press Release #165. United States Department of Justice. April 15, 1996. http://www.justice.gov/opa/pr/1996/April96/165.cr.htm.

31. Three Oglala Women who wish to remain anonymous in discussion with author, 2011.

32. Southern Poverty Law Center, Hate Map. http://www.splcenter.org/get-informed/hate-map.

33. Church followers believe the white race is nature's highest creation, while Jews and nonwhites, mud people, are their natural enemy.

34. Center for New Community, the Montana Human Rights Network, and the Northwest Coalition for Human Dignity, "Creating a Commotion: Matt Hale and the World Church of the Creator." January 7, 2003. http://www.buildingdemocracy.org/reports/commotion.pdf.

35. Steve Hendricks, *The Unquiet Grave: The FBI and the Struggle For the Soul of Indian Country.* (New York: Thunder's Mouth Press, 2006), p. 26.

36. Personal knowledge of the author.

37. While Yellow Thunder did receive some help from the dancers in hiding his nakedness and leaving the building, neither dancers nor the deputy called for any medical attention for the bloody, beaten man.

38. Leslie Hare was convicted of manslaughter and sentenced to six years with a $500 fine. His brother, Melvin, received two years with a $500 fine.

39. Dale Mason, "You can only kick so long, AIM leadership in Nebraska 1972-79." http://www.dickshovel.com/lsa23.html

40. Christine Rose, Students and Teachers Against Racism. Press release: "The Mysterious Death of Jay Spotted Elk." September 18, 2005. http://mostlywater.org/node/3356

41. *Eastman* v. *County of Sheridan,* United States District Court. Fifth Amended Complaint: 07CV05004 (D. Neb 2007). http://www.clearinghouse.net/chDocs/public/JC-NE-0005-0001.pdf

42. *Rapid City Journal,* "Sheridan County Settles Lawsuit on Inmate Suicide." May 11, 2010. https://www.prisonlegalnews.org/(S(cxriybf5fay3mvb04emm1q45))/displayListServ.aspx?listid=5351&AspxAutoDetectCookieSupport=1.

43. *Eastman* v. *Sheridan County*: 07CV05004 (D. Neb 2007). http://www.gpo.gov/fdsys/granule/USCOURTS-ned-7_07-cv-05004/USCOURTS-ned-7_07-cv-05004-0/content-detail.html.

44. Steve Russell, "In Memory of Jay Spotted Elk," The Rag Blog, August 9, 2010. http://indiancountrytodaymedianetwork.com/ictarchives/2010/08/06/russell-in-memory-of-jay-spotted-elk-81104.

45. Rose, Students and Teachers Against Racism. Press Release.

46. Vincent Schilling, *Indian Country Today,* "Whiteclay Fallout: Women's Day of Peace march ends with arrests and youth being maced." August 29, 2012. http://battleforwhiteclay.org/?p=2057.

47. Schilling, *Indian Country Today.*

48. Nicholas D. Kristof, *The New York Times Sunday Review,* "A Battle with

the Brewers," May 5, 2012. http://www.nytimes.com/2012/05/06/opinion/sunday/kristof-a-battle-with-the-brewers.html?_r=0.

49. Sandy Sauser, personal observation, 2008.

Chapter Six

1. Bill Harlan, "Thirty-Five-Year-Old Memories Still Drive Flood Debate." *Rapid City Journal,* October 1, 2007. Quote attributed to a late Rapid City economist, Earle Hausie, who studied Lakota history.

2. Fort Laramie Treaty, April 29, 1868. http://www.puffin.creighton.edu/lakota/1868 la.html.

3. There was some doubt that Custer's party had actually found enough gold to make mining in the Black Hills profitable. In June of 1875, William Jenney, a geologist, led another expedition into the area and confirmed the gold strike was more than a figment of Custer's imagination.

4. Thadd Turner, *Wild Bill Hickok: Deadwood City—End of Trail.* (USA: Universal Publisers/uPUBLISH.com), 26.

5. Edward Lazarus, *Black Hills, White Justice: The Sioux Nation Versus the United States, 1775 to the Present.* (New York: HarperCollins Publishers, 1991), p. 83.

6. Rapid City: History. "Cities of the United States, 2006." http://encyclopedia.com/doc/1G2-3441801864.html.

7. "Rapid City, South Dakota, AKA: skinhead central, U.S.A." http://www.mindspring.com/-mike.wicks/rapidcity.html.

8. South Dakota Advisory Committee to the United States Commission on Civil Rights. *"Native Americans in South Dakota: An Erosion of Confidence in the Justice System,* 2000," p. 20. http://www.usccr.gov/pubs/sac/sd0300/ch1.htm/.

9. "Rapid City, South Dakota, AKA: skinhead central, U.S.A."

10. The list, notes, and the death of each man are a compilation of several sources, including "Rapid City, South Dakota, AKA: skinhead central, U.S.A.";
Keohane, "Deaths of Homeless Investigated." *Nativenews.* September 6, 1999; and Chet Brokaw, "Officials Look for Answers in Rapid Creek Mystery Deaths 10 Years Later," *The Associated Press,* June 22, 2009. http://www/rapidcityjournal.com/articles/2009/06/22/news/local/doc4a3e7725727c140737691.txt

11. Chet Brokaw, "Officials Look for Answers ..."

12. Chet Brokaw, "Officials Look for Answers ..."

13. When Glassgow served as sheriff of Custer County, South Dakota, Dennis Banks of the American Indian Movement asked him to negotiate conditions of a peaceful protest when the Lakota marched to Whiteclay, Nebraska, after the deaths of Black Elk and Hard Heart.

14. DeWayne Glassgow, in discussion with the author, 2009.

15. Jon Lurie, Lakota Student Alliance, "Harvest of Death." http://www.thepeoplespaths.net/Articles2000/LSA0000312Harvest.htm.

16. Eric Slater, "A Quiet Creek in S.D. Becomes River of Death," *Los Angeles Times*, May 20, 2000. http://articles.latimes.com/2000/may/20/news/mn-32030.

17. Terry Johnson, "Reward Offered to Solve Mysterious Death," *Indian Country Today*, September 19, 2004.

18. Terry Johnson, "Reward Offered."

19. Jenifer Peterka, "Aura of Slayings in South Dakota," *Native News*, August 5, 1999. http://www.mail-archive.com/nativenews@mlists.net/msg03784.html.

20. South Dakota Advisory Commission, 18.

21. South Dakota Advisory Commission, 17.

22. "Rapid City, South Dakota, AKA: skinhead central, U.S.A."

23. David Melmer, "Two Suspects Charged in Johnson Murder: Both Could Face Death Penalty." *Indian Country Today*. High Beam Research. http://www.highbeam.com/doc/1P1-79288722.html

24. DeWayne Glassgow, in discussion with the author.

Chapter Seven

1. Two Oglala women who wish to remain anonymous in discussion with the author, 2009.

2. Sheriff Robbins in discussion with the author, 2009.

3. Jomay Steen, "Murder Confession a Rumor," *Lincoln Star Journal*, April 15, 2006.

4. The Carpenter Guy in discussion with the author, 2009.

5. Ibid. He wrote on Myspace, "not a one comes close to the one who taught me, a man named Morris, who lived a perfect life." 2009.

6. Myspace. 2009. Interests column.

7. The Carpenter Guy in discussion with the author.

Chapter Eight

1. Larry Salway, "The Medicine Wheel: Sacredness of the Sacred Hoop," *Outline of Lakota Culture 110*. http://lifeinitiativesinc.org/trainingculture110.html.

By keeping the hoop whole, the people "… walk in Wisdom (or Peace), Beauty, Harmony, Balance, and Love."

2. Among the Lakota, each tribe was divided into smaller units known as an Oyate. Each Oyate contained several Tiospaye, usually no more than several hundred people and usually all related. After Bull Bear's death, the band changed their name to Ki-ya-ksa or "bitten in two"; this has been translated to "Cut Off."

3. Francis Parkman, *The Oregon Trail* (Boston: Little, Brown, and Company, 1883; Mineola: Dover Publications, Inc. 2002), p. 147. Citations are to the Dover edition.

4. Ibid, p. 147.

5. R. Eli Paul, ed. *Autobiography of Red Cloud: War Leader of the Oglalas* (Helena: Montana Historical Society Press, 1977), p. 69.

6. The band moved to the Red Cloud Agency located near Crawford, Nebraska. They did not move onto the Pine Ridge, forty miles northeast, until 1878.

Before 1872, the agency had been located along the Platte River. Red Cloud's people, remaining free and nomadic, used it as a place to pick up their rations.

7. Rumors and stories of mineral wealth in the Black Hills had been around for years before Custer's expedition. Custer pushed for the expedition believing he would find gold. However, his superiors justified the excursion differently: General Sheridan proclaimed he had been interested in building a military post in the hills for several years to better control the Indians, while Terry announced he could find no offense to the Lakota by Custer's expedition.

8. Edward Lazarus, *Black Hills White Justice: The Sioux Nation Versus the United States, 1775 to the Present* (New York: HarperCollins Publishers, 1991), p. 81–82.

The Lakota were divided on the question of sale. Little Big Man yelled at the meeting of commissioners and Lakota, "I will kill the first chief who speaks for selling the Black Hills!" Crazy Horse said, "One does not sell the land the people walk on." However, chiefs like Spotted Tail and Red Cloud saw the sale as an opportunity to provide for their people for generations. They asked for $70,000,000.

9. Beard died in 1955 at the age of ninety-nine. Una's great-uncle and Leonard Little Finger's grandfather, he was also known as Iron Hail. After meeting Admiral Dewey, he adopted the name Dewey Beard. Beard was the last surviving participant of the Battle of the Greasy Grass or the Little Big Horn.

10. Fort Fetterman, named after Captain Fetterman who once claimed that with eighty men he could ride through Lakota country, and whose entire command, including himself, of eighty men was killed near Fort Phil Kearney in the foothills of the Big Horn Mountains in 1866, causalities of Red Cloud's successful war to close forts along the Bozeman Road.

11. Leonard Little Finger (Beard's grandson), in discussion with the author, 2010. As a youngster at a pow wow near the Greasy Grass, Leonard Little Finger was excited when his grandfather, Beard, offered to show him around the battlefield. However, his father said he had to stay and dance.

12. There is no evidence they were swimming in the same hole, but Black Elk had been swimming when the attack began.

13. John G. Neihardt, *Black Elk Speaks: Being the Life Story of a Holy Man of the Oglala Sioux* (New York: William Morrow & Company, 1932; New York: Pocket Books, 1972), p. 91. Citations are to the Pocket Books edition.

14. Gregory F. Michno, *Lakota Noon: The Indian Narrative of Custer's Defeat* (Missoula: Mountain Press Publishing Company, 1997), p. 30.

Michno's account does not agree with Little Finger's. He writes that Beard had joined a younger brother herding horses at the time of the attack.

15. Little Finger, Interview.

Again, Michno disagrees (*Lakota Noon*, p. 73). He uses David Humphrey Miller, "Echoes of the Little Bighorn" (*American Heritage* 22, no. 4 (June 1971), p. 28–39 as a source. According to Michno, Beard had caught his favorite war pony, a small buckskin mustang called Little Yellow Horse, and mounted him for battle. He braided his tail, mixed white paint and daubed spots of hail-stone on his own forehead and gathered up his bows and arrows.

16. David Humphreys Miller, *Custer's Fall: The Native American Side of the Story* (New York: Meridian, 1992), p. 92.

17. Little Finger, Interview.

18. Ibid.

19. Neihardt, *Black Elk Speaks*, p. 91–104.

20. The Lakota are one of three groups of confederated tribes who speak different dialects. The other two are the Dakota and the Nakota.

21. Philip Wells, "Ninety-Six Years Among the Indians of the Northwest—Adventures and Reminiscences of an Indian Scout and Interpreter in the Dakotas as told to Thomas E. Odell." The authors used a copy of the work passed through Sandy Sauser's family. The work was also published in *North Dakota History*, 15 (Jan-Oct 1948).

22. Buffalo, source of all things to the Lakota, were already in decline when Red Cloud defeated the army. Tongues were considered delicacies in eastern and European cities; hides tanned and cut into strips became long-wearing factory belts to power the industrial revolution. As civilized man's insatiable need for top hats brought the beaver population near extinction, the demand for buffalo skin brought the shaggy beasts even closer.

When Lewis and Clark explored the West there may have been thirty to seventy million buffalo. This number fell to a low of 300 before conservation measures began to restore them.

General Sheridan was plainly outspoken. Never known for his sympathy to the original inhabitants, he summed up the judgment of many of his time: "These men [the buffalo hunters] have done more in the last two years to settle the vexed Indian question than the entire regular army has done in the last forty years. They are destroying the Indian's commissary. And it is a well-known fact that an army losing its base of supplies is placed at a great disadvantage. Send them powder and lead if you will, but for the sake of a lasting peace let them kill, skin, and sell until the buffalo are exterminated. Then your prairies can be covered with speckled cattle and the festive cowboy who follows the hunter as the second forerunner of an advanced civilization." General Sheridan, as quoted in, Christopher Ketcham, "They shoot buffalo don't they; Hazing America's last wild herd," *Harper's Magazine* June, 2008. http://harpers.org/archive/2008/06/0082064.

23. Captain Richard H. Pratt, who founded the U.S. Training and Industrial School in Carlisle, Pennsylvania, in 1879, where many Lakota children were sent, often against family wishes, in 1892 expressed clearly what he, and many others, thought of the culture of the original inhabitants: "A great general has said that the only good Indian is a dead one, and that high sanction of his destruction has been an enormous factor in promoting Indian massacres. In a sense, I agree with the sentiment, but only in this: that all the Indian there is

in the race should be dead. Kill the Indian in him, and save the man." http://
historymatters.gmu.edu/d/4929/.

24. Dee Brown, *Bury My Heart at Wounded Knee* (New York: Henry Holt
and Company, 1970), p. 425–26.

Chapter Nine

1. James Mooney, "The Ghost-Dance Religion and the Sioux Outbreak of
1890," Fourteenth Annual Report of the Bureau of Ethnology, 1892-93, pt.2 (Washington, D.C., 1896). Reprinted as: *The Ghost Dance Religion and Wounded Knee*
(New York: Dover Publications, 1973) p. 820. Citations are to the Dover edition.

2. Mooney, *Ghost Dance Religion*, p. 780. There are significant disagreements
about the date the letter was received by the Oglala. Short Bull says the Oglala read
the letter before the second group of emissaries was sent to visit Wovoka. Short
Bull's testimony, handwritten by an unnamed translator, is found in the Buffalo
Bill Memorial Museum in Golden, Colorado. According to Mooney, "Black Short
Nose, a Cheyenne, took from a beaded pouch and gave me a letter, which proved to
be the message or statement of the doctrine delivered by Wovoka to the Cheyenne
and Arapaho delegates, of whom Black Short Nose was one, on the occasion of
their last visit to Nevada, in August, 1891, and written down on the spot, in broken
English by one of the Arapaho delegates."

3. Short Bull Testimony, Buffalo Bill Memorial Museum, Golden, Colorado.

4. William S.E. Coleman, *Voices of Wounded Knee* (Lincoln: University of Nebraska Press, 2000), p. 30–31.

5. Mooney, *Ghost Dance Religion*. p. 1061.

6. Elaine Goodale Eastman, *Sister to the Sioux: The Memoirs of Elaine Goodale
Eastman, 1885–1891* (Lincoln: University of Nebraska Press, 1978), p. 137.

7. Donald Danker, ed., *The Wounded Knee Interviews of Eli S. Ricker*,
Nebraska History 62 (Summer 1981), p. 224. Reservation clerks and inhabitants questioned Royer's honesty as well as his courage. Robert O. Pugh, Issue Clerk, accused him of stealing wood, hay, and grain, and understating the
weight of cattle meant for the Oglala, allowing his and his partners to sell off
$40,000 worth of beef at a profit.

8. Dr. Daniel F. Royer, Agent, Pine Ridge Agency. Telegram sent to Bureau of
Indian Affairs, Washington D.C. November 15, 1890. http://www.omaha.lib.ne.us/
transmiss/congress/activities.html.

9. "Fifteen Thousand Braves. The Indians Could Do Much Harm If So Disposed," *The Salt Lake Tribune*, November 18, 1890. http://newspaperarchive.com.

10. "Expect To Be Killed: Citizens of Mandan Anticipate an Attack by Frenzied
Sioux Braves," *St. Paul Daily Globe*, November 18, 1890. http://chroniclingamerica.
loc.gov/lccn/sn99021999/issues.

11. *New York Times*, November 20, 1890. The *Times* article blamed Agent
Royer's desertion of his post as a main cause of the excitement and talk about an
imminent uprising. http://query.nytimes.com/gst/abstract.html?res=9404E6DF1E

3BE533A25753C2A9679D94619ED7CF&scp=39&sq=December+20%2C+1890 &st=p.

12. "Indians Ready to Fight: A Squaw's Warning," *Omaha Daily Bee*, November 20, 1890. http://chroniclingamerica.loc.gov/lccn/sn 99021999/1890-11-20.

13. "Indians Ready To Fight," *New York Times*, November 22, 1890. http://query.nytimes.com/mem/archive-free/pdf?r=1&res=9C04E2DF1E3BE533A2575 1C2A9679D94619ED7CF

14. "Red Devils Rampant," *St. Paul Daily Globe*, November 27 1890. http://chroniclingamerica.loc.gov/lccn/sn90059522/1890-11-27/ed-1/seq-1/; words=Phillips+Scotty.

15. Red Cloud, *Chadron Democrat*, November 20, 1890. Quoted in William S.E. Coleman, *Voices of Wounded Knee* (Lincoln: University of Nebraska Press), p. 93.

16. Red Cloud, *New York World*, November 23, 1890. Quoted in Coleman, *Voices of Wounded Knee*, p. 96.

17. "The Ghost Dance: The Indians Keep It Up and Get Excited," *Salt Lake Herald*, November 22, 1890. http://chroniclingamerica.loc.gov/lccn/ sn85058130/1890-11-22/ed-1/seq-1/;words=reds+Cloud+Red+red.

18. Richard E. Jensen ed., *The Indian Interviews of Eli S. Ricker, 1903–1919* (Lincoln: University of Nebraska Press, 2006), p. 151.

19. "Fearing an Outbreak: Trouble is Apprehended Among the Sioux," *Arizona Republican*. October 28, 1890. http://chroniclingamerica.loc.gov/lccn/ sn84020558/1890-10-28/ed-1/seq-1/;words=Laughlin+Agent+Mc.

20. L. W. Colby, "The Sioux Indian War of 1890–91." *Transactions and Reports of the Nebraska State Historical Society 3*, (1892), p. 151.

21. "The Last of Sitting Bull," *St. Louis Republic*, December 17, 1890. http:// www.dickshovel.com/greasy.html.

22. Jensen, *The Indian Interviews of Eli S. Ricker*, p. 209. Dewey Beard told Ricker the full text of the letter: "My Dear Friend Chief Big Foot. Whenever you receive this letter, come at once. Whenever you come to our reservation a fire is going to be started and I want you to come and help us put it out and make a peace. Whenever you come among us to make peace we will give you 100 head of horses."

23. Ibid, p. 209.

24. "The Hostiles Combining," *New York Times*, December 19, 1890. http:// query.nytimes.com/gst/abstract.html?res=9904E7D81E3BE533A2575AC1A9649 D94619ED7CF&scp=13&sq=December+19%2C+1890&st=p

25. Robert M. Utley, *The Last Days of the Sioux Nation*, 2nd ed. (New Haven: Yale University Press), p175.

26. Jensen, *Indian Interviews*, p. 194–195.

27. "Bull's Warriors Surrender: Big Foot and a Band of Hostiles Headed Off by Colonel Sumner," *Omaha Daily Bee*, December 23, 1890.

This statement was from General Miles regarding the rebellion by the Santee Dakota against the United States. It has been estimated that between 400 and 800 settlers were killed. Thirty-eight Indians were hanged, the most people executed on one day in American History. http://chroniclingamerica.loc.gov/lccn/sn99021999/1890-12-23/ed-1/seq-1/;words=troubles+Minnesota.

28. Proceedings of an Investigation Made Pursuant to Special Order No. 8, Headquarters, Division of the Missouri, in the Field, Pine Ridge, South Dakota, Jan. 4, 1891. Quoted in Jeffry Ostler, *The Plains Sioux and U.S. Colonialism from Lewis and Clark to Wounded Knee* (Cambridge: Cambridge University Press, 2004), p. 334.

29. Jensen, *Indian Interviews*, p. 216.

30. Ibid., p. 216.

31. Proceedings of an Investigation Made Pursuant to Special Order No. 8, Headquarters, Division of the Missouri, in the Field, Pine Ridge, South Dakota, Jan. 4, 1891. Quoted in Utley, *Last Days of the Sioux Nation*, p. 197.

32. U.S. Senate. Hearing before the Select Committee of Indian Affairs, 102 Congress, 1st sess., April 30, 1991. Washington DC: GPO, 1991. Quoted in William S. Coleman, *Voices of Wounded Knee* (Lincoln: University of Nebraska Press, 2000), p. 274.

33. U.S. Senate. Hearing before the Select Committee of Indian Affairs, 101 Congress, 2nd sess., September 25, 1990. Washington DC: GPO, 1991. Quoted in Coleman, *Voices*, p. 273.

34. Jensen, *Indian Interviews*, p. 217.

35. Ibid, p. 199.

36. Ibid, p. 218.

37. Wells, *Ninety-Six Years*.

38. Jensen, *Indian Interviews*, p. 219.

39. Ibid, p. 209.

40. Wells, *Ninety-Six Years*.

41. Jensen, *Indian Interviews*, p. 200–219. Both Joseph and Dewey Beard told Ricker that Black Coyote's rifle pointed harmlessly into the air toward the east.

42. Wells, *Ninety-Six Years*.

43. Jensen, *Indian Interviews*, p. 220–225.

44. *Army and Navy Journal,* January 24, 1891, Quoted in Coleman, *Voices*, p. 322.

45. While the name Maya Owichapaha is well recorded in written sources, it is a mystery to some modern Oglala who refer to her only as "The Grandmother."

46. L. Frank Baum, Editorial, *Aberdeen Saturday Pioneer*, January 3, 1891, Quoted in A. Waller Hastings, "L. Frank Baum's Editorials on the Sioux Nation." http://www.history.ox.ac.uk/hsmt/courses_reading/undergraduate/authority_of_nature/week_7/baum.pdf.

Chapter Ten

1. Irma R Miller, *French Indian Families in America's West*, 2nd, Ed. (Westcliffe: Trafford Publishing, 2005), p. 37. "This was the woman whose haunting beauty was painted in life and in death, profiled against a fur robe background

overlooking a saddened Henri. The collage-like painting hangs in upper hall of the original portion of the house that Chatillon built. The house, purchased by a Dr. Demenil and enlarged, is now an historical site in St. Louis, Missouri."

2. Matthew C. Field, *Prairie and Mountain Sketches*. ed. Kate L. Gregg and Francis McDermott (Norman: University of Oklahoma Press, 1957), p. 163.

3. Miller, *French Indian Families*, p. 41. "Since some frontiersmen spoke English, some French, and all a little Lakota, the Lessert name took several permutations. To show his family relationship to his father, Ben became known as petit Clement to the French and young Clement to the English. Since the name Clement in French is pronounced 'Cle'mon,' many variations such as Clemoo, Claymon, and Claremore were used until Claymore evolved. Lessert was not used in the mountains."

4. "Exterminate Them!" *Rocky Mountain News*, March 24, 1863. "They are a dissolute, vagabondish, brutal, and ungrateful race and ought to be wiped from the face of the earth." http://www.yellowstone-online.com/buffalo/october12genocidedestructionandimperialismslideshow.pdf.

"The Battle of Sand Creek," *Rocky Mountain News*, December 17, 1864. http://www.kclonewolf.com/History/SandCreek/sc-reports/rocky-editorials.html.

5. Miller, *French Indian Families*, p. 67.

6. Ibid, p. 70.

7. Richard E. Jensen ed., *The Settler and Soldier Interviews of Eli S. Ricker, 1903-1919* (Lincoln: University of Nebraska Press, 2006), p. 182. Ricker records the man's name as Cogill while Miller lists it as Cowgill.

8. Ibid, p. 258.

9. Miller, *French Indian Families*, p. 104.

10. Progressive and traditional became more attitude than physical description.

11. David W. Daily, *Battle for the BIA: G.E.E. Lindquist and the Missionary Crusade against John Collier* (Tucson: The University of Arizona Press. 2004) p. 13.

12. In 1891, Pine Ridge residents created the Oglala Council along traditional lines, even writing and adopting a constitution under the presidency of James Red Cloud.

Chapter Eleven

1. Holland, Michigan. *The Holland Evening Sentinel*. Wednesday, February 28, 1973. https://www.google.com/?gws_rd=ssl#newwindow=1&q=Federal+officers+exchanged+gunfire+today+with+between+200+and+300+militant+Indian+who%09seized+the+settlement+of+Wounded+Knee.

2. Aaron Running Hawk in discussion with the author, 2010.

3. Pete S. Catches, Sr., *Sacred Fireplace* (Oceti Wakan), ed. Peter V. Catches (Santa Fe: Clear Light Publishers, 1999) p. 63.

Indian religion is unique; it is something that Wakan Tanka gave to us. We do not need X-rays, modern techniques, and the latest in modern powerful drugs to cure our ills. Instead, we ask the Great Spirit, the creator of all things, to make us whole, to cure us. His word is medicine. His word is healing. We Are Truly the Children of the Great Spirit Because He watches over us, He takes care of us, and I know He loves us.

4. Aaron Running Hawk in a sweat lodge, talking to his sweat group, October 2010.

5. Aaron Running Hawk, discussion. Aaron passed away shortly after the interview. His obituary appeared in the *Lakota Country Times*. Perhaps symbolic of the dilemma of acculturation faced by the Oglala, the man who wanted to forsake everything wasicu had a funeral held at the Inestimable Gift Church. http://www.lakotacountrytimes.com/news/2011-07-06/The_Holy_Road/Aaron_William_Running_Hawk.html.

6. Arlette Loud Hawk in discussion with the author, 2009.

7. Akim D. Reinhardt, *Ruling Pine Ridge: Oglala Lakota Politics From the IRA to Wounded Knee* (Lubbock: Texas Tech University Press, 2007) p. 29.

8. United States Department of the Interior, Office of Indian affairs. Constitution and by-laws of the Oglala Sioux tribe of the Pine Ridge Reservation South Dakota. Washington: United States Government printing office, p. 2.

9. Reinhardt, *Ruling Pine Ridge*, p. 93.

10. Paul Robertson, *The Power of the Land: Identity, Ethnicity, and Class Among the Oglala Lakota,* ed. John R. Wunder and Cynthia Willis Esqueda (New York: Routledge, 2002), p. 194.

11. Russell Means, *Where White Men Fear To Tread: The Autobiography of Russell Means* (New York, 1995) p. 106.

12. Ibid, p. 196.

13. Minutes of the Oglala Sioux Tribal Council, November 8, 1972, Box 12, Folder Council Proceedings 1972, Records of the Oglala Sioux Tribe, Oglala Lakota College Achieves, Oglala Lakota College, Kyle, SD.

14. Rolland Dewing, *Wounded Knee II* (Chadron: Great Plains Network, 2000), p. 37.

15. Oglala Sioux Tribal Council, November 10, 1972, Box 12, Folder Council Proceedings 1972, Records of the Oglala Sioux Tribe, Oglala Lakota College Achieves, Oglala Lakota College, Kyle, SD.

16. Reinhardt, *Ruling Pine Ridge*, p. 153.

17. Russell Means in discussion with the author, 2010.

Means might have let on more than he intended, or perhaps he just spoke as a traditional, but AIM did have a reputation for male chauvinism. A lawyer for AIM wrote about women and work: "As we talked, I felt comfortable enough to criticize two things about AIM. 'Lots of women do the best work,' I said '... But once the men came onto the scene, the women were pushed into the kitchen or entirely out of the picture.'" Kenneth S. Stern, *Loud Hawk.* (Norman: University of Oklahoma Press, 1994), p. 140.

18. Birgil Kills Straight in discussion with the author, 2010.

19. Ellen Moves Camp quoted in *Voices From Wounded Knee: The People Standing Up* (Rooseveltown: Akwesasne Notes), p. 14.

20. Reinhardt, *Ruling Pine Ridge*, p. 137.

21. Catches, *Sacred Fireplace*, p. 104.

22. Rienhardt, *Ruling Pine Ridge*, p. 178.

23. Means, *Where White Men Fear to Tread*, p. 151.

24. Bill Zimmerman, *Airlift to Wounded Knee* (Chicago: The Swallow Press, 1976), p. 78.

25. Means, *Where White Men Fear to Tread*, p. 252.

26. Dewing, *Wounded Knee*, p. 33.

27. Charles Trimble: "Facts and Truth of Wounded Knee" Indianz.Com. Monday, March 9, 2009. http://64.3812.138/news/2009/013480.asp.

28. Means, *Where White Men Fear to Tread*, p. 263.

29. The brothers from Oklahoma were products of what the Lakota believe to have been a liaison the general conducted with Monaseetah, a seventeen-year-old Cheyenne girl captured during his pre-dawn raid on her village along the Washita in Kansas.

30. Richard Janis in discussion with the author, 2009.

31. Birdie Mesteth, phone call with the author, 2009.

Chapter Twelve

1. Rita Long Visitor in discussion with the author, 2010.

2. David Weir and Lowell Bergman, "The Killing of Anna Mae Aquash," *Rolling Stone*, April 7, 1977, p. 55.

3. Joseph H. Trimbach, *American Indian Mafia: An FBI Agent's True Story About Wounded Knee, Leonard Peltier, and the American Indian Movement (AIM)* (Denver: Outskirts Press, Inc. 2008), p. 57.

4. Ibid., p. 486.

5. Ibid., p. 79.

6. Ibid., p. 375.

7. Ibid., p. 158.

8. Ibid., p. 68.

9. Ibid., p. 489.

10. Akim D. Reinhardt, *Ruling Pine Ridge: Oglala Lakota Politics From the IRA to Wounded* Knee (Lubbock: Texas Tech University Press, 2007) p. 168.

   In fact, Eugene Rooks went on a nationwide speaking tour condemning AIM for its communist principles. So did Douglas Durham, the FBI infiltrator who said AIM was prepared to indiscriminately kill whites in an attack on the 1976 Bicentennial.

11. Trimbach, *American Indian Mafia*, p. 7.

12. Ibid., p. 72.

13. Rita Long Visitor in discussion with the author, 2010.

14. Nathan Blindman, "Letter to the Editor," *Rapid City Journal*, December 31, 2001.

15. Rita Long Visitor in discussion.

16. Gladys Bissonette quoted in *Voices From Wounded Knee: The People Standing Up* (Rooseveltown: Akwesasne Notes) p. 57.

17. Grace Black Elk quoted in *Voices From Wounded Knee: The People Standing Up*, p. 154.

Chapter Thirteen

1. Arlette Loud Hawk in discussion with the author, 2009.

2. Debbie Lang, "The Battle of Wounded Knee 1973, Resistance Stories of Lakota People," *Revolutionary Worker* #1038, January 16, 2000. http://revcom.us/a/v21/1030-039/1038/wknee.ht

3. Ibid.

4. Wallace Black Elk quoted in *Voices From Wounded Knee: The People Standing Up* (Rooseveltown: Akwesasne Notes) p. 179.

5. Joseph H. Trimbach, *American Indian Mafia: An FBI Agent's True Story About Wounded Knee, Leonard Peltier, and the American Indian Movement (AIM)* (Denver: Outskirts Press, Inc. 2008), p. 376.

   Defense department records identified him as Frank Clear, 49, a Caucasian from Virginia, inducted into the army in 1943. Tried by the army for running from his company in the face of the enemy in Italy, he was dishonorably discharged.

6. Rolland Dewing, *Wounded Knee II* (Chadron: Great Plains Network, 2000), p. 120.

7. Phyllis Shock, Letters to the Editor, *Spokesman Review Forum*, May 7, 1973. http://lookingbackwoman.wordpress.com/2012/12/17/leo-wilcox-editorial/.

8. Dewing, *Wounded Knee II*, p. 97.

9. Stanley David Lyman, *Wounded Knee: A Personal Account* (Lincoln: Bison Books, 1991), p. 22.

   Ironically, only a few days before his death he said, "We have got to stop this brother fighting brother."

10. Susan L.M. Huck, "Renegades: The Second Battle of Wounded Knee," *American Opinion Magazine*, May, 1973, p. 4. http://federalexpression.files.wordpress.com/2012/10/197305-renegades.pdf.

11. Carson Walker, "Slain Activist Had Roots In Civil Rights Movement," *News From Indian Country*, November, 6, 2004. http://www.indiancountrynews.com/news/investigations/ray-robinson.

12. Ibid.

13. Barbara Deming, quoted in Walker, "Slain Activist."

14. Editors Note, "Bernie Lafferty Speaks About Perry Ray Robinson's Killing Inside Wounded Knee 1973, *News From Indian Country*, 2007. http://www.indiancountrynews.com/news/investigations/ray-robinson

15. Leon Eagle in discussion with author, 2010.

16. *Voices From Wounded Knee: The People Standing Up*, p. 191.

17. Dewing, *Wounded Knee II*, p. 116.

18. Ibid.

19. Editors Introduction, Anna Mae Timeline I-Wounded Knee, Indian Country News.com, January, 1997.http://www.indiancountrynews.com/index. php/annie-mae-special-features-58/additional-aquash-articles-1999-2011-special-features-108/47-articles-related-to-aquash-2007-2011/2101-annie-mae-timeline-i-wounded-knee?showall=&start=1.

20. Ward Churchill and Jim Vanderwall, *The Cointelpro Papers: Documents From The FBI's Secret Wars Against Dissent In The United States* (Cambridge: Sound End Press, 2002), p. 249.

21. Bruce Johansen and Roberto Maestas, *Wasi'chu: The Continuing Indian Wars* (New York: Monthly Review Press, 1979), p. 83.

22. "New Report: U.S. Homicide Rate Falls To Lowest In Four Decades," Department of Justice, http://blogs.justice.gov/main/archives/1765.

23. "Amid Drug War, Mexico Homicide Rate Up For Fourth Straight Year," *Los Angeles Times*, August 21, 2012. http://latimesblogs.latimes.com/world_now/2012/08/in-midst-of-drug-war-mexican-homicide-rate-increase-for-fourth-straight-year.html.

24. Duane Brewer in discussion with the author, 2008.

25. Tim Giago, "Whatever Happened To The So-Called Goons? *Huffington Post*, September 16, 2007. http://www.huffingtonpost.com/tim-giago/whatever-happened-to-the-_2_b_64611.html

26. Tim Giago, "Bringing A Dark Chapter In Oglala History To An End," *Huffington Post*, September 6, 2007. http://www.huffingtonpost.com/tim-giago/bringing-a-dark-chapter-i_b_63346.html

27. Dewing, *Wounded Knee II*, p. 155.

28. Paul DeMain, Comments on book cover, Trimbach, *American Indian Mafia.*

29. Trimbach, *American Indian Mafia*, p. 9.

30. Arlette Loud Hawk in discussion with the author, 2009.

31. Ward Churchill, *From A Native Son: Selected Essays in Indigenism, 1985–1995.* (Cambridge: South End Press, 1996).

Chapter Fourteen

1. Mary Ann Little Bear, a young Oglala girl shot in the eye as her family returned home from an outing, quoted in Steve Hendricks, *Unquiet Grave: The FBI and Struggle for the Soul of Indian Country* (New York: Thunder's Mouth Press, 2006), p. 81.

2. Federal Bureau of Investigation, "Report for Pine Ridge Indian Reservation, South Dakota: Accounting for Native American Deaths Pine Ridge Indian Reservation," May 2000.

3. Ward Churchill, "Analysis and Refutation of the FBI's 'Accounting' for

AIM Fatalities on Pine Ridge, 1973–1976." http://www.noparolepeltier.com/churchill.html.

4. FBI, "Report for Pine Ridge."

5. Ward Churchill, *From A Native Son: Selected Essays in Indigenism, 1985–1995* (Cambridge: South End Press, 1996), p. 257–260.

6. Debbie Lang, "Reign of Terror After 1973 Wounded Knee: Resistance Stories of the Lakota People," *Revolutionary Worker* #1039, January 23, 2000. http://revcom.us/a/v21/1030-039/1039/wknee2.htm.

7. FBI, "Report for Pine Ridge."

8. Ibid.

9. Churchill, "Analysis and Refutation."

10. The Bissonette name has been associated with the Lakota since the first trappers and traders lived among them. Joseph Bissonette, eighteen years old, left St. Louis in 1836 for fortune and adventure on the plains. He married Nellie Plenty Brothers, an Oglala woman. After accompanying Spotted Tail and Red Cloud to Washington, D.C. in 1875, he died in 1894 among his adopted people on the Pine Ridge. http://boards.ancestry.com/surnames.bissonette/9.10.13.1/mb.ashx

11. Frank Bissonette in discussion with author, 2012.

12. FBI pictures show the bullet hole near the key slot on the back of the trunk. The autopsy showed the slug that killed Jeanette traveled downward at a 20-degree angle. Apparently she was lying down in the seat, really slouched over, or the bullet deflected, splintered, and entered her body at that angle.

13. Report of REDACTED, to USA, Sioux Falls, South Dakota, Attention: AUSA REDACTED. August 16, 1976. Unknown Subject: Mrs. Jeanette Bissonette nee Jeanette Waters. Field Office File #70-9815.

14. Memorandum: SAC Minneapolis to Director, FBI, March 26, 1975. Mrs. Jeanette Bissonette nee Jeanette Waters—Victim. Field Office File #70-9815.

15. Memorandum: From SAC Minneapolis, to Director (Attn: FBI Laboratory) April 2, 1975. Mrs. Jeanette Bissonette nee Jeanette Waters—Victim. Field Office File #70-9815.

16. Report of REDACTED, to USA.

17. Memorandum: ASAC Rapid City, to Director, FBI, January 20, 1977. Mrs. Jeanette Bissonette nee Jeanette Waters—Victim. Field Office File #70-9815.

18. Memorandum: SAC Minneapolis, to Director, FBI, December 28, 1981. Mrs. Jeanette Bissonette nee Jeanette Waters—Victim. Field Office File #70-9815.

19. ICMIPRO1: Source From Which Property Acquired, FBI Laboratory, PCR Extracted DNA Tubes and Amplified DNA Tubes from Cigarette Butts. April 18, 2002. Case# 198A-MP-5674. ICMIPRO1: Description of Property: One Styrofoam Coffee Cup. January 13,2004. Case# 198A-MP-5674.

20. Levi Rickert, "37 Years Later, Jeanette Bissonette's Son Wants Answers and Closure to Her Death," *Native News Network*. June 13, 2012. http://www.nativenewsnetwork.com/37-years-later-jeanette -bissonette-son-wants-answers.

21. Report of REDACTED, to USA.

22. Joseph Trimbach, *American Indian Mafia: An FBI Agent's True Story*

About Wounded Knee, Leonard Peltier, and the American Indian Movement (Denver: Outskirts Press, 2008) p. 28, 295.

23. Ibid., 592.

24. Report of REDACTED, to USA.

25. Ward Churchill, *Since Predator Came* (Oakland: AK Press, 2005), p. 214.

26. FBI, "Report for Pine Ridge."

27. Ibid.

28. Churchill, "Analysis and Refutation."

29. Oglala woman who wished to remain anonymous, in discussion with the author, February 2012.

30. Report of REDACTED, to Sioux Falls, South Dakota, AUSA Boyd, October 15, 1975. Title: Benjamin Sitting Up (Deceased), Isabelle Sitting Up. Field Office File #: 70-10021.

31. Ibid.

32. Memorandum: SA REDACTED, to SAC Minneapolis (198-1384), August 21, 1975. Subject Benjamin Sitting Up (Deceased), Isabelle Sitting Up.

33. Mary Crow Dog, *Lakota Woman* (New York: Harper Perennial, 1990), p. 193.

34. Leonard Crow Dog and Richard Erdoes, *Crow Dog* (New York: Harper Perennial, 1995), p. 67.

35. Trimbach, *American Indian Mafia*, p. 410.

36. Letter received by author from the FBI.

37. FBI, "Report for Pine Ridge."

38. Ibid.

39. Oglala woman who wished to remain anonymous, in discussion with author, 2012.

40. FBI, "Report for Pine Ridge."

41. Churchill, "Analysis and Refutation."

42. Bud Merrill in discussion with the author, 2012.

43. FBI, "Report for Pine Ridge."

44. Alex White Plume in phone discussion with the author, 2012.

45. FD-302: File # MP-70-8216. September 25, 1973.

46. Verola Spider in discussion with author, 2012.

47. FD-302. September 28, 1973. File # MP-70-8216.

48. FD-302. September 24, 1973. File # MP-70-8216.

49. FD-302. June 14, 1974. File # MP-70-8216.

50. Memorandum: SAC Omaha, to SAC Minneapolis. August 22, 1974. Melvin Spider—victim. 70-1705.

51. Ibid.

52. FD-302. April 30, 1974. File # MP-70-8216.

53. Memorandum: SAC REDACTED, to SAC Minneapolis, February 18, 1975. Melvin Spider—Victim. File # MP-70-8216.

54. FBI, "Report for Pine Ridge."

55. Churchill, "Analysis and Refutation."

56. Hand Written Statement: Aloysius White Crane. February 2, 1976. With REDACTED BIA Criminal Division.

57. Report of REDACTED, to Sioux Falls, South Dakota, Attn: AUSA, Rapid City South Dakota. April 27, 1976. Aloysius White Crane; Cleveland Emmitt Reddest—victim (Deceased).

58. FD-302. May 10, 1976. File # RC-70-11602.

59. Report of Redacted, to ASAC Rapid City. August 9, 1976. Betty Means—victim. File # 70-11739.

60. Report of REDACTED, to AUSA Sioux Falls. November 12, 1976. Betty Lou Means—victim. File # 70-1139.

61. Report, August 12, 1976.

62. Report, November 12, 1976.

63. Report, August 12, 1976. The autopsy also found Betty had active tuberculosis in one lung.

64. Letter: David V. Vrooman United States Attorney, to REDACTED Assistant Special Agent in Charge, Rapid City. August 22, 1978.

65. FBI, "Report for Pine Ridge."

66. Churchill, "Analysis and Refutation."

67. FBI, "Report for Pine Ridge."

68. Ibid.

69. Report of REDACTED, to AUSA Sioux Falls, South Dakota. May 16, 1975. Hilda Rosa Good Buffalo—victim. File # 70-9834.

70. Ibid.

71. Report of Redacted. Minneapolis Office. December 5, 1975. Hilda Rose Good Buffalo—victim. File # 70-64972.

72. Report of REDACTED. To AUSA Sioux Falls, South Dakota, April 30, 1976. Hilda Rose Buffalo—victim. Field Office File # 70-9834.

73. W.O. Brown, M.D. Autopsy Report. Good Buffalo, Hilda Rose, April 5, 1975.

74. Letter: Norman A Zigrossi, Assistant Special Agent in Charge, to REDACTED Agency Special Officer, Pine Ridge BIA, December 6, 1976.

75. Churchill, "Analysis and Refutation."

76. Report, Hilda Rose Good Buffalo. April 30, 1976.

77. Letter: Zigrossi to Pine Ridge BIA.

78. Rex Wyler, *Blood of the Land: The Government and Corporate War Against the American Indian Movement* (New York: Vintage Books, 1982), p. 106.

79. FBI, "Report for Pine Ridge."

80. Bud Merrill in discussion with the author.

81. Steve Hendricks, *The Unquiet Grave: The FBI and the Struggle for the Soul of Indian Country* (New York: Thunder's Mouth Press, 2006), p. 91.

82. Peter Matthiessen, *In the Spirit of Crazy Horse* (New York: Penguin Books, 1992), p. 99.

83. Ibid.

84. Wyler, *Blood of the Land*, p. 109.

85. FBI, "Report for Pine Ridge."

86. Ibid.

87. Crow Dog and Erdoes, *Crow Dog,* p. 216–218.

88. Ibid., 217.

89. *U.S.* v. *Paul Duane Herman,* 5:77-cr-50032.

90. *U.S.* v. *Paul Duane Herman,* 5:91-cr-50017.

91. Richard A. Serrano, "Pine Ridge Indian Homicide Cases Get New Scrutiny," *Los Angeles Times,* August 8, 2012. http://articles.latimes.com/2012/aug/08/nation/la-na-pine-ridge-20120809.

92. Charles Michael Ray, "Pine Ridge Reservation Deaths To Be Reinvestigated," National Public Radio. http://www.npr.org/2012/08/18/159058219/near-wounded-knee-years-of-alleged-injustice.

The 1998 murders were actually the killings of Hard Heart and Black Elk, which occurred in 1999.

Chapter Fifteen

1.Leon Eagle in discussion with the author, 2010.

2. Johanna Brand, *The Life and Death of Anna Mae Aquash* (Toronto: James Lorimer & Company, 1993), p. 18.

Candy Hamilton went to the location to confirm her burial after she had been identified. She was struck by the irony of the Catholic burial of her friend who was a devout follower of traditional Indian religion and hated Christian churches.

3. Ibid., p. 21–22.

When informed of his mistake, Brown still insisted Anna Mae died from exposure, even if the bullet initiated the mechanism of death. "Why all the interest in this case?" He asked. "It seems awfully routine, you know. So they found an Indian body—so a body was found."

4. "Statement From The Family of Anna Mae Pictou Aquash: Ann Mae Begins Her Journey Home." *Indigenous Women for Justice,* April 2004. Indigenous womenforjustice.org/home.html/

5. Mike Cassidy and Will Miller, "A Short History of FBI COINTELPRO," *Monitor.* http://www.monitor.net/monitor/9905a/jbcointelpro.html.

6. Final Report of the Select Committee to Study Governmental Operations with Respect to Intelligence Activities. United States Senate, 94th Congress, 2nd Session, April 26, 1976. Book III, "Supplementary Detailed Staff Reports on Intelligence Activities and Rights of Americans," p. 5.

7. Brian Glick, *War at Home: Covert Action Against U.S. Activists and What We Can Do About It* (Cambridge: South End Press, 1989), p. 10.

8. Ibid., p. 60.

Former GOONs tend to keep their silence about the Time of Troubles. One incident Duane Brewer and Bud Merrill are quick to discuss is the beating that WKLDOC lawyers received at the Pine Ridge Airport. The group of men and women had flown in to Pine Ridge to conduct interviews. When they returned to their car, they found it shot full of holes. They stayed in their vehicle as carloads of GOONs arrived. When Oglala Tribal President Dick Wilson got there he said to the effect, "Stomp them."

Duane Brewer says he started the beating by jumping on the hood of the car and kicking the windshield in while yelling, "If you want to be an Indian then you can drive an Indian car." One woman required two days hospitalization, the rest were treated for lacerations and contusions from the beating. Bud Merrill and Duane Brewer, in discussion with author, 2012.

9. Final Report of the Select Committee to Study Governmental Operations with Respect to Intelligence Activities. United States Senate, 94th Congress, 2nd Session, April 26 (legislative day, April 14), 1976. http://www.aarclibrary.org/pub-lib/contents/church/contents_church_reports.htm.

10. The Federal Bureau of Investigation, FBI Records: The Vault, COINTEL-PRO. http://vault.fbi.gov/cointel-pro.

11. The dangerous weapon of Jimmy Eagle's is another source of controversy. Matthiessen, *In The Spirit of Crazy Horse*, made reference to a clasp knife he says Jimmy never pulled (page 210). However, the *No Parole Peltier* website, http://www.noparolepeltier.com/faq.html#17, lists a 2005 interview with Jerry Schwarting, the victim, who said he was beaten, slashed with knives, had guns fired over his head and threatened with castration. Leon, Jimmy's brother, said he had never heard that story and did not believe it.

12. Peter Matthiessen, *In the Spirit of Crazy Horse* (New York: Penguin Books, 1992), p. 212.

13. Ibid., p. 334.

14. According to Leon, neither he nor Jimmy ever got along with their wintke (homosexual) uncle. Leon Eagle in discussion with the author, 2013.

15. Matthiessen, *Spirit of Crazy Horse*, p. 575.

16. Leonard Peltier, *Prison Writings: My Life Is A Sun Dance* (New York: Crazy Horse Spirit, Inc., 1999), p. 142.

17. "The Manipulation of Myrtle Poor Bear." http://www.dickshovel.com/affa.html.

18. Memorandum: to Assistant Director, Federal Bureau of Investigation. 'Leonard Peltier.' May 15, 1979.

"The inconsistency between the first affidavit and the subsequent two affidavits is believed to be the result of Myrtle Poor Bear's initial reluctance to fully cooperate because of her legitimate fear for her own personal safety."

19. The inclusion of the escape route in Poor Bear's affidavit would seem to be the bureau's excuse for the ease in which AIM members made their way out of the compound while hundreds of armed men searched for them.

20. Myrtle Poor Bear, Sworn Affidavit. United States District Court, District of South Dakota, February 19, 1976. http://law2.umkc.edu/faculty/projects/ftrials/peltier/poorbearaffidavits.html.

21. Myrtle Poor Bear, Sworn Affidavit. United States District Court, District of South Dakota, February 23, 1976.

22. Myrtle Poor Bear, Sworn Affidavit. United States District Court, District of South Dakota, March 31, 1976.

23. Marty Poor Bear in discussion with the author, 2010.

24. Ibid.

25. Ibid.

26. Cory Johnson, "The Case of Leonard Peltier: Notorious Frame-up of Native American Activist Returns to Public Spotlight." *World Socialist Web Site,* December 14, 2004. http://www1.wsws.org/articles.2000/dec2000/pelt-d14.shtml.

27. Marty Poor Bear in discussion.

28. Matthiessen, *Spirit of Crazy Horse,* p. 347.

29. Ibid, p. 366.

30. *Richard Marshall* v. *State of South Dakota.* No. 12982. 1981. S. D. 302 N.W. 2d 52 (VersusLaw).

31. Marty Poor Bear, in discussion.

32. Michael Kuzma, "Where are the FBI files concerning Myrtle Poor Bear?" *Censored News,* April 17, 2013. http://bsnorrell.blogspot.com/2009/01/where-are-fbi-files-concerning-myrtle.html.

33. Johnson, "The Case of Leonard Peltier."

34. Peltier, *Prison Writings,* p. 142.

35. Johanna Brand, *The Life and Death of Anna Mae Aquash* (Toronto: James Lorimer & Company, 1993), p. viii.

36. Final Report of the Select Committee to Study Governmental Operations with Respect to Intelligence Activities. http://www.aarclibrary.org/publib/contents/church/contents_church_reports.htm.

37. *U.S.* v. *Robert Eugene Robideau and Darrelle Dean Butler,* USDC, (N.D.I.), Cedar Rapids Division, No. CR-76-11, July 1976. This is a story told by Anna Mae. Price arrested her in the raid on Crow Dog's Paradise in 1975. Price always disputed the story.

John Trudell, former AIM leader testified at the trial of Robideau and Butler for the murder of the FBI agents: "She told me she had been arrested at Crow Dog's and ... Price saw her and when he saw her he shined his flashlight on her and when he saw who she was he said, 'There you are. We have been looking for you,' and that is all the conversation that took place there. They took them all to Pierre and she said during her interrogation by Price and another agent ... that Price had told her he knew that she knew who shot those agents, and that she could—should cooperate, and if she would, she would get a new identity, and she would get a new place to live ... She cussed at him and he told her that if she wanted to have that attitude **he would see her dead within a year**. ... The last time I saw her was the first—very first part of October, I believe—in Los Angeles. She told me at the time that she would go back to court and then the next time I saw anything, I saw her on TV in Oregon, three days before she was going to appear in court, and she had been arrested with Kamook Banks and Russell Redner and Kenneth Loud Hawk in Oregon and that was the last time I ever saw her."

38. Angie Cannon, "Healing Old Wounds: An Indian Woman's Murder Goes to Trial—Too Many Years Later." *U.S. News and World Report,* December 14, 2003. www.usnews.com/usnews/news/articles/031222/22woundedknee.htm.

39. *U.S. v. Fritz Arlo Looking Cloud,* U.S. Dist. Ct. S. Div. S.D., CR 03-50020, (2004). http://www.grahamdefense.org/200402cloud-transcript/index.htm.

40. Ibid.

41. Ibid.

42. Ibid.

43. David Seals, "Arlo Looking Cloud Interview," *Dakota-Lakota-Nakota Human Rights Advocacy Coalition.* February, 2004. http//www.dlncoaliton. org/arlo_looking_cloud_interview.htm.

Arlo Looking Cloud told David Seals that Richard Two Elk lied about everything. "I barely knew him. We never grew up together or anything else."

44. An urban Chicano organization led by Corky Gonzales.

45. *U.S. v. Looking Cloud.*

46. David Seals, Arlo Looking Cloud Interview, February, 2004.

47. "Commemorating Anna Mae," *John Graham Defense Committee,* November 2004. http://www.grahamdefense.org/200411investigatethefeds.htm.

48. Ibid.

49. Interview of Fritz Arlo Looking Cloud. Robert Ecoffey, Director BIA Office of Law Enforcement Services and Detective Abe Alonzo, Denver Police Department. March 27, 2003. *Justice for Anna May and Ray.* www.jfamr.org/doc/arlo. html.

50. Dave Kolpack, "Witness: Man supplied gun in 1975 S.D., slaying." *The Associated Press.* www.woodlandindians,org.forums/viewtopic.php?id=7677.

51. Heidi Bell Gease, "Witness Points to gunman accomplice in AIM slaying," *Rapid City Journal,* April 16, 2010. http://rapidcityjournal.com/ /news/witness-points-to-gunman-accomplice-in-aim-slaying/article_9e71af06-48bb-11df-b695-001cc4c03286.html.

He identified Charles Abourezk, the son of Senator James Abourezk.

52. Richard Marshall's Trial: Day 6. *KEVN, Black Hills Fox,* April 21, 2010. www.blackhillsfow.com/Archive/2010/0422/Richard-marshalls-trial-day-6.

53. Heidi Bell Gease, "Trial begins for man accused of AIM activists death," *Rapid City Journal,* April 14, 2010. www.woodlandindians,org.forums/viewtopic. php?id=7677.

54. Richard Marshall's Trial: Day 7.

55. Richard Marshall's Trial: Day 4.

56. Heidi Bell Gease, "Witness in 1975 AIM slaying trial recalls a fractured AIM, Peltier admission," *Rapid City Journal,* April 20, 2010. http://www. rapidcityjournal.com/news/article-8556940-4cc11-df-a293-001cc403286

57. Richard Marshall's Trial: Day 7.

58. *U.S. v. Fritz Arlo Looking Cloud,* U.S. Dist. Ct. S. Div. S.D., CR 03-50020,

(2004). Memorandum In Support Of Defendant Graham's Motion To Compel Discovery. http://grahamdefense.org/courtdocs/document252.pdf.

59. *South Dakota* v. *John Graham A/K/A John Boy Patton,* CRIM. NO. 09-3593, (7ᵗʰ Judicial District) 2010.

60. "Who In The Hell Murdered Native Activist Annie Mae Aquash? Indian Country Wants Justice Now." Peace & Collaborative Development Network. http://www.internationalpeaceandconflict.org/profiles/blogs/who-in-the-hell-murdered#.UW8dTrUsl8E

61. Rex Weyler, "Who Killed Anna Mae," *Vancouver Sun,* January 8, 2005. http://www.grahamdefense.org/20050108weyler-van-sun.htm.

62. Heidi Bell Gease, "Graham Sentenced to Life in Prison," *Rapid City Journal,* January 24, 2011.

63. *South Dakota* v. *John Graham.*

64. Ibid.

65. During the same session Looking Cloud asked her how many people he should implicate in the murder. She replied, "Only John Boy."

66. *South Dakota* v. *John Graham.*

67. Vernon Bellecourt and Ward Churchill, interview by Harlan McKosato, *Native America Calling,* November 4, 1999.

68. "The Denver Press Conference," *News From Indian Country,* November 3, 1999. www.indiancountrynews.info/denverpress.cfm.htm.

69. Vernon Bellecourt and Ward Churchill interview.

70. Clyde Bellecourt, telephone interview by author, April, 2013.

71. Is this one and the same person? You decide. aimovement.org/mckiernan.html.

72. Matthiessen, *In the Spirit of Crazy Horse,* p. 194.

73. Ward Churchill and Jim Vander Wall, *The COINTELPRO Papers; Documents From the FBI's Secret Wars Against Dissent in the United States* (Cambridge: South End Press, 2002) p. 277–280.

Dog Soldiers were elite Cheyenne warriors. They wore a long sash and during battle they would impale it to the ground with a sacred arrow and never retreat.

74. "FBI Chief: No Proof of U.S. Indian Plot," *Oakland Tribune,* July 7, 1976.

75. Trimbach, *American Indian Mafia,* 18.

76. *U.S.* v. *Arlo Looking Cloud.*

77. "Anna Mae Pictou Aquash Timeline: An Investigation by News From Indian Country." *News From Indian Country.* January 1997. http://www.dickshovel.com/time.html.

Chapter Sixteen

1. Of course, no one knows what Jancita's last hours were like. Was she terrified, angry, drunk? The facts of her death, hit by a car in Nebraska are indisputable. No one has said why she was there or even how she got there. The story of her drive from Valentine is only mine.

2. Report of the Federal Bureau of Investigation, Minneapolis Division. "Accounting For Native American Deaths, Pine Ridge Reservation, South Dakota," U.S. Department of Justice, Federal Bureau of Investigation.

3. Ida Marshal, Lakota Rosebud resident, in discussion with the author, 2011.

4. In Late Defense of Jancita Eagle Deer: Her Own words vs. William Janklow. *The Doomsday Diet.* https://thedoomsdaydiet.wordpress.com/2011/12/07/in-late-defense-of-jancita-eagle-deer-her-own-words-vs-william-janklow.

5. Ibid

6. Ibid.

7. Ibid.

8. Ida Marshal, in discussion.

9. Janklow claimed in his lawsuit against Viking Press and Peter Matthiessen that the use of this term evinces malice. *William Janklow, Plaintiff and Appellant, v. The Viking Press and Peter Matthiessen, Defendants and Appellees.* Supreme Court of South Dakota. 1990.SD.104, 495 zn.E.2d415. http://sd.findacase.com/research/wfrmDocViewer.aspx/xq/fac.19900718_0006.SD.htm/qx.

10. "GOP official admits moving Janklow file." *Huron Daily Plainsman*, October 10, 1974.

11. "Shoot Gunmen: Janklow Explains Bank's Quote." *The Daily Republic*, (Mitchell, SD.) March 23, 1976.

http://www.newspaperarchive.com/. Dennis Banks, quoting verbally from an affidavit signed by John Gridley, a South Dakota attorney. Janklow made the statement to him at a coffee party in Sioux Falls a month before the election.

Janklow denied he ever made that statement but claims instead to have said, "Anybody who threatens another person with a gun or uses a gun on another person should have a bullet put in him."

12. Dennis Banks and Richard Erdoes, *Ojibwa Warrior: Dennis Banks and the Rise of the American Indian Movement* (Norman: University of Oklahoma Press, 2004), p. 271.

13. Ibid., p. 272.

14. Paula Giese, "Douglass Durham and the Death of Jancita Eagle Deer: Your Tax Dollar at Work." *North County Anvil.* No. 17. March-April 1976, p. 5.

15. Ibid., p. 7.

16. "Janklow denies raping woman," *Huron Daily Plainsman* (Huron, SD), October 29, 1974.

17. Ibid.

18. Ibid.

19. Steve Hendricks, *Unquiet Grave: The FBI and Struggle for the Soul of Indian Country* (New York: Thunder's Mouth Press, 2006), p. 154.

20. Melvin J. Williams, Examiner. *Rosebud Sioux Tribal Court, Plaintiff* v. *William Janklow, Defendant.* Rosebud Reservation. October 31, 1974. http://ishgooda.org/peltier/eagledeer/jancitapolygraph.jpg.

21. Mario Gonzales, Rosebud Tribal Judge. In Re: Disbarment of William

Janklow: Memorandum Decision. Rosebud Sioux Tribal Court. http://ishgooda. org/peltier/eagledeer/jancitapolygraph.jpg.

22. Affidavit of Robert G. Philbrick, *Tribal Court* v. *Janklow.*

23. Harley D. Zephier, Acting Area Director to Norman Beare, Rosebud, South Dakota. Andrew Bogue, United States District Judge. Writ of Habeas Corpus. United States District Court for the District of South Dakota, Central Division. http://ishgooda.org/peltier/eagledeer/jancitapolygraph.jpg.

24. Mario Gonzales, Rosebud Tribal Judge. Warrant to Apprehend. *Tribal Court* v. *Janklow.* http://ishgooda.org/peltier/eagledeer/jancitapolygraph.jpg.

25. Paula Giese, *Secret Agent Douglass Durham and the Death of Jancita Eagle Deer: Your Tax Dollar at Work.* (Millville, MN: Anvil Press, 1976), p. 9.

26. Banks, *Ojibwa Warrior*, p. 281.

27. Ibid., p. 11.

28. Nick Lamberto, "Grand Jury's 10-X Report Chides City," *Des Moines Register* (Des Moines, IA) June 21, 1972. http://www.newspaperarchive.com/.

29. Giese, "Douglass Durham," p. 3.

30. *William Janklow, Appellant,* v. *Newsweek, Inc. Appellee.* United States Court of Appeals: Eighth Circuit. 755 F. 2d 1300. http://law.justia.com/cases/ federal/appellate-courts/F2/788/1300/300888/.

31. *William Janklow, Plaintiff and Appellant,* v. *The Viking Press and Peter Matthiessen, Defendants and Appellees.* Supreme Court of South Dakota. 1990. SD.104, 495 zn.E.2d415. http://sd.findacase.com/research/wfrmDocViewer.aspx/ xq/fac.19900718_0006.SD.htm/qx.

32. *Janklow* v. *Newsweek.*

Who acknowledged Jancita's claim to be false? Certainly, she nor Pitchlynn nor the American Indian Movement, nor her relatives ever acknowledged her claim to be false. This statement seems to derive entirely from the FBI "investigation."

33. Ibid.

34. *Janklow* v. *Viking Press.*

35. Frederick W. Lambrecht, Administrative Law Judge to Administrator, Wagner Public Health Service Hospital. http://ishgooda.org/peltier/eagledeer/jll. jpg.

36. Richard Meryhew, "Janklow's Law License Restored a Year Early." *Star Tribune* (Minn. St. Paul), January 25, 2006. http://www.startribune.com/templates/ Print_This_Story?sid=11610806.

37. Sarah Deer, "Toward an Indigenous Jurisprudence of Rape." William Mitchell College of Law Open Access. http://open.wmitchell.edu/cgi/.

Chapter Seventeen

1. Loren Black Elk in discussion with the author, 2009.

2. Memory-of.com, Shelli Poor Bear (1979-2005).

3. Babe Poor Bear in discussion with the author, 2010.

4. Memory-of.com, Shelli Poor Bear (1979-2005).

5. *U.S. v. Jessica Lou Twiss*: 5:06CR50020-1 (D-South Dakota 2006).

6. Memory-of.com Shelli Poor Bear (1979-2005).

7. Ibid.

8. Pte San Win in discussion with the author.

9. Ibid.

10. Memory-of.com, Shelli Poor Bear (1979-2005).

Chapter Eighteen

1. Royal B. Hassrick, *The Sioux: Life and Customs of a Warrior Society* (Norman: University of Oklahoma Press, 1964), p. 12.

"The family of man, wife, and children, while a biological reality, was not of particular sociological importance. Brothers and sisters were the family of significance. As the sons or daughters of a leader, as the co-operative partners in a closely related team of hunters and warriors, the family survived not so much as result of marital co-operation as of sibling co-coordination."

2. Marla says she has been taught that hiding the children beneath the baggage in the face of enemies was a customary practice.

3. Ben Black Elk and Marla Under Baggage in personal discussion with the author, 2012.

4. The man's father claims Jolene started the violence, usually by hitting her husband. He said she had the knife first and his son took it away from her. Duane Brewer, Sr. in phone call with the author, 2012.

5. "On the Bootleggers Trail in Indian Country." *Indian Country Today Media Network,* http://indiancountrytodaymedianetwork.com/ictarchives/2010/10/11/on-the-bootleggers%25e2%2580%2599-trail-in-indian-country-76523.

Jolene Black Elk points to the scar on her neck, an inch from her windpipe, where she says her boyfriend stabbed her in an alcohol-fueled rage. She talks about her teenage years on the "rez," drinking and drugging, and the night she was raped. As night descends on Whiteclay, she warns a writer and photographer to stay close: "You guys are gonna get ganged."

6. Jolene Black Elk in personal discussion with the author, 2012.

Chapter Nineteen

1. Monica and Carrie Titus in discussion with the author, 2011.

2. Don Titus in phone discussion with the author, 2012.

3. Mary in phone discussion with the author, 2012.

4. David M. Hardy, Section Chief, Record/Information Dissemination Section, Records Office Management Division, FOIPA Request No.: 1180674-00, Subject: Daniel Duane Titus, to Alan Hafer, January 23, 2012.

Chapter Twenty

1. Alex White Plume in discussion with the author, July 2011. Also, David Melmer, "Oglala Sioux President Alex White Plume sees the old ways as better." *Indian Country Today,* August 28, 2006.

2. White Plume, discussion.

3. The Papal Bulls as Pertaining to the Americas. http://bullsburning.itgo.com/essays/Caetera.htm.

4. Alex on Christianity: "They wrote their spirituality down on a piece of paper—this is what this guy did, and this is what that guy did—and they wrote a Bible. So for two thousand years, they didn't follow their spirituality, but they followed their book and their little rules to the T. Every hundred years or so, Mother Earth shifts, she changes. And when she shifts and changes, you have to be on her, you have to be ready to be in on the scheme of the new changes. ... The Lakota people have been doing that. But when you have yours written down, it eventually becomes real obsolete. It doesn't keep up with the natural cycle of Mother Earth.

5. Dan Skye, "America's Only Hemp Farmer." *HighTimes.com.* May 29, 2003. http://hightimes.com/news/dskye/367.

6. Jeremy Briggs, "Wahupta Ska Pejuta," Hemphasis. http://www.hemphasis.net/History/history.htm.

"You have to have respect for the dirt, for the soil, it's alive. The Oglala words for the dirt are 'Ma Kanea,' and the dirt is very important to the Oglala." Alex White Plume in discussion with the author. Also, "Meet Alex White Plume," *The Free Press,* April 3, 2010. http://freepress.org/departments/display/8/2010/3774.

7. With a THC level so low, as people who have tried ditchweed know, this *Cannabis* plant can be smoked all day, and all you get is a headache.

8. AZ-Hemp, Arizona Industrial Hemp Council. http://azhemp.org/Archive/Package/Legal/legal.html.

9. Briggs, Hemphasis. http://www.hemphasis.net/History/history.htm.

10. Ibid.

11. Title 21 United States Code (USC) Controlled Substances Act Section 802. Definitions. http://www.deadiversion.usdoj.gov/21cfr/21usc/802.htm.

12. Heidi Bell Gease, "Manderson area family havests hemp crop." *Rapid City Journal,* August 2, 2002. http://newsfeed.rootsweb.com/th/read/NATIVE-AMERICAN-NEWS/2002-08/1028931890.

13. Robert J. Miller, "Treaty Interpretation: Judicial Rules and Canons of Construction," *Legal Research Paper Series. Paper No. 2009 – 24.* Lewis & Clark Law School. http://papers.ssrn.com/sol3/papers.cfm?abstract_id=1355227.

14. *U.S.* v. *White Plume,* CIV 02-5017 (D-South Dakota, 2006). http://64.38.12.138/docs/court/whiteplume/usacomplaint0809.pdf.

15. *U.S.* v. *White Plume.*

The Eighth Circuit dealt with this issue in different language. "The language of the Treaty as Written is not ambiguous on the matter of farming hemp because the Treaty is not written in the context of permitting the cultivating of particular crops." *United States* v. *White Plume*, 447 F.3d 1067 (8th Cir. 2006).

16. Fort Laramie Treaty of 1868, U.S.-Sioux Nation, art. VIII, April 29, 1868. http://www.pbs.org/weta/thewest/resources/archives/four/ftlaram.htm.

17. Thomas Ballanco quoted in David Rooks, "DEA and FBI agents raid family crop," *Indian Country Today,* September 6, 2000.

18. Briggs, Hemphasis.

19. U.S. Census Bureau, 1850 Census. http://www.census.gov/prod/www/abs/decennial/1850.html.

20. Lori Murphy, "Enough Rope: Why United States v. White Plume Was Wrong On Hemp And Treaty Rights, And What It Could Cost The Government," *American Indian Law Review 35.* Am. Indian L. Rev. 767. 2010-2011. 6. https://litigationessentials.lexisnexis.com/webcd/app?action=DocumentDisplay&crawlid=1&doctype=cite&docid=35+Am.+Indian+L.+Rev.+767&srctype=smi&srcid=3B15&key=386738f885e96e82224346880604795d.

21. Murphy, "Enough Rope," p. 3.

Chapter Twenty-One

1. Robert Ecoffey in discussion with the author, 2009.

2. Police supervisor (who wished to remain anonymous) in discussion with the author, 2008.

3. Sheridan County Sheriff Homer Robbins in discussion with the author, 2008.

4. Tom Poor Bear in discussion with the author, 2009.

5. Alex Dillon, Wild Boyz, in discussion with the author, 2011.

Chapter Twenty-two

1. Bud Merrill in discussion with author, 2012.

2. Tony Yellow Hawk in discussion with author, 2012.

3. Marty Red Cloud in discussion with author, 2012.

4. Ben Mesteth in discussion with author, 2011.

5. Hunka phone call with author, January, 2012.

6. Hunka in discussion with author, 2012.

7. Babe Poor Bear in discussion with author, 2012.

8. Hunka in discussion with author, February, 2012.

9. Ben Black Elk phone call with author, 2012.

10. Tom Poor Bear phone call with author, 2012.

11. Hunka in discussion with author, 2012.

Chapter Twenty-three

1. CAMP JUSTICE Home Page, 2. http://85.173.132/search?=cache:n9-t3T2904J:www.aics.org/justice/camp.html+ca.

2. Vincent Schilling, Oglala Sioux President Arrested at Whiteclay Protest, *Indian Country Today Media Network,* June 19, 2013. http://indiancountrytodaymedianetwork.com/2013/06/19/oglala-sioux-president-arrested-whiteclay-protest-149982.

3. Oglala Sioux president arrested in Whiteclay, *Rapid City Journal,* June 17, 2013. http://rapidcityjournal.com/news/local/oglala-sioux-president-arrested-in-Whiteclay/article_ca60e806-3531-5ee9-ba48-0fb32155ae8f.html.

4. "Oglala Sioux President Squanders Chance to Talk with Nebraska Governor," *Madville Times,* July 9, 2013. http://madvilletimes.com/2013/07/oglala-sioux-president-squanders-chance-to-talk-whiteclay-with-nebraska-governor/.

5. Joe Duggan, "Meeting on Whiteclay alcohol sales ends quickly with no progress," *Omaha World Herald,* July 9, 2013. http://www.omaha.com/article/20130708/NEWS/707099997.

6. United States Department of Commerce, United States Census Bureau, State and County Quick Facts. http://quickfacts.census.gov/qfd/states/46/46113.html.

Bibliography

"1850 Census." CENSUSRECORDS.COM. Accessed July 2, 2011. http://www.censusrecords.com/content/1850_census?gclid=CPC3jab6y7kCFQJqMgoda TYA5Q

Abbott, E. C., and Helena Huntington Smith. *We Pointed Them North; Recollections of a Cowpuncher.* Norman: University of Oklahoma Press, 1955.

"AIM Reaction." *American Indian Movement: Still Strong.* Accessed November 23, 2012. http://mail-archive.com/nativenews@mlists.netmsg04577.html.

Allen, Charles Wesley. *From Fort Laramie to Wounded Knee: In the West That Was.* Edited by Richard E. Jensen. Lincoln: University of Nebraska Press in Association with the Nebraska State Historical Society, 1997.

Allport, Gordon W. *The Nature of Prejudice: Abridged.* Garden City, NY: Doubleday, 1958.

Ambrose, Stephen E. *Undaunted Courage: Meriwether Lewis, Thomas Jefferson, and the Opening of the American West.* New York: Simon & Schuster, 1996.

"America's Only Hemp Farmer." *High Times.* May 28, 2003. http://hightimes.com/news/dskye/367.

"Amid Drug War, Mexico Homicide Rate up for Fourth Straight Year." *Los Angeles Times,* August 21, 2012. http:/latimesblogs.latimes.com/world-now/2012/08/in-midst-of-drug-war-mexican-homicide-rate-increase-for-fourth-straight-year.html.

Anderson, Gary Clayton, and Alan R. Woolworth. *Through Dakota Eyes: Narrative Accounts of the Minnesota Indian War of 1862.* St. Paul: Minnesota Historical Society Press, 1988.

Andrist, Ralph K. *The Long Death: The Last Days of the Plains Indian.* New York: Collier Books, 1993.

Archuleta, Margaret, Brenda J. Child, and K. Tsianina Lomawaima. *Away from Home: American Indian Boarding School Experiences, 1879–2000.* Phoenix: Heard Museum, 2000.

Ardrey, Robert. *The Territorial Imperative: A Personal Inquiry into the Animal Origins of Property and Nations.* New York: Atheneum, 1966.

"Autopsy Report: Good Buffalo, Hilda Rose." W.O. Brown, MD. April 5, 1975.

"AZ-Hemp." Arizona Industrial Hemp Council. Accessed September 3, 2011. http://azhemp.org/Archive/Package/Legal/legal.html.

Bailey, Thomas Andrew. *The American Pageant: A History of the Republic.* Boston: D. C. Heath, 1965.

Banks, Dennis, and Richard Erdoes. *Ojibwa Warrior: Dennis Banks and the Rise of the American Indian Movement.* Norman: University of Oklahoma Press, 2004.

Baum, L. Frank. Editorial. *Aberdeen Saturday Pioneer,* January 3, 1891. http://history.ox.ac.uk/hsmt/courses-reading/undergraduate/authority-of-nature/week=7baum.pdf.

Beasley, Conger. *We Are a People in This World: The Lakota Sioux and the Massacre at Wounded Knee*. Fayetteville: University of Arkansas Press, 1995.

Becher, Ronald. *Massacre Along the Medicine Road: A Social History of the Indian War of 1864 in Nebraska Territory*. Caldwell, ID: Caxton Press, 1999.

Berkhofer, Robert F. *The White Man's Indian: Images of the American Indian from Columbus to the Present*. New York: Knopf, 1978.

Bettelyoun, Susan Bordeaux, Josephine Waggoner, and Emilie Levine. *With My Own Eyes: A Lakota Woman Tells Her People's History*. Lincoln: University of Nebraska Press, 1998.

Black Elk DeSersa, Esther, Olivia Black Elk Pourier, and Arron DeSersa, Jr. *Black Elk Lives: Conversations with the Black Elk Family*. Edited by Hilda Neihardt Petri and Lori Utecht. Lincoln: University of Nebraska Press, 2000.

Black Elk, Wallace H., and William S. Lyon. *Black Elk: The Sacred Ways of a Lakota*. San Francisco: Harper & Row, 1990.

Blindman, Nathan. Letter to the Editor. *Rapid City Journal*, December 31, 2001.

Boller, Paul F., and John H. George. *They Never Said It: A Book of Fake Quotes, Misquotes, and Misleading Attributions*. New York: Oxford University Press, 1989.

Bourke, John Gregory. *On the Border with Crook*. Lincoln: University of Nebraska Press, 1971.

Brady, Cyrus Townsend. *Indian Fights and Fighters*. Lincoln: University of Nebraska Press, 1971.

——. *The Sioux Indian Wars: From the Powder River to the Little Big Horn*. New York: Indian Head Books, 1992.

Brand, Johanna. *The Life and Death of Anna Mae Aquash*. Toronto: J. Lorimer, 1978.

Brave Bird, Mary, and Richard Erdoes. *Lakota Woman*. New York: Grove Weidenfeld, 1990.

Bray, Kingsley M. *Crazy Horse: A Lakota Life*. Norman: University of Oklahoma, 2006.

Brayton, Matthew. *Kidnapped and Sold By Indians: True Story of 7-Year-Old Settler Child*. E-Book Edition, 2010.

Briggs, Jeremy. "Hemphasis.net ~ Hemp Paper." Accessed September 10, 2011. http://www.hemphasis.net/History/history.htm.

Brokaw, Tom. "Officials Look for Answers in Rapid Creek Mystery Deaths 10 Years Later." *Rapid City Journal*, June 22, 2009. http://rapidcityjournal.com/news/local/officials-look-for-answers-in-rapid-creek-mystery-deaths/article_42a62a1b-9d23-54d0-b145-86675f854e73.html.

Brooks-Gun, Jeanne, and Greg J. Duncan. "The Effects of Poverty on Children." The Future of Children. Summer 1997. http://futureofchildren.org/futureofchildren/publications/docs/07_02_03.pdf.

Brown, Dee Alexander. *The Fetterman Massacre*. Lincoln: University of Nebraska Press, 1971.

——. *Bury My Heart At Wounded Knee: An Indian History of the American West*. New York: Henry Holt and Company, 2007.

"Bull's Warriors Surrender: Big Foot and a Band of Hostiles Headed off by Colonel Sumner." *Omaha Daily Bee*, December 23, 1890. http://chroniclingamerica. loc.gov/lccn/sn99021999/1890-12-23/ed-1seq-1;words=troubles=Minnesota.

Burton, Richard Francis. *The Look of the West, 1860: Across the Plains to California*. Lincoln: University of Nebraska Press, 1963.

Cahill, Cathleen D. *Federal Fathers & Mothers: A Social History of the United States Indian Service, 1869–1933*. Chapel Hill: University of North Carolina Press, 2011.

"Camp Justice Home Page." Camp Justice. Accessed May 19, 2009. http://85.173.132/ search?=cache:n9-t3T2904J:www.aics.org/justice/camp.html+ca.

Cannon, Angie. "Healing Old Wounds: An Indian Woman's Murder Goes to Trial—Too Many Years Later." *U.S. News and World Report*, 2003.

Cassidy, Mike, and Will Miller. "A Short History of FBI COINTELPRO." Accessed September 13, 2010. http://www.monitor.net/monitor/9905a/ jbcointelpro.html.

Catches, Pete. *Sacred Fireplace (Oceti Wakan): Life and Teachings of a Lakota Medicine Man*. Edited by Peter Catches. Santa Fe: Clear Light Publishers, 1999.

Chavers, Dean. *Racism in Indian Country*. New York: Peter Lang, 2009.

Cherokee Nation v. Georgia, 30 U.S. 1 (1831).

Chief, Eagle D. *Winter Count*. Lincoln: University of Nebraska Press, 2003.

Churchill, Ward. "Analysis and Refutation of the FBI's Accounting for AIM Fatalities on Pine Ridge, 1973–1976." *No Parole Peltier Association* (web log). Accessed June 2012. http://wwwnoparolepeltiercom-justice.blogspot.com/.

———. *From a Native Son: Selected Essays in Indigenism, 1985–1995*. Boston: South End Press, 1996.

———. *Since Predator Came: Notes from the Struggle for American Indian Liberation*. Littleton, CO: Aigis Publications, 1995.

Churchill, Ward, and Jim VanderWall. *The COINTELPRO Papers: Documents from the FBI's Secret Wars against Dissent in the United States*. Cambridge: South End Press, 2002.

Coel, Margaret. *Chief Left Hand, Southern Arapaho*. Norman: University of Oklahoma Press, 1981.

"COINTELPRO." FBI. Accessed September 13, 2010. http://vault.fbi.gov/ cointel-pro.

Colby, L. W. *The Sioux Indian Wars of 1890–91*. Transactions and Reports of the Nebraska State Historical Society 3, 1892.

Coleman, William S. E. *Voices of Wounded Knee*. Lincoln: University of Nebraska Press, 2000.

Collier, John. *The Indians of the Americas*. New York: W.W. Norton, 1947.

———. *On the Gleaming Way: Navajos, Eastern Pueblos, Zunis, Hopis, Apaches, and Their Land and Their Meanings to the World*. Denver: Sage Books, 1962.

Commager, Henry Steele. *Documents of American History*. New York: Appleton-Century-Crofts, 1963.

"Commemorating Anna Mae." John Graham Defense Committee. November 2004. http://www.grahamdefense.org/200411investigatethefeds.htm.

Connell, Evan S. *Son of the Morning Star: General Custer and the Battle of the Little Bighorn*. New York: Harper Perennial, 1991.

Controlled Drugs and Substances Act, SC 1996, C 19. http://www.deadiversion.usdoj.gov/21cfr/21usc/index.html

Crow Dog, Leonard, and Richard Erdoes. *Crow Dog: Four Generations of Sioux Medicine Men*. New York: HarperCollins Publishers, 1995.

Crow Dog, Mary, and Richard Erdoes. *Lakota Woman*. New York: Harper Perennial, 1991.

Custer, George A. *My Life on the Plains, Or, Personal Experiences with Indians*. Norman: University of Oklahoma Press, 1962.

Daily, David W. *Battle for the BIA: G.E.E. Lindquist and the Missionary Crusade against John Collier*. Tucson: University of Arizona Press, 2004.

Danker, Donald Floyd, ed. *The Wounded Knee Interviews of Eli S. Ricker*. Lincoln: Nebraska State Historical Society, 1981.

"Dark Side of the Force." Wookieepedia: The Star Wars Wiki. Accessed June 21, 2013. http://starwars.wikia.com/wiki/Dark_side_of_the_Force.

Davis, Eric. "Lawyers File Briefs in Many Horses Case." *Native News*, September 14, 1999. http://www.mail-archive.com/nntivenews@mlists.net/msg0428.html.

Davis, Theodore R. "A Stage Ride to Colorado Across the Great Plains of Kansas, 1865." *Harper's New Monthly Magazine*, Vol. XXXV, 1867.

"DEA and FBI Agents Raid Family Crop." Indian Country Today Media Network.com. September 6, 2000. http://indiancountrytodaymedianetwork.com/ictarchives/2000/09/06/dea-and-fbi-agents-raid-family-crop-86551.

de Tocqueville, Alexis. *Democracy in America, And Two Essays on America*. Edited by Isaac Kramnick. Translated by Gerald Bevan. London: Penguin, 2003.

Deer, Sara. "Toward an Indigenous Jurisprudence of Rape." William Mitchell College of Law Open Access. 2004. http://open.wmitchell.edu/cgi/.

Degler, Carl N. *Out of Our Past: The Forces That Shaped Modern America*. New York: Harper, 1959.

Deloria, Vine. *The Indian Reorganization Act: Congresses and Bills*. Norman: University of Oklahoma Press, 2002.

DeMallie, Raymond J., ed. *The Sixth Grandfather: Black Elk's Teachings Given to John G. Neihardt*. Lincoln: University of Nebraska Press, 1984.

"The Denver Press Conference." *News From Indian Country*. Novemeber 3, 1999. http://www.indiancountrynews.info/denverpress.cfm.htm.

Department of Justice. "New Report: U.S. Homicide Rate Falls to Lowest in Four Decades. http://blogs.justice.gov/main/archives.1765 (web log). Accessed February 2010.

Dewing, Rolland, *Wounded Knee II*. Chadron, NE: Great Plains Network, 1995.

Dickson, Albert Jerome. *Covered Wagon Days: A Journey Across the Plains in the*

Sixties, and Pioneer Days in the Northwest. Lincoln: University of Nebraska Press, 1989.

Dippie, Brian. "Its Equal I Have Never Seen." *Columbia Magazine,* Summer 2005. http://www/friendslittlebighorn.com?Georgecuster.htm.

DiSilvestro, Roger L. *In the Shadow of Wounded Knee: The Untold Final Chapter of the Indian Wars.* New York: Walker, 2005.

"DLN Issues: Jancita Eagle Deer." Jancita Eagle Deer Polygraph Regarding Alleged Rape by Janklow and if He Threatened to Kill Her. Accessed May 2, 2011. http://www.dlncoalition.org/dln_issues/janklowpolygraph.htm.

——. Judge Frederick Lambrecht Letter to Wagner Service Health Service. Accessed May 1, 2011. http://www.dlncoalition.org/dln_issues/janklowlambrechtletter.htm.

——. Judge Gonzales Finding of Probable Cause of Assault with Intent to Commit Rape by William Janklow and Carnal Knowledge of a Child Under the Age of 16 Years. Accessed May 1, 2011. http://www.dlncoalition.org/dln_issues/janklowwarranttoapprehend.htm.

——. Judge Mario Gonzalez's Disbarment Order of William Janklow from Practicing Law in Rosebud Sioux Tribal Court. Accessed May 2, 2011. http://www.dlncoalition.org/dln_issues/janklowgonzalezorder.htm.

——. Letter from Bureau of Indian Affairs (BIA) Aberdeen Area Director Harley Zephier to BIA Rosebud Officer. Accessed May 1, 2011. http://www.dlncoalition.org/dln_issues/janklowzephierletter.htm.

——. Robert G. Philbrick Statement. Accessed May 1, 2011. http://www.dlncoalition.org/dln_issues/janklowphilbrick1.htm.

Donovan, Jim. *A Terrible Glory: Custer and the Little Bighorn—The Last Great Battle of the American West.* New York: Little, Brown and Company, 2008.

Duggan, Joe. "Meeting on Whiteclay Alcohol Sales Ends Quickly with No Progress." *Omaha World Herald,* July 9, 2013. http://www.omaha.com/article/20130708/NEWS/707099997.

——. "Rally Leaders Promise to Return." *Lincoln Journal Star,* June 28, 1999. http://www.dickshovel.com/wc3.html.

——. "They Searched for Their Dead Brothers." *Lincoln Journal Star,* June 27, 1999. http://www.journalstar.com/articles/2007/09/24special-reports/whiteclay/p6/doc4286955a8c20a147804020.txt.

Duncan, D. M. "In Jancita Eagle Deer's Own Words v. William Janklow." The Doomsday Diet. 2007. http://www.operationmorningstar.org/In_Jancita_Eagle_Deer's_Own_Words_vs._William Janklow.

Duthu, N. Bruce. *American Indians and the Law.* New York: Viking, 2008.

Eastman, Charles Alexander. *The Soul of the Indian: An Interpretation.* Lincoln: University of Nebraska Press, 1980.

Eastman, Elaine Goodale, and Kay Graber. *Sister to the Sioux: The Memoirs of Elaine Goodale Eastman, 1885–91.* Lincoln: University of Nebraska Press, 1978.

Editors Note. "Anna Marie Timeline 1-Wounded Knee." *News From Indian*

Country, December 16, 2007. http://www.indiancountrynews.com/index. php/investigations/286-aquash-peltier-timeline-1975-2010/2101-annie-mae-timeline-i-wounded-knee.

Editors Note. "Bernie Lafferty Speaks about Perry Ray Robinson's Killing inside Wounded Knee 1973." *News from Indian Country Today*, July 17, 2007. http://www.indiancountrynews.com/news/investigations/ray-robinson.

Embry, Carlos B. *America's Concentration Camps: The Facts about Our Indian Reservations Today*. New York: D. McKay, 1956.

Erdoes, Richard, and Alfonso Ortiz, eds. *American Indian Myths and Legends*. New York: Pantheon Books, 1984.

Ex Parte Crow Dog, 109 U.S. 556 (1883).

"Expect to Be Killed: Citizens of Mandan Anticipate an Attack by Frenzied Sioux Braves." *St. Paul Daily Grove*, November 18, 1890. http://chroniclingamerica. loc.gov/lccn/sn99021999/issues.

"Exterminate Them." *Rocky Mountain News* (Denver), March 24, 1863. http://www.yellowstone-online.com/buffalo/october12genocidedestructionand imperialismslideshow.pdf.

"FBI Chief: No Proof of U.S. Indian Plot." *Oakland Tribune*, July 7, 1976. http://newspaperarchive.com/oakland-tribune/1976-07-07?tag=american+indian+m ovement+dog+soldier+memo&rtserp=tags/american-indian-movement-dog-soldier-memo.

"FD-302." Federal Bureau of Investigation. June 14, 1974. File # MP-70-8216.

"FD-302." Federal Bureau of Investigation. May 10, 1974. File # MP-70-8216.

"FD-302." Federal Bureau of Investigation. May 10, 1976. File # RC-70-11602.

"FD-302." Federal Bureau of Investigation. September 28, 1974. File # MP-70-8216.

"FD-302 (REV.11-27-70)." Letter from Federal Bureau of Investigation. May 10, 1974.

"FD-302." Federal Bureau of Investigation. April 30, 1974. File # MP 70-8216.

"FD-302." Federal Bureau of Investigation. September 24, 1973. File # MP-70-8216.

"Fearing an Outbreak: Trouble Is Anticipated among the Sioux." *Arizona Republican*, October 28, 1890. http://chroniclingamerica.loc.gov/lccn/ sn84020558/1890-10-28/ed-1/seq-1/;words=Laughlin+agent=Mc.

Feraca, Stephen E. *Wakinyan: Lakota Religion in the Twentieth Century*. Lincoln: University of Nebraska Press, 1998.

Field, Matthew C. *Prairie and Mountain Sketches*. Edited by Kate Leila Gregg and John Francis McDermott. Norman: University of Oklahoma Press, 1957.

"Fifteen Thousand Braves: The Indians Could Do Much Harm If So Disposed." *Salt Lake Tribune*, November 18, 1890. http://newspaperarchive.com.

Finerty, John F. *Warpath and Bivouac*. University of Oklahoma Press, 1961.

Fletcher, Alice C., and Francis La Flesche. *The Omaha Tribe*. Lincoln: University of Nebraska Press, 1972.

Flood, Reneé S. *Lost Bird of Wounded Knee: Spirit of the Lakota*. New York: Da Capo Press, 1995.

"FOIPA Request No.: 1180674-00, Subject: Daniel Duane Titus." David M. Hardy to Alan Hafer. January 23, 2012.

Fort Robinson Illustrated. Lincoln: Nebraska Game and Parks Commission, 1986.

Franklin, Benjamin. *Autobiography and Other Pieces.* Edited by Dennis Sydney Reginald Welland. London: Oxford University Press, 1970.

Frazier, Ian. *On the Rez.* New York: Farrar, Straus and Giroux, 2000.

Gagnon, Gregory O. *Pine Ridge Reservation: Yesterday and Today.* Interior, SD: Badlands Natural History Association, 1992.

Gease, Heidi B. "Graham Sentenced to Life in Prison." *Rapid City Journal*, January 24, 2011.

——. "Trial Begins for Man Accused of AIM Activists Death." *Rapid City Journal*, April 14, 2010. woodlandindians.org.forums/viewtopic.php?=7677.

——. "Witness in AIM Slaying Trial Recalls a Fractured AIM, Peltier Admission." *Rapid City Journal*, April 20, 2010. http://www.rapidcityjournal.com/news/article-8556940-4cc11-df-a293-001cc403286.

Giago, Tim. "Bringing a Dark Chapter in Oglala History to an End." *Huffington Post* (web log), June 09, 2007. http:www.huffingtonpost.com/tim-giago/bringing-a-dark-chapter-i_b_63346.html.

——. "Whatever Happened to the So-called Goons." *Huffington Post* (web log), September 16, 2007. http://www.huffingtonpost.com/tim-giago/whatever-happened-to-the_2_b_64611.html.

Gibbon, Guy E. *The Sioux: The Dakota and Lakota Nations.* Malden, MA: Blackwell Pub., 2003.

Gibson, Arrell Morgan. *The American Indian: Prehistory to the Present.* Lexington, MA: D.C. Heath, 1980.

Giese, Paula. *Secret Agent Douglass Durham and the Death of Jancita Eagle Deer: Your Tax Dollar at Work.* Millville, MN: Anvil Press, 1976.

——. "Witness Points to Gunman Accomplice in AIM Slaying." *Rapid City Journal*, April 16, 2010. http://rapidcityjournal.com/ /news/witness-points-to-gunman-accomplice-in-aim-slaying/article_9e71af06- 48bb-11df-b695-001cc4c03286.html.

Glick, Brian. *War at Home: Covert Action Against U.S. Activists and What We Can Do about It.* Boston: South End Press, 1989.

Glover, Vic. *Keeping Heart on Pine Ridge: Family Ties, Warrior Culture, Commodity Foods, Rez Dogs, and the Sacred.* Summertown, TN: Native Voices, 2004.

Gonzalez, Mario, and Elizabeth Cook-Lynn. *The Politics of Hallowed Ground: Wounded Knee and the Struggle for Indian Sovereignty.* Urbana: University of Illinois Press, 1999.

"GOP Official Admits Moving Janklow File." *Huron Daily Plainsman*, October 27, 1974. http://newspaperarchive.com/huron-daily-plainsman/1974-10-27/page-11?tag=gop+official+admits+moving+janklow+file&rtserp=tags/?pc=13622&pci=7&plo=gop-official-admits-moving-janklow-file&psi=88&pt=15164.

Hall, Philip S. *To Have This Land: The Nature of Indian/White Relations, South Dakota, 1888–1891.* Vermillion: University of South Dakota Press, 1991.

Hamilton, William Thomas, and E. T. Sieber. *My Sixty Years on the Plains*. Alexandria, VA: Time-Life Books, 1982.

Hardorff, Richard G. *The Death of Crazy Horse: A Tragic Episode in Lakota History*. Lincoln: University of Nebraska Press, 2001.

Harlan, Bill. "Thirty-Five-Year-Old Memories Still Drive Flood Debate." *Ra*, October 1, 2007.

Harring, Sidney L. *Crow Dog's Case: American Indian Sovereignty, Tribal Law, and United States Law in the Nineteenth Century*. Cambridge: Cambridge University Press, 1994.

Hassrick, Royal B. *The Sioux: Life and Customs of a Warrior Society*. Collaboration with Cile M. Bach and Dorothy Maxwell. Norman: University of Oklahoma Press, 1964.

"Hemp vs. Marijuana." Accessed September 3, 2011. http://azhemp.org/Archive/Package/Legal/legal.html.

Hendricks, Steve. *The Unquiet Grave: The FBI and the Struggle for the Soul of Indian Country*. New York: Thunder's Mouth Press, 2006.

———. "Promised Land." *Orion*, July/August 2005. http://www.stevehendricks.org/writings/promised-land.pdf.

"History—Incident at Wounded Knee." U.S. Marshals Service. Accessed September 2010. http://www.justice.gov/marshals/history/wounded-knee/.

Hittman, Michael. *Wovoka and the Ghost Dance*. Edited by Don Lynch. Lincoln: University of Nebraska Press, 1997.

Hogan, Lawrence J. *The Osage Indian Murders: The True Story of a Multiple Murder Plot to Acquire the Estates of Wealthy Osage Tribe Members*. Frederick, MD: Amlex, 1998.

Hollow, Robert C., and Herbert T. Hoover. *The Last Years of Sitting Bull: June 1–September 30, 1984, North Dakota Heritage Center, State Historical Society of North Dakota*. Bismarck: Museum Division, North Dakota Heritage Center, 1984.

Huck, Susan L.M. "Renegades: The Second Battle of Wounded Knee." *American Opinion Magazine*, May 1973. Http://federalexpression.files.wordpress.com/2012/10/197305-renegades.pdf

"HUD Accepts New Census Numbers—Population Soars from 15,000 to 28,000." *Village Earth*, September 18, 2007. <http://villageearth.org/pages/global-affiliate-network/projects-pineridge-reservation/hud-accepts-new-census-numbers-population-soars-from-15000-to-28000>.

Hyde, George E. *Spotted Tail's Folk: A History of the Brulé Sioux*. Norman: University of Oklahoma Press, 1961.

"ICMIPRO1: Description of Property: One Styrofoam Coffee Cup." January 13, 2004. Case #198A-MP-5674.

"ICMIPRO1: Source from Which Property Acquired, FBI Laboratory, PCR Extracted DNA Tubes and Amplified DNA Tubes from Cigarette Butts." April 18, 2002. Case #198A-MP-5674.

"Income." *Table C3. Per Capita by County: 1959, 1969, 1979, and 1989.* Accessed September 15, 2007. <http://www.census.gov/hhes/www/income/data/historical/county/county3.html>.

"Indians Ready to Fight." *New York Times*, November 22, 1890. http://query.nytimes.com/mem/archive-free/pdf?r=1&res=9C04E2DF1E3BE533A25751C2 A9679D94619ED7CF.

"Indians Ready to Fight: A Squaw's Warning." *Omaha Daily Bee*, November 20, 1890. http://chroniclingamerica.loc.gov/lccn/sn99021999/issues.

"Inter Caetera." Accessed September 5, 2012. http://bullsburning.itgo.com/essays/Caetera.htm.

"Interview of Fritz Arlo Looking Cloud." Justice for Anna Mae and Ray. 2003. www.jfamr.org/doc/arlo.html.

"Janklow Denies Raping Woman." *Huron Daily Plainsman*, October 29, 1974. http://newspaperarchive.com/huron-daily-plainsman/1974-10-29?tag=janklow+denies+raping+woman&rtserp=tags/?pep=janklow-denies-raping-woman.

"Jankow's Law License Restored a Year Early." *Star Tribune* (Minneapolis), January 25, 2006. http://www.startribune.com/templates/Print_This_Story?sid=11610806.

Jensen, Richard E., ed. *The Indian Interviews of Eli S. Ricker, 1903–1919.* Lincoln: University of Nebraska Press, 2005.

——. *The Settler and Soldier Interviews of Eli S. Ricker, 1903–1919.* Lincoln: University of Nebraska Press, 2005.

Johansen, Bruce E., and Roberto Maestas. *Wasi'chu: The Continuing Indian Wars.* New York: Monthly Review Press, 1979.

"John Graham Defense Committee. Trial Transcripts and Other Court." John Graham Defense Committee. February 26, 2012. http://www.grahamdefense.org/courtdocs/John_Graham_Trial20101201-10Vol_07.pdf.

Johnson, Cory. "The Case of Leonard Peltier: Notorious Frame-up of Native American Activist Returns to Spotlight." World Socialist Web. 2004. http://www1.wsws.org/articles.2000/dec2000/pelt-d14.shtml.

Johnson, Terry. "Reward Offered to Solve Mysterious Death." *Indian Country Today,* September 19, 2004.

Johnson, Virginia Weisel. *The Unregimented General: A Biography of Nelson A. Miles.* Boston: Houghton Mifflin, 1962.

Kadlecek, Edward, and Mabell Kadlecek. *To Kill an Eagle: Indian Views on the Last Days of Crazy Horse.* Boulder: Johnson Books, 1981.

Kehoe, Alice Beck. *The Ghost Dance: Ethnohistory & Revitalization.* Long Grove, IL: Waveland, 2006.

Kelly, Fanny. *My Captivity Among the Sioux Indians.* New York: Carol Pub. Group, 1993.

Kenny, Colleen. "Standing at the Crossroads." *Lincoln Journal Star,* May 15, 2005.

Keohane, Sonja. "Deaths of Homeless Investigated." *Native News,* September 6, 1999.

Ketcham, Christopher. "They Shoot Buffalo Don't They: Hazing America's Last

Wild Herd." *Harper's Magazine*, June 2008. http://harpers.org/archive/2008/06/0082064.

Kilborn, Peter T. "Life at the Bottom—America's Poorest County/A Special Report; Sad Distinction for the Sioux: Homeland Is No. 1 in Poverty." *The New York Times*. September 20, 1992. Accessed September 2007. http://www.nytimes.com/1992/09/20/us/life-bottom-america-s-poorest-county-special-report-sad-distinction-for-sioux.html.

"Kill the Indian, and Save the Man: Capt. Richard H. Pratt on the Education of Native Americans." Accessed September 10, 2009. http://historymatters.gmu.edu/d/4929/.

Kinsley, D. A. *Custer, Favor the Bold: A Soldier's Story*. New York: Promontory Press by arrangement with Henry Holt & Company, 1988.

Kipp, Woody. *Vietcong at Wounded Knee*. Lincoln: University of Nebraska Press, 2004.

Kolpack, David. "Witness: Man Supplied Gun in 1975 S.D., Slaying." *Associated Press*, 2010. Woodlandindians.org.forums/viewtopic.php?id=7677.

Kuzma, Michael. "Where Are the FBI Files Concerning Myrtle Poor Bear." Censored News. 2013. http://bsnorrell.blogspot.com/2009/01/where-are-fbi-files-concerning-myrtle.html.

Lakota Country Times. June 07, 2011. [obituary] http://www.lakotacountrytimes.com/news/2011-07-06/The_Holy_Road/Aaron_William_Running_Hawk.html.

Lamberto, Nick. "Grand Jury's 10-X Report Chides City." *Des Moines Register*, June 21, 1972. http://www.newspaperarchive.com.

Lame Deer, Archie Fire, and Richard Erdoes. *Gift of Power: The Life and Teachings of a Lakota Medicine Man*. Santa Fe: Bear and Company, 1992.

LaMere, Frank. "Frank LaMere Speaks about Whiteclay." Common Ground Common Sense On Line Community (web log). Accessed October 19, 2009. http://www.commongroundcommonsense.org/forums/lofiverson/index.

Lang, Debbie. "The Battle of Wounded Knee: The People Standing Up." *Revolutionary Worker* #1038, January 16, 2000. http://revcom.us/a/v21/1030-039/1038/wknee.ht.

———. "Reign of Terror After 1973 Wounded Knee: Resistance Stories of the Lakota People." *Revolutionary Worker #1039*, January 23, 2000. http://revcom.us/a/v21/1030-039/1039/wknee2.htm.

Larson, Robert W. *Red Cloud: Warrior-statesman of the Lakota Sioux*. Norman: University of Oklahoma Press, 1997.

Laymon, Oliver E. *Survey of the Constitution and By-laws of the Oglala Sioux Tribe*. Vermillion: University of South Dakota, 1955.

Lazarus, Edward. *Black Hills/White Justice: The Sioux Nation versus the United States: 1775 to the Present*. New York: HarperCollins, 1991.

Legends of the Mighty Sioux. Interior, SD: Badlands Natural History Association, 1987.

Lewis, Meriwether, and William Clark. *The Journals of Lewis and Clark*. Abridged by Anthony Brandt. Washington, D.C.: National Geographic Adventure Classics, 2002.

Lewis, Thomas H. *The Medicine Men: Oglala Sioux Ceremony and Healing*. Lincoln: University of Nebraska Press in Cooperation with the American Indian Studies Research Institute, Indiana University, 1990.

Louis, Adrian C. *Skins: A Novel*. New York: Crown Publishers, 1995.

Luna-Firebaugh, Eileen. *Tribal Policing: Asserting Sovereignty, Seeking Justice*. Tucson: University of Arizona Press, 2007.

Lurie, Jon. "Harvest of Death." First Nations Issues of Consequence (web log). http:www.dickshovel.com/lsa.html.

Lyman, Stanley David. *Wounded Knee 1973: A Personal Account*. Edited by Floyd A. O'Neil, June K. Lyman, and Susan McKay. Lincoln: University of Nebraska Press, 1991.

Maddra, Sam. *Hostiles?: The Lakota Ghost Dance and Buffalo Bill's Wild West*. Norman: University of Oklahoma Press, 2006.

Magnuson, Stew. *The Death of Raymond Yellow Thunder and Other True Stories from the Nebraska-Pine Ridge Border Towns*. Lubbock: Texas Tech University Press, 2008.

Mancall, Peter C. *Deadly Medicine: Indians and Alcohol in Early America*. Ithaca: Cornell University Press, 1995.

Marshall, Joseph, III. *Keep Going: The Art of Perseverance*. New York: Sterling Pub., 2006.

———. *The Day the World Ended at Little Big Horn: A Lakota History*. New York: Penquin Books, 2008.

———. *The Lakota Way: Stories and Lessons for Living*. New York: Penquin Compass, 2002.

———. *Walking With Grandfather: The Wisdom of Lakota Leaders*. Boulder: Sounds True, 2005.

Matthiessen, Peter. *In the Spirit of Crazy Horse*. New York: Penguin Books, 1992.

McGaa, Ed, John F. Bryde, and John McGaa. *Crazy Horse and Chief Red Cloud: Warrior Chiefs, Based on Warrior Interviews*. Sioux Falls, SD: Four Directions Pub., 2009.

McGillycuddy, Julia B. *Blood on the Moon: Valentine McGillycuddy and the Sioux*. Lincoln: University of Nebraska Press, 1990.

McGinnis, Anthony. *Counting Coup and Cutting Horses: Intertribal Warfare on the Northern Plains, 1738–1889*. Evergreen, CO: Cordillera Press, 1990.

McLaughlin, Marie L. *Myths and Legends of the Sioux*. Lincoln: University of Nebraska Press, 1990.

McMurtry, Larry. *Crazy Horse*. New York: Viking, 1999.

Means, Russell. *Where White Men Fear to Tread: The Autobiography of Russell Means*. Edited by Marvin J. Wolf. New York: St. Martin's Press, 1995.

"Meet Alex White Plum." Free Press email update. 2010. http://freepress.org/departments/display/8/2010/3774.

Melmer, David. "Oglala Sioux President Alex White Plume sees the old ways as better." *Indian Country Today*, August 28, 2006. http://intercontinentalcry. org/oglala-sioux-president-alex-white-plume-sees-the-old-ways-as-better/.

——. "Two Suspects Charged in Johnson Murder: Both Could Face Death Penalty." *Indian Country Today*. Accessed November 13, 2009. http://highbeam. com/doc/1P1-79288722.html.

"Memorandum." ASAC Rapid City to Director, FBI. January 20, 1977. Mrs. Jeanette Bissonette Nee Jeanette Waters—Victim. Field Office File #70-9815.

"Memorandum." Federal Bureau of Investigation to SAC Minneapolis. February 18, 1975. Melvin Spider—Victim. Field Office File #70-8216.

"Memorandum." Letter to Assistant Director, Federal Bureau of Investigation. May 15, 1979. http://law2.umkc.edu/faculty/projects/ftrials/peltier/affidavit explanation.jpg.

"Memorandum." SAC Minneapolis to Director (Attn: FBI Laboratory) April 2, 1975. Mrs. Jeanette Bissonette Nee Jeanette Waters—Victim. Field Office File #70-9815.

"Memorandum." SAC Minneapolis to Director, FBI. December 28, 1981. Mrs. Jeanette Bissonette Nee Jeanette Waters—Victim. Field Office File#70-9815.

"Memorandum." SAC Minneapolis to Director, FBI. March 26, 1975. Mrs. Jeanette Bissonette Nee Jeanette Waters—Victim. Field Office File #70-9815.

"Memorandum." SAC Omaha to SAC Minneapolis. August 22, 1974. Melvin Spider—Victim. Field Office File #70-8216.

"Memorandum: Subject Benjamin Sitting Up (Deceased), Isabelle Sitting Up." SAC Minneapolis to SAC Minneapolis. August 21, 1975. Field Office File #70-10021.

Meryhew, Richard. "Janklow's Law License Restored a Year Early." *Star Tribune* (Minneapolis) January 25, 2006. http://www.startribune.com/templates/Print_ This_Story?sid=11610806.

Michno, Gregory. *Lakota Noon: The Indian Narrative of Custer's Defeat*. Missoula, MT: Mountain Press Pub., 1997.

Michno, Gregory, and Susan Michno. *A Fate Worse than Death: Indian Captivities in the West, 1830–1885*. Caldwell, ID: Caxton Press, 2007.

Miller, David H. "Echoes of the Little Bighorn." *American Heritage* 22, no. 4 (June 1971).

——. *Custer's Fall: The Native American Side of the Story*. New York: Meridian, 1992.

——. *Ghost Dance*. Lincoln: University of Nebraska Press, 1959.

Miller, Irma R. *French-Indian Families in America's West: Lessert (aka Claymore), Roy, Chatillon, Delor, Royer*. Victoria, B.C.: Trafford, 2005.

Miller, Robert. "Treaty Interpretation: Judicial Rules and Canons of Construction." Lewis and Clark Law School. Accessed April 6, 2011. http://papers.ssrn. com/sol3/papers.cfm?abstract_id=1355227.

Monroe, Mark. *An Indian in White America*. Edited by Carolyn Reyer. Philadelphia: Temple University Press, 1994.

Mooney, James. *The Ghost-dance Religion and Wounded Knee*. New York: Dover Publications, 1973.

Murphey, Lori. "Enough Rope: Why United States v. White Plume Was Wrong on Hemp and Treaty Rights." *American Indian Law Review* 35, No. 2 (2011).

Murray, Jim. *Wasicu in Indian Country*. www.Xlibris.com, 2012.

"Myrtle Poor Bear Lies ..." Accessed August 8, 2010. http://www.dickshovel.com/affa.html.

"Myrtle Poor Bear's Three Affidavits in the Peltier Case." Accessed May 12, 2008. http://law2.umkc.edu/faculty/projects/ftrials/peltier/poorbearaffidavits.html.

Nadeau, Remi A. *Fort Laramie and the Sioux Indians*. Englewood Cliffs, N.J.: Prentice-Hall, 1967.

"Native America Calling." Transcript, Native American Public Telecommunications. November 4, 1999. http://www.indiancountrynews.info/nativecalling3.cfm.htm.

Neihardt, John Gneisenau. *Black Elk Speaks: Being the Life Story of a Holy Man of the Oglala Sioux*. New York: Pocket Books, 1972.

New York Times. November 20, 1890, [no title]. http://query.nytimes.com/gst/abstract.html?res=9404E6DF1E3BE533A25753C2A9679D94619ED7CF&scp=39&sq=november+20%2C+1890&st=p.

Nixon, Barbara. *Mi' Taku'ye-Oyasin: Letters From Wounded Knee—The Native American Holocaust*. www.Xlibris.com, 2012.

Norgren, Jill. *The Cherokee Cases: Two Landmark Federal Decisions in the Fight for Sovereignty*. Norman: University of Oklahoma Press, 2004.

"Officials Look for Answers in Rapid Creek Mystery Deaths 10 Years Later." *Rapid City Journal*, June 22, 2009. http://www.rapidcityjournal.com/articles/2009/06/22/news/local/doc4a3e7725727c140737691.txt.

"Oglala Sioux President Arrested in Whiteclay." *Rapid City Journal*, June 17, 2013. http://rapidcityjournal.com/news/local/oglala-sioux-president-arrested-in-Whiteclay/article_ca60e806-3531-5ee9-ba48-0fb32155ae8f.html.

"Oglala Sioux President Squanders Chance to Talk Whiteclay with Nebraska Governor." *Madville Times*, July 9, 2013. http://madvilletimes.com/2013/07/oglala-sioux-president-squanders-chance-to-talk-whiteclay-with-nebraska-governor/.

"Oglala Sioux Reservation Sealed Off." *The Holland Evening Sentinel*, February 28, 1972.

Oglala Sioux Tribal Council. November 10, 1972, Box 12, Ed. Folder: Council Proceedings. Records of the Oglala Sioux Tribe, Oglala Lakota College Archives, Kyle, S.D."

Oglala Sioux Tribal Council. November 8, 1972, Box 12, Ed. Folder: Council Proceedings. Records of the Oglala Sioux Tribe, Oglala Lakota College Archives, Kyle, S.D.

"On the Bootleggers Trail in Indian County." Indian Country Today Media Network.com. 2011. http://indiancountrytodaymedianetwork.com/ictarchives/2010/10/11/on-the-bootleggers%e2%80%99-trail-in-indian-country-76523.

Ostler, Jeffrey. *The Lakotas and the Black Hills: The Struggle for Sacred Ground.* New York: Viking, 2010.

———. *The Plains Sioux and U.S. Colonialism from Lewis and Clark to Wounded Knee.* Cambridge: Cambridge University Press, 2004.

Parkman, Francis. *The Oregon Trail.* Mineola, NY: Dover Publications, 2002.

Paul, R. Eli, ed. *Autobiography of Red Cloud: War Leader of the Oglalas.* Helena: Montana Historical Society Press, 1997.

Peltier, Leonard. *Prison Writings: My Life Is My Sundance.* Edited by Harvey Arden. New York: St. Martin's Press, 1999.

Peterka, Jennifer. "Aura of Racism in Rapid Creek Deaths." *Indian Country Today*, August 5, 1999. http://www.mail-archive.com/nativenews@mlists.net/msg03557.html.

Petrillo, Larissa, Melda Trejo, and Lupe Trejo. *Being Lakota: Identity and Tradition on Pine Ridge Reservation.* Lincoln: University of Nebraska Press, 2007.

Philbrick, Nathaniel. *Mayflower: A Story of Courage, Community, and War.* New York: Viking, 2006.

Powers, Thomas. *The Killing of Crazy Horse.* New York: Alfred A. Knopf, 2010.

Powers, William K. *Oglala Religion.* Lincoln: University of Nebraska Press, 1977.

———. *Yuwipi, Vision and Experience in Oglala Ritual.* Lincoln: University of Nebraska Press, 1982.

Price, Catherine. *The Oglala People, 1841–1879: A Political History.* Lincoln: University of Nebraska Press, 1996.

"Rapid City: History: Cities of the United States." 2006. http://encycpedia.com/doc/1G2-3441801864.html.

"Rapid City, South Dakota, AKA: Skinhead Central, USA." Accessed December 21, 2009. http://mindspring.com/-mike.wicks/rapidcity.html.

Ray, Charles M. "Pine Ridge Reservation Deaths To Be Reinvestigated." National Public Radio. August 18, 2012. http://www.npr.org/2012/08/18/159058219/near-wounded-knee-years-of-alleged-injustice.

Record, Ian. "A Fire That Burns: The Legacy of Wounded Knee 1973." *Native Americas Magazine*, Spring 1988. http://www.oocities/crazyoglala/WK73to98_record.html.

"Red Devils Rampant." *St. Paul Daily Grove*, November 22, 1890. http://chroniclingamerica.loc.gov/lccn/sn90055922/1890-11-27/ed-1/seq-1/; words=phillips=Scotty.

Red Star, Nancy. *Star Ancestors: Indian Wisdomkeepers Share the Teachings of the Extraterrestrials.* Rochester, VT: Destiny Books, 2000.

Reinhardt, Akim D. *Ruling Pine Ridge: Oglala Lakota Politics from the IRA to Wounded Knee.* Lubbock: Texas Tech University Press, 2007.

"Report for Pine Ridge Indian Reservation, South Dakota." Federal Bureau of Investigation. Accessed September 11, 2010. http://www.fbi.gov/.

"Report." Redacted to AUSA Sioux Falls, South Dakota. April 30, 1976. Hilda Rose Good Buffalo—Victim. Field Office File #70-9834.

"Report." Redacted to AUSA Sioux Falls, South Dakota. May 16, 1975. Hilda Rosa Good Buffalo—Victim. Field Office File #70-9834.

"Report." Redacted to Minneapolis Office. 1975. Hilda Rose Good Buffalo—Victim. Field Office File #70-64972.

"Report." Redacted to Sioux Falls, South Dakota, Attn: AUSA, Rapid City South Dakota. April 27, 1976. Aloysius White Crane; Cleveland Emmitt Reddest—Victim. Field Office File #70-11558.

"Report." Redacted to Sioux Falls, South Dakota, AUSA Boyd. August 21, 1975. Title: Benjamin Sitting Up (Deceased), Isabelle Sitting Up. Field Office File #70-10021.

"Report" Redacted to USA, Sioux Falls, South Dakota, Attention: AUSA Redacted. August 16, 1973. Unknown Subject: Mrs. Jeanette Bissonette Nee Jeanette Waters. Field Office File #70-9815.

"Report." Redacted to USA Sioux Falls, South Dakota. August 12, 1976. Betty Lou Means—Victim. File #70-11739.

"Report." Redacted to USA, Sioux Falls, South Dakota. September 22, 1977. Betty Lou Means—Victim. File #70-68538.

"Report." Redacted to AUSA Sioux Falls. November 12, 1976. Betty Lou Means—Victim. File #70-1139.

"Request No.: 1180674-00, Subject: Daniel Duane Titus." David M. Hardy to Alan Hafer, January 23, 2012.

Richard Marshall, Petitioner and Appellant v. State of South Dakota, Appellee (May 20, 1981), FindACase.

"Richard Marshall's Trial: Day 6." KEVN, Black Hills Fox. April 21, 2010. www.blackhillsfox.com/Archive/2010/0422/Richard-marshalls-trial-day-6.

Richardson, Heather Cox. *Wounded Knee: Party Politics and the Road to an American Massacre.* New York: Basic Books, 2010.

Richmond, Robert W., and Robert W. Mardock, eds. *A Nation Moving West: Readings in the History of the American Frontier.* Lincoln: University of Nebraska Press, 1966.

Rick, Lynn T. "Rape on the Reservation: Criminal Convictions Tough to Come By." *Rapid City Journal,* November 2, 2010. http://rapidcityjournal.com/news/rape-on-the-reservation-criminal-convictions-tough-to-come-by/article_c77c315e-e60a-11df-80d0-001cc4c002e0.html.

Rickert, Levi. "37 Years Later, Jeanette Bissonette's Son Wants Answers and Closure to Her Death." Native News Network. June 13, 2012. http://www.nativenewsnetwork.com/37-years-later-jeanette -bissonette-son-wants-answers.

Robertson, Paul. *The Power of the Land: Identity, Ethnicity, and Class Among the Oglala Lakota.* New York: Routledge, 2002.

Robinson, Doane. *A History of the Dakota or Sioux Indians from Their Earliest Traditions and First Contact with White Men to the Final Settlement of the Last of Them upon Reservations and the Consequent Abandonment of the Old Tribal Life.* Minneapolis: Ross and Haines, 1956.

Ross, Dennis. "Janklow Seeks Meeting." *Rapid City Journal,* May 3, 2000.

Royer, Daniel F., Agent, Pine Ridge Agency, Telegram Sent to Bureau of Indian Affairs, Washington, D.C. November 15, 1890. http://www.omaha.liv.ne.us/transmiss/congress/activities.html.

Ruby, Robert H. *The Oglala Sioux: Warriors in Transition*. Lincoln: University of Nebraska Press, 2010.

Russell, Don. *The Lives and Legends of Buffalo Bill*. Norman: University of Oklahoma Press, 1960.

Salway, Larry. "The Medicine Wheel: Sacredness of the Hoop." Outline of Lakota Culture. Accessed September 2009. http://lifeinitiativesinc.org/trainingculture 110.html.

Sandoz, Mari. *Crazy Horse, the Strange Man of the Oglalas: A Biography*. Lincoln: University of Nebraska Press, 1992.

———. *Old Jules*. Lincoln: University of Nebraska Press, 1985.

Schiller, Lawrence. *Perfect Murder, Perfect Town*. New York: HarperCollins, 1999.

Schilling, Vincent. "Oglala Sioux President Arrested at Whiteclay Protest." Indian Country Today Media Network.com, 2013. http://indiancountrytodaymedianetwork. com/2013/06/19/oglala-sioux-president-arrested- whiteclay- protest-149982.

Schultz, James Willard. *My Life as an Indian*. New York: Fawcett Columbine, 1981.

Scott, Sir Walter. *Marmion: A Tale of Flodden Field*. Edited by Henry Morely. Vol. Canto 6, XVII. P&R Samizdat Express, 2008. Kindle Ed.

Serrano, Richard A. "Pine Ridge Indian Homicide Cases Get New Scrutiny." *Los Angeles Times*, August 8, 2012. http://articles.latimes.com/2012/aug/08/ nation/la-na-pine-ridge-20120809.

"Shannon County Quick Facts from the U.S. Census Bureau." Accessed September 14, 2013. http://quickfacts.census.gov/qfd/states/46/46113.html.

"Shelli Poor Bear (1979–2005)." Accessed June 2010. http://shelli-poor-bear. memory-of.com/About.aspx.

"Shoot Gunmen: Janklow Explains Banks' Quote." *Mitchell Daily Republic*, March 23, 1974. http://newspaperarchive.com/mitchell-daily-republic/1976-03-23?ta g=janklow+banks+explains&rtserp=tags/janklow-banks-explains.

Sides, Hampton. *Blood and Thunder: An Epic of the American West*. New York: Doubleday, 2006.

Slater, Eric. "A Quiet Creek in S.D. Becomes River of Death." *Los Angeles Times*, May 20, 2000. http:articles.latimes.com/2000/may/20/news/mn-32030.

Smith, Rex Alan. *Moon of Popping Trees*. New York: Reader's Digest Press, 1975.

Smith, Scott L., and Fay Kuhlman. *Gray Wolves, Indians, and Buffalo Bones: True Stories of the Old West*. Bearcreek, MT: Banner Press, 1969.

Smith, Victor Grant. *The Champion Buffalo Hunter: The Frontier Memoirs of Yellowstone Vic Smith*. Edited by Jeanette Prodgers. Helena, MT: TwoDot, 1997.

South Dakota Advisory Committee to the United States Commission on Civil Rights. Office of Civil Rights. "Native Americans in South Dakota: An Erosion of Confidence in the Justice System." 2000.

Spring, Agnes Wright. *The Cheyenne and Black Hills Stage and Express Routes*. Lincoln: University of Nebraska Press, 1967.

Standing Bear, Luther. *My People, the Sioux*. Lincoln: University of Nebraska Press, 1975.

Stanklo, Rudy (Butch). *The Score: An Autobiography Exposing the Forces That Remain Studiously Concealed and Masked*. Gering, Nebraska: R. Stanko, 1986.

Starita, Joe. *The Dull Knifes of Pine Ridge: A Lakota Odyssey*. Lincoln: University of Nebraska Press, 2002.

"Statement from the Family of Anna Mae Pictou Aquash." Indigenous Women for Justice. 2004. http://indigenouswomenforjustice.org/.

Steen, Jomay. "Murder Confession a Rumor." *Lincoln Journal Star*, April 15, 2006.

Steinberger, Ruth. "Juvenile Justice." *Native Times*, September 2002. http://dlncoalition.org/din-coalition/2002septgodfrey.htm.

———. "The Strange Case of Adelia Godfrey Supports Suspicions." *Lakota Journal*, September 27, 2002. http://www.dlncoalition.org/dln-coalition/2002septgodfrey. htm.

Stern, Kenneth S. *Loud Hawk: The United States versus the American Indian Movement*. Norman: University of Oklahoma Press, 1994.

"The Battle of Sand Creek." *Rocky Mountain News* (Denver), March 17, 1864. http://www.kclonewolf.com/History/SandCreek/sc-reports/rocky-editorials. html.

"The Death of Robert Many Horses." In *20/20*, ABC.

"The Ghost Dance: The Indians Keep It up and Get Excited." *Salt Lake Herald*, November 22, 1890. http://chroniclingamerica.loc.gov/l/sn85058130/1890-11-22/ed-1/seq-1/words=reds+Cloud+Red+red.

"The Hostiles Combining." *New York Times*, December 19, 1890. http://query. nytimes.com/gst/abstract.html?res+9904E7D81E3BE533A2575AC1A9649D 94619ED7CF&scp=13&sq=december+%2C+1890&st=p.

"The Last of Sitting Bull." *St. Louis Republic*, December 17, 1890. http.www. dickshovel.com/greasy.html.

"The Manipulation of Myrtle Poor Bear." Dick Shovel. Accessed June 6, 2009. http://www.dickshovel.com/affa.html.

"To Raise Up an Interesting Commonwealth: Jackson's Reaction To Worcester and Nullification," Jeff Mather's Home Page. Accessed November 10, 2009. http:// jeffmatherphotography.com/jeff/.

Treaty with the Sioux-Brule, Oglala, Miniconjou, Yantonai, Hunkpapa, Blackfeet, Cuthead, Two Kettle, San Ars, and Santee and Arapahoe, National Archives General Records of the United States Government, Record Group 11 (1868).

Tremblay, William. *The June Rise: The Apocryphal Letters of Joseph Antoine Janis*. Golden: Fulcrum, 1994.

"Tribes Charges Double Standard Used." *Associated Press*, March 4, 2002.

Trimbach, Joseph H., and John M. Trimbach. *American Indian Mafia: An FBI Agent's True Story about Wounded Knee, Leonard Peltier, and the American Indian Movement (AIM)*. Denver: Outskirts Press, 2008.

Trimble, Charles. "Facts and Truth of Wounded Knee." Indianz.com. Accessed March 9, 2009. http://www.indianz.com/News/2009/013480.asp.

Turner, Thadd. *Wild Bill Hickok: Deadwood City—End of Trail.* USA: Universal Publishers/uPUBLISH.com, 2001.

Tuttle, Edmund B. *Three Years on the Plains: Observations of Indians, 1867–1870.* Norman: University of Oklahoma Press, 2002.

United States Department of the Interior: Indian Affairs. *Constitution and By-Laws of the Oglala Sioux Tribe of the Pine Ridge Reservation.* United States Government Printing Office.

United States Federal Bureau of Investigation. Report for Pine Ridge Indian Reservation, South Dakota: Accounting for Native American Deaths, Pine Ridge Indian Reservation. 2000.

"United States of America vs. Fritz Arlo Looking Cloud Court Trial Transcripts." February 2004. http://www.grahamdefense.org/200402cloud-transcript/index.htm.

United States Senate Committee on Indian Affairs. Oversight Hearing on Indian Housing. Testimony given by John Yellow Bird Steele, President of the Oglala Sioux Tribe. March 22, 2007. http://Indian.senate.gov/public/-files/steele0322.

United States v. Kagama, 118 U.S. 375 (1886).

Unrau, William E. *White Man's Wicked Water: The Alcohol Trade and Prohibition in Indian Country, 1802–1892.* Lawrence: University Press of Kansas, 1996.

U.S. Congress. *Final Report of the Select Committee to Study Governmental Operations with Respect to Intelligence Activities, United States Senate: Together with Additional, Supplemental, and Separate Views.* S. Bill. Washington: U.S. Government Printing Office, 1976.

U.S. v. Jessica Twiss (U.S. Dist. Ct. Div. S.D.) 5:06-cr-50020.

U.S. v. Paul Duane Herman (U.S. Dist. Ct. S. Div. S.D) 5:77-cr-50032.

U.S. v. Paul Duane Herman (U.S. Dist. Ct. S. Div. S.D) 5:91-cr-50017.

U.S. v. Rogers, U.S. 567 (1846).

U.S. v. White Plume, CIV 02-5017 (U.S. Dist. Ct, Div. S.D.) CIV 02-5017.2002. http://search.comcast.net/?cat=web&oqry=http%3A%2F%2F64.38.12.138%2Fdocs%2Fcourt%2Fwhiteplume%2Fusacomplaint0809.pdf&con=betac&form_submit=1&q=http%3A%2F%2F64.38.12.138%2Fdocs%2Fcourt%2Fwhiteplume%2Fusacomplaint0809.pdf&top_SearchSubmit=&search_type=new.

"U.S. v. White Plume." Indian Country Today Media Network.com. 2006. http://indiancountrytodaymedianetwork.com/ictarchives/2000/09/06/dea-and-fbi-agents-raid-family-crop-86551.

Utley, Robert M. *The Last Days of the Sioux Nation.* New Haven: Yale University Press, 1963.

VanDevelder, Paul. *Savages & Scoundrels: The Untold Story of America's Road to Empire Through Indian Country.* New Haven: Yale University Press, 2009.

Vaughan, Alden T. *New England Encounters: Indians and Euroamericans Ca. 1600-1850 : Essays Drawn from The New England Quarterly.* Boston: Northeastern University Press, 1999.

Vaughn, J. W. *Indian Fights: New Facts on Seven Encounters.* Norman: University of Oklahoma Press, 1966.

Vestal, Stanley. *New Sources of Indian History, 1850–1891: The Ghost Dance, the Prairie Sioux, a Miscellany.* Norman: University of Oklahoma Press, 1934.

Voices from Wounded Knee, 1973, in the Words of the Participants. Rooseveltown, NY: Akwesasne Notes, 1974.

"Wahupta Ska Pejuta." Hemphasis.net ~ Hemp Paper. Accessed September 10, 2011. http://www.hemphasis.net/History/history.htm.

Walker, Carson. "Slain Activist Had Roots in Civil Rights Movement." *News From Indian Country,* November 6, 2004. http://www.indiancountrynews.com/news/investigations/ray-robinson.

Walker, J. R. *Lakota Society.* Edited by Raymond J. DeMallie. Lincoln: University of Nebraska Press, 1982.

Wallace, Anthony C. *Jefferson and the Indians: The Tragic Fate of the First Americans.* Cambridge: Belknap Press of Harvard University Press, 1999.

Weir, David, and Lowell Bergman. "The Killing of Anna Mae Aquash." *Rolling Stone,* April 7, 1977.

"Welcome to News From Indian Country." Accessed November 3, 1999. http://www.indiancountrynews.info/denverpress.cfm.htm.

Wells, Phillip. *Ninety-six Years among the Indians of the Northwest: Adventures and Reminiscences of an Indian Scout and Interpreter in the Dakotas.* Compiled by Thomas E. Odell. Unpublished.

Wetmore, Helen Cody. *Buffalo Bill, Last of the Great Scouts.* Lincoln: University of Nebraska Press, 2003.

Weyler, Rex. *Blood of the Land: The Government and Corporate War against the American Indian Movement.* New York: Everest House, 1982.

White Crane, Aloysius. Hand-written Statement. February 4, 1976. Federal Bureau of Investigation, File #70-11558.

"Who in the Hell Murdered Native Activist Annie Mae Aquash? Indian Country Wants Justice Now." Peace & Collaborative Development Network. Accessed January 18, 2012. http://www.internationalpeaceandconflict.org/profiles/blogs/who-in-the-hell-murdered#.UW8dTrUsl8E.

William Janklow v. *Newsweek, Inc.,* 788 F2.d 1300 (8th cir 1986).

William Janklow v. *Viking Press and Peter Matthiessen,* 1990.SD.104. http://versuslaw.com. 459 N.W.2d 415. http://sd.findacase.com/research/wfrm-DocViewer.aspx/xq/fac.19900718_0006.SD.htm/qx.

Williams, Lee. "Adelia Won't Be Tried as an Adult." *Argus Leader,* April 20, 2002.

___. "Teen's Jailing Angers Tribe." *Argus Leader,* April 20, 2002.

Worcester v. *Georgia,* 31 U.S. 515 (1831).

Zigrossi, Norman A. Special Agent in Charge to Redacted Agency Special Officer, Pine Ridge BIA Memorandum. December 6, 1976.

Zimmerman, Bill. *Airlift to Wounded Knee.* Chicago: Swallow Press, 1976.

Index